RETURN

LORD HAILSHAM

LORD HAILSHAM

A Life

Geoffrey Lewis

JONATHAN CAPE
LONDON

First published 1997

1 3 5 7 9 10 8 6 4 2

© Geoffrey Lewis 1997

Geoffrey Lewis has asserted his right
under the Copyright, Designs and Patents Act 1988
to be identified as the author of this work

First published in the United Kingdom in 1997
by Jonathan Cape
Random House, 20 Vauxhall Bridge Road, London SW1V 2SA

Random House Australia (Pty) Limited
20 Alfred Street, Milsons Point, Sydney
New South Wales 2061, Australia

Random House New Zealand Limited
18 Poland Road, Glenfield,
Auckland 10, New Zealand

Random House South Africa (Pty) Limited
Endulini, 5a Jubilee Road, Parktown 2193, South Africa

Random House UK Limited Reg. No. 954009

A CIP catalogue record for this book is available from the British Library

Papers used by Random House UK Limited are natural,
recyclable products made from wood grown in sustainable forests.
The manufacturing processes conform to the environmental
regulations of the country of origin

ISBN 0-224-04252-1

Typeset by Deltatype Ltd, Birkenhead, Merseyside

Printed and bound in Great Britain
by Mackays of Chatham PLC

Contents

Illustrations

Quintin Hogg (1845-1903)
Myssie Brown at her marriage to Archibald Marjoribanks
Douglas Hogg (1872-1950) in the Temple
Neil and Quintin Hogg, and Edward and Isabel Marjoribanks
Neil Hogg
Eton Collegers in 1921
"My Contemporaries": The Earl of Birkenhead's article (*Churchill College*)
Edward Marjoribanks (*Churchill College*)
Quintin in the Alps
Natalie
The Oxford By-election (*Getty Images*)
Quintin Hogg canvassing laundry girls
Quintin Hogg and Lord Hinchingbrooke (*Getty Images*)
Mary
Quintin Hogg in 1938
As First Lord of the Admiralty
Brighton Conference, 1957
At home at Carters Corner
With Averell Harriman (*Getty Images*)
With Khrushchev and Gromyko (*Getty Images*)
Consulting with Harold Macmillan (*National Portrait Gallery*)
Harold Macmillan at the christening of the Hailshams' youngest daughter
Macmillan and Home
At the Blackpool Conference, 1963 (*Getty Images*)
With Rab Butler (*Getty Images*)
Applauding Butler at Blackpool (*Getty Images*)
Applauding Home at Blackpool (*Getty Images*)
Lord Hailsham and Lord Denning

George Thomas and Lord Hailsham
Deirdre
At his daughter's wedding, 1987
The Maastricht Treaty Debate
On the Woolsack

(Unless otherwise acknowledged, all the photographs come from Lord Hailsham's private collection)

Introduction

I had never met Lord Hailsham when I set out on this book. But I had heard that he could be difficult: opinionated, rude and liable to sudden bursts of rage. None of this was untrue, although I never experienced anything but calm seas. In any case, there was so much else. The conversations I had with him, enlivened with anecdote and the occasional vulgar shaft, became a source of pleasure, at least to me. He enjoyed talking about the past and the things he loved. Dogs, for instance. A Jack Russell was his constant companion and there was a sort of mutual respect and distance between the two of them. Once the little dog sat on the sofa beside me and began to growl in a menacing way. 'Don't say that!' said his master with distaste.

The thing that impressed me more and more as I got to know him and worked through his papers, was how the world of his childhood and education had moulded his life through to its last phase. He continued to draw on his knowledge of the classical age and apply its lessons, particularly the consequences of moral decline, to current affairs. This greatly attracted Margaret Thatcher. So too the virtuous certainties of his home lasted for the rest of his life. He made me realise how distant is the time when religious belief was a reality in public and in private, and not just the object of an occasional genuflexion. So far as I know, he has never cut a corner in anything he has done. In that equivocal and fluctuating relationship with Harold Macmillan, on which his career eventually turned, it was the durability of Hailsham's values which most appealed to his leader. No foolishness, no extravagance of behaviour, came near to destroying the bond of a common inheritance which joined the two men.

Most public figures leave some legacy, an event or an achievement which is and remains linked with their name, but I prefer to think of the constancy and worth of Lord Hailsham's principles in almost fifty years of public service as his real monument.

I must record my thanks to everyone who has helped me with the writing of this book. Philip Ziegler suggested Lord Hailsham as a subject and Patrick Neill smoothed the path. Lord Hailsham and his family all gave encouragement and time without stint. I had unrestricted access to the Hailsham papers in the Churchill Archives Centre in Cambridge and at Putney. Fortunately, my subject's often-repeated warning that his papers contain nothing of interest proved not to be true. But the nuggets lie deep under strata of gardening accounts and the other debris of daily life.

I found Lord Hailsham invariably helpful and friendly, but while I was writing he never evinced the slightest curiosity in what I might say about him. Nor did he read or comment on any part of the manuscript. There seemed to be a tacit understanding that, apart from the sacrosanctity of facts, I could do what I liked with the information he supplied. A biographer could not ask for better.

A public career as long and varied as his was bound to lead to meetings and correspondence with all sorts and conditions of men and women. In the notes I have listed some eighty names. These encounters are one of the most enjoyable aspects of biography. All whom I met were considerate, usually deprecating what they could contribute. Most, particularly the women, were frank. But their frankness gave rise to a familiar dilemma, which I never felt I could completely resolve: how to draw a fair picture without abusing confidence. At the risk of invidious selection, I must mention particularly Derek Oulton, a former Permanent Secretary to the Lord Chancellor, who was my constant guide to the arcane processes of his Department; Ian Gilmour who permitted me to quote from his inimitable diary and who with Dennis Walters, knew Lord Hailsham's political outlook through and through; Norman Turner who was the Official Solicitor at the time of the dockers' cases in 1972 (discussed in Chapter 22 and Appendix 1) and whose extraordinary memory for detail helped greatly in unravelling a tangled episode; Cyril Glasser, whose encyclopaedic knowledge of Legal Aid did not obscure his very clear views on the subject; and some of my own family who acted from time to time as critics and researchers.

I have naturally leant on the skill and experience of librarians and archivists. Although Lord Hailsham's papers in Churchill have not yet been catalogued, I was able to work from a provisional listing with guidance that seemed sometimes to be inspired from Alan Kucia, the Archivist, and his staff, and with help from the Keeper, Correlli Barnet. Thomas Legg, the present Permanent Secretary to the Lord Chancellor, kindly made the Departmental records available, notwithstanding the thirty year rule. This was an unexpected bonus, and Enid Smith and her staff at the records section helped me to thread a way through the awesome volume of papers there. I am grateful to the Trustees of the Harold Macmillan Archive and their archivist for making their invaluable papers available: to Miss Louise Davis for information about Lord Hailsham's mother and her Tennessee family; also to the librarians of the Public Record Office; the Cambridge University Library; the Bodleian; Trinity College, Cambridge; Southampton University, and the University of East Anglia; the Keeper of Eton College Collections, and the archivists of the Conservative Party, the Conservative Research Department, the BBC, the Oxford Union, Christ Church, Oxford, the English Province of the Society of Jesus, and the Drapers' Company; to the Chief Executive of the Bar Council for information relating to chapters 23 and 24; and to the late Victor Montagu's (Viscount Hinchingbrooke's) family for access to his private archive.

I visited the Kennedy Library in Boston and the Library of Congress in Washington D.C., and with much help from Stephen Columbia, I investigated the American side of the negotiations leading to the nuclear test ban treaty in 1963. These American libraries were a revelation: models of efficiency and professionalism which can be achieved only when funds on a scale unknown in Britain are forthcoming. I also had valuable help from Professors Arthur Schlesinger Jr. and Carl Kaysen, who were both members of the Kennedy Administration.

Finally I thank Charles Elliot and Tony Whittome, my editors, and Xandra Bingley, my agent, who seemed always able to supply sympathy and objectivity in equal shares; and Marion Spring whose dedication transformed a thoroughly confusing manuscript into clean and tidy type.

1

Family and Beginnings

EDWARDIAN England, the brief interlude which separated the end of Victoria's reign and the First World War, has about it a peculiar nostalgia. For the upper classes it was a good time to be alive. Those who were comfortably circumstanced were indeed comfortable. The picture is always of long summer afternoons. Servants relieved the tedium and friction of domestic tasks. The country stood at the head of the greatest empire since Rome and might sail on serenely for ever. The noble melodies of Edward Elgar, the nation's favourite composer, seemed to give voice to these certainties. But the music was elegiac too. There were few who glimpsed the seeds of disintegration germinating within, or the menace to come from outside, which in a few brief years would wipe out a whole generation.

Quintin McGarel Hogg was born into that age, on 9 October 1907, with almost every advantage that nature, birth and circumstance could grant. It would soon emerge that he had as good an academic intellect as any of his generation, as well as superb means of expressing his mind in speech and writing. His father, Douglas Hogg, was a highly successful barrister whose talent would shortly carry him into the upper reaches of his profession and of government. 'Hogg looked like Mr Pickwick,' wrote Lord Denning, 'and spoke like Demosthenes.' Quintin's mother was a beauty from Nashville, Tennessee, a woman of acuity who could and did make trenchant political speeches of her own.

Quintin first saw this world from a well-ordered Edwardian nursery at 5 Cleveland Square, Bayswater. Shortly afterwards the family moved to 46 Queen's Gate Gardens. The household had no less than eight living-in servants who were paid next to nothing but lived like fighting cocks. The children were segregated under a professional nanny in the day and night nurseries. Her edicts on behaviour were law, against which there was no appeal. Questions of what was done and not done were derived from Nanny rather than parents. But her charges were fond of Nanny. 'I loved my Nanny,' Lord Hailsham told the *Daily Express* reporter seventy years on. 'You don't easily forget somebody who has been so important and cared for you and controlled you when you were young. . . . I saw her on a Sussex beach many years later and we recognised each other and were warmly affectionate.' Occasionally the children were brought out on display and granted affection by their parents. Father would look into the nursery just after breakfast and then Mother would come and play, and perhaps sing a spiritual. One hour was about the limit of her patience. Quintin was not destined to be musical, but he knew what he liked. When he became a castaway on the BBC programme, *Desert Island Discs*, his first choice was a 1910 recording of *I do like to be beside the seaside*. It reminded him of his nursery and the wind-up gramophone which was kept there. On some days the children were brought down to see Father after tea. There was rather more contact on Sundays when the children were dressed up to be exhibited at teatime.

In this closed regimented world children had to make their own lives and character formed early. Quintin had not left the nursery before a disturbing trait emerged: consciousness of his own superiority. His brother, Neil, $2\frac{1}{2}$ years younger, discovered that Quintin was not willing to put up with a less intellectual child at close quarters. The elder boy turned on those who differed from him with scorn and ridicule. Under such circumstances, the nursery was a swamping experience for Neil. The strain of arrogance and intolerance which he discovered so early in his elder brother would not have mattered in the long run, for they became fast friends, had not the nursery characteristic persisted into adult life where it eventually threatened Quintin's political and professional career.

How did their parents appear to these young boys? Neil thought of them as *Olympians*. He meant this in the sense used by Kenneth Grahame who in *The Golden Age* charged his own parents with the usual offence of being out of touch. 'It was a perennial matter for amazement,' Grahame wrote, 'how these Olympians would talk over our heads – during meals for instance – of this or the other social or political inanity, under the delusion that these pale phantasms of reality were among the importances of life. We *illuminati*, eating silently, our heads full of plans and conspiracies, could have told them what real life was. We had just left it outside, and were all on fire to get back to it . . .'

The Hogg boys' mother had an aura of beauty, a subject for a Sargent portrait, had Father been able to afford the commission. She was vivacious with a very mobile face, and understood English social conventions perfectly. She had a very quick mind, and wrote a good strong hand, often taking down Father's opinions for him. Father was not so easy to describe. He was a shy, rather ponderous man who felt strongly but could not express his emotions. Although nominally an Anglican, he had been brought up in a powerfully evangelical tradition. He never took Communion and had a deep antipathy to Roman Catholicism. His outlook would have been close to the Presbyterianism of his own mother, but he never discussed religion with the boys. This was a Christian household and religion was a pervasive presence at home. Quintin described both his parents as 'conventionally devout', but Neil considered this unfair to his father. However that may be, the household were agreed on one thing: 'The Church of Rome was corrupt, superstitious, idolatrous, and much to be distrusted.'

The Hogg family were linen merchants in Ulster, among the early Protestant settlers coming from Scotland in the seventeenth century. In 1869, a relative by marriage researched the history of the family in Ireland: 'I have always heard the Hogg family was from Scotland and that their ancestor . . . was a Presbyterian imbued with the opinions prevalent at the time and that he established himself at Lisburn, or Lisnagarvey as it was then called'.[1] According to the family historian, 'Hogg could not well have settled before 1621'. Some later members of the family were Quakers and Church of Ireland. Quintin was brought up as an Anglican but the fundamentalism of his earliest Hogg forebears was not far away. His great-aunts believed in direct verbal inspiration and gave examples to the credulous small boy. Quintin liked to describe these Hoggs as humble folk, but they were not, at least from the time of James Weir Hogg. He was born in 1790 and won a gold medal for oratory at Trinity College, Dublin. He became a student at Gray's Inn, and according to his diary[2] was called to the Irish Bar at the age of twenty-three. The next summer he applied for permission from the East India Company to practise at the Calcutta Bar, and boarded the East Indiaman *Rose* in March 1815 to make his career in the Company's territory. This extraordinarily able and energetic man was a severe judge of himself, complaining of his own 'beastly indolence' and the passing of youth. But his career belied his self-doubt. He practised at the Calcutta Bar for eight years and built up a lucrative connection. He returned to England in 1833 and shortly afterwards was returned to Parliament for Beverley as a supporter of Peel. Elected a director of the East India Company, he became its Chairman and chief spokesman in the Commons. He was made a Baronet and a Privy Councillor and died in 1876. Sir James Weir Hogg was the first of a long line whose energy and abilities impelled them to high places and who thus became great public servants. The subject of this book is the most recent example.

The seventh son and fourteenth child of Sir James was the first Quintin Hogg, born in 1845. His unusual name came into the family through his godfather, Mr Quintin Dick, a parliamentary friend of Sir James. The first Quintin was a man in the awesome tradition of Victorian philanthropy, that tiny number of men and women who alone saw how urgent were the country's social problems which formed the dark shadow of her industrial greatness. Lord Hailsham, his grandson, described it thus:

> . . . it was perhaps this handful of men and women who more than any other – more than the Dizzies and Palmerstons, the Tennysons, Roebucks, Brights, perhaps more than the Darwins and the Huxleys – lent to the Victorian age its peculiar flavour, at once the glory and the despair, the pride and the butt of their successors.[3]

While he was at Eton, in the bullying and largely pagan school atmosphere of the day (Arnold of Rugby was still to come), the first Quintin Hogg showed unusual religious and compassionate leanings. He started a Bible class among the sceptics and scoffers of his House. It needed courage, but he was a powerful boy and his physical strength helped. As soon as he left school to work at a City tea merchant, he began to put his ideas into practice among the desperate, nomadic children of London. In his own words:

> The seedling first saw the light just after Christmas, 1863, when the writer took two crossing-sweepers into the Adelphi arches, which were then open to the river, and with a beer bottle and a tallow candle for the entire lighting apparatus, a couple of Bibles wherewith to teach the letters of the alphabet as the entire school furniture, the two crossing-sweepers as the total of the scholars, and himself as the teaching staff, commenced a very elementary ragged school. This grew until it needed a home of its own, which was secured in 'Of Alley' off the Strand, a court forming part of the estate of the great Duke of Buckingham, and marking the site of his river house, the streets George Court, Villiers Street, Duke Street, Of Alley and Buckingham Street giving the name of the nobleman in question.[4]

In the London of that time children of the homeless poor could earn a few coppers sweeping refuse from the streets to make a passage for others to cross. The 'Ragged schools' to which Hogg referred were voluntary schools for destitute urchins originated by John Pounds of Portsmouth about 1818. Primary education for all children was not introduced until W. E. Forster's Education Act of 1870.

In parallel with his teaching, the young Hogg organised his ragged friends into a battalion of bootblacks, kitted out with red coats and tins of polish in order to give them decent employment. On two or three nights a week, their organiser sallied forth himself in their livery to learn more of their life and gain their confidence.

From these humblest beginnings Quintin Hogg established a home for boys, moving several times to successively larger premises in the slum areas around Covent Garden. Finally, in 1882, he moved to his permanent site in Regent Street above Oxford Circus. Here the old 'Polytechnic institution' unexpectedly came on the market. It had been open for fifty years as a place where children of the well-to-do could be taken to be amazed and amused by the wonders of Victorian science. Quintin Hogg had other plans for it, for the benefit of those with fewer advantages. He was now, although still under forty, a great merchant and a man of wealth. Through the influence of his brother-in-law Charles McGarel, he had been taken into the firm of Bosanquet, Curtis and Company, and rapidly became senior partner. The business, which owned sugar estates in the West Indies, prospered under his direction and was renamed Hogg, Curtis & Campbell. Hogg bought the lease of the old Polytechnic for £15,000 (about £600,000 in value in 1997).

His idea was of a place where unprivileged men 'would find a reasonable outlet for any healthy desire, physical, spiritual, social, or intellectual, which he possessed'. The Poly, as it became known, was an immediate, stunning success. The great hall was opened on Sunday 25 September 1882, crowded with 1500 young men met to celebrate the event. Quintin Hogg had seen every boy individually as he joined. By 1889, 70,000 had enrolled as members or students. The technical education in every craft and skill from electrical engineering to tailors' cutting was not compulsory, but Hogg reckoned that six-sevenths of the members took classes. In 1890 an American magazine published an admiring description of the facilities at Regent Street:

Membership . . . entitles to the use of all the club-rooms and facilities of the place and gives admission to such classes as the member may choose to attend at about two-thirds the regular class fees. The social and refreshment room ... is sixty feet long by forty-eight feet wide and is the general lounging and rallying place ... The daily papers lie about on the tables, the latest notices of the various athletic clubs are posted on bulletin boards ... and the place has an air of a very comfortable and hospitable living-room for a club of democratic but decent young men. ... Easily accessible is the lending library of several thousand volumes, freely at the service of all members; and in a separate room ... is the reading library supplied with books, reference works and a large number of periodicals. ... The swimming bath is one of the finest in England, being beautifully walled with decorated tiles. ... The recreative side of life at the Polytechnic is no wild pretence, but a very robust reality. ... Mr Hogg has provided for sports by securing a place at Wimbledon known as Merton Hall with nearly thirty acres of land, and it has been converted into a cricketing ground and general playground that is, I am told, the finest in the Kingdom. Mr J. E. K. Studd, the famous cricketer and muscular Christian of Cambridge University, has become one of Mr Hogg's right-hand men in two parts of the Polytechnic's work, namely the sporting and the religious.[5]

This was a University, no less, and it is not surprising that the Regent Street Polytechnic became the model for the entire polytechnic movement. Today, a hundred yards from the old Poly, the benign bearded figure of its founder, seated and reading the Bible to two boys, still looks down on Portland Place to remind Londoners of what could be achieved by the imagination and drive of a single man.

The Polytechnic entered the bloodstream of the Hogg family, passing from generation to generation. Lord Hailsham, the second Quintin Hogg, visited Regent Street first when he was less than three years old. He became a Governor when he was less than thirty, and then Vice-President. His grandfather founded it, his godfather was the second President. His brother Neil's godfather was the first Secretary. His father, Douglas Hogg, sat in the Chair. It was the family monument.

Though he never knew his grandfather, the second Quintin derived something else from the first. This was the force and tendency of his beliefs. Religion had been the spring of the first Quintin's life. It was not a narrow, sectarian creed. He despised dogmatic disputation, believing instead in a broad intellectually-based religion. After his death in 1903 an unfinished letter to a young friend was found on his desk.

My precious boy,

I was very much touched by your letter and the thought which led you to come back to me with the doubts and difficulties which have cropped up since you went out into the greater world outside the Poly. Do you remember sonnie how in old days I advised you to stick to essentials. This *one* thing I *know* is better than a dozen creeds. Whatever else may be shaken there are some [facts] stablished beyond the warring of theologians. Forever virtue is better than evil – truth than falsehood, kindness than brutality. These, like love, 'never fail'. So you must not let your doubts lead you to a wrong life. Do not confuse theology and religion. The one is a science to be proved or disproved – the other is a life to be lived. I am writing this in the early morning hours and will try to run out and catch the 3 a.m. post so that it may reach you in the morning. You say you are free all day. Come any time.[6]

Lord Hailsham thought this letter 'very moving, expressing truths so profound that it just stops short of revelation'.[7] Quintin Hogg's faith was at the root of his grandson's belief in the intellectual framework of all religion. He returned to it again and again. In his Corbishley Memorial Lecture of 1977 he made a plea for the *philosophia perennis*, a phrase not much used nowadays, but indicating the central core of philosophical truths that are generally accepted, regardless of time or place, and which underly all true religious belief. For the second Quintin this was precisely the same as his grandfather's unfinished letter.

While Quintin never knew his grandfather Hogg, he certainly knew and remembered Alice Hogg, his saintly grandmother, whose devotion to the young was as great as her husband's, for he and his brother Neil were her favourite grandsons. A deeply religious Scots Presbyterian, she was the main spiritual influence in the nursery life of the boys. Nanny was, of course, influential too. She was a High Church Anglican of melancholy disposition, and taught the boys the Creed, the Lord's Prayer and the Catechism. But it was Alice Hogg whose teaching went deepest and lasted longest. The boys saw a good deal of her. 'She was by far the greatest and most loving woman I can remember ever having known', wrote her grandson in *The Door Wherein I Went*. She introduced the boys to the Titan characters and spellbinding stories of the Old Testament, and she showed them the incomparable beauty of the Authorised Version. These things left indelible impressions. The poetry spoke and the narrative gripped Quintin's forming mind. He continued to draw on the stories throughout his life, and they helped to form his belief that the Old and New Testaments were a single body of evolving religious truth.[8]

Douglas McGarel Hogg, the first Viscount Hailsham, was born in 1872, the eldest son of Quintin. He was educated at Eton, and his father sent him some stern but doubtless practical advice on arriving at school:

> You can be civil and companionable with all, but give your real friendship only to those whose life and conversation are such that they will be helps and not hindrances to you. .... As for yourself *do nothing* and *say nothing* which you would not like your mother and sisters to see and hear. You have a mother such as few are blessed with. She has given you of her time, her love, her prayers – she has borne with you when you were fretful and passionate – what return will you make?[9]

Quintin the philanthropist was fond of underlining, and even making allowances for the period (1885) this was austere stuff. It was partly the example and character of his father which helped to make Douglas reserved. But for the second Quintin, these letters of his grandfather were, of their kind, 'as good as anything I have seen'; and his aunt, Ethel Wood, niece and biographer of the philanthropist, wrote that 'they bring out the fervent heat of his conviction that love alone can lead us to the solution of both personal and general problems'.[10]

For some unknown reason, perhaps parsimony, his father did not send Douglas to University, but packed him off immediately to the family sugar estates in British Guiana owned by Hogg, Curtis and Campbell. This hurt Douglas but he never complained. Only the youngest son Malcolm was sent to University and became known in the family as 'Benjamin Our Ruler'. Douglas did not enjoy life in the West Indies and became ill. He volunteered for the South African war and had to bribe the medical panel because his eyesight was not up to scratch. When his father died, Douglas threw himself into the work of the Polytechnic, and remained absorbed in it for the rest of his life.

After the war, Douglas read for the Bar and was called in 1902. He was an immediate success, although starting late, and quickly built up a strong commercial practice. He had the necessary qualities, as they were described in the conventional obituary language of Lord Simon's entry in the *Dictionary of National Biography* – a powerfully analytical mind which he could bring to bear on complex sets of facts, grasp of legal principle, dedication to his chosen profession, a conciliatory manner in Court and, perhaps most important, a robust attitude to any situation he might meet. 'They pay for your opinions, not your doubts,' he was fond of saying to his own son, Quintin. His son considered, rightly, that Douglas had better natural equipment for the Bar than he had, although not a scholar. The father possessed notably better judgment of a point.

In 1922, when Quintin was only fifteen, Douglas was hijacked into politics when Bonar Law invited him to become Attorney-General. He had taken silk only five years previously. The change of direction was permanent and he never afterwards left the political life. He was a natural Conservative of right-wing, although not rabid, views: a socialist government was for him an unthinkable disaster. Quintin, who became interested in politics from an unusually early age, had long conversations with his father. He was quite clear that it was their talks which led him to become a Conservative. His father was a compelling advocate. As Lord Hailsham acknowledged very fairly later in life, the origin of beliefs is fortuitous, however logical and systematic they may eventually become. 'I make no doubt at all that if I had been born into another family I would very likely have had different opinions and very likely would have been sucked into the general left-wing trend to which most intelligent young people of my generation subsequently succumbed'. Later he felt the force of loyalty. With a father prominent in Conservative politics, he could have caused him embarrassment by publicly taking a different stance.

★

On 14 August 1905, Douglas married Elizabeth Trimble Brown, the daughter of Judge Trimble Brown of Nashville, Tennessee, and young widow of Archibald Marjoribanks.

'Myssie' Brown* was a grey-eyed Southern belle whose marriage to Marjoribanks in 1897 was so splendid an affair and so consistently made the front pages of the Nashville press that it became known simply as 'The Wedding'. 'In importance, the event has scarcely been equalled in the social history of Tennessee,' claimed the local organ: 'the marriage is one of international importance.'[11] Marjoribanks was the son of Lady Tweedmouth, and his party, which included his brother-in-law Lord Aberdeen, the Governor-General

---

* Myssie was the name given to Elizabeth Brown by her black nurse, and by which she was invariably known in Nashville. Lord Hailsham remembers his father using the name once only, at her funeral, when he said, 'Poor Myssie, she always hated crowds'.

of Canada, arrived by special train. The bride wore diamonds and aquamarines given her by Lord and Lady Aberdeen. She was reported to have 'carried herself with an independent and queenly air that wins instant admiration'. The reporter was not mistaken. Recalling his mother for the author of an article in a Nashville magazine in 1957, Lord Hailsham described her as having had an extraordinary magnetic and high-spirited personality. But Marjoribanks was not outdone by this Southern splendour. Tall, with a high-domed head and dashing moustache, he was in full military regalia and kilt, as were his party. When the bride entered the reception to cut the cake, a military band played 'God Save the Queen' and 'Dixie'.

Myssie's grandfather was Neill S. Brown, the youngest ever Governor of Tennessee and the first Ambassador of the United States to Imperial Russia from 1850 to 1853. Lord Hailsham had a complete collection of the Ambassador's reports from Russia and was struck both by the forthright language and by how changeless Russia seemed. 'The Government of Russia is consistent,' wrote Ambassador Brown, 'it promises no freedom and gives none.' Hailsham commented: 'Here you have my great grandfather writing of the Imperial Czarist regime more than a hundred years ago in terms which might well have been used of Khrushchev and Bulganin. He is appalled by the same hatred of freedom, the same secrecy, the same distrust of strangers, especially from the West.'[12]

Neill Brown's family were small farmers of Scotch-Irish descent and had moved to Tennessee from North Carolina in the early years of the nineteenth century. Brown's own grandfather had served in the Revolutionary War and was a strong Presbyterian. Neill practised law in Pulaski, Tennessee, but finding little work entered politics as a Whig. He was elected Governor at the age of thirty-seven. His wife was Mary Ann Trimble, the daughter of a judge. He was altogether a picturesque and highly respected figure in Tennessee history, renowned for his strength of character. Tennessee was a border state in the Civil War, nominally part of the Confederacy, and the Browns' sympathies lay with the Confederates, having lost their home in a fire started by Federal soldiers.[13] Myssie's father, Judge Trimble Brown, was only thirty-six when he suffered a fatal stroke in the midst of what was expected to be a successful campaign for election as attorney-general of the state, so she spent much of her childhood in her grandfather Neill's house. She thus grew up in a highly articulate, political household, and early acquired knowledge which she later put to good use.

Having dished Myssie's many Nashville beaux, Marjoribanks

carried his bride off to a home near his mother's estates in the west country of England and little more was heard of her in Nashville. She sent pictures home of her two children, Edward and Isabel. But the marriage which had begun with such magnificence was not destined to last. Marjoribanks died suddenly and his widow, who had taken so readily to English life, and her two young children made their home with Lady Tweedmouth, Marjoribanks' mother. The young widow threw herself into Liberal politics in the city of Bath and proved an excellent public speaker. When Lord Hailsham visited Bath in 1956 as First Lord of the Admiralty, some people he met could still remember her political speaking from the years 1902–1904.

★

Douglas Hogg and Archibald Marjoribanks were first cousins, since Lady Tweedmouth, acknowledged by all to be the uncrowned Queen of Bath, was a daughter of Sir James Weir Hogg and Douglas's aunt. Douglas was soon invited to one of her functions. There he met the young widow and they quickly fell in love. As was seemly, the wedding did not rival the splendours of the Nashville nuptials. It was a harmonious marriage of the conventional and the eccentric. Believing that one should only employ specialists, Quintin's mother engaged the services of a rabbi to circumcise her younger son. Douglas would not have done that. And it was she who experimented with early motor cars and took her husband on a motor tour of East Anglia in 'a beautiful contraption with a brass bonnet'.

The rhythmic tenor of Edwardian nursery life permitted annual digressions to the sea, usually the dreary Bristol Channel town of Weston-super-Mare. Inside the nursery, Quintin and Neil had for companions their mother's two children by her first marriage, Edward and Isabel. Their half-sister seems not to have figured much in the boys' memory, and soon dropped out of the Hogg family life. Edward was a different matter. A brilliant, highly strung character whose life ended in early tragedy, he was a formative influence on the young Quintin. In a family photograph of the four children, reproduced in this book, Edward, his hair plastered down and parted in the middle and with starched spreading Eton collar, cut-away jacket and (of all things) a medal, gazes confidently at the camera. He holds the hand of an uncharacteristically shy Quintin, nearly eight years his junior, dressed in a velvet Fauntleroy suit and lace collar fastened with a small jewelled brooch. Edward was a romantic figure,

11

much of whose magnetism for Quintin was his success. The ambitions of the younger boy and their consistent realisation as he grew older were strongly influenced by the careers of his father and his half-brother. But Edward was the closer and Quintin could daily observe his natural gifts and the intense application with which he employed them. Quintin consciously imitated him and deferred to his opinions. The intimacy continued. Many years later, in wartime Cairo, he told his cousin Elizabeth Gwynne (who became the cookery writer Elizabeth David) that 'though Edward had died more than ten years ago, I did not think of him as dead. I still sometimes mentally continue the arguments I had with him, and if he came into the room now I would not be alarmed but would start again just where we had left off.' His mother, too, cared about academic success and was hard on Quintin if he did not come top. It would have been an uncomfortable nursery for any child who was not naturally in the 'A' stream.

That feature of preparatory school would not hold any fears for Quintin, whose nursery governess had taught him all the declensions of Latin nouns and the four conjugations of verbs before he was nine. Other terrors, however, awaited the small boy as he got ready to face what Cyril Connolly called 'that incubator of persecution mania, the English private school'.[14]

2

School

NOTHING in the tranquil world of the nursery prepared a small boy for the rigours of a private preparatory boarding school. Sent away from home at the age of eight, few small boys could begin to understand why their parents subjected them to brutal partings, long separations, and the substitution for their comfortable homes of a regime that was cold and hostile in equal parts. Quintin could not even tie his tie. In the school dormitory the boys hunted down and exposed to derision the slightest deviation from what they decreed to be the norm. The sanitary arrangements were so unspeakable that it was probably only the English climate which fended off epidemics. All this was in the name of 'character' in general, and that stoicism in particular which was so prized by the governing classes.

Such was the preparatory school at Sunningdale to which Quintin was despatched, but in this unpromising environment he encountered a teacher of real genius. Gerard Alston Ling was the embodiment of the admired stoicism. When he returned from the First World War in 1917 (Quintin's second year) he had one arm paralysed and one eye shot out. It was not until Quintin's own son was at Sunningdale that he discovered that the eye which had been lost was the good eye, and that Ling had been nearly blind the whole time he was teaching. Ling gave Quintin his command of Latin, and, to a lesser extent, Greek, both of which he retained throughout his life. He was the best teacher Quintin ever had, and he revered his memory. In 1912, his brilliant teaching had won Edward the top scholarship to Eton, as it had for many boys from the school.

In 1955 when Ling was seventy-six and, being completely blind and crippled, was compelled to retire, Lord Hailsham discovered from a chance conversation with the headmaster that his only means of support was a First World War disability pension. Stoicism had now to deal with poverty. He had never earned more than £500 in any year in his life. An appeal was launched by Hailsham and others, and raised enough to ensure a minimum level of comfort. It is difficult now fully to appreciate what boys learned through classical language and literature. It is true that they were being 'hotted up' for scholarships; but from Ling at any rate, Quintin and his contemporaries learned the meaning of civic and personal virtue as those concepts were understood by the two closed civilisations they were studying. 'But for his example, these stirring sentiments might have fallen on deaf ears. Years later, I learned to my sorrow that he had no religious beliefs. This too has been a lesson to me. If heroism counts for anything, he is sure of his place in heaven.'

In 1920, aged thirteen, Quintin moved on to Eton. As a scholar he went into College and so became a member of the school's academic élite. Eton was a religious foundation which included within its structure a school for seventy 'poor scholars' (the epithet is invariable) who constitute College. The Collegers live and eat separately and have their own library, all under the jurisdiction of the Master in College and a professional matron. The boys are set apart and encouraged to think of themselves as chosen. Few in this closed society made real friends in the school outside College and, according to one old Etonian whose retrospect was unsentimental, few easily made the transition to the outside world.

The rest of the boys at Eton, the vast majority of a thousand or so, are known as 'Oppidans' (literally townsmen). The Oppidans live outside College in Houses. In the first Quintin's time the Houses were licensed to private owners who might or might not be masters at the school, and whose care of the boys might or might not be tender. The licensees were known as tutors or dames. By Douglas's time this haphazard arrangement had gone, replaced by the present system in which each housemaster is a teacher at the school, and each House is regulated by the school. The Oppidans, who had originally paid board to the private owners of the Houses as well as fees to take advantage of the school facilities, continued to pay fees, whereas the Collegers receive grants. Oppidans might be able boys but they do not experience the benefits, if such they are, of the intellectual forcing house that College is and was.

The Masters in College in Quintin's time were J. F. Crace and H. K. Marsden. He remembered Crace as 'bald, short and friendly', and Marsden as 'tall, gangling and dedicated'. Crace was admired as a scholar, but 'he had none of Alington's [the Headmaster's] flair for handling high-mettled scholars'.[1] His was the era of liberation or, if you preferred, licence, associated with the names of George Orwell and Cyril Connolly, and recalled afterwards as 'the Reign of Love'. Marsden, his successor and universally known as 'Bloody Bill', was as different as could be. A mathematician of outstanding ability, the beginning and end of his landscape was Eton. Some thought him a sadist and he certainly set about tightening things up. 'Regulations, and the penalities attendant on their infringement, were his ruling passion'.[2] According to Richard Ollard, a writer who was at Eton much later, Quintin was regarded by his contemporaries as the leader of the reaction against laxity. In any event, he co-operated enthusiastically in Marsden's disciplinary reforms.

A body of contemporaries too big and too unanimous to ignore recollect that Quintin beat other boys frequently and with gusto. His half-brother, Edward Marjoribanks, who was eight years Quintin's senior as captain of the school, had a reputation for sadism which lived on. He was singled out in Cyril Connolly's book *Enemies of Promise* as a 'passionate beater'. Connolly wrote as a victim (his book dwells lovingly on corporal punishment) but his conceit of the masters as the medieval church and the boys as a feudal hierarchy, is more entertaining than objective. Connolly worked out the analogy in some detail. A boy had two loyalties, to his tutor and his fagmaster or feudal overlord. Sometimes the church could protect a young clerk. It depended on the balance of power. Sometimes 'the housemaster was powerless, the "church" weak and unable to control the feudal barons. At other times there were struggles between master and boy which ended in Canossa.' There is however no doubt that beatings, which were the universal rule in English public schools, encouraged sadism and perhaps other undesirable proclivities. Flogging was a rite of passage and its erotic connotations were well known. It cannot have been good for a boy of Quintin's character to be encouraged to believe he was a member of the chosen and to be given unchecked powers of physical chastisement.

For all that, Eton was a civilising influence. Quintin's classical tutor, the man in charge of his studies and, to a degree, his general upbringing, was A. W. Whitworth, a charming and cultivated man with whom Quintin apparently got on well. Whitworth is supposed to have said that Quintin was too clever for him. Whether true or not, his academic progress was unimpaired and everything his tutor could desire. According to the narrow English tradition, Quintin became a classics specialist as a junior boy, and his work was singled out to be sent to the Headmaster no fewer than 21 times.* Arriving

---

* This is known as 'Sent up for Good'. If it happens three times, the boy is given a prize. Unfortunately, Quintin's work which was sent up does not survive. For one boy's work to be sent to the Headmaster on twenty-one occasions is believed to be an Eton record.

at Eton in 1920 with the top scholarship, he won prizes in Latin, French or Divinity in almost every year and a Declamation Prize in 1926. In 1925 he won the supreme academic prize and became Newcastle Scholar. The competition for this last was a gruelling affair consisting of ten papers in classics and religious studies including such recondite exercises as rendering an English poem into Greek iambics. When he left he was in Sixth Form Division 1 and first in the School Order. As a consequence of this position, and being in College, he became captain of the school (a purely academic qualification) as his half-brother Edward had been before him.

These triumphs of scholarship brought him into closer touch with the remarkable Headmaster, Dr Cyril Argentine Alington. Alington was a highly articulate and enthusiastic spirit. He was ambitious too and understood Eton's unique position in the social structure of the country. He had striking looks, and could hold the chapel spellbound with his mellifluous voice and dramatic presence aloft in a pulpit lit only by a candle. As if to balance these gifts, he also wrote for the evening newspapers. Both Alington and his wife had the candour which encouraged friendships with the boys. Quintin liked him, and as captain of the school dined from time to time in his house. But he was not universally admired. He was not a great scholar and some boys regarded him as sanctimonious, referring to him as 'Creeping Jesus', according to Tim Card's history, *Eton Renewed*. But no headmaster worth his salt would aspire to be loved by all.

Alington personified part of the genius of Eton, that respect for the individual which was more important even than learning. In fostering the development of a boy's personality, the school encouraged independence of mind and did not frown on idiosyncrasy. In bringing boys to realise that there was no sanctity in conformity, Eton made possible the ease and freedom which comes from self-assurance. This characteristic distinguished the school from most, if not all, others. It was a distinction which mattered.

Fortunately for posterity, *The Eton College Chronicle* 'conducted by present Etonians' gives information on activities outside academe.* From this we learn that Hogg excelled in declaiming speeches. He read Burke's *Letter to a Noble Friend* 'in a high and unnatural pitch which made the words seem harsh, but the vigour of his delivery overcame this'. There would be speeches in later life which could be

---

* For those who knew Lord Dilhorne as an advocate and judge it will be interesting to learn that the Chronicle described Manningham-Buller (12st. 5lb.) as 'rather a rough oar'.

so described. He read Pericles' funeral oration in Greek and held 'in respectful silence the many in his audience who knew little or no Greek'. In the Wall Game, that mysterious and brutal ritual which was Quintin's only serious sporting activity, he was 'amazingly strong for his size and weight; has an uncanny ability for staying on the ball'. Those who believe that organised games illuminate character have a point. As captain of the school, Quintin became ex officio a member of the Eton Society, or 'Pop'. Originally a debating society, it became the self-elected inner aristocracy of the school. The glamour of Pop was that it was the focus for the natural snobbery of school society. Everyone wanted to be a member: even Connolly grovelled and gratified to get in, and his own description, which may be overheated, was: '. . . Pop were the rulers of Eton, fawned on by masters and the helpless Sixth Form. Such was their prestige that some boys who failed to get in never recovered . . .' In Quintin's time its membership had extraordinary and arbitrary powers of punishment and fagging. They wore fancy waistcoats and walked arm in arm. Pop epitomised the Englishman's insatiable longing to be an insider.

What sort of schoolboy was this scholastic prodigy? He described himself as 'prickly' and 'too clever – not by half, but I was too critical by half'.[3] Contemporaries' adjectives include 'ambitious, even ruthlessly so', 'obstreperous', 'loud', 'aggressive', 'exuding hubris'. A picture of a thoroughly nasty schoolboy emerges: small, assertive, bumptious. But there were other more sympathetic voices. Anthony Martineau, who was second in the Sixth Form order to Quintin, remembers him as very clever, but 'a boy who was not able to wear his cleverness lightly'. Sir Robin Brook, who was one year his junior and befriended him when his mother died, thought that Quintin had got himself rather isolated at the time. To Brook he was a very successful young scholar who meant to be outstanding and could be pugnacious about it. He could be easily upset and might react with unexpected force. His intellectual standing did not have the effect of making him aloof. Brook's account was perceptive as well as understanding, as he discerned a trait of character which others missed. Quintin was emotionally vulnerable and lacked friends.[4]

A year before he left Eton, he sustained his first shock of bereavement. Two years earlier, his mother had had a stroke and it had affected her personality. 'Where on the whole she had been light-hearted and sparkling, she became irritable, short-tempered and hypercritical.' Her sons did not understand what had happened and Quintin's relations with his mother suffered. Her death in May 1925, announced abruptly by Edward to Quintin and Neil while they were both in the college sickroom, came out of a blue sky. Quintin was unprotected from the grief which overwhelmed him. He realised that his religious faith offered him no comfort. There followed five years of drift and unbelief. For the present, he rebuffed anyone who offered spiritual solace. 'In the afternoon the headmaster came in to comfort me. He was a gentleman and a Christian. He sought to console me with talk about the afterlife. I was discourteous. I suddenly realised that I did not believe a word of what he was saying, and I told him so. I said that I believed that when we died we were nothing. "Like the animals," I said for good measure. He was angry and went away.' Where his mother's brilliant personality had been, there was now a vacuum. Douglas too was unprotected and the emotion which had been suppressed under an austere carapace for so long burst surface and engulfed him. 'He could be heard at night from his bedchamber, literally shouting with agony.' Quintin's response to his wife Mary's sudden death fifty years later was to bear a painful resemblance.

Although academic success continued, culminating in the top Classical Scholarship to Christ Church, Oxford, Quintin's remaining year at Eton passed unhappily. Damaged by his mother's death, he described himself as morose and neurotic. Sir Robin Brook recalls taking long walks with him and allowing him to talk about himself. There were very few others in whom he could confide.

3

Oxford

QUINTIN was not tempted by the frivolous life on offer at Oxford, and was never even on the fringe of Evelyn Waugh's 'Bright Young People' who introduced a new jargon into the language. His ambition was too serious and too strong. During his time at Christ Church between 1926 and 1930 the essential priorities were academic success, then a career at the Bar and in Conservative politics. The four-year course in 'Mods' and 'Greats' came first. The formidable curriculum for these 'schools' (or courses) was: Honour Moderations ('Mods') in Greek and Latin literature: composition and translation; set classical texts; a general paper on the classical civilisations; and Honour School of Literae Humaniores ('Greats'): Greek and Latin languages; history of Greece and Rome; philosophy, including logic and moral and political philosophy. After this academic assault course, in order of importance, came the Union, the self-conscious replication of the Palace of Westminster as debating chamber and political nursery; then social contacts which could be helpful later. It sounds cold-blooded, but it was a conventional programme for those who had ambitions to move events. In this picture, Douglas Hogg and Edward Marjoribanks, father and half-brother, were dominant figures in the foreground. Quintin was watching and consciously modelling himself on both of them.

A look backwards at the career of Quintin's father ought now to be taken. After one unsuccessful foray into politics as parliamentary candidate for Marylebone East in 1909, he devoted himself to his practice at the Bar with the single-mindedness which that jealous goddess always exacts from its successful votaries. He took silk in 1917 and in the years of boom in litigation which followed the war his earnings rose to levels seldom equalled in his profession.[1] In 1917 he bought 'Carters Corner Place', near Hailsham in Sussex. This was a house dating back to Elizabeth's time, with farming land, which Myssie set about restoring bit by bit. Quintin came to love this country home. But the watershed event in Douglas's career was the collapse of the Coalition Government in October 1922. Among the casualties were the Law Officers, Ernest Pollock and Leslie Scott, who declined to serve on under the new, unknown Prime Minister, Bonar Law. There was a story, almost certainly apocryphal, that while the government was struggling with its initial difficulties, Lord Derby suggested Douglas Hogg for Attorney-General. 'I know the very man,' he is supposed to have said. 'Someone was telling me about him the other day, a fellow called Pig.'[2] However the talents and steady Conservatism of Douglas Hogg were brought to the attention of Bonar Law, the fact was that within the space of one month he entered the House of Commons and became a Knight, a Privy Councillor and Attorney-General. He quickly proved himself in debate and in less than a year, according to Professor Heuston, the biographer of modern Lord Chancellors, he was recognised by all as the Government's most powerful debater. 'Hogg, as you know, is turning out to be a real discovery . . . I hope to be able to use him a great deal,' Bonar Law told Curzon.[3]

After the short and unhappy life of the first Labour Government in 1924, Baldwin made Douglas Hogg Attorney-General once more and brought him into the cabinet, an unusual distinction. He left him some of the most difficult assignments to face the government. Among them was the Electricity Supply Bill, which established a national grid and was bitterly opposed by a group of Tory backbenchers who thought it smelled of socialism. Then came the General Strike, and Douglas was one of the government's strong men in the House.

The General Strike of May 1926 brought to a climax years of industrial unrest and attempts by the miners to gain support for their grievances from their fellow workers. Threatened by wage cuts, the miners finally persuaded the Trades Union Congress to call out the transport workers, printers, builders and men in the heavy industries. The Baldwin Government, with Winston Churchill in the van, reacted sharply and with unexpected resolution. It commandeered the information services, including radio, used troops to distribute food, and recruited volunteers to maintain other essential services. The TUC was ill prepared for this response and surrendered abjectly after nine days, but the miners stayed out – in vain – until August. The Strike left a legacy of bitterness, not least between the betrayed miners and the TUC. It was also a stinging reverse for the whole trade union movement.

Like many young men of his background, Quintin did voluntary work during the Strike and had some fun with it. This was in the summer before he went up to Oxford. He returned from a Mediterranean cruise in the middle of the stoppage and was determined to do his bit. He became a vehicle mechanic for a few weeks, maintaining a fleet of ancient lorries on refuse collection duty in Marylebone. He was supremely unqualified for the job, but it did not matter. Somehow the lorries remained on the road and the grateful citizens of Marylebone plied their rescuers with frequent stimulants. Quintin doubtless learned something about the internal combustion engine. It is not difficult to imagine the excitable young Hogg making a great deal of noise about his vehicle maintenance. But neither he nor his father seem to have been moved by the fact that it was in the end hunger which drove the miners back to work.

In the aftermath of the Strike Douglas was given responsibility for drafting and steering through the Commons the controversial Trade Disputes Bill which outlawed any strike 'designed or calculated to coerce the government or to intimidate the community'. Douglas declined to agree publicly with Sir John Simon's solemn denunciation of the General Strike as illegal, and probably disagreed with it.[4] But there is no evidence that he had any qualms about the Bill which gave statutory sanction to Simon's view. Indeed, he advised Quintin to defend the Bill in a speech at Oxford as being necessary in view of the Strike experience.[5] In any event, he carried the Bill in the Commons with skill and resolution against every known tactic of obstruction. When the House was aroused, his style was always to meet uproar with calm, a style which Baldwin justifiably preferred to either the flamboyance of Birkenhead or the pugnacity of Churchill.

Douglas having become Baldwin's close confidant, it was no surprise that he was offered the Lord Chancellorship when Lord Cave died suddenly in March 1928. He accepted after Birkenhead had declined, but it seems that he was bounced into it by Baldwin persuading him that it was his duty to take it on. By doing so, and thus accepting a peerage, he deprived himself of the chance of becoming Prime Minister.

Neville Chamberlain, for one, was dismayed. He wrote to his sister: 'I regard his promotion as rather a calamity and it was all rushed through in a very unfortunate way . . . Poor Douglas was very unhappy, for he had realised when it came to the point he wanted to continue his political career and of course the tragedy is that he is now barred from the chance of becoming P.M. when S.B.

retires. To my mind this is a great misfortune for I believe he would have had a very good chance and I am sure he is the best man we have for such a position . . . I would gladly serve under him as I believe he would under me . . ."[6] With Douglas Hogg out of the Commons for ever, Chamberlain himself became Baldwin's heir and the repository of Conservative orthodoxy. Douglas became a peer without a proper opportunity to think through the consequences: his son would be compelled to leave the Commons without any opportunity at all.

From Eton and Oxford, Quintin watched these developments in his father's career with the closest attention. Douglas wrote to him at Oxford once a week. Quintin was speaking at the Union and Conservative clubs and his father supplied him with material. When the Electricity Supply Bill was going through, he sent him copies of the Bill and other parliamentary papers with his own detailed commentary. He advised him how to explain the Trade Disputes Bill to best tactical advantage. He even attended a Conservative Party Conference at Yarmouth in 1929, and spoke. This precocious politician of twenty-two years was not abashed by the occasion and was described, beyond even the limits of journalistic licence, as 'impetuous youth, a blue eyed boy with a cupid's bow of a mouth'. He did have good looks and an engaging flamboyance, and while he was saying that many of the new women voters would be little older than himself, a woman's voice called out to loud laughter, 'You'll do all right!' He also began writing for the press. In the same year the *Sunday Times* published his piece on 'Why I am a Conservative'.

Douglas's letters to his son described the life he was leading as Attorney-General. 'I'm living at so much strain that I hardly know when I last wrote to you! What with Revenue papers in Court,* 3 speeches, 2 cabinets and about 2–3 hours a day of Imperial Conference Committees, this week has been terrible: and next week Electricity in the Commons will make things even worse'.[7] The letter was written in a few snatched moments from Chequers. After a hard day in Court, Douglas had to face the Commons; then often out to dinner with a speech to make, or an event at the Polytechnic; finally before bed he would be obliged to work on his papers for two or three hours. It was little wonder that his health gave way.

The tone of the exchanges was of friendly men on equal terms. Quintin was encouraged to, and did, proffer his own view. This intercourse between the successful father and the son full of promise was evidently a source of satisfaction to both. When Lord Cave was

---

* The Attorney-General used to lead for the Crown in tax appeals, before Attorneys became more politician and less lawyer.

known to be dying, and Baldwin was seeking to persuade Douglas to accept the Woolsack, Quintin urged his father to decline. He did not like the idea of being placed in line for a hereditary peerage which might well stunt his own career, and did not see why it was necessary simply to spare Baldwin temporary embarrassment. He felt sure that his mother would have dissuaded her husband; but Mildred Lawrence, whom Douglas was about to marry, was strongly in favour. And Douglas was impelled by a sense of duty. The actual news of his father's appointment as Lord Chancellor reached Quintin while he was on holiday abroad. 'Melancholy congratulations. Reform Lords,' he wired home. He followed this with a letter which elaborated these sentiments: 'Some are born unto titles; some achieve them and some have them thrust upon them. Pity the poor third class!' The letter went on to canvass some possible titles. 'Might I suggest Hurstmonceux ... Hailsham is possible ... Polegate is doubtful (Do you know Polegate? Such a nice little man!).' Hailsham it was. Quintin did not think his father had chosen wisely in his own interests and he resented the consequences for himself. But he could not know the precise way in which the fateful inheritance would bring him down at the last fence. Nor could he guess that he would follow his father as Lord Chancellor, an office of which he was then largely ignorant.

Edward Marjoribanks continued to be a model for Quintin. He had a flamboyant manner, seeing himself, Quintin recalled, as a Byronic figure. Edward's industry was prodigious. He had been a scholar at Eton, a scholar at Christ Church, a double first in Mods and Greats (Quintin's subjects), President of the Oxford Union, and was as well a fine oarsman. He had a large circle of famous friends which included Marshall Hall, the great histrionic advocate whose biography he was to write, Lady Cunard, the redoubtable hostess, and Lord Beaverbrook. He had himself embarked on what promised to be a starry career at the Bar and in politics. Quintin could not fail to be magnetised by such an heroic brother. But Edward was also possessed of a temperament which swung erratically from elation to depression. Perhaps because of it this romantic figure was unfortunate in love. All his affairs were disasters. He would dazzle at first encounter but the courtship which followed would be stormy. In the interval between Eton and Oxford Quintin witnessed at close quarters the end of Edward's affair with his first love, Pamela Beckett. Both appeared unexpectedly on a Mediterranean cruise which Douglas had arranged for Quintin as a reward for winning the Newcastle. Pamela, 'like some delicate Cartier jewel full of beauty and appeal', jilted Edward in mid-voyage, causing him to leave the ship in Athens abruptly and without explanation. She went on jilting and died unhappy.[8] For Edward, his unstable temperament and his failures in love led directly to the final tragedy of his suicide in 1932.

★

The University of Oxford, like Cambridge, is a loose confederation of self-governing colleges. Founded at different times over at least seven centuries (the origins of the oldest are obscure), each has its own character. Quintin's college, Christ Church, is the grandest. The founder of its predecessor, Cardinal College, was Thomas Wolsey, the most powerful man in the land after the King. The college has its own cathedral, thirteen Prime Ministers have been Christ Church men,* and Charles I made the college his palace during the Civil War. For centuries it has had a social pre-eminence, a cachet which has drawn the privileged to it. If there is such a thing as 'the Establishment', Christ Church is part of it. So too is All Souls, to which Quintin Hogg later won a coveted Prize Fellowship. All Souls is the most idiosyncratic of all. Founded in the fifteenth century as a place where priests could pursue theological studies and where prayers were to be offered for the souls of Henry V, the Duke of Clarence and the English captains who had fallen in the French wars, it has no undergraduates and has become a focus for advanced studies. Its Fellows are distinguished men and women from diverse fields who are mainly non-resident and gather in college at weekends.

Quintin loved Christ Church and was to love All Souls, but how he was affected by his Oxford experience is harder to say. Certainly, he shed some of the raw bumptiousness of his Eton days, without loss of that life force which buoyed him up always. However, the evidence of what he did and how he lived beyond the confines of his academic and political preoccupations is sparse and anecdotal. In one episode, he returned to his rooms late one night to find some rowdies in possession, on a wrecking raid. They ran off when discovered. He pursued them, shouting, tried unsuccessfully to involve a policeman, and chased them alone until they dispersed. He was physically brave, and doubtless would have taken them on, had he had an opportunity. In his first year he was chosen as one of a

* George Grenville, the Earl of Shelbourne, the Duke of Portland, William Grenville, the Earl of Liverpool, George Canning, Sir Robert Peel, the Earl of Derby, W. E. Gladstone, the Marquis of Salisbury, the Earl of Rosebery, Sir Anthony Eden, and Sir Alec Douglas-Home. A fourteenth, William Pulteney, Earl of Bath, was asked to form a government in 1742, but refused.

series of 'Idols' for the undergraduate magazine *Isis*. This was no sillier than most student forays into journalism, but it shows that he was already prominent in the University. The reporter noted that he had made his debut at the Union, where all aspiring politicians ought to show their paces, in his first term and forecast a career of public office. But his scout (the servant allotted by the college to look after the needs of a group of undergraduates) did not share in the optimism. '"Mr Hogg has made a bad start," he said, mournfully surveying the disarray of morning.'

Quintin Hogg was never under any illusion about the capacity of his mind. He described it best in *The Door Wherein I Went*.

> I acquired, and have retained, an almost unlimited capacity to absorb information, great power of concentration, and meticulous habits of scholarship, marred only by the occasional carelessness caused by the speed at which I work. I was academically exceptionally gifted, and being intensely ambitious and competitive by nature, made full use of this gift. Moreover, being extremely clumsy and unathletic, although robust and healthy, I had no other field in which to excel.

Although Quintin knew that his work at Oxford came first, he took chances with it. His tutor for the Honour Moderations course, J. G. Barrington-Ward, described him in a letter written in 1928 to Douglas as 'the ablest boy – and one of the most industrious – that I have come across since the war';[9] but Douglas worried about the distractions of the Union and politics. 'I'm a little afraid your club and Union duties may crowd out necessary work; but you must judge best about Oxford, as I never had that advantage'.[10] He did have cause for concern. In a wildly over-confident flight of fancy Quintin stood as candidate for President of the Union in his very first term. He was quite unknown, the Union was dominated by Liberals when he stood as a Conservative, and he was bound to lose. It might have ruined his chances later on, and in retrospect he simply did not know how he had the gall to do it. However, the throw gave him the chance to take part in the Presidential debate, the most important of the term, which was attended by the legendary F. E. Smith.* When the votes were counted, Quintin was not last but

* Frederick Edwin Smith, first Earl of Birkenhead 1872–1930. Barrister, politician, horseman; a brilliant, swashbuckling orator with a reputation for reckless partisanship, his maiden speech in the Commons in 1906, contrary to convention, was highly controversial. Attorney-General (1915); Lord Chancellor (1919); Secretary of State for India (1924).

third out of four, the winner being Dingle Foot, with Richard Acland bottom of the poll In the end the attempt did him no harm: 'this ludicrous foray in the field of calculated risk was one of the factors which set me on the road to become President in 1929.'

He liked calculated risks. Elizabeth Harman, who later married Frank Pakenham and became Lady Longford, bet him a pound that he would not leave one of the translation papers in the Greats examination an hour early, thus, as she thought, reducing his chances of getting an alpha double plus. He duly won his bet and got his First. 'I'll never forget his wonderful smirk', she wrote, 'as he walked down exactly an hour early.'[11]

Barrington-Ward did not doubt his ability to get a First in any course except the most technical ones, 'so that if he took Modern Greats I am sure he would come out top there . . . The future which I have had in mind for him from the beginning was that he should get his First and then an All Souls Fellowship.' Quintin took advice from his father: the advice was that he should read Law, but if he would not do that it should be Greats rather than Modern Greats.[12] 'The latter was only intended for people who wanted to read philosophy and couldn't do Greek – not your case! It is nothing thought of by old Oxfordians, and has nothing like the same prestige as Greats. You throw away all the great advantages of your classical scholarship, and have to take up modern languages of which you know practically nothing, and all for the sake of reading political economy, which is a very vague science . . .' Edward was reported to have concurred in this view emphatically and was 'really shocked that you should throw away the advantage of Oxford . . .' This was good advice forcefully expressed, and Quintin took it. He worked hard, especially in the vacations, and got his double first in Mods and Greats. Douglas, however, agreed with Barrington-Ward about going for an All Souls Fellowship. He thought it 'the Oxford distinction which mysteriously – here I speak with knowledge – is the most esteemed and the one of practical value in after life'. All Souls was already a force in the Conservative Party, a gathering place at weekends for the hierarchy. In the thirties, the College's association with the Chamberlain Government's policy of appease-ment became notorious.

Although he was not particularly social, Quintin naturally widened his circle during his four Oxford years. Gilbert Ryle, the distinguished philosopher who was not yet thirty at the time, taught him for Greats. He got to know David Cecil and Randolph Churchill, and in Lindemann's rooms at Christ Church ('the Prof', as he was always known, was professor of experimental philosophy, i.e. physics) he met F. E. Smith and Winston Churchill. The prickly, brilliantly clever Lindemann, who was a friend of Edward's, had right-wing views and believed in a hierarchical society, inherited wealth and white supremacy. It is perfectly believable that the gatherings in his rooms produced 'quite extraordinary evening colloquies'. Churchill and F. E. Smith gave firework displays of eloquence and wit for the delectation of the Prof's young friends.

Although Eton more nearly resembles Oxford than do other schools, the release from a stratified male society had a beneficial effect on Quintin, as his Oxford friends attest. Who were those friends? He himself described this as a difficult question to answer. They certainly included Denys Page and Donald Allen, both classicists, who after Christ Church had distinguished academic careers; Richard Best, the son of a Northern Ireland judge; and Billy Loudon and Hilary Magnus. These last two remained his closest friends for life. They did not share his ambitions and were not his academic equals, but there was a bond between them, rare in Quintin's case, which proved indissoluble. The three continued to like larking about together; their company brought out the best of Quintin's raucous, mischievous side and his strongly marked sense of the ridiculous.

There seem to have been no girl friends, and certainly he did not fall in love. Elizabeth Harman, admired and aspired to by so many male contemporaries, was reading Greats at the same time as he was. She was a Zuleika Dobson figure, for whom men competed to hold her umbrella. She met her future husband, Frank Pakenham, at a New College Ball. They each had different partners. Pakenham fell asleep on a sofa. She woke him up with a kiss. On rousing he said, 'I'm afraid I can't kiss you,' and resumed unconsciousness. From this unlikely beginning, they never looked back. Lord Hailsham, who was also at the Ball, gives a different account of Pakenham's words: 'I'd like to, but what would your friends think?' As the first version is Lady Longford's own, and given in her memoirs, *The Pebbled Shore*, its authenticity is beyond challenge. But Hailsham's apocryphal version has a certain charm. Lady Longford remembered that she enjoyed being with him. 'He was a very cheerful and amusing companion, but I always thought one had to be a bit careful. He was more conventional than you would think.' She liked his generosity of character, 'not financially because he always regarded himself as poor, and I think still does,' but in his willingness to help her with her work and to give time. 'He laughs so much himself and makes sure you laugh too'.[13]

Helen Asquith was a second cousin and they met just before they both went up to Oxford, when he was invited by his great aunt, Frances Horner, to stay at her house in Somerset for a ball at Longleat. They became close friends and met frequently at Oxford where they pursued the same studies and went to the same lectures. It was an affectionate relationship and Helen found him a very congenial intellectual influence. 'He had great vitality, and a sort of masculine toughness of mind which was stimulating and provocative.'[14]

In 1929, Douglas remarried, to Mildred Lawrence, the widow of the King's Proctor. The boys did not like their stepmother at first, 'a Memsahib type', Quintin described her; she thought him a cocky young man. Quintin confided in Helen Asquith about his hurt feelings. She saw, as Robin Brook had at Eton, that underneath his pugnacious exterior he was emotional and vulnerable. Helen Asquith was the daughter of Raymond Asquith, the Prime Minister's son, who was killed on the Somme: and Katherine Horner, whose own mother was a younger sister of Alice Hogg, Quintin's grandmother. Katherine Asquith had earlier become a Roman Catholic, and while Quintin was at Oxford her three children, including Helen, followed her into the Catholic church.

Quintin was brought into touch with the Jesuits of Campion Hall, where Helen Asquith attended seminars. But she did not introduce him. The circumstances of the introduction were odd, the consequences far-reaching. He and his friend, Richard Best, received an invitation out of the blue in the summer of 1928 to a meal at Campion Hall. The Campion Hall Journal for 22 June 1928 reads: '*St Aloysius Wine*. Guests: Q. Hogg: Ric. Best: & McElwee. Undergraduates from Ch. Ch. Wine dessert, Coffee Smokes. Benediction: *Te Deum* and Thanksgiving.'

Quintin had never heard of the place. He found out many years afterwards that the object of the invitation was to cure two young Jesuit students, who were living there, of their ignorance and suspicion of Protestants and public schoolboys.[15] One of the two was Tom Corbishley, who became a lifelong friend and was later Master of Campion Hall. Quintin never discovered why or how he and his friend Best, the son of an Orangeman, had been selected to demonstrate that their species was human after all. He was not an obvious candidate himself. 'I do not think that I was all that bad as young men go. But I was certainly not good and not becoming better, which is to say that I was going down hill. My contact with the Church of my baptism and confirmation was purely formal. My faith had dwindled into agnosticism.'[16]

Ringing the bell at Campion Hall, he felt a thrill of danger. Fr

Martin D'Arcy met him at the door. He was not yet Master but was already the moving spirit in contacts between the Jesuit community and the University. This remarkable man had a large and diverse circle of Oxford friends. At first, Quintin found Fr D'Arcy frightening rather than attractive. 'The only adjective which really serves, God save the mark, is Mephistophelean, aquiline, dark, handsome with a friendly but apparently sinister grin, redeemed, but only at a second glance, by gentleness and compassion.'[17] That was his description, forty years after their first meeting. Martin D'Arcy became one of the profound influences in his life. Their friendship was untroubled, until D'Arcy's death in 1976. Quintin turned to him always, and later to Tom Corbishley as well, in every moral or emotional crisis: 'over the years I have come to him with problems as diverse and as poignant as any penitent in the confessional'.

The irony in the friendship was evident. Quintin had been brought up to believe that the Pope was anti-Christ. The Jesuits were the shock troops of Roman Catholicism, whose supposedly unscrupulous methods of obtaining conversions were a legend. Douglas was anxious when he heard that his son was spending time at Campion Hall. But his fears were groundless. Quintin found that the Jesuits were neither designing nor ruthless. Martin D'Arcy never played unfair. Always uncompromising and occasionally stern, he gave his help 'unstintingly, generously, understandingly', in Quintin's words; and he made him feel ashamed that he was unable to repay the kindness in the coin that D'Arcy would most have wished. There was, however, no serious question that he would ever become a Catholic.

D'Arcy's conversation was allusive and cryptic, 'betraying often that he knew more of the world than one did oneself'. (Alone among Quintin's friends, he was to foresee the result of the 1945 General Election. Are you quite sure, he asked with characteristic obliqueness, that it is not going to be a landslide for Labour?) Quintin believed that he would not have returned to his Christian beliefs without D'Arcy's guidance. By argument and by example, he taught Quintin that the Christian faith, Catholic or Protestant, was intellectually respectable. Quintin emphasised this in his tribute on Fr D'Arcy's eightieth birthday: 'But there is a Christian philosophy as well as a Christian religion, that there is a Christian cultural inheritance as well as a Christian ethic, that Christianity is not just a comforting fable to be dismissed with the other illusions of childhood, are truths which, more than to any other man, I owe to Fr D'Arcy.'[18]

The Catholic hierarchy gave a dinner for Fr D'Arcy when he

ceased to be Provincial and Quintin was asked. 'Odd to find you here,' remarked one of the establishment. It was not odd at all. The friendship with Martin D'Arcy and Tom Corbishley was for life. When Corbishley was dying in 1976, Lord Hailsham visited him. 'As I said goodbye,' he wrote in his diary, 'I said "Get Well". He said, "I will. I cannot say I shall." So we parted. Left bottle Glenfiddich.'[19]

These friendships were the main reasons for the restoration of Quintin Hogg's faith. But he also ascribes this to his own philosophical speculations, which are traced in *The Door Wherein I Went*. According to his account, the barren years of unbelief were brought to a sudden end during a three-hour paper on Logic, when he was twenty-three, and writing his 'Greats' examinations.

A very odd thing happened to me in this examination. I had entered it, as I believed, exceptionally well prepared, and there were few of the questions I could not have attempted except the one or two designed for candidates interested particularly in music or the arts. But the strange thing was that I had only attempted to answer two of the questions about which I thought I knew so much. Most of the time I had spent in attempting to answer a question about which I knew nothing, and about which in fact I knew rather less than this. It was a question about mysticism, which I was ignorant enough to equate with belief in God. It was this strange episode in my intellectual history which, I believe, proved the turning-point in the slow recovery of my Christian faith.

These speculations, recalled in chapter 3 of *The Door Wherein I Went*, led him to the conviction that if there was no reason why an intelligent, rational man should believe in God, there was equally no reason why he should not. But it is open to question whether they were as potent an influence on the young man's spiritual life as the blossoming friendship with the Jesuits. They did, however, lead him back to the thinking of his grandfather, the first Quintin, and his belief in the universal validity of virtue: 'Whatever else may be shaken there are some [facts] stablished beyond the warring of theologians. Forever virtue is better than evil − truth than falsehood, kindness than brutality.' (See p. 7.) The second Quintin Hogg was one of the very few public figures of the age to continue to practise and profess his Christian faith. It never wavered again.

★

When Quintin finished his Oxford studies at the age of twenty-three, he had been studying the classics continuously for sixteen years. From the age of seven, the Greek and Latin languages and cultures had been his staple. With Enoch Powell he became one of the few people in public life to have been educated in this way, to follow the course of studies which had sustained first the church and then the administrators and governing classes in England since the Reformation, but which was in the process of being gradually abandoned. Today it seems almost perverse to have concentrated so much toil on the history, philosophy and tongues of two civilisations long since dead, and pagan too. Was it absurd? In common with all others who have been brought up in this school, he thought not. He argued that his studies had a strong moral content, both as regards individual and civic virtue. Moreover, the classical historians wrote often to show the lessons of history, and he continued to draw parallels between contemporary circumstances and the events described by Thucydides and Livy. 'The ancient world has much to teach us about the dangers of social disintegration and permissiveness, of treachery and cowardice.' There were to be many occasions when the future Lord Hailsham would give public warning against social disintegration and permissiveness. In the gathering crisis which afflicted and then destroyed the Heath Government of 1970–74, he saw the dominant cause as moral, not economic. Insurrection in Ulster, lawlessness among the dockers and miners, irresponsibility in parliament – all to him were aspects of the same malaise, a want of belief in country, party or indeed anything. The Greek and Roman historians would have recognised the symptoms. He did not add, but could have done, that his immersion in the disciplines of Greek and Latin, in which he produced weekly prose and strictly metred verse in both languages, although not of much utilitarian value, was as good training for the mind as could be devised. He did not lose his facility with the dead languages. In 1994, at the age of 86, he went to Eton for the reopening of the Montague James Schools of the Classics Department. *The Times* reported him as saying, 'My own classics are as rusty as an old sword in a scabbard'; and then addressing the assembled dignitaries in fluent Latin. The study of the classics was certainly no disadvantage in the long and arduous professional and public life on which he now embarked.

4

The World Outside

IN the twenties and thirties the transition from Eton to Oxford to the Bar looked easy, at any rate for the gifted. The worlds appeared comfortingly similar. One lived and worked in a collegiate atmosphere among old buildings arranged in courts and cloisters and staircases. One's colleagues were friends and acquaintances, or at least from recognisably similar homes. But the last stage masked a real change. Quintin Hogg had to earn his living in a highly competitive profession where even the ablest spent their first years on or near the subsistence level. The picture which he draws in his autobiography of a profession that is chivalrous and generous is affected by a rosy afterglow. There were, and are, high standards of integrity and practitioners offer each other courtesies in their dealings. But chivalry was an exaggeration. Beneath the surface of conventional urbanity, advantages could be taken which were certainly not chivalrous. Quintin Hogg himself did not shrink from doing so. Lord Lester, then a young junior, remembers being led by him when he was suffering from such a disturbed digestive tract that throughout his opponent's speech he lay across the desk moaning softly. No one ever knew how far this was forensic, although it would be fair to Lord Hailsham's reputation to say that his junior added: 'Quintin Hogg was a formidable and very perceptive advocate. He had mastered the legal issues thoroughly and was realistic about the prospects of success or failure, but above all he had the courage of a lion in the way in which he argued the case in spite of the fact that he was very sick throughout the hearing.'

Before he entered this world, however, there was one more Oxford prize. His Tutor had recommended that he go in for a Fellowship at All Souls and his father had enthusiastically concurred. He determined to do so. As Douglas Hogg advised his son, the

College possesses unrivalled prestige. It awards Prize Fellowships each year on All Souls' Day, regarded as the ultimate testimonial to academic achievement. Neither Quintin's father, who had not been to University, nor his half-brother Edward had been awarded an All Souls' Fellowship; so he was breaking fresh ground.

Because his father had taken the hereditary peerage in 1929, Quintin knew that he must hasten his call to the Bar; that in turn would hasten his entry into politics. His father was fifty-seven when he became a Peer; when he died the son would be forcibly carried up to the Lords. His projected time in the Commons was therefore at best limited and might be cut away at any moment. At worst there might be no time at all. He would have to establish himself at the Bar before attempting to fight a seat in the Commons. It was hard to foresee how long that might take. These considerations closed off the possibility that he should compete for the All Souls Fellowship in the subjects for which he was best qualified: ancient history and philosophy. He had to start reading for the Bar immediately and the subject for All Souls would have to be law, of which he knew practically nothing. He therefore determined to compete in 1931, the year after he took his first in Greats, and at the same time as he was preparing for his Bar examinations. This double hurdle in an unknown field perhaps represented the toughest test he had ever set himself, and he worked day and night for it. The result was triumph. Edward wrote: 'My very dear Quintin, You are as I always thought, undefeated. I think on the whole success is better for you than failure, so I am unreservedly delighted with and proud of you . . .'[1] He was awarded his Prize Fellowship in preference to Richard Wilberforce and Herbert Hart, two of the most distinguished legal figures of their generation, and the following year he came top in the Bar Finals. He became Junior Fellow at All Souls and there began an attachment which was one of the most agreeable of his life. His stipend of £400 (£11,000 in 1990s values) was granted for an initial period of two years. Thereafter, it was reduced to £50 since he was not pursuing an academic career. For the same reason, the Fellowship was not renewable after its initial term of seven years. But his association with the College continued and he was elected to a Distinguished Fellowship in 1961.

Hogg's unbroken line of success did not prepare him for the misfortunes which fell on him in the year after Oxford, and whose long echoes sounded for the rest of his life. The first was the suicide of his admired brother, Edward. The circumstances of his death are described in distressing detail in *A Sparrow's Flight*. The brilliance of Edward's career, which had by now taken him into the House of

Commons, where he gravitated to the Beaverbrook-Empire Crusader wing of the Conservative Party, was marred by his fragile temperament. He had been unwell for some time and become insomniac. The melodramatic affair with Pamela Beckett was repeated with the daughter of the chairman of his own constituency party. She accepted his proposal and then, finding his highly charged personality too much for her, broke off the engagement. Quintin was warned by his brother's doctor that Edward should not be left alone. He never afterwards was able to forgive himself for having left Edward in the care of his father while he went off to pursue his own courtship; or for having left the gun room at Carters Corner unlocked. Edward shot himself with Quintin's own much-prized shotgun. The unbalanced Edward would most likely have taken his life anyway, and his brother could not have done more than delay the inevitable. But afterwards he could never think or speak of Edward without guilty emotion and he was left with a peculiar horror of suicide.

A little earlier in the same year of 1932 he met Natalie Antoinette Sullivan. He was speaking for the Conservative candidate at Salisbury and she was the Party agent for the constituency. Although the daughter of an American mother and a Canadian father, she lived with her family in Kent. She was a converted Catholic, a little older than he, acute, highly ambitious and highly sexed. There was a glamour and excitement about her, also a certain *hauteur* which hinted at a harder, unforgiving side. She was fascinated by politics and longed to be at the centre of events.[2] It was his first real affair and he was susceptible. He looked young beside his *mondaine* bride. Quintin's stepsister, Domini, went to the wedding. She was only four years old, but she took away a vivid impression of the bride which remained with her throughout her childhood. Natalie was 'a glittering figure, very accomplished socially, but she had no time for small children.'[3]

There was an immediate mutual attraction between the two. Quintin was courting Natalie when Edward took his own life, and she comforted him. On the day of the memorial service, 5 April 1932, she wrote him a loving letter. 'You have not been out of my thoughts since you left yesterday morning. All my love has been sent through the air to you to give you strength through these terrible days.'[4]

Quintin's successes in male society did not forearm him against the possibility of failure in his first serious encounter with the opposite sex. In *A Sparrow's Flight* Lord Hailsham warned his readers that he did not intend to be wholly candid about his marriage to Natalie. He remained raw and hurt about it for the rest of his life, and he omitted the marriage from his entry in *Who's Who*. His children did not learn of it until quite late in his life.

The couple became quickly engaged. He learned that it was impossible for her to bear children. He was not willing to make the promises required of him by the Catholic Church. For either or both these reasons, he asked her to release him; but she would not. A sense of honour made him go on; ambition impelled her. It was the worst possible start. They were married on 12 November 1932 at Holy Trinity, Marylebone. Those who were closest to the bride and groom felt an atmosphere of foreboding, and the *Marylebone Chronicle* reported that the marriage would take place quietly, no invitations had been issued but all friends would be welcomed at the church. The ceremony was Anglican. Natalie did not ask for a dispensation to marry in the Church of England, so the marriage could not be recognised by Rome. It was therefore valid for him but not for her. In 1933 she rejoined the Anglican community. This apparently cavalier attitude to faith, and the bizarre consequences to which it led, were distressing to him.*

The couple set up home in a little house in Victoria Square which had been Edward's and which Douglas Hogg gave them as a wedding present. The first Lord Hailsham was generous to his son. He gave him £10,000 (nearly £300,000 in 1997) on his majority, and when Natalie's father promised a fund to bring in £100 a year, Hailsham agreed to match it. The marriage lasted ten years. As well as the inauspicious circumstances in which it was made, there were differences in temperament and in expectation. She needed a masterful partner, he wanted a loving wife. He demanded affection but could not easily give it. His egocentricity made him rarely capable of imaginative sympathy. She became resentful and looked elsewhere. He described the marriage as 'probably an error from the start'. Yet there was real affection. Relations veered between warmth and rancour, but the letters between them and the diary he kept in wartime attest beyond argument to the affection.

---

* In 1978 he was prompted by a speech made by Prince Charles about the folly brought about by bickerings over doctrine, to write to *The Times* about his own experiences. He pointed out that after his marriage to Natalie had been dissolved, he wished to marry an Anglican (his second wife, Mary). They were not able to marry in Church and had to settle for Caxton Hall. If Mary had been either a Catholic or a Presbyterian there would have been no difficulty about the wedding being in church. If, he said, he had listened to the theologians instead of his father, he might not have married Mary. 'And when the poor sheep happen to belong to different folds, whilst their warring pastors argue with one another as to which of their unverifiable propositions is true, many go unfed altogether, and others are allowed to wander away into the wilderness.' (*The Times*: 7 July 1978)

Douglas Hogg thought his son was marrying too soon. It was certainly early in his career, within a few months of his Bar Finals. Douglas wrote to his brother-in-law, General Lytle Brown, in the United States: 'My son, Quintin, has got engaged to be married to a Canadian girl . . . and their wedding is to be on 21st December. I could have wished that he had waited until he had been better established in life, but young people are apt to take these matters into their own hands.'[5] Natalie was dogged by ill health and the threat of surgery. In 1934 Douglas wrote to a friend that there was talk of an operation, and again in 1939, this time a hysterectomy. It was naturally affecting the couple: 'Quintin has been having the devil of a time; everything he does is wrong and Natalie is undoubtedly suffering and nervy. He finds his work has suffered and has practically dried up, and he is very sorry for himself.'[6]

Quintin was difficult to live with and Natalie stood up to him. She told him what she thought of his insensitivity. But she was vulnerable too, particularly about her inability to bear children.[7] The same inability touched his pride, and to assuage it he could occasionally draw attention to his wife's barrenness in conversation around the dinner table with friends. Some demon drove him on. The fact that she had forced him into marriage and her recurrent ill health made the friction worse. She was unfaithful, although on how many occasions is uncertain. He knew of at least one episode and blacked the interloper's eye. He was naïve and inexperienced; the idea of divorce was repugnant, socially unacceptable. All these things festered and turned a possible mistake into a certainty. This was the sadder because she could and did help him to further his political ambitions; but the early years of his career were made much more anxious by the absence of peace and security at home; and by a sense of failure.

By the time of his wedding and aged twenty-five, Quintin Hogg had been called to the Bar by Lincoln's Inn and was pupil to the celebrated Theo Mathew, best known as the author of *Forensic Fables*, a series of gently satirical pieces on life at the Bar, originally published with his own illustrations in the *Law Journal*. Apart from examinations, his only earlier contact with the profession was through having acted as marshal to Mr Justice Roche in the previous year. The marshal was the junior member of the itinerant household that accompanied a Judge on circuit. His main task was to see that the great man encountered no tedious little problems which might interfere with the workings of his mind. The marshal had a few ceremonial duties and was expected to keep the judge company. Roche was a forbidding figure who expected his marshal to go hunting with him between cases. He was a Trollopian character, a hard-riding judge who would get out in the field whenever a gap appeared in his list. He surprised his young companion by commenting not only on the cases themselves, but also by his critical appraisals of counsel's performances. Marshalling was a typical instance of the Bar's preference for teaching by example and personal contact rather than by the book.

Theobald Mathew never took silk. By the time he took on Quintin Hogg as a pupil (he had upwards of 200 pupils in all) he 'was so senior he had run through several, quite different, Common Law practices'. At that period he was concentrating on libel. Mathew had a deep respect for the traditions of the Bar but, according to his clerk, Sydney Aylett, had become crotchety. Quintin later drew a picture of him in verse:

> Hands clasped backwards, tilted hat,
> Humming voice, abstracted pose,
> Pince-nez spectacles that sat
> Halfway down the lifted nose.

The young Hogg, described by Aylett as 'a tousle haired, fresh-faced, ungainly figure', did not get on particularly well with Mathew. Nor did he ever satisfy his clerk as to the standards of his dress. Surprising as it may seem, barristers' clerks used not to hesitate to arrogate to themselves the right to vet the appearance of their charges, particularly when attending Court. None the less, Aylett had a high opinion of him. He records that the first Lord Hailsham visited him personally to arrange the pupillage and that he, Aylett, disregarded the opinion of those who warned him that young Hogg was conceited and too clever. Aylett gladly took him in to his chambers again much later in 1947 and was not disappointed. His own judgment was that Mr Hogg had star quality. Aylett was 'ready to accept the temperamental behaviour that is expected from those who breathe a rarer atmosphere ... His [Hogg's] occasional eccentricities, which were part of the whole man, were taken by some out of context and portrayed as absurdities.'[8] Perhaps Aylett was too indulgent towards the awkward young customer who was still the lowest form of legal life, but he was an understanding clerk, one of a small number who justified by their personal example the bizarre system by which barristers' work was organised and their fees negotiated with solicitors by a group of men of little formal education who knew no law but had sharp wits.

After pupillage, Hogg left Theo Mathew's chambers for the

chambers of Freddie Van den Bergh, a busy commercial silk. He could not recall much about his early work. 'Curiously enough, I remember little of my early cases at the Bar and, although my practice was mainly civil, most of my recollections are of a sort of bargain basement in crime.' In his first two or three years he took some 'dock briefs', for which the arrangement was that young barristers attended Court on a speculative basis, and the prisoner selected his advocate from those present. The remuneration was £1.3s.6d., later increased to £2.4s.6d., half a crown (2s.6d. or 12½p) going to the barrister's clerk. A similar system operated for some small prosecution briefs, which the Clerk at the Old Bailey distributed. These were known as 'soup', because the brief was regarded as a soup ticket. He also represented private charities which supported poor litigants in the magistrates' and county courts. These included the Roman Catholic *Our Lady of Good Counsel* 'which meant, alas, generally young and inexperienced counsel'. In addition, Hogg went down to Deptford once a fortnight to an advice centre where he gave his services free. Most of the questions were about the Rent Acts and most of his clients could not, or did not want to, pay their rent. This 'bargain basement' gave him a first-hand insight into the conditions under which those at the bottom of the pile were living out their lives. The experience undoubtedly influenced his political outlook. The idea that the social order for the thirties would have to be changed was already germinating in his mind. He began to think of himself as a young Conservative who, like the stranger in Disraeli's *Sybil*, perceived that England was not one but two nations. But he did not yet give voice in public to these thoughts. In *One Year's Work*, an account of what he had said and done in 1943, he looked back on the pre-war years. 'I am sure that the deep cleavage which divided the nation between the wars must be healed. The cleavage was the real bar to progress . . . This country cannot be united without extensive social reform.'

★

In 1936 Hogg wrote a textbook on arbitration, a subject of which, according to his own recollection, he had little practical experience. He recalls having been briefed in only one case in the field, concerning the coal industry, the solicitor being Ernest Jacobson, whose son later became a close friend in the army. Hogg collected David Jacobson's personal effects when he was killed in the Western Desert, and tried unavailingly to console the widowed father, whom he described as a 'vast old Maccabee'. He wrote the text book because, he thought, the subject was in a small compass and the existing rivals were poor books. The book was a well-ordered treatise on the law through decided cases, and his father wrote a brief foreword, wishing it every success. It is a pity that the work never went to a second edition after the war when the law of arbitration was consolidated in an Act of 1950, for it might have then become the leading text on the topic. *Hogg on Arbitration* is still used and thought well of by specialist practitioners who are concerned to trace the history of a point.

Hogg had more than the superficial acquaintance with arbitration that he remembered. In 1937/8 he took an active part in fending off a proposal to bring Britain into a scheme for international arbitration, and lobbied his Lord Chancellor father on the subject. He explained in a long handwritten letter[9] that an attempt was being made by a body called the Institute of Private International Law with headquarters in Rome 'inappropriately enough' to introduce what he described as 'a Convention which would impose as compulsory the foreign system of "conciliation" instead of the English system of "arbitration" in commercial contracts'. He expounded the difference between the two to his father as if the Lord Chancellor were a law student:

> An English arbitrator, although chosen by the parties, is still a judge in the sense that he must administer the law . . . He has no right to carve out a new contract for the parties, or to suggest 'reasonable' or 'equitable' courses. He is there to determine the dispute by deciding which party is right. The Latin system of 'conciliation' is based on a totally different conception. The referee thereunder undertakes the good offices of a friend . . . He is not limited to decide the dispute according to the rights of the parties or even to decide who is in the right at all. His object may be equally to effect a compulsory compromise, and he may therefore by his award direct the parties to do that which they have never agreed . . .'

The young barrister told his father that the idea coming from Rome was regarded with suspicion by the City fraternity, who feared that the scheme would undermine the reputation of London as the pre-eminent place to settle international trading disputes. They had decided to ask the Foreign Office to oppose the draft Convention, but Anthony Eden, the Foreign Secretary, had said that he would not move unless advised to do so by the Lord Chancellor's Department. Hence Hogg's appeal to his father.

In the event, the proposal died a natural death and Britain was not alone in opposing it. The time was not yet ripe for the harmonising of national laws on dispute resolution. Nor were lawyers in the City of London yet ready to face the question whether, in trying to help businessmen settle their disputes, they should not simply apply the law but also assume 'the good offices of a friend', as Hogg had termed it.

His father watched his progress with some anxiety. 'Quintin is not getting much work at the Bar, which is disturbing as he seems to do well what he does get. Outside the Bar he is looked on as one of our promising young men; for instance the BBC has asked him to speak as the representative of youth in a series entitled "Whither Britain".'[10] This was part of a series in which Churchill and Lloyd George were also participating. Hogg's contribution was printed in *The Listener* for 21 January 1934. It wears the confident air of a man who knew what to prescribe for the disease. It also contained a denunciation of hatred and violence which drew praise from the press, and of which the *Jewish Chronicle* for 2 March 1934 said, 'These words of a young man carry a well-timed rebuke to many among us of maturer years.' Hogg had said: 'Do not believe a man who says he hates the Jew and loves the Christian, or hates the rich and loves the poor. The man who hates the Jew is the enemy of the Christian.' Even the *Jewish Chronicle* did not know how precisely apposite these sentiments were in 1934. Hogg advised his listeners that if war broke out between France and Germany, Britain should stay out: the Locarno Treaty and the Covenant of the League of Nations would accordingly have to be re-negotiated. We should co-operate with the United States so as not to be 'called on to fight for someone else's King and Country'. At home, he thought that in order to maintain freedom from fear the working man must own property and not be under threat of a week's notice to quit. Employers should be required to set aside funds from their profits to protect the unemployed. These liberal views were to recur and to be developed with conviction during the war and in its immediate aftermath. The later picture of Hogg as a politician of right-wing inclinations was always unjust.

*

Neil, who had been forced to leave Eton because of asthma to continue his schooling in Switzerland, was an excellent correspond-ent. 'I trust you perceive an improvement in my literary style,' he wrote to Quintin from his pension-like academy in Chillon, 'as I have been reading wads of Scott. This, I find, has a soothing effect and produces the replete feeling that a heavy suet pudding will produce, if taken in large quantities.' Later he joined the Foreign Office and during the war kept in touch with Natalie, sending reports to his brother. 'She seems to miss you; I can't think why.' Of their father, who had by then had a stroke, he wrote: 'The old boy is looking a little like St Peter without the beard; charming but not so hearty as I had hoped . . . the lower part of his face is very fallen away.' And of their stepmother, Mildred, 'Every day she gaily plunges into a complicated mass of plans.'[11] Neil was not only a good letter writer. Among his many talents was a considerable gift for poetry. A limited edition of his verse was published under the title *Zodiac with Interludes* and he also published a free translation of some Arabic poems entitled *The Notebook of Abu Nuwas*, somewhat in the style of Edward Fitzgerald. Quintin thought him 'the most talented human being I have known'.[12]

Quintin could not rival this light touch and was not a good letter writer, but one long letter to his father of 1938 survives.[13] From its opening, it suggests that this was a very rare occurrence: 'You asked for a long letter and you shall have it; it is only because I am only too aware that my epistolary style is devastatingly dull that I don't inflict more on you.' The letter describes his summer holiday spent climbing in Wales and the Alps (he and Natalie took holidays separately). He had been introduced by his father to mountain walking and climbing at the age of thirteen, and it had become a life-long passion until a weakness in his ankles stopped him. This was congenital: what he thought were sprains were probably fractures. The weakness became steadily worse. Climbing was the only physical recreation he enjoyed. He disliked ball and team games and was bad at them, the Eton Wall Game apart. He had tried rowing at Eton and Oxford and enjoyed it, but it was not a passion. Edward had introduced him to a Balliol history don, Francis Urquhart, who had reading parties at his chalet in the French Alps. Climbing was forbidden until after the academic studies were done, but afterwards the undergraduates were encouraged to use the services of a local guide. Hogg described these reading parties as some of the happiest days of his life; they deepened his passion for the grandeur of the mountains and the exhilaration of climbing.

In his letter to his father he narrated in detail the climb he made at Chamonix with Hilary Magnus, his brother-in-law, Matthew Sullivan, 'a leading light of that suicidal institution, the Oxford Mountaineering Club', and a friend of Sullivan's called Ronnie Symonds, thought to be a complete novice but a man of good nerve. Hogg had diarrhoea and sickness but characteristically he pressed on cheerfully. He was always a good man to have in a tight corner. The party was delayed at the summit and ran out of time and daylight on the way down. They were forced to make their bivouac on a rock ledge exposed to the wind. 'It was a narrow bed and a hard one, but we had to lie on it.' The party slept fitfully, changing positions and clutching each other for warmth. A thunderstorm got up but fortunately passed overhead, leaving only drizzle after sleet. At 2 a.m. they gave up any pretence of sleeping and betook themselves to song until it was light enough to move. In the grey light of dawn the downward route looked impossible. They were too weak to climb, and there was no way down. Eventually they were rescued by another climbing party. The experience, described in a flat, factual way in the letter, marked itself in his mind. He described it again in his wartime diary. He wrote also about his feelings for the mountains. 'There is much joy in the high hills. There is fear and laughter; there is labour and hunger and thirst; there is friendship; there is triumph, weariness and mystery; and there is release from trouble, and peace.' (*Diary*, 23 January 1942).

★

In February 1933, Hogg took part in the notorious Oxford Union debate on the motion, 'That this House will in no circumstances fight for its King and Country'. As one of the visiting speakers, he spoke fourth against the motion, Professor C. E. M. Joad speaking fifth in favour. The resolution was carried by a large majority. The result afterwards became a fertile source of legend, although at the time it attracted little attention. None of the London newspapers bothered to send a reporter. In 1927 the Cambridge Union had passed a pacifist motion to similar effect;[14] and the Oxford debate might have gone as unnoticed, had not Randolph Churchill attempted to have the proceedings expunged from the Union records. Before he could move the expunging motion, a gang of undergraduate rowdies, supposed to be supporters of Mosley's Fascist party, forced their way into the Union, tore the offending pages from the minute book and burned them at the Martyrs' Memorial. When Randolph Churchill's motion came on for debate a fortnight later, supported by Hogg, Frank Pakenham and others, opinion had turned against them, partly as a result of the intervening incident, and partly because members felt the proceedings of the Society should not be interfered with. The would-be expungers were roughly handled and heavily defeated.

By now, public interest was aroused. For some, it showed that something was rotten in Britain's youth. The *Daily Express* put the result down to 'practical jokers, woozy-minded communists and sexual indeterminates'. The effects went further than that. The press whipped up the affair and Randolph Churchill's failed motion made matters worse. The debate came to assume a symbolic importance and to epitomise the corrupting weakness of the thirties. It was apparently noticed in Germany. The historian of the Union quotes Professor Beloff, who was one of the tellers in the debate, as saying later that 'it was one of the things that made it plausible for Ribbentrop and other people to report back that Britain wasn't ready to fight.'[15] And in *The Left was Never Right*, Hogg quoted the experience of a Liberal MP who visited Germany a year after the debate. A prominent young Nazi asked him about the debate, and commented 'with an ugly gleam in his eye: "The fact is that you English are too soft." '[16]

Recalling the debate thirty years later,[17] the then Lord Hailsham thought that those who voted for the motion, although genuinely horrified by the still fresh memory of trench warfare, and sincere in their pacifism, defiled themselves none the less. He recalled that this was the era of 'the fetish-worshippers of disarmament, of the Peace Ballot, whose words may have spoken of collective security, but whose whole effect was to weaken democracy'. Joad, a very wily debater indeed, 'advanced a series of sophistical paradoxes designed to show the stupidity and contradictions of all save out and out pacifists'. But Hogg was right to say that the Labour and Liberal left were infected by a sentimental brand of pacifism. At the time when Hitler was just coming to power, disarmament became the main plank in the foreign policy of the Left.

Were the Conservative mainstream equally deluded? We have seen that, in the year following the Union Debate, Hogg defended patriotism in his radio talk, but that did not mean fighting for *someone else's* King and Country. His father, who inhabited the heartland of Conservative orthodoxy, could be relied on to speak with its authentic voice. He and his second wife, Mildred, were Neville Chamberlain's first guests at Chequers when he became Prime Minister. His views on the abdication crisis of 1936 were sternly ultramontane. He wrote to the Governor-General of New Zealand: 'I think it is a dreadful thought that anyone who had so much personality and promise as the present King, and such unrivalled opportunity for strengthening the position of the Crown and linking up the Empire should have been the one to deal such a blow; and it is a bitter thought that this prospect should have been ruined by an adventuress like Mrs Simpson.'[18]*

When the National Government was formed under Ramsay Macdonald in August 1931, Douglas had been left out. He was objectionable to the Labour Party for his part in carrying through the Trade Disputes Act after the General Strike. But following the October election of the same year he was included in the second National Government as Secretary of State for War. He appears to have felt that war with Germany was inevitable, at least from the time when she walked out of the Disarmament Conference in October 1933 and then immediately left the League of Nations. According to Professor Heuston, 'Whatever was done to maintain our defences between 1931 and 1935 was due to the joint efforts of Chamberlain and Hailsham.'[19] Hogg agreed always and wrote in 1965: 'My father at least was not blind to the dangers of German aggression. He spoke to me about it in season and out of season . . . He fought a lonely battle in the Cabinet . . . and his one ally was the much maligned Chamberlain.' Douglas thought that Hitler only kept his word when it suited him. But he failed to draw the inevitable conclusions from this sound premise. In 1935 he wrote to his brother-in-law in America:

> It really looks as if Germany were still pining for that world domination which brought about the last war, and that she is gambling on the unwillingness of the Western Powers to face another conflict to enable her to arm so strongly as to be in a position of definite superiority over the rest of the world. I wish I could see more clearly the right policy. I know that in this country the lesson we have learnt from the Great War is a profound conviction of the senselessness and cruelty of warfare as a means of settling differences.[20]

That is probably as clear a reflection as could be found of the muddled state of mind which led to Munich. It was difficult to re-arm when it appeared to be the duty of those who desired peace to see that their own government did not have the means of making

* A glimpse of the formality attaching to the contemporary life of senior public figures is also revealing. A letter from an Equerry about a forthcoming visit to Sandringham by Lord and Lady Hailsham reads: '. . . I feel a word on the subject of clothes might be of assistance. For dinner – trousers, white tie and decorations. On Sunday top hats are usually worn for Church, but in the case of stormy weather bowlers are worn. If you wear an overcoat for Church (which will hide the coat underneath) there is no need to bring a frock or tail coat, the ordinary short day coat will meet the situation.' (HAIL 1/3/2: 18 Jan. 1934).

war. Appeasement was not yet a dirty word, and only Churchill and his small band of followers saw the fatal contradiction in the thinking of the Conservative hierarchy. For if Chamberlain distrusted Hitler, how could he think that Munich would lead to a durable settlement? Douglas used the same language as his leader. After seeing Chamberlain off at Heston airport to his fateful encounter with Hitler, he wrote to Neil: 'I think that Neville will bring back peace from Munich and I hope it will be peace with honour.'[21] As late as January 1939 he was telling Neil that: 'Everybody in England seems to have got nerves . . . personally I don't share their apprehensiveness, as I don't believe that German incursions into Eastern Europe can produce war . . .'[22]

★

Hogg was to be called upon to defend the Munich agreement and Chamberlain's conduct of affairs sooner than he could have imagined. For the time being, however, he accepted his father's advice that he should establish himself at the Bar before attempting a foray into politics. He could do no other because he relied on Douglas to put up the necessary money. It was impossible in the thirties to become a Conservative MP without making a substantial contribution to the funding of the local constituency association. This was not ended until 1948. On the recommendation of a committee chaired by Sir David Maxwell Fyffe, Conference in that year abolished the arrangements by which candidates virtually bought their seats. The motives for reform were mixed: first, abolition would mean that financial considerations would no longer inhibit the choice of candidates; and second, it would induce constituencies to collect funds more widely from local supporters. The first Lord Hailsham therefore controlled the timing of his son's entry.

As early as 1931, when he was only twenty-four but already known as an outstanding young speaker and writer, Hogg had been invited by the Pontypool Division Unionist Association to allow his name to go forward for nomination. In 1935, it was again suggested that he should stand, this time for Twickenham in the General Election, but Douglas wrote 'I am afraid . . . that there can be no idea of my son entering the House of Commons at present. His mind is set upon making his way at the Bar and until he has established himself there I do not think he will or can undertake any constituency.'[23] Hogg did not chafe about this. He loyally accepted his father's view as of a man who knew best. The exit from politics is often unceremonious and brutal, and it is wise to have a job to go back to. In any case, loyalty to his father, a true filial piety, was paramount.

When the government was reconstructed in June 1935, Douglas became Lord Chancellor for the second time at the age of sixty-three. A year later he suffered a serious stroke, became paralysed down his right side and could no longer use his right hand. He had to learn to write with his left, and his speech was badly affected. Baldwin continued him in office but his convalescence was slow and uncertain. In January 1937 he wrote to the Canadian Prime Minister, R. B. Bennett, regretting that he had not been able to preside in the important series of Canadian constitutional appeals which had been heard by the Privy Council. 'I was taken very ill at the beginning of last July . . . and I have ever since been fighting a severe illness. I am only now convalescent . . . I have done my first Cabinet today; I shan't tackle any judicial work for some weeks to come.'[24]

Douglas's illness and incapacity changed everything. It looked likely that he would have to leave public life, and that his own life expectancy would be drastically shortened. Nevertheless, he stayed on as Lord Chancellor into Chamberlain's Government until March 1938 and then agreed to take the sinecure office of Lord President. No one could have foreseen that he would live on until 1950, least of all Quintin, distressed by his father's pitiable state. Some time in late 1936 he pressed his father, whose mind remained quite clear, to let him try for the Commons, arguing that at least a short period there before he succeeded to the peerage would be an asset. To his surprise, his father agreed. But it was not so easy. Although Hogg was on the party's list of approved candidates for both the next General Election and any by-election which might arise, the constituency parties were reluctant. They have never taken kindly to having a headquarters candidate foisted on them, and the circumstance that Douglas was a member of the inner circle of the government made this antipathy the stronger. An unspoken but potent factor was the threat that if a constituency put up Quintin, he might be removed to the Lords at any time. In the result only one constituency, East Willesden, even short-listed him; and then it preferred an experienced businessman. 'By the summer of 1938 I had virtually given up hope of ever serving in the Commons before succeeding to my father's two peerages'. Life at the Bar was difficult too. 'He [Quintin] told me', Douglas reported to Neil in May 1938, 'that he was in the depths of the worst slump he had ever known at the Bar, and had practically no work, and was earning no money.'[25]

It was in these wholly unpromising circumstances that the least expected occurred.

5

The Oxford By-Election

IN August 1938 Bobby Bourne, the Member for Oxford City,* died suddenly while walking on the Scottish moors. He was just fifty years old. Douglas wrote to his son: 'I notice from the papers that Bourne is dead. I don't know whether you have ever contemplated the thought of becoming his successor in Parliament. Oxford City would be a nice seat, and you would be an eminently suitable person to represent it. I only throw out the idea . . .'[1] Quintin already knew and had thought about it. He too was walking and shooting in Scotland and heard the news of Bourne's death over the radio. Alexander Spearman, who was his host, persuaded him to apply for the Conservative nomination and to send a telegram from the nearest post office. As his father said, there were good reasons to do so. He was well-known in Oxford and had even spoken for Bourne at the last general election. At that moment there was nothing to set the forthcoming by-election apart, as the Munich agreement still lay a month in the future. Hogg was duly adopted at a meeting presided over by Alderman Mrs Townsend, who described him as the ideal candidate, and was later to play an important role in his life. His father transferred £800 to his account for election expenses, saying, 'I hope you will regard it as my birthday present.'[2] The election was to be a three-cornered fight with Patrick Gordon-Walker (defeated in the last general election) as the official Labour candidate, and the Liberal Ivor Davies. Nomination day was 19 October and polling was on the 27th. 'It all looked as if we were in for a fairly dull time, arguing about local issues like the Cutteslowe

* At that time, as well as the City seat, the University had two seats, as did Cambridge University. By tradition the Universities' Members were Independents and were a source of strength and diversity in the House. A. P. Herbert represented Oxford University for many years.

Walls, or travelling round the weatherbeaten track of unemployment, housing, rearmament, Abyssinia and the League of Nations.' However, this was not to be.

Through the second half of September, Neville Chamberlain had been negotiating with Hitler about the fate of Czechoslovakia. This small nation had been created in the last weeks of the First World War. For the Czech people, it was the fulfilment of centuries of national aspiration. As the Austro-Hungarian Empire was breaking up the new state was proclaimed by the two patriots, Tomas Masaryk the Slovak and the Czech Josef Benes.* Due to their extraordinary efforts, Czechoslovakia was immediately recognised by the victorious powers and took its place with them at the Peace Conference in 1919. The Versailles conference decided to draw the Czech frontier along the ancient mountain boundary of Bohemia in spite of there being left within the frontier nearly four million Germans living mainly in the area known as the Sudetenland. Winston Churchill described the dilemma which the drawing of this frontier posed: 'To exclude the German-speaking population was deeply and perhaps fatally to weaken the new state; to include them was to affront the principle of self-determination.'[3] The grievances, actual or manufactured, of the Sudeten Germans led directly to the Munich crisis.

Chamberlain's policy was to make peace in Europe by redressing German grievances left over from the Treaty of Versailles. This became known by the now discredited word 'appeasement', but in its inception there were few politicians in London and Paris who did not accept it as right. In relation to Czechoslovakia, appeasement meant negotiating with Hitler the concessions to be made to the Sudeten Germans and persuading the Czechs to accept them. It meant also making clear to Hitler the point beyond which Britain was not prepared to go, and at which she would be willing to stop Germany by force. It was therefore a mixed policy of conciliation and sanction.

Appeasement was not only a policy: it was also an attitude. The memory of the slaughter of the First World War made dreadful the thought of another round. The efficiency with which the Nazis were reviving Germany's economy and its people's morale was enviable. Widespread anti-semitism, more often latent than overt, bred indifference to the fate of the German Jews and the other dark aspects of the Third Reich. People preferred not to know. Appeasement therefore agreed with the national mood, and the few

---

* After Munich, with characteristic instinct for his prey's weakness, Hitler fomented a Slovak separatist movement, which assisted his aim of destroying Czechoslovakia, accomplished in March 1939.

who raised their voices against conciliating the dictators and warned of the perils of making concessions were thought of as irresponsible scaremongers.

In pursuit of his policy, Chamberlain eventually became so mesmerised by the mirage of peace that conciliating Hitler blotted out sanction, and towards the Czechs persuasion became bullying. His delusion was driven by the impossible belief that Hitler was a man with whom he could do business. From the middle of the fateful month of September 1938, Chamberlain resolved to realise his purposes by personal diplomacy. His assessment of his man was therefore crucial. After the first meeting at Berchtesgaden, he told his Cabinet that at first sight Hitler struck him as 'the commonest little dog'.[4] But to his sister he wrote at the same time: 'In short I had established a certain confidence, which was my aim and, in spite of the hardness and ruthlessness I thought I saw in his face, I got the impression that here was a man who could be relied upon when he had given his word.'[5] Tragically, he never disabused himself.

Chamberlain could also be ruthless – and obstinate. He continued to press for a negotiated peace with Hitler in spite of mounting evidence that any such settlement was an illusion; and he found ways to evade the objections of his Cabinet colleagues. The dissentients were not only hawks like Duff Cooper but also, after Hitler's outrageous demands at Godesberg, his closer allies, Halifax the high-minded Foreign Secretary, and Hailsham.

The melancholy story of Chamberlain's three visits to Hitler at Berchtesgaden, Godesberg and Munich while Europe teetered on the edge of war has often been told. The images are vivid ones: Chamberlain with his aide, Sir Horace Wilson, making their journeys with 'the bright faithfulness of two curates entering a pub for the first time';[6] Masaryk and Benes pleading vainly against the dismemberment of their young country; Chamberlain at Heston airport waving his scrap of paper. After the agreement was signed at Munich between Britain, France, Germany and Italy on 30 September, and the Czechs, who had not participated in the talks, were told the fate of their doomed nation, Chamberlain flew home. The agreement meant that German troops would be in the Sudetenland within days. In the evening Chamberlain appeared at the window of No. 10 and said: 'This is the second time that there has come back from Germany to Downing Street peace with honour. I believe it is peace for our time.' The language was almost identical to that used by Lord Hailsham to his son Neil written one day earlier after seeing Chamberlain off to Munich (See page 45).

Did Chamberlain really believe that he had secured a lasting peace and not just a breathing space? The story that in the car travelling back from the airport to Downing Street he said to Halifax, 'All this will be over in three months,' was later said by Halifax not to mean that Chamberlain had no faith in the Munich settlement, and that meaning of the famous phrase should probably be discounted. Hogg believed that 'peace with honour' did not truly represent Chamberlain's state of mind and that 'he was carried away on the balcony at Downing Street in the euphoria of his own relief and that of the cheering crowds that he had brought back peace with honour'. The point is of some importance in assessing Hogg's consistent defence of Munich. He may himself have believed at the time that the real case for the settlement was that it gave an opportunity for Britain to prepare herself both morally and defensively for the life-and-death struggle to come. But that was not Chamberlain's position. Throughout the Czech crisis, he never understood that Hitler's appetite grew by what it fed on. He recognised the urgent need to rearm, but thought, as he told the Cabinet just after Munich, 'that we were now in a more hopeful position, and that the contacts which had been established with the Dictator Powers opened up the possibility that we might be able to reach some agreement with them which would stop the armament race.'[7]

The atmosphere in London to which Chamberlain returned was feverish. There were trenches in Hyde Park, gas masks had been fitted and London children were preparing to leave. The palpable gust of relief which greeted Chamberlain's return and the announcement that after all there would not be war soon gave way to deep divisions, between friends and within families. Wherever people met, argument was hot and angry. There was a strong and growing sense of humiliation, that Czechoslovakia had been thrown to the wolves to save the skins of Britain and France. This was the atmosphere in which the Oxford by-election was to be fought, and there could be only one issue.

While the European drama was unrolling, manoeuvres were on foot in the Oxford City constituency. On 13 October *The Times* reported that a month earlier, on 12 September, the Liberal candidate had offered to withdraw in favour of an Independent if the Labour candidate would do the same; and that Dr Lindsay, the Master of Balliol, would be willing to stand as an 'Independent Progressive'. The following day, readers of *The Times* were told that the proposal had come to nothing because the National Executive of the Labour Party would not agree to any withdrawal. But when nominations went in on October 19, Quintin Hogg as a National Conservative pledged to support the Prime Minister's efforts in the cause of peace, and Dr A. D. Lindsay, a member of the Labour Party but campaigning under the style of an Independent Progressive, were the only candidates.

The account of what happened in *A Sparrow's Flight* is that both opposition candidates withdrew, the Liberal willingly, and Gordon-Walker unwillingly under the compulsion of his party. Hogg suspected that this was masterminded by Frank Pakenham, by now the husband of his Oxford friend, Elizabeth Harman, and an Oxford City Councillor and Secretary of the local Labour Party. The object of the plan was for Pakenham to obtain the reversion to the constituency. A respected candidate, Dr Lindsay, was therefore found who could unite the opponents of the Munich settlement, and who was willing to stand down at the next General Election, expected in 1940 at the latest. Pakenham would then become the official Labour candidate in a constituency whose boundaries were, it was thought, to be redrawn to include the working class areas of Headington and Cowley.*

There was evidence to support the supposed plot. Gordon-Walker was certainly forced against his will to stand down, and wrote an open letter to the *Daily Herald* to say so. 'I maintained that it was a betrayal of the Labour Party at such a moment as this not to go on with the fight.'[8] Pakenham was a friend, former pupil and colleague of Lindsay in the Workers' Educational Association. In the spring of 1939, the local Labour Party adopted Pakenham as its candidate, and this was confirmed by Transport House. Neither Lindsay nor Gordon-Walker was heard of again as a possible Labour candidate. This does not quite add up to the story put forward in *A Sparrow's Flight*, but it is close. According to Pakenham's own account, the coup was engineered by the Oxford communists who had infiltrated the local Labour Party, 'with the rest of us more or less starry-eyed dupes'. For Pakenham himself the affair was 'the political step which I would most prefer to "have back" if I could have my time over again'. He thought at the time that, 'in spite of many paradoxes of alignment', there was scope for an anti-Chamberlain alliance with the Communists on one wing and Churchill leading from the other.[9] Lady Longford agrees in her memoirs that the dumping of Gordon-Walker was shameful; but 'there was no question of his being re-adopted or indeed accepting a constituency so riddled with Communism.'[10]

Lindsay thus became a candidate for the Popular Front. While his

---

* In fact the boundaries were not redrawn until the 1950 election. Pakenham contested the 1945 election in the Labour interest and his wife the 1950 election. Both were beaten by Hogg.

supporters were the heterogeneous collection that such fronts habitually gather, it has to be remembered that for many, particularly the young, such a grouping was unified by hatred and fear of Fascism. Sandy Lindsay was a Christian Socialist, a widely respected and well-known Oxford figure who had just finished his term as Vice-Chancellor, but a man without experience of electioneering. His entry in the *Dictionary of National Biography*, written by a later Master of Balliol, says 'there was something grand and, some felt, even saintly about his imaginative sympathy'. There was also a touch of the authoritarian prig about him, as if he had a direct line to the Almighty. He was an improbable figure to lead a crusade against a peace initiative, but the first Lord Hailsham had no doubt that he would be a tougher proposition than Gordon-Walker and Ivor Davies. He wrote to his son: 'I heard on the wireless yesterday that after all the Socialists and Liberals were combining to support Lindsay: I am afraid it means a much stiffer fight for you, because Lindsay is a very formidable opponent, and naturally would rally some dissident Conservative opinion . . . I do wish you luck with all my heart.'[11]

He enclosed *Hints for Speakers no. 17* on the European Crisis issued by the Conservative Central Office[12] 'which Natalie thought you might not have'. This document ran to 55 pages and is instructive to read now. It began with the history of the German minority in Czechoslovakia. The 3.9 million Sudeten Germans were included within the national boundaries in order to provide natural strategic frontiers for the new state. Benes, the Czech leader, had given assurances in 1919 that minority rights would be respected, and that the country would be developed on the Swiss cantonal model. 'These pledges unfortunately were not carried out.' Speakers might think from this that they were being encouraged to advance the argument that Munich was a just settlement. The paper then shifted its ground in a section epitomised by the sentence, 'The choice that really confronted Czechoslovakia was, therefore, between ceding a portion of its territory or risking certain destruction in a world war.' This was an appeal to the arguments of *realpolitik*: the Germans would destroy Czechoslovakia unless it allowed itself to be dismembered; but it was open to the obvious rejoinder that the object and effect of the dismembering was to save the Western powers. Finally, Chamberlain is quoted as having said on 6 October: 'One good thing at any rate has come out of this emergency . . . It has thrown a vivid light upon our preparations for defence, on their strength and on their weakness.' Conservative speakers could be forgiven for wondering which of these arguments they should run:

for it would be difficult to argue them all in parallel. The document exemplifies the confused thinking at the heart of the policy of appeasement.

The thrust of Hogg's campaign was that in Neville Chamberlain the country had a leader it could trust, who had averted war and would now work towards a general settlement in Europe, in which Munich was only the first step. On the advantage of a breathing space to improve Britain's defences, the only argument upon which Munich could possibly be justified in hindsight, and the one which is relied on in *A Sparrow's Flight*, his election address said: 'With all its hopes of a general settlement, the Munich Agreement will not be justified unless our state of preparedness is developed until it appears from their actions that all the parties to it are acting in good faith . . .'[13] The point was fairly made.

For his part Lindsay announced that, if elected, he would not take the whip of any party and that his purpose in standing would be defeated if he did. He admitted candidly that he had 'shared the universal relief' that war had been averted; yet he 'deplored the irresolution and tardiness of a government which never made clear to Germany where the country was prepared to make a stand'. The nation could not unite behind Mr Chamberlain because it did not know what his policy was. He asked whether that policy was not peace at any price? This was fair enough, but Lindsay was weaker on the positive policy which he would himself support. It seemed to be: rebuild the League and in the meantime act on its principles.[14] But the League's recent performance was not encouraging. It had failed to save China from Japan and Abyssinia from Mussolini; it had sat on its hands while Hitler incorporated Austria into the German Reich. There was little here on which to place trust. Hogg was quick to exploit the weakness and he pointed out that a vote for Lindsay, however well intended it might be, was a vote for chaos and a vacuum in leadership.

Hogg entered the campaign with advantages which were probably decisive. There had been a large Conservative majority in the constituency in the latest general election of 1935, and a Conservative had been returned at every election since 1885 except in 1922 and 1923. He himself was a Scholar of Christ Church, a Fellow of All Souls and a President of the Oxford Union. *The Times* observed that he had practised as a 'poor man's lawyer' and had acquired a wide knowledge of working-class conditions and problems. As Douglas recognised, and Quintin generously allowed in his autobiography, Natalie was a real asset. An attractive and energetic wife, she spoke herself and could not have done more to help, being well-informed about election tactics and procedures. When he fell ill during the campaign with a chill, which later developed into pleurisy, she nursed him and kept him operational. Hogg was always a good campaigner and his boyish good looks and energy were electoral assets. He was in any case a political orator, much better on the hustings than his opponent. This election cut across party lines, and he had to expect attacks from every quarter, including the Conservative dissidents against whom his father had warned. He enjoyed this sort of thing and the noisy meetings and occasional rough houses brought the best out of his naturally pugnacious instincts.* By contrast, Lindsay was 'both too amateurish and too lofty' for the in-fighting. He was shocked by some of the tactics adopted in his name, 'notably our masterpiece: "A vote for Hogg is a vote for Hitler"',' as Elizabeth Pakenham recalled.[15] Quintin simply responded with, 'Vote for Hogg and Save your Bacon'.

As was to be expected, University opinion was noisy and divided. In a letter to *The Times* published on 20 October, eighteen academics led by C. K. Allen, the Warden of Rhodes House, were at pains to point out that just because Lindsay had been Vice-Chancellor of the University (a tenure that had recently ended) his views did not necessarily command wide support among its senior members. Sir Charles Oman, the Professor of Modern History, Sir William Holdsworth, Vinerian Professor, Mr J. C. Masterman, Mr J. G. Barrington-Ward, Quintin's ertwhile tutor, and a large number of other distinguished academics signed a 'manifesto' supporting him. On the other side were ranged Professor Gilbert Murray, Sir William Beveridge, the Master of University College, Maurice Bowra, the Warden of Wadham, Roy Harrod and Sir Arthur Salter, one of the Members for the University. It is doubtful whether these partisan and sometimes sententious sallies from the Senior Common Rooms in the end made much difference to the result. But they added to the excitement.

The voices of Conservative dissidents were more significant. Among them were an undergraduate from Balliol (Lindsay's college)

---

* He never lost his enthusiasm for taking hecklers head on. In a speech at Goldsmiths' Hall in 1976 he was interrupted by a 'loud, articulate and unmistakable monosyllable BALLS'. He rejoined: 'I do not know whether the interruption was a boast of sexual prowess or a criticism, however indirect, and courteously expressed of my current remarks. But in case it was the latter I will bring my speech to a close'. The by-election spawned legend. More than 50 years on, Radio Oxford asked Lord Hailsham to confirm a story that at the Pressed Steel works, his car had been overturned by an anti-Munich mob, and that he had responded by saying, 'Thank you for making a platform for me.' He said there was not a word of truth in it and Pressed Steel was not even in the constituency.

named Edward Heath, and Captain Harold Macmillan, one of a small band of MPs deeply shamed by Munich, who was reported to have said at a meeting for Lindsay on 25 October: 'They could always appease lions by throwing Christians to them, but the Christians had another word for it.'[16]

As polling day approached, the temperature rose and hyperbole increased. Two of Hogg's friends wrote: 'I hope you lick hell out of that prunes-and-rice-pudding old fool'; and Frank Pakenham: 'Wishing you the best of luck personally and the worst of luck politically'.[17] On the eve of the poll Hogg described Munich as 'the greatest miracle of modern times performed by a single man', and his supporters had devised a campaign song to the tune of 'The Lambeth Walk', whose deplorable lyric ran: 'Every pretty Oxford girl, In the High or in the Turl, You'll find them all, Voting for Quintin Hogg'.

Polling day, 27 October, was one of intense activity. Some 75 per cent of the electorate voted. Everywhere the red, white and blue favours of Hogg clashed with the red and yellow of Lindsay's side. The *Oxford Times* reported that the nurses from St Giles, coming off night duty, were among the earliest voters, many wearing favours. There were over 420 cars at the disposal of the candidates, 274 of them Lindsay's, to help carry voters to the polls. During the evening, an expectant crowd gathered outside the Town Hall where the result was to be announced. By 9 o'clock there was a huge press, and many were crushed and had to be hauled inside the iron gates where they could be treated by St John Ambulance men. At last, at 11.15, the Mayor appeared and announced the result: Quintin Hogg 15,797; A. D. Lindsay 12,363. Hogg's majority was reduced but still decisive. The result was greeted with a great cheer, as the two candidates stepped on to the balcony with their wives. The four stood for over five minutes acknowledging the cheers. There were tributes from each candidate to the other. The cheering and shouting went on until the defeated candidate told the crowd that he was very tired, and that they should follow his example and get some sleep.[18]

For an hour after the declaration, roads near the centre of the city were blocked by crowds of pedestrians as the victor set off for a tour of his committee rooms. There were many letters of congratulation, but a few contained warnings. Roy Harrod wrote from Christ Church: '. . . as things go from bad to worse and the rotten-ness in the state of Denmark is more fully exposed, you may yet be of service to the cause which I regard as right'.[19] Another letter from a relative: 'Personally I don't feel as certain as you do about Neville's performance and the antics of Hitler – I just wonder if he, Hitler, did not make rings round him, which will shortly encircle us – I am prepared for an argument!'[20]

But Hogg, never one to concede an argument, even when it was fifty years old, went on, almost alone, defending Munich to the end of his days. Chamberlain's choice at Munich, he argued, was either to start a world war for which Britain was woefully unprepared, or to make an agreement to serve as 'an acid test, a trip-wire, a litmus paper which would determine the possibility of maintaining peace decisively, once and for all, and fighting a year later if the wire was tripped'. He had no doubt that Chamberlain made the right choice; and when the wire was duly tripped the following March on Hitler's marching into Prague, he knew that war was inevitable. He knew also that the Fuhrer's word was worth nothing; but he continued to claim that Britain could not have defended herself when the trial came in 1940 had Chamberlain not won the country time to mend its dykes, and to unite the country in war.

In *The Left was Never Right*, a polemic published in 1945 to demonstrate that the 'Guilty Men' were to be found on the left rather than the right, Hogg observed that criticisms of Munich have altered as the years have passed. 'Whatever we do, whatever we say, Aunt Agatha tells us it isn't the way.' To the extent that hindsight improves argument, the point was fair; but it could be turned round and made to face the other way. Munich was intended to bring peace to Europe: it did not, but the breathing space it offered, although appreciated and used by Hogg in his election speeches, looked better and better as an argument the further the event receded into the past. In his book Hogg recalled that he had to face three principal arguments in the by-election: 1: The dictators are only bluffing; stand up to them and the cowards will run away. 2: Munich is only a prelude to further and worse concessions. 3: Munich was right, but the Conservative Party ought not to have got us into this mess. Rightly, he thought the third was the only argument which deserved to be taken seriously.

Curiously, Hogg was never tarred by his association with the discredited policy of appeasement, as was R. A. Butler, then Under-Secretary of State at the Foreign Office, and Lord Home who, as Lord Dunglass, was one of Chamberlain's Parliamentary Private Secretaries. Lady Longford, formerly Elizabeth Pakenham, had thought that Hogg's character might have brought him in on their side and against Munich; but she reckoned without the spirit of loyalty within him, one of the most consistent themes of the public life on which he was just embarking.[21]

6

The Onset of War and the Norway Debate

PUBLIC life was soon to be interrupted by war. Hogg barely had time to find out how difficult life could be for a young barrister trying also to make his way in the House. Lord Hailsham wrote to his sister Elsie: 'I think Quintin's politics are rather interfering with his legal enthusiasms, which I always feared would be the case if he got into the H. of C.'[1] There was nothing insouciant about the first Lord Hailsham. A wry pessimism was more in character: 'Quintin had a triumph in the Special Jury list yesterday. He was defending in a slander action about which he was very troubled when he spent the weekend at Carters Corner about ten days ago, but he succeeded in getting a clear judgment. I hope that his experience will not be mine when I advised against my client and won, and the solicitor decided never to brief me again because, he said, that when I *do* get a winner I don't know it.'[2] Hogg himself did not usually allow that he was content with the state of his practice, but times were particularly difficult in the immediately pre-war period and there was a slump in the volume of work coming into the Bar. On the other hand, Natalie had got over the scare of a serious operation in February 1939 and by the summer when she visited Neil, then posted in Lisbon, the atmosphere at home had improved. 'I dined with Quintin and Natalie,' Hailsham wrote to Neil, 'and found them much less nervy than I had seen them.'[3] While Natalie was in Portugal, her husband went climbing with friends in Snowdonia and Norway. The holiday was interrupted by the announcement of the Hitler-Stalin pact which made war not only certain but imminent. Hogg had been waiting for war since Czechoslovakia was obliterated in March. Now it would be only weeks, if not days, before the two dictators carved up Poland and plunged Europe into conflict. He did not volunteer for the army until the actual outbreak of war for 'the

58

plain fact was that I had to earn a living at the Bar as well as carry on my duties in the House of Commons.'

Hogg had made his maiden speech in the House on 29 November 1938. The subject was the Criminal Justice Bill. As is conventional, it was not a contentious address; but it did contain some interesting remarks. The most arresting were his views on corporal punishment. He complained that the King's Bench Judges, whose view it was that flogging for robbery with violence had a deterrent effect, had been ignored and his suggestion was that instead of abolishing flogging altogether, as the Bill proposed, 'there might be a trial of this completely revolutionary proposal in English jurisprudence.'[4] Even allowing for contemporary thinking on corporal punishment, its abolition in 1938 was hardly 'revolutionary'. Hogg was a hard-liner on violent crime, and his schooldays, when he flogged frequently and *con brio*, may have left him feeling that the King's Bench Judges were right. But his speech was balanced for all that. He argued generally for leniency in punishment on the ground that it 'does on the whole tend to prevent the repetition of offences more adequately than a policy of undue severity.' If that were a doubtful proposition, he moved to firmer ground. His experience was that juries sometimes failed to convict not because of rational doubt 'but because they objected to the severity of the penalty which had to be imposed in the case of conviction'.

★

When war was declared in September, Hogg set about joining up. At thirty-two he was old for a subaltern but too young, he felt, honourably to avoid active service. In any case he wanted to fight. He had no special qualifications for army service and, but for the intercession of his Oxford friend, Hilary Magnus, he would have found it difficult to get into a good infantry regiment. Magnus got him into the Tower Hamlets Rifles, later absorbed into the Rifle Brigade, where he immediately found himself among friends from school and Oxford. After a short spell guarding 'strategic points' in the East End, the battalion moved to Lincolnshire. Here, bereft of any weapons, equipment, transport or training which would have made it of any use in a shooting war, it stayed on, Hogg with it, through the 'phoney war' into the early summer of 1940. In a mood of deep discontent with the conduct of affairs, he decided to travel down to Westminster to take part in the momentous Norway Debate on 7 and 8 May.

The deplorable failure of the amphibious operations in Norway, designed to deny Germany control of the long indented coastline dominating the North Sea and access to Scandinavian iron ore, was for many inside and outside the House of Commons the last straw in a story of weakness and indecision which had characterised the first eight months of the war. The Labour and Liberal parties stood outside the Chamberlain Government and there was a growing number of Conservative rebels. The House of Commons was irritable and factious. Attlee, the Labour leader, epitomised the frustration felt by Members on all sides: 'It is not Norway alone. Norway comes as the culmination of many other discontents. People are saying that those mainly responsible for the conduct of affairs are men who have had an almost uninterrupted career of failure. Norway followed Czechoslovakia and Poland. Everywhere the story is "Too late".'[5]

Hogg was one of a group of young Tory officers whose intervention in the debate made it one of the turning points in British parliamentary history. Their votes against Chamberlain and their own Government ensured its fall and the formation in its place of the great wartime coalition under Winston Churchill. But the occasion presented Hogg with an extraordinarily painful dilemma and by his own reckoning, the most difficult political decision he ever had to take.[6] He had been elected, little more than a year earlier, to support Neville Chamberlain, and he had no sympathy for the faction in the party which was attacking the Prime Minister with what he thought almost pathological hatred. He and his family were on warm personal terms with Chamberlain. On the other hand, and in common with his brother officers, he considered that the conduct of the war thus far was nerveless and ill prepared. There was a desperate need for stronger leadership and unity of purpose.

To make this dilemma worse, Hogg was given the unusual courtesy of a personal interview with the Prime Minister before the debate to explain his discontent. But when asked what the particular complaint was, 'I could only blurt out some relatively trivial matters affecting my own unit. These were most conscientiously, and crossly, investigated to destruction by the Secretary of State for War.' The new young Member was quite unable to get across the real burden of complaint. 'I remember now the gentleness, courtesy and generosity with which the doomed man treated his inarticulate and presumptuous young supporter who ventured to question his authority and make his task more difficult.'[7] This is a warmer picture of Chamberlain than the conventional one of a starchy, unsociable leader.

It became clear on the first day of the debate, 7 May, that there was a major political crisis on hand. Chamberlain's speech was unconvincing, and he was severely damaged by speeches from Sir Roger Keyes, in full uniform as Admiral of the Fleet,* and Leo Amery, an old friend of the Chamberlain family. Amery quoted with devastating effect Cromwell's report of his conversation with Hampden when the Parliamentarians were being badly cut about by the Royalist cavalry: 'I said to him, "Your troops are most of them old, decayed serving men and tapsters, and such kind of fellows . . . You must get men of spirit that are likely to go as far as they will go, or you will be beaten still." ' And he ended by pointing directly at the Prime Minister, employing Cromwell's imperious words to the Long Parliament: 'You have sat too long here for any good you have been doing. Depart, I say, and let us have done with you. In the name of God, go.'[8] The atmosphere in the House was charged, and Hogg intervened twice, once, when a government supporter was assuring the House that it had the confidence of the country, to declare: 'No, a thousand times no. And not one serving member holds that view either.'[9]

On the following day, Herbert Morrison gave notice that the opposition would press to a vote its criticisms on the whole conduct of the war. The dilemma which Hogg had felt, submerged by the drama in the House, now returned in a more acute form, for he would have to decide whether to join the Conservative dissidents and add his name to those seeking to bring Chamberlain down. If Chamberlain fell, his likely successor was Churchill. There was a strong feeling that Churchill's genius was flawed by a wayward judgment. Hogg did not think that; he knew that Churchill's greatness could unite the country behind him; but there was another difficulty. The man whom he had come down from Lincolnshire to help proclaim as the new national leader was First Lord of the Admiralty, primarily responsible for the Norwegian fiasco, and would wind up for the government. Hogg drew a vivid picture of the old lion 'scowling, crouching and snarling at the despatch box', as he dealt with the charges of incompetence and irresolution. Churchill was in no mood to conciliate the critics, still less to play politics by riding a wave of popularity. His words seemed to brand Hogg, if he voted against the government, as a renegade.

Hogg wanted to speak in the debate so that his personal position would not be misunderstood, but the Speaker did not call him. In *A Sparrow's Flight* he describes this as providential: 'As I should

---

* Keyes 'supported the complaints of the Opposition with technical details and his own professional authority in a manner very agreeable to the mood of the House.' (Churchill: *The Gathering Storm*, p.520)

certainly have made a fool of myself, it is fortunate that my guardian angel again came to my rescue'. This, however, was retrospect. At the time, he was impatient to be on his feet; and on the day after the debate he wrote to Margesson, the Chief Whip, to complain about not being called.

> Last night the chair was discriminating against calling men in khaki, as Col. Clifton Brown told one of my colleagues. Do you seriously think that this is a proper or advisable attitude? Can't you trust us to be slightly more discreet in public than the men they do call. Do you seriously want the PM to be supported by nobody but fools and crooks? Or that the voice of serving men should never be heard?[10]

The letter, while exculpating Chamberlain, ('the one figure in politics for whom I have a feeling of personal loyalty and affection') levelled harsh criticism at his government and showed his frustration. 'The fact is that there is no young officer whom I know who can wholeheartedly support the government so long as our men are neglected and betrayed by the administration for which the government are responsible. Even those who voted for it agree with this.'

As there is no doubt that he felt very strongly about the direction of the war by Chamberlain's government (the letter to Margesson makes it clear enough), it is hard to see how he could at the same time acquit its leader. It was hardly adequate to blame the 'fools and crooks' of Chamberlain's administration (whoever they were) and acquit the Prime Minister himself of all blame. But he did, and he hesitated to the end before casting his vote. Last into the 'No' lobby just before the door was locked, he went on arguing with himself until it was almost too late whether he could vote against his leader and the government which he had been elected to support.

Many of those who took part in the debate which brought Churchill to power, including Quintin Hogg, were aware that the war in the west was about to begin in earnest – as it did with stunning ferocity less than 48 hours after the vote. When the result was known, a reduced but still substantial government majority of 81, Hogg felt that his gesture had been futile. The Administration which he had dared to criticise had survived. He was wrong. Chamberlain was quickly persuaded that he could no longer carry on or command the support of the other two parties. Churchill, who wrote that all his past life 'had been but a preparation for this hour and this trial', became leader of the new coalition on 9 May.

Both Hogg and his father wrote letters of sympathy to Chamberlain. Within six months, the defeated Prime Minister was dead. Hogg returned north to his unit, enduring as he went the bleak prophecy of Walter Liddall, the Member for Lincoln, that he would regret his vote for the rest of his life. To judge from his post bag, most of his constituents agreed.

★

Hogg remained in Lincolnshire with the Tower Hamlets Rifles through the summer of 1940. Disaster followed disaster. Belgium, Holland and France fell with lightning speed, and by the end of May the British Expeditionary Force was penned into a small perimeter around the Channel port of Dunkirk. The deliverance of more than 300,000 troops from that precarious and exposed beach was completed by the first days of June. Britain's fate now depended on victory in the air, and the Blitz began in July. During this grim time, equipment in the form of machine guns and armoured carriers began at last to arrive in Lincolnshire and Hogg acquainted himself with, and taught, such forgotten skills as the maintenance of a Bren gun and double-declutching. His infantry career was, however, interrupted by a summons from the War Office to join the Intelligence Directorate in London, to work with scientific and technical experts on the development of new weapons. Here he learned something else that was to prove useful later – the workings of a land-mine. He was also ordered to write an appreciation of the entire war situation and given a week's leave to do it. The report, unfortunately now lost, found its way ultimately to Hugh Dalton at the Ministry of Economic Warfare, who offered him a job on the strength of it. He declined.[11]

Until the end of the year he was able to live at home with Natalie in Victoria Square, and so experience the full force of the Blitz on central London. He left the Intelligence Directorate at his own request, hoping to rejoin the Tower Hamlets Rifles who were going to the Middle East. Back-room jobs and reserved occupations in wartime were not to his taste.

It was in December, just before he left to join his troopship, that a bomb fell on the old Carlton Club in Pall Mall where he and his father were dining. The occasion was a farewell party for which his father, now very immobile and disabled, had travelled up from the country. The Club was full and while father and son 'were consuming roast partridge and a bottle of claret, things became a good deal more exciting'. The dining room was first lit up in a lurid glare by magnesium flares and then plunged into dust and darkness as the bomb exploded inside the building. In what must have been a memorable tableau, Hogg carried his crippled father on his shoulders out of the smoking remains of the Club, causing Winston Churchill to remark in his memoirs that the scene called to mind Aeneas carrying his own infirm father, Anchises, from the flaming ruins of Troy. The Chief Whip stood on the pavement counting the diners as they came out into the rubble-strewn street. Mercifully no one was killed. Hogg left London and Natalie a few days later to join his ship at Liverpool. Hoping to get to the fighting, he cannot have imagined that the next two years would provide him, for the first time in his life, with much enforced idleness and time to think.

7

Middle East

THE troopship *Britannic* pursued a circuitous course to Egypt, sailing far out into the Atlantic before doubling back to Sierra Leone and then round the Cape. A young officer in the 7th Hussars called Robert MacGill was also on board and chance brought Hogg and him together at a shore party in Durban. The meeting quickly blossomed into friendship. MacGill was thirteen years the younger and came to look on Hogg as a father. On his side, Hogg was captivated by the younger man's sunny disposition and deep instinctive loyalty. The friendship was to become one of the most poignant in the older man's life.

The long voyage ended in March 1941 and Hogg found himself in a transit camp in the Canal Zone. His hopes of rejoining the Tower Hamlets Rifles were frustrated and it was not clear what his military fate was to be; but the network of friendly contacts came to his aid. The Commanding Officer of the Second Battalion of the Rifle Brigade, who had known Edward Marjoribanks, was recruiting after having taken part in Wavell's advance to Benghazi. Although relatively old and quite untried, Hogg was selected. This was a crack unit and he was fortunate. His Company was composed in equal halves of regular soldiers from India and boys only just over half his age from England. He was the junior subaltern and the oldest officer in the Battalion but for the Colonel and the Second-in-Command, both already war heroes, and the latter of whom, Hugo Garmoyle, had sat next to Hogg in class at Eton. He was going to have something to prove, and quickly, for the Battalion was almost immediately moving up into the desert to help stem the sudden advance of Rommel, newly arrived in North Africa to stiffen up the Italians. The regimental history of The Rifle Brigade records: 'New officers, among them Quintin Hogg, and a draft of riflemen arrived

. . . It was on the 30th April that the 2nd Battalion once more took its way along the road to the Pyramids while the bougainvillaea was in flower and the orange blossom smelt its strongest, turned to the right before it reached Mena and left civilization firmly behind it for the second time.'[1]

A Subaltern who commanded a platoon in the same Company knew Quintin Hogg well in this period. 'He was undoubtedly the worst-dressed Rifleman in the whole Battalion . . . a very good companion, there were gales of laughter although he could be irascible . . . not really cut out to be a soldier'.[2] Hogg would not have wanted to disagree. The fact that he was a barrister and MP brought on a good deal of derision and he described his own active service as 'my inglorious career as a fighting soldier'. Military life encouraged the larking side of him. While the Battalion was pausing near the Pyramids, he conceived the absurd idea that his men would benefit from a route march to the top of the Great Pyramid and down again: '. . . the officers and men of "S" Company were soon festooned at various points of ascent and descent like the animals on the Mappin terraces at London Zoo. I ought, of course, to have known better.'

Rommel had by now invested Tobruk and was at the Egyptian frontier, threatening to sever the vital Canal and perhaps drive on to India or Southern Russia. The Battalion moved up to Buq Buq, close to the Libyan border where the plateau runs down to the sea in a narrow defile at Halfaya Pass. The main objective was to raise the siege of Tobruk. There was however no major engagement while Hogg was at the front. He enjoyed the life of the desert. Wildlife was plentiful, and he secured a variety of game suitable for the pot: bustard, gazelle, fox and hare. These exploits with a rifle made him popular with his platoon. The brilliant night skies were of a beauty he had never seen, and occasionally, after rain, the sand would become bright with asphodel.

The knowledge of land-mines that he had acquired while in Whitehall came to be useful when he was given the task of clearing the road in the defile of mines laid by his Scots Guards predecessor, who was unable to help him by indicating how many and exactly where they were. They had first to be found and then disarmed. This nerve-wracking, sweaty task was made the more deadly because the detonators, which had first to be removed, were highly sensitive, and capable alone of blowing off a limb without any help from the main charge. Hogg never lacked physical courage. He decided to attempt to disarm the first mine himself so that he could then instruct his platoon how to do it. He scrabbled away gently and warily in the sand with a bayonet until the first mine showed itself. It was of a type unfamiliar to him, and he had to work out how to proceed by the light of nature. Near the bottom of the case was a bayonet fitting like a light bulb, which he figured would have to be pushed in to release. He paused to collect his thoughts and say a short prayer before embarking on this perilous gambit. Fortunately, it worked and the sinister detonator was revealed. Having completed the pilot scheme successfully, Hogg's platoon then safely disarmed some 150 of these mute enemies.

In May the Battalion took part in a limited offensive action and captured a large number of Italian prisoners. This was much to Hogg's taste. 'Quintin Hogg', records the regimental history, 'dressed in ill-fitting shirt and shorts and a topi, brandishing his pistol in a very dangerous way, took charge of them. (Not every constituency was represented by its member at the front)'.[3] The menace offered to the doubtless apprehensive prisoners was not confined to gestures: '*Morte a Mussolini porco,*' he declaimed at them. But his 'inglorious career' was nearly over. At the end of May he was discovered alone in an exposed desert position, armed only with a sand-jammed Bren gun, by three Messerschmitts roaming about the sky looking for just such a target. He was shot up first by cannon, then by machine gun fire, and finally by a stick of anti-personnel bombs. Only when the planes were leaving the scene did the wretched Bren finally come to life. Hogg found his desert boot full of blood. He wrote a poem about his airborne assailants in his diary early the following year:

> They were so beautiful, they scarcely seemed
> To hold the menace that I knew was there.
> Graceful and confident, their bodies gleamed
> Serenely circling in the desert air.

The wound, to his knee, almost cost him his right leg. After going back to the Casualty Clearing Station and two weeks' convalescent leave in Jerusalem, he rejoined his unit. But not for long. Being then thirty-four, and not yet in command of a company, he was decreed too old for the desert, or as he put it, 'undesertworthy'. It was a blow. So, in August 1941, he was posted to Cairo with the rank of Captain, his active service over, and condemned to a year and a half of back-room life in the Middle East. The excitement, camaraderie and sheer fun of regimental life was a thing of the past. This was not what he had joined the Army for and he was not happy. Neither fighting nor looking after his constituents, he felt he was in a soft job while others were hazarding their lives.

He was in Cairo until the end of October sharing a too comfortable flat, as a staff officer with responsibility for communications. This was not much of a job, but there was a consolation. Many people of political consequence passed through, and Hogg was able to see them and keep in touch. He saw Walter Monckton, then Minister of State in Cairo, on several occasions. They corresponded after Hogg left Egypt. Hogg wrote to him about the inclusion of Stafford Cripps in the Cabinet in January 1942. Cripps had been sent on a mission to Russia in the summer of 1940 and had become identified with the increasingly popular view that Britain was not doing enough to support the Russian war effort. In the first half of 1942, while Cripps' star was rising, Churchill's popularity sank to its lowest ebb. These factors, together with Churchill's policy of presenting himself as the nation's warrior chief and paying little attention to home affairs, combined to make Cripps' claim to a seat in the Cabinet irresistible. Monckton, who admired Cripps and even thought of him as a possible successor to Churchill,[4] replied: 'I can well understand your anxieties. I do not think that you need worry about the price paid for Stafford Cripps. So far as I have been able to judge, it was essential to get him into the Cabinet in order to satisfy critics of the government who felt that they were content with less than 100% of the war effort. There is at home the same feeling which I find among many of the troops here that hitherto we have not done all we can to grasp the hand of the Russians. I have no doubt that there is a big swing to the left in England . . .'[5] This last remark did not pass unnoticed. Hogg asked Monckton's advice about returning home; Monckton thought this would be useful 'for a month or two', if he could be spared: 'you would have a chance of contributing to political thinking at a critical moment and your contribution would be the better because you have been away from Parliament for some time'. This was not what Hogg meant. He was chafing to go home for good; but he was at least keeping his contacts warm. He also saw Randolph Churchill, Anthony Greenwood and Oliver Baldwin.

However, not all political preoccupations were serious. Hogg recorded a story in his diary about Eden sending in a report to Churchill on his Middle East tour. 'Winston read it, and then said, "Capital. There are only two clichés you have forgotten: God is love, and Please adjust your dress before leaving".' (*Diary* 28 Dec. 1941.)

In October, Hogg's network of friends rescued him again from boredom and frustration. General H. M. Wilson (universally known as 'Jumbo') was G.O.C. 9th Army with headquarters in Brumana, a pleasant airy resort above Beirut. Wilson was intensely loyal to his regiment, the Rifle Brigade, and could hardly bear to accept anyone in his entourage who was not a 'black button' (so named after the distinctive buttons on the service dress of the Brigade). Fortunately, Hogg satisfied the essential qualification and was offered a job acting as liaison officer between Wilson and Sir Edward Spears' political mission to the Free French.

The situation in Syria and the Lebanon was complicated and explosive. French influence in the area went back at least a century and had been formalised after the First World War when Syria and Lebanon were mandated to France by the League of Nations. The French were now divided into the Free French, led by De Gaulle, and the collaborationist Vichy Government. De Gaulle was well aware of the labyrinthine politics of the Levant, and in a famous phrase in his war memoirs, he described his visit there in March 1941: 'Towards the complex Orient I flew with but simple ideas'. The simplest was that French influence in the region should be unimpaired, come what may.

Two months later, in May 1941, the Vichy Admiral, Darlan, met Hitler at Berchtesgaden and agreed to place the Syrian airbases at the disposal of the Axis powers. British forces under Wilson invaded Syria to head off the threat. Ill-advisedly but on the prompting of De Gaulle, a Free French contingent was included in the force, and as a result there was savage fighting between the two French camps before the Vichy forces were defeated. On crossing into Syria, the allied forces promised independence to Syria and the Lebanon. But, as he made plain in his war memoirs,[6] De Gaulle had no intention of relinquishing the French mandatory's ultimate power in the Levant until the war was won. To do so, he thought, would have been to deliver the Middle East to British influence. When independence came, to Syria in October and Lebanon in December of 1941, the French felt outmanoeuvred and betrayed. There were many angry episodes. Of one meeting between himself and De Gaulle, Oliver Lyttleton, the British Minister resident in Cairo, wrote, 'The discussion degenerated into what women call a scene'. De Gaulle never forgave Britain.

Catroux, the able and urbane Free French representative in Beirut, did what he could to carry out De Gaulle's bidding with tact; but he could not conceal French resentment about British pro-Arab primacy in the region and French detestation of '*ces petits Lawrences*'. Of De Gaulle, Hogg shrewdly observed: 'a great man with an almost unlimited ability to take advantage, like Hitler, of British weakness'. (*Diary* 14 Nov. 1941.)

The already difficult situation was aggravated by poor relations between Wilson and Spears. Spears, an admirer and lover of French civilisation, had got De Gaulle out of France to London as darkness descended in 1940 and could claim to be the midwife of the Free French. But De Gaulle's independent policies antagonised Britain, and Spears was under instructions from Churchill to counteract French procrastination and machination. Spears was capable of violent likes and dislikes, and towards the French he now displayed the symptoms of a scorned lover. His object became to foil the French and advance British influence – into the post-war world, if possible. Wilson, who in Hogg's view was a fine and much-loved soldier, was concerned with law and order, disliked politicking, and thought that animosities between Britain and France should not be allowed to interfere with war aims. It looked as if there would be plenty for Hogg to do as liaison officer between the two. He hoped also that the Levant, with its long, chequered history and myriad minorities and religious sects, would at least absorb his interest while he was in Brumana.

On 5 November, he met Charles Mott-Radclyffe, from whom he was taking over, at Lydda airport. They had an affable conversation over two small ginger ales. Mott-Radclyffe warned his successor that relations between Spears and Wilson were not good. 'Jumbo is a soldier, a damn good soldier, but he does not pretend to understand the political aspect of affairs . . . Spears on the other hand gets a rush of blood to the head once a week . . . when he tries to send off terrible signals which have to be stopped by me . . . I gather that trouble between Spears and Jumbo is worst when they do not meet.' (*Diary* 5 Nov. 1941.) Mott-Radclyffe knew Spears well enough to contribute his entry in the *Dictionary of National Biography* but, in Hogg's view, he underestimated Wilson's political gifts. In the disputes between Wilson and Spears, Hogg unhesitatingly took Wilson's part. 'Rightly, in my opinion, Jumbo believed that the French (of both factions) and Spears were foolishly preoccupied by securing advantages for their respective countries after the war in circumstances which at that time neither could predict, and were ignoring the immediate future . . .' Hogg spent more than a year in the Lebanon trying to promote peace between all parties. Whatever the measure of his success in this diplomatic task, he managed to maintain excellent personal relations with Catroux and his staff at the Grand Serail in Beirut, and with both Wilson and Spears. Spears' wife, the novelist Mary Borden, ran an ambulance unit for the Free

French with exemplary efficiency, and both she and her husband offered Hogg much kindness and hospitality.

Hogg lived well in the beautiful surroundings of Beirut. The diary contains entries giving details of excellent lunches and dinners provided by the Commissariats of Catroux and Spears. Both approached the subject of food and wine in the French manner. Peace broke out sometimes too, at least socially. On one occasion Wilson, Spears and Catroux all attended the races together, travelling in an impressive motor cortege. The races were mixed horse and mule.

Between October 1941, when he was in Cairo, and the end of 1942, when he returned home to England, Hogg kept a regular diary for the only time in his life. He had tried to do so once or twice before, but all attempts failed after a few days. At the end of the diary, and after re-reading it, he gave it a savage review: 'A humiliating experience. This diary has gone on for over a year . . . I found it dull, inconsequent, and mawkish in parts. Some of it, but far less than I hoped, was interesting. In general all intentional jokes were in bad taste, and all attempts at serious discussion were half-baked. All the same, as a form of catharsis I have found it useful.' (*Diary* 25 Nov. 1942.) Some of the entries are embarrassing, but the diary was not intended for anyone else's eyes and the strictures are too severe. It is an unusual diarist who confides his thoughts and is not occasionally betrayed into sentimentality. And he was too hard on his own jokes. For example, he recorded a story of two Australian sappers who were at large for 374 days in Crete after the German occupation.

They worked for the Boche with pick and shovel on an aerodrome. Nearby they saw a ragged shepherd tending his sheep. They came up and, as they were very short of food, asked to buy one of his beasts in their extremely bad Greek. He, apparently in fear, would have nothing to do with them. Then they said that as they were really desperate, if he would not sell willingly, they would make him, using as much force as necessary. The tattered shepherd replied, 'You can have the whole fucking lot if you want. I'm sick of the bastards.' A Greek shepherd had been killed in the blitz and a soldier had taken his sheep and his clothes as a disguise. They joined forces and lived on the sheep for some time. (*Diary* 6 Oct. 1942.)

The diary contains digressions on disparate topics: saints, physical courage, war crimes, a plan for demobilisation. There are also conversations with brother officers about the post-war period world to which they looked forward. But the mood of the diarist is one of nagging frustration. In *A Sparrow's Flight* Lord Hailsham described his time in the Lebanon and Syria as 'an unforgettable interlude in a political and legal life'; but the diary gives only occasional hints of the pleasures of living and travelling in the Levant. He thought his life there futile and he wanted to be somewhere in the thick of things. 'Wired Father whether or not it was my duty to come home,' he recorded on 20 February 1942. It was hard to bear that his regimental colleagues were being decorated for bravery in the Western Desert, and that he could neither join them nor return to the Commons. There were divided views on whether he should come home. On 16 March the diary shows that Natalie (always called 'Tony' by her husband) had advised against return, Beaverbrook was for it, Amery against. The reasons were not given, but on the same day: 'I have now made up my mind about myself. I must return and as soon as opportunity offers . . .' No opportunity arose, and in September he was still kicking at his life. 'Extremely bored, no work for the past few days . . . I want to go. Where? To Persia with Jumbo – back home to my constituency – to the desert with the regiment. Anywhere, except here, which is incidentally one of the pleasantest spots in the whole world.' (*Diary* 4 Sep. 1942.) He still had four months to wait for his opportunity for release, and that would be presented only by illness.

Two women who knew him in his Cairo and Beirut days, although not well, had similar impressions. One was Hermione, Countess of Ranfurly, whom Hogg admired greatly and who wrote a vivid diary of life in Cairo and Jerusalem at this period in *To War with Whitaker*. Both thought him good company, but lonely and inclined to be withdrawn. He enlisted sympathy and responded to friendship; an older man, and different from 'the other blades that one knew'. There was something strangely touching about him which stayed in the mind. All this would tally with his dissatisfaction with his life and, perhaps, anxiety about the state of his marriage. Both women had the clear impression that he was leading a celibate life – which cannot have been usual in wartime Cairo or Beirut, but was all of a piece with the stern personal morality which he imposed on himself all his life.[7]

John Hackett, the celebrated and much decorated soldier, was a contemporary of Hogg's at Oxford and they met again in the Lebanon and saw each other from time to time, becoming close friends. Both were believing Christians and enjoyed philosophical discussion. Hogg recorded a long talk over an al fresco lunch in

Beirut. 'Lunch Belvedere, Shan Hackett. Little fishes, risotto, cake, and rough wine. We ate in the sun, the first time this year. We talked first of his trouble [Hackett had difficulty getting permission to marry the Austrian internee who later become his wife], which is terrible, and then of religion. He said his only prayer was for strength. I said I was praying for light which he called spiritual pride, and moral weakness.' (*Diary* 14 March 1942.) Hackett remembered the conversation too and said that his own experience of hiding in a house in Holland after Arnhem, described in his book *I was a Stranger*, had greatly borne out what Hogg had said about prayer. He also recalled that each had discovered something about the other: he had always wanted to be a classical scholar and Hogg had a secret longing for blood and sand.[8] Hogg saw him again in Cairo on his way back to England in November and heard how Hackett in a solitary vehicle armed with a 37 mm. gun had nearly captured two German guns of enormous size.

> Then, he said, it came on him like a flash, just as when a child, taken out by its aunt, looking into a shop window, suddenly realises that there is one thing he really wants . . . I realised that I had all my life wanted those two lovely guns. I came up to them and jerked my thumb for them to follow . . . they were drawn by two tracked vehicles with two rows of men like choirboys seated on a knife board seat. One crew abandoned ship. The other stayed on board. Both obeyed his summons. The leading one was driven by an old disillusioned man with a helmet, much too big, over his ears.

Hackett was finally chased away by some Mark III Tiger Tanks. He told Hogg that it was a lesson to him. ' "Life is never perfect" said Shan, "You will never be allowed to take it home. Break it there." ' The conversation then turned and Hogg said that this war should have its Thucydides to do justice to the story: 'Churchill . . . his defects which reserved him to the right moment, to be comprehended in a few sentences . . . Roosevelt – *his* qualities, so cunningly stage managing his great historical comedy, the entry of the U.S. into the war – complete without Pearl Harbor which was a gift from Heaven, all the world knowing what he was about, and none able to stop him.' (*Diary* 25 Nov. 1942.) It was an exhilarating friendship of fellow spirits.

Hogg took trouble with the friends of his army life. Harold Terry, who had been junior clerk in his Chambers and was now a lance-corporal, corresponded regularly. Hogg thought him 'above his own education' and his letters 'warmed the heart' with their 'natural taste in the things he says'. The letters which survive are of an easy but respectful informality. 'Your assurance about my future and your wish that we should again work together is all to me . . .'[9] Terry was killed in Sicily.

On 14 December 1941, Hogg received news that Robert MacGill, the young friend he had first met in Durban, was reported missing at Sidi Rezegh in the Western Desert, and on Christmas Eve he had one of his letters returned marked 'missing, believed killed'. He was distraught and, as so often when faced with a personal crisis, he wrote a long letter to Father D'Arcy at Oxford, 'setting down at last what it all meant in order'. He and MacGill had seen a good deal of each other in Cairo. Hogg wrote that he believed he had never had a greater affection for any friend, and confessed that he 'loved him like a brother, or rather, almost like an adopted son'. The diary continues: 'After all this chance a Providence gave me what my heart desired in a strange guise; for it was suggested to me by him that I had found someone at last whom I could really regard as a child.' On 28 December he received a letter from an officer in the 7th Hussars saying that a corporal had seen MacGill being taken away in a German staff car. He resolved to go to Cairo at once to find out if he could whether his friend was alive or dead.

The city was far worse than he had thought it would be. Ghosts of MacGill were in every corner, in every bar and even in the decrepit taxis. He contacted an officer in the 3rd Hussars who had also been at Rezegh. Gradually another sinister story unfolded itself. A youthful corpse had been found in a shallow grave in a likely spot at Rezegh. There were no marks of identity, which was consistent with the dead man having been in enemy hands. The description of the face, though not exact, 'succeeds in giving an impression of Robert'. The regiment were inclined to think it was he. He thought of going out to the desert to disinter the corpse but the spot had not been marked sufficiently clearly and there were too many graves. So he got hold of a photograph of MacGill and took it to the 3rd Hussars. His diary for 4 January reads: 'Well, I did it. I went into the Mess as if into the consulting room of a specialist expecting to be told I was suffering from cancer.' Hogg's contact told him that the dead officer was not the one in the photograph – so far as he could say.

Hogg left Cairo in a state of wracking uncertainty. Some of the following diary entries are heavily crossed out, an indication of the torment he was undergoing. However, in the ensuing weeks reports that MacGill had been lightly wounded and captured gained conviction, and eventually he felt able to write to MacGill's widowed mother to say that he thought her son was alive. Early in March, Hogg received a peremptory wire from Headquarters, Second Echelon, Ninth Army: 'War Office state you informed NOK [next of kin] that Lt. RC MacGill seen in enemy hands. Wire gist report confirmed by signed statement. Officer now reported killed in action. Very urgent.' He sat down at once and wrote out his statement, but he feared he might be court martialled for what he had done. 'This sort of thing knocks the spirit out of a man,' reads the diary, 'I fear so much that the most sincere thing I have done to help those I love has turned rotten and evil in my hands.' But relief was near and the drama was finally resolved within days. In the office he found a wire from Mrs MacGill: 'Robert written. Wounded prisoner.'

Hogg thought that an inscrutable providence was at work in the whole episode. The innocent friendship with the younger man was unlike anything else in Hogg's life. His more perceptive friends at school and afterwards discerned that he did not make deep friendships easily. His egocentricity prevented it. But here Hogg committed himself without reserve. He loved MacGill as he would a son. The young man released emotions that belong to a father, and which, because of Natalie's inability to bear children, had till then been pent-up. She knew about the friendship and realised that it might help her husband to reconcile himself to the idea of adoption. The diary shows that he realised it too. On Christmas Day, 1941, while stunned by the blow of his young friend's apparent death, he wrote:

> I had always desired a son of my body. Next when this failed I thought of adopting one, and perhaps I shall after the war, for Tony's sake. But the deliberate method of selection in this caused me to shrink; a child must always be the gift of God, in a sense. Only so comes the spontaneous love which leaps over shortcomings and achieves perfect sympathy.

Within five months Natalie, then undergoing a serious operation and under severe stress herself, made it clear to her husband that only adoption could save their marriage. But in spite of the experience of his friendship with Robert MacGill, Hogg's doubts about adoption remained and he could not bring himself to do it for his wife's sake.

★

As soon as he heard that MacGill was missing, Hogg wrote a short poem in his diary.

> Yes, I must talk, and I must laugh and eat
> As if the world were still the same today
> As when, together in that sunny street
> We said goodbye, and each went on his way . . .

Although he had been writing Latin or Greek verse since the age of ten, he wrote none in English until 1940. Edward, his half-brother, had fancied himself as a poet and Neil wrote good verse, but for some reason he himself had not attempted English verse until he was in his thirties. The 1941–2 diary contains much of the little collection that was published under the title *The Devil's Own Song* in 1968. The rigours of a classical education had given him a feeling for the choice of words, and for the music and metre of verse. Some of the best in the collection are the compressed translations from the Latin. In *An emperor's reflection*, he rendered the lament of the Emperor Hadrian which had inspired *Lycidas*.

> Poor little laughing soul of mine,
> Companion and co-tenant of my clay,
> Oh, whither now departest thou
> And wanderest away,
> Stiff, naked, old, pale, weak and cold
> Forsaking all thy play?

His artistic leanings were exclusively literary and he knew the power of poetry to excite tears and laughter. What perhaps brought him to write poems during his time in the Middle East was both that he had time to indulge this innocent pastime ('as natural to man as singing in his bath'), and that it was for him a period when his emotions, never far below the surface, often broke through. He thought too that versifying was a salutary discipline, and wrote in the introduction to his poems: 'If I were asked to give a single reason for the decline of the English language into the flaccid, inaccurate, verbose, windy, and pompous vehicle of speech it is becoming in the hands of civil servants, politicians, lawyers and journalists, I would say it is because the art of verse writing has fallen into a decline.'

It is a pity that he did not develop his natural talent for verse parody. When Sir John Betjeman, the Poet Laureate and a friend, produced his dire tribute for Princess Anne's Wedding in 1973: 'Hundreds of birds in the air, And millions of leaves on the pavement . . .' which merited a *Daily Express* headline 'Going from Bad to Verse', Lord Hailsham doodled in his Lord Chancellor's engagement diary:

> Hundreds of birds in the air, and thousands of tarts on the
>   pavement
> Down the processional route hobbles old Hailsham along.
> Bravely he marches on to the gay flags joyous enwavement
> Lurching from side to side, and singing this dubious song:
> 'You know what to do with your bells and your birds and your
>   holy enslavement,
> 'Hailsham has come to take over; hark to the kettledrum's throb.
> 'Hailsham's the laurelled brow, and the sack barrel's drunken
>   enstavement
> 'Betjeman's no good at all; Hailsham's the man for the job.'[10]

★

Hogg travelled a good deal while he was on Wilson's staff, to Jerusalem, occasionally to Cairo, and into Syria. The road to Homs and Aleppo through the Bekaa valley took him past the great Graeco-Roman temples of Baalbek where he used to stop to eat his sandwiches. His first visit was in December 1941 and there is a good descriptive entry in his diary. In the temple of Bacchus, he saw that a fragment of roof on the outer colonnade was decorated with the star of David, 'said to have been wrought by Jewish slaves, but possibly an example of the Roman Imperial practice of universalising religion – of which the identification of Jupiter with Baal is clearly a striking example'. (*Diary* 8 Dec. 1941.)

In August 1942, he unexpectedly got fourteen days leave and decided to take a walking tour in the Lebanon mountains, the first holiday of that sort since the Hitler-Stalin Pact had interrupted his climbing trip in Norway. There is a gap in his diary here and the account which he kept at the time in a separate notebook is lost. But he recorded his experiences in an article in the *Geographical Magazine* published in March 1943. He was accompanied by an undersized but observably virile donkey called George. After the trip he learned that George had been the pet of an English lady: 'His work for me was apparently his first excursion into sordid business life.' In the magazine article he explains how the Christian enclave in the Lebanon was left intact when Islam swept over the Roman world, advancing down the Bekaa valley and through the Homs-Tripoli gap to the coast. 'When the horsemen of the first crusade came down the coastal road in the 11th century, strange bearded figures descended from the mountains, making the sign of the cross.'

His route from Broumana was north by mule-tracks close to the summit of the mountains on the seaward side, as far as the great cedars. He lay on his back and drank in the inimitable scent of the trees. The country was recognisably Christian and delightful 'with the familiar church and shrines of Catholic Europe; while the agriculture – vines, terraces and cereal crops – reflects the simple cultivation of medieval Italy or Provence.' From the cedars he passed through the mountains and returned quickly by the Bekaa. One night the party got lost and had to knock up the muktar of a Moslem village. He gave them shelter and an excellent meal; but Hogg drank large quantities of water, and became infected with hepatitis. Early in September he had to go into a New Zealand military hospital. The debilitating disease kept him confined there until the end of October, when he was discharged nearly forty pounds lighter in weight. He was medically downgraded and could no longer hope to serve in an active theatre. This was the opportunity to return home, long hoped for but not in this depleted way.

The military interlude was over. It had been a disappointment because he had wanted to fight and, but for a few months, could not. But as perhaps he did not then realise, his two years abroad had given him much: freedom from the confines of a professional routine; companionship which flowered in a few cases into life-long friendships; the satisfaction of living and breathing the air of the Eastern Mediterranean; and perhaps most worthwhile of all, a time to reflect.

8

Homecoming

IN the last days of October 1942 Hogg was out of hospital and on sick leave, spent under the Spears' hospitable roof, 'eating heavily and writing little'. Thence to Alexandria to put in his application to go home. The desert battle had begun and the diary is sprinkled with news and comment about Alamein. On 16 November he heard a lecture on the battle and thought: 'This was a battle which was very nearly lost.' Later, in Cairo, he discussed Montgomery's performance with Hackett and Douglas Darling, who had been his company commander and who now had command of the 7th Battalion, Rifle Brigade, at the age of twenty-eight. Both were critical. They considered that when Rommel turned tail, the pursuit had been bungled and an opportunity to cut off the retreat had been lost. Darling also thought that at the crisis of the battle 100 tanks had been sacrificed in the punch through, owing to Montgomery's failure to realise that 'it is no good sending armour across a minefield in face of 88 mm. guns'. 'All this is sad,' Hogg commented, 'crabbing as it does a brilliant victory and the man who made it.' Darling doubted if Montgomery would improve with experience: he was too conceited. These were not armchair critics.

By 25 November he was in Shepheard's Hotel in Cairo. He noticed a change in the atmosphere in the bar. 'Last year it was carefree, irresponsibly youthful. Now droves of serious faced young gentlemen drink whiskies and sodas with solemn looks. Is this an improvement? The fact is that they are different people. Our people escaped out of blitzed England to smite the enemy, almost gaily. The new arrivals are austerity minded – that is not that they do not take their pleasures, but that they take them less pleasurably.' (*Diary* 25 Nov. 1942.) (However, one who took his pleasures pleasurably was Mark Chapman Walker. Hogg was told that a friend once remonstrated with him while he was in the bath in a Cairo hotel and said he was sure that sooner or later he would come to grief. 'Mark replied from the soap suds with a glass of champagne in his hand: "Well, when I think of all you chaps wisking your lives up in front, I feel I ought to take a few wisks back here".') Hogg saw as many people as he could while he was in Cairo, awaiting transport. Among them was Lord Moyne, the deputy Minister of State, who was later assassinated in Palestine: 'an agreeable, if somewhat elderly man'. At Moyne's dinner table he met John Winant, the United States Ambassador to Britain, who impressed him as 'very courteous and polished', and Air Chief Marshal Tedder, who did not – 'gauche and awkward, and, in spite of his opportunity with Winant, said nothing worth saying'.

On 3 December the saga of his journey home began. He was to travel by air with a weight limit of 40 lbs. He rushed about buying presents. After much indecision he acquired 3 metres of pink silk and an amethyst brooch for Natalie. There was a series of false starts, but he finally got off in his Liberator aircraft with a bare minimum of clothing and personal possessions. He lay in the bomb bay 'like Jonah in the belly of the fish'. There was a stop in Gibraltar, 'a hive of activity, packed with travellers'. He stayed at Government House, and then moved on. In the early afternoon of 12 December, he happened to go up into the observation dome of the aircraft: 'after two years [I] saw again that holy thing with green and brown criss crossed in patchwork pattern and the afternoon sunlight on the winter water.' But there was no time to become sentimental about homecoming. They ran into rough air and were 'thrown about like corks on a rough sea' as they came down.

★

The grievous story of the end of Quintin Hogg's first marriage is told in *A Sparrow's Flight*. It is the same story that he recorded in the last entry in his diary written a month after his homecoming, when he first felt able to put pen to paper. Arriving late in the evening, weary from his journey from Cairo without luggage, clean clothes or money, and still with traces of jaundice, he appeared unannounced at 1 Victoria Square, to find Natalie with a Free Frenchman called François Coulet, General de Gaulle's *chef de cabinet*, in the house. When Hogg had told a brother officer in the Western Desert that he kept his front door key always with him and intended to surprise Natalie by arriving suddenly, his friend had tried to dissuade him, saying that it was unfair to his wife who would want to prepare for his return. Although Hogg disregarded this excellent advice, it would have made no difference, for the marriage was over. After a few painful weeks Natalie left and spent the rest of her life with Coulet. Hogg had always rejected divorce as an option, but he was now persuaded by his father and his brother Neil, who was fortunately in London, to free himself, rather than be condemned to a lonely life in which solace and sexual companionship would have to be always illicit.

He wrote to Tom Corbishley, who had just been ordained, not for advice, but out of the need to confide in a friend. 'I have I fear sad news to tell you. My wife, who had been writing affectionate letters all the time I was away, bolted from me on my return with abusive words. She had been living in my own house for fourteen months with a Free French officer, and seems to regard this as somehow my fault. However, she's gone, and I am alone.'[1]

In his last diary entry he attempted a post mortem on his marriage. The attempt was bound to be a failure, for who can look with detachment on his own marriage? He remarked that, in the Old Testament, Hosea's conclusion was that it was his own fault, for lack of affection, that his wife became a whore. But he did not think he could convict himself of blame. There was as usual more to be said. Natalie, who was energetic and did not lack the common touch, had been working hard while her husband was away, nursing his constituency and organising Red Cross canteens in Shoreditch, for which she was publicly praised by the Mayor. She wanted to join the A.T.S. (women's army corps) and she sought Hogg's approval. 'Received this day a wire from dear Tony asking if she should take a job as A.T.S. education officer. She has had my December letters. Wired back "yes".' (*Diary*, 24 Feb. 1942.) With good reason, she thought that her Shoreditch job had given her first-hand experience of the Blitz, and she wanted to use it by visiting Air Raid Posts and the Fire Services in the Oxford constituency. For this she needed the help of the Conservative agent. This got her into trouble with Lady Townsend, the Constituency Chairman, who wrote to Quintin: 'Mrs Hogg unfortunately thought the agent should do various personal errands for her . . . I fear she did not like it when I told her . . .'[2] Natalie protested to her husband: 'Nor would I have wanted to do any of these things in any other capacity than as the MP's wife and deputy.' The reverberations from the clash of these Tory ladies are almost palpable. Hogg agreed with his wife but thought it more prudent not to upset the local potentates.

The diary records affectionate messages. 'Remember 12 Nov. 1932. No regrets', she wired on their wedding anniversary; and:

'*Ayez confiance en moi*. All love, Rosca Tosca'; but the assurance did not prevent him, from time to time, from feeling anxiety about her constancy. In May 1942 she had to have a serious operation for the removal of a growth affecting her bladder and womb. She described the operation as 'necessary 1939' and it confounded her plan to join the A.T.S. The operation precipitated an emotional crisis and she wrote a three page airgraph (a letter sent in the form of a microfilm) to her husband.

Dearest Quaggers, 'The best laid plans of mice and men' – ! . . . My war effort, which promised so well, is in limbo. When I am fit again I will find another outlet for my ideas and renewed energy, I hope in the A.T.S. as I am sick of the 1914 ideas of the Red Cross!'

She then gave her husband details of the operation, saying

What it all amounts to is about 3 months hors de combat, 3–4 weeks in hospital, then Mildred says [I] can go to C.C. [Carters Corner] . . . I leave it to your imagination what I am suffering mentally and the great thing that sustains me is your love for me and the hope that you will redeem your promise to adopt a child, for without confidence in your word – to adopt in spite of any financial considerations, as though it were our own, I will be quite lost and without hope. Quaggers, I trust in you, for if you forsake me in this project I am afraid, even though the whole affair is *my* fault – our mutual interests and affection would not be sufficient to bind us. Your feelings for Robert [Robert MacGill] may have prepared you for such a step . . . I've resigned Commandant and so should wear the 'prison blue' instead of my lovely scarlet! It's rather sad, it was *so* becoming. The R.X. [Red Cross] *couldn't* have been more NASTY about my going into the A.T.S. although they offered no reasonable employment. However, I am told I remain 'The Angel of Shoreditch'! Please, dear husband, write me and cable me very often. I need your understanding help and love very desperately.

Fond love, Tisca.[3]

Unhappily, Hogg received this desperate appeal in parts. On receipt of the second page, by itself, containing no reference to adoption, he immediately wired 'Will not forsake'. Then he realised, when he had pages 1 and 3 later, that his wife was making their marriage depend on his agreement to adopt. He noted in his diary, 'I cannot in the present state wire cancelling. Very difficult. Must leave it to time to pan out.' (*Diary*, 25 June 1942.)

Natalie's airgraph coincided with news of the fall of Tobruk and Sir John Wardlaw-Milne's motion in the Commons of 'no confidence in the central direction of the war'. The diary shows that the airgraph did not drive public affairs from Hogg's mind. On the same day as he sent his wire to Natalie, he also wired to the Prime Minister: 'Feel it necessary at this time to reaffirm my support for Govt., though *not* uncritical. Good luck.' He commented: 'I think this sums up my real view.' Did Churchill feel that his young supporter was a whit patronising? In any case, Churchill survived the vote of censure with ease; and the debate turned into farce when Wardlaw-Milne suggested that the Duke of Gloucester be made Commander-in-Chief.

It is impossible to read Natalie's letter and her husband's diary entries without being moved. The two, separated by distance, but much more by an inability to make emotional contact, were bound to go separate ways. Hogg could not bring himself to believe that he could love an adopted child as his own: his wife, unable to bear children, was making adoption a condition of the continuation of their marriage. Her shout could not be heard across the divide; he thought he could temporise. The blow each struck at the other, her infidelity and his incapacity to respond, was mortal.

Natalie made a rapid recovery. She was looked after well by her father-in-law who paid her medical expenses, and by Mildred. They all kept Hogg informed of her progress by frequent letters and cables. On 14 June: 'wire from dear T: "Record Recovery".' But the end was inevitable. On 17 December, he wrote in his diary: '. . . after fumbling up the steps in the dark I opened the door with a lump in my throat. The kind of welcome I got when I came in had better not be described here.'

9

Beveridge and the Tory Reform Committee

THE break-up of Quintin Hogg's first marriage was boyhood's end. The woman who had challenged his supremacy and did not shrink from undermining his self-respect damaged him badly. He never lost his zest for life or his sense of mischief, but nor could he obliterate the shadow of failure which Natalie had thrown across his life. None the less, he came to recognise later that he had been more fortunate than he knew. Natalie remarried almost at once and there were no children. A clean break was achieved. Now he had to get over his ordeal and put his life together. 'The great thing at present is not to let this disaster get me down. I am seeing as much as possible of my friends, and living as full a life as possible from the point of view of my work.' (*Diary* 22 Jan. 1943.) Within days of touching down in England, he saw Churchill, who gave him a cigar. He kept the sodden stub as a memento, 'a piece of vulgarity of which I am somewhat ashamed'. Winston was kind. He showed Hogg the 'Sit Map', and told him that he was justified in resuming parliamentary duties: 'no one should presume to say after two years' foreign service and a wound that I was trying to shirk.' (*Diary* 17 Jan. 1943.)

From the time when Hogg was in hospital in the Lebanon with jaundice, he had been making longer, speculative entries in his diary and preparing for his return to England and political life. A reading of *English Saga* by Arthur Bryant, an author he did not much admire, provoked the comment that 'the great virtue of the Conservative Party has always seemed to be its opportunism: at any rate its freedom from theories'. Hogg was shortly to develop this thought and turn it into a coherent political philosophy in *The Case for Conservatism*.

Lady Spears had kept him supplied with reading matter, including two old copies of *The Spectator*. A letter from a lance-corporal to the editor impressed him. Hogg was troubled by public morale at home. 'We have appeared to achieve in our hour of peril, almost without effort, the spirit of battle, which arose spontaneously and rallied and crystallised quite naturally around the fighting personality of Winston Churchill. We lacked all along and we lack now the spirit of victory – that effortless feeling of self-confidence which seems to be so largely the secret of success.' (*Diary* 23 Oct. 1942.) Prophetic words, at a time when ultimate victory at last began to look secure. The lance-corporal darkened his premonitions by analysing what was missing: lack of emotional allegiance to the Empire or any traditional British institution; lack of faith in social change; lack of faith in individual futures.

The diary commented that war had brought men and women of all classes together, so that differing points of view were better understood, and 'the actual exigencies of warfare' had driven the nation to make social and political experiments from which lessons were beginning to emerge. The full implications of this thought were probably better understood outside government than in. All classes shared the same air raid shelters; food rationing spread deprivation evenly, and meant that poorer people were better nourished than in peacetime; the evacuation of children brought them into contact with people whose lives were not dreamed of. The mixing of all sorts and conditions of men was going on in parallel in the armed forces. Here were the springs of the social upheaval which was to break surface so dramatically in the 1945 election.

Hogg noted in his diary that he wanted to see an inter-party committee of young MPs who would produce an agreed programme of minimum requirements 'sufficient to satisfy all doubts that, whatever party held power after the war, certain measures of social justice could be regarded as secure'. (*Diary* 23 Oct. 1942.) This may not have been practical politics but it showed which way he would want to push his own party. Interestingly, Herbert Morrison, a very practical politician, floated a similar idea the following year: the three parties would conduct their election campaigns on the basis of an agreed minimum programme; there would be normal contests in which each party would add its own emphasis to the minimum programme; and the new composition of the House after the election would determine the balance and policies of the resultant coalition. This idea, probably inspired by the conviction that Churchill must win the next election, ran into the sand.[1] Shortly after his return to England, Hogg was a fellow guest at a dinner party with Aneurin Bevan. Bevan talked about his own political aims regarding the structure of society; to Hogg's surprise, they were almost the same as his own.

These musings all pointed one way: in the direction of radical change. They were brought sharply into focus by the publication of the Beveridge Report in November 1942 while Hogg was still in the Middle East. He had not then read the Report but he was aware of the extraordinary impact it had made in the armed forces. Beveridge caught a flood tide, coinciding with the turning point of the war against Germany. After Stalingrad, Alamein and the American landings in North Africa, victory was not in serious doubt, and the conception of a post-war world moved into the foreground of popular thinking. Even so, the dramatic effects of the publication of the Report were quite unforeseen. The task which Sir William Beveridge had undertaken in 1941 was to tidy up a confused mass of social and medical insurance schemes, all of which were individually inadequate. No one expected much from such a tedious piece of work. No one except Beveridge himself thought he would start a social revolution. The work was described in his entry in the *Dictionary of National Biography* as 'an obscure interdepartmental inquiry'. But within a few days of starting, Beveridge had convinced himself that it offered the opportunity he had been looking for to re-shape British society after the war.

Beveridge was an unlikely figure for a prophet. White haired and slight, he had a curiously bird-like profile and a high pitched, fastidious Oxford accent. But he was determined to carry through the root and branch reform which was his own. The face and the voice were 'flashed by Pathé News into every cinema in the country'.[2] The report was an instant best seller. It sold 250,000 copies before the end of the year and a summary was translated by the BBC into 22 languages. A Gallup poll taken at the time indicated that 95 per cent of the population knew about it and approved of its recommendations. There has never, before or since, been anything like it to come out of the government bookshop.

Although the Report was written in the desiccated language of the professional administrator, it still caught the public imagination; and it began with a call for revolutionary change, not just patching. It was an attack on Want, its author declared, with conscious overtones of Bunyan. 'Want is one only of five giants on the road to reconstruction and in some ways the easiest to attack. The others are Disease, Ignorance, Squalor and Idleness.'[3] Beveridge proposed the unification of all schemes for health, unemployment, retirement and other social benefits. In return for one flat-rate weekly contribution in the same amount, everyone in the land would receive a subsistence payment whenever his employment was interrupted or ended.

While Hogg was waiting in Cairo for transport to take him home, he learned that there was to be a three-day debate on the Report in the following March. He put down some thoughts in his diary, which he afterwards had typed, perhaps for use with his political friends. He included these in *One Year's Work*, an account of what he had done during 1943. This curious piece of self-advertisement was published in 1944 with a blurb which read: 'In this book can be seen the steps Quintin Hogg has taken, by word and pen, in one year to show a new light, uphold a new beacon to all who waver in their belief in the British way of life.' It contains the text of many of his speeches and articles given and written during 1943. The piece on Beveridge welcomed the report for its moral effect. It was to be translated and broadcast in many languages, 'so that it is apparent that the government has decided to back it'. (In the event, the government's rapture was far too modified for the taste of Hogg and his friends.) The moral effect of the report would be felt particularly in the fighting services who were not merely soldiers, sailors and airmen, 'but a cross-section of the whole community, violently interested in the future of their country'. The real cause of social insecurity before the War, he felt sure, was unemployment. 'It was the existence of this social evil which had such a depressing effect not merely on the unemployed themselves, but on the conditions and rewards of employment itself; it was this too which led to the fear of sickness and old age; and the feeling of moral responsibility for the fate of the unemployed which interfered so largely with the natural and healthy optimism of the British community.' (*Diary* 3 Dec. 1942.)

Hogg thought that if it were to succeed, Beveridge must be adopted abroad as well as at home. Only in that way could our exports compete in overseas markets: 'we shall then combine our interests with our humanitarian duty.' The export of the Beveridge scheme was particularly important in the Commonwealth, to avoid mass immigration. That lesson was not learned, or even preached. He also feared a mistake of emphasis in the Report. 'Too much stress is laid upon providing a safe and comfortable haven for a rapidly aging population of adults. Too little upon providing a brilliant and profitable equality of opportunity for enterprising youth.'

These were very preliminary views, but his political instincts were clear. The opportunity to follow them came in his first week home. In that week, he attended the Commons three times, and also saw the Speaker, Leslie Hore-Belisha, Alexander Spearman and Viscount

Hinchingbrooke. Hinchingbrooke asked him to join a group of young Conservative members who dined every week. 'We are busy trying to get down our political aims on paper, but this is not easy. We start with few prejudices – and progressive ideals. But we are still in the thinking stage.' (*Diary* 22 Jan. 1943.) The little group consisted of Alfred Beit; Hogg's old friend and fellow-pupil at the Bar, Peter Thorneycroft; Hogg and Hinchingbrooke. Hugh Molson joined a little later. The moving spirit was 'Hinch', the quintessential English backbencher, generous, erratic, and independent minded, 'the best loved of us all'. The first meetings were in a little restaurant behind Charing Cross Road, but the group soon moved to the grander Connaught Hotel where Beit arranged the commissariat. There was a dinner in February to discuss the debate on the Beveridge Report, which was to take place in the next few days. The hosts were the industrial insurance offices and arrangements were made through Alec Spearman, a friend who always seemed at hand at turning points in Hogg's career. (It had been on his initiative that Hogg had first put forward his name for nomination in the Oxford City by-election.) Hogg spoke up forcibly for unequivocal acceptance of the Beveridge Report, arguing particularly for the immediate establish-ment of a Ministry for Social Security. His hosts had something of a vested interest in the status quo and were not enchanted by Hogg's uncompromising views. According to him, the genesis of the Tory Reform Committee was in this discussion around the dinner table. It was then that the little group decided to use the forthcoming debate to go flat out for Beveridge.

The Committee was launched formally at the House of Commons on 17 March with Hinchingbrooke as Chairman, and Thorneycroft and Molson as Secretaries. Hogg was an enthusiastic leading light from the outset. He had decided not to return to the Bar while the war was on. He came home to serve his constituents and to speak for the armed forces. 'My whole activity was directed in politics, and in politics my whole thought was towards post-war reconstruction.' The young officers who made up the group were on terms of easy friendship. Peter Thorneycroft recalled that it was 'a wonderful happy time for all the members; we were friends doing an exciting thing, contributing to the building of the post-war world'.[4] Hogg thought that membership of the Committee had taught him to work in Parliamentary harness with other people. 'Hitherto I had been a lone wolf arriving at my own decisions and rather despising committee work. Basically, I think this may still [1965] be my tendency.'[5] The experience of the Tory Reform Committee helped him with Parliamentary tactics when he later came into government.

The work required prolonged discussion, compromise and the loyalty due to friendships. None of this came easily to him, but the excitement of being part of a ginger group was very congenial.

The Beveridge Report struck Hogg as being not well written and containing a fair amount of muddled thinking and incautious optimism. But it was an initiative about which it was impossible to be neutral. There seemed to be only three options: 'to attack it, to praise it with faint damns, or to go bald-headed for its adoption'.[6] The decision to go bald-headed fixed his course for the next three years. He had already made that decision by the time he joined the Tory Reformers. The persistent pool of unemployment before the war, and the poverty and despair which it brought had preoccupied him then. Families lived under the twin threat of dismissal and eviction. Those who were out of work could neither save for old age, nor provide for sickness, nor bring up their families in decency. Even those who were in work had had the level of their wages depressed by the very existence of the pool. These preoccupations had been strongly reinforced by the views he had encountered in the army and by his own reflections.

Beveridge had not relied on his scheme to speak for itself. He and his colleagues took evidence across the widest spectrum of opinion and had found very general approbation. The outright opponents were an anachronistic minority, exemplified by the Confederation of British Employers, whose Director told the Committee: 'we did not start this war with Germany in order to improve our social services . . . we entered it to preserve our freedom and to keep the Gestapo outside our houses.'[7]

Opinion within the coalition government was different. There were none unalterably against, but there were elements advising caution and qualification. There was the strongest feeling that unity within government in order to achieve victory was paramount. Until now all policies had been bipartisan: the massive figures of Churchill and Bevin had seen to that. In any case, Churchill regarded all domestic issues as secondary and potentially divisive. Hogg thought that the Great Man had a curious deafness to the demand for social justice and that the government's 'pussy-footing over the Beveridge Report was unduly unconstructive and unimaginative.'

Churchill, however, had reason to be cautious. He had commissioned a secret report from a committee of Tory MPs chaired by the Party Chairman, Ralph Assheton, to advise him on Conservative reaction to Beveridge in the House.[8]* The report, an important

* Details were first published in *The Road to 1945* by Paul Addison (1975). The members of the Committee were: Ralph Assheton (Chairman), Sir Arnold Gridley,

document in the history of the party, was delivered on 19 January 1943, and was a good deal less than enthusiastic. The Committee complained that they had been given inadequate time to cope with a subject of such significance. They accepted some of Beveridge's proposals, but they rejected the key recommendations that all benefits should be at subsistence level, and that they should be paid to everyone. At the root of their reservations was the financial commitment. They pointed out that the plan was for limited contributions by employer and employee, but imposed unlimited liability on the state; and they asked, 'Is the state justified in assuming a liability of this kind to meet not only want but also to assure benefits to those not in need?' They did not think that long-term unemployment was an insurable risk and proposed to limit unemployment benefit as of right to six months. And in two sentences which surely would have been anathema to the Tory Reformers, had they read them, they declared: 'It is essential to preserve the incentive to work and it is necessary, therefore, that benefit should as a rule be substantially lower than wages. As it is impossible to forecast the level of wages, so it is impossible to fix in advance the appropriate rate of unemployment benefit.'

This fell short of outright opposition, but it was tepid water. If, as seems likely, it represented the general mood in the parliamentary party, it goes far to explain Churchill's unwillingness to 'go bald-headed' for Beveridge. To add to the Assheton paper was the traditional Treasury view of Kingsley Wood, Chancellor of the Exchequer and an apostle of financial rectitude. He had advised the Prime Minister when the Beveridge Report was published that the scheme would involve 'an impracticable financial commitment'.[9]

On 14 February, the eve of the debate on the Report, Churchill circulated a note to the Cabinet in which he outlined the way in which Beveridge should be handled.[10] 'This approach to social security, bringing the magic of averages nearer to the rescue of the millions, constitutes an essential part of any post-war scheme of national betterment.' He had no doubt that the report should be implemented – but not yet. Not until after a General Election. 'There should be a body – if necessary a Commission – set up to work from now till the end of the war, polishing, reshaping, and preparing for the necessary legislation ... We cannot however initiate the legislation now or commit ourselves to the expenditure involved. That can only be done by a responsible Government and a House of Commons refreshed by contact with the people.'

Florence Horsburgh, Dr A. B. Howitt, Alice Johnston, Dr Clive Saxton, Spencer Summers, and Sir Herbert Williams.

Ever since December, when he had heard in Cairo that there was to be a debate on the Beveridge Report, Hogg had been eagerly waiting. The Government's line would not begin to satisfy the enthusiasm which he and his fellow Tory Reformers felt about it. Arthur Greenwood, occupying the impossible position of official leader of the opposition, moved an anodyne motion welcoming the Report 'as a valuable aid in determining the lines on which developments and legislation should be pursued'.[11] Sir John Anderson, the Lord President, followed for the government with a bloodless effort, saying, 'It has been my duty to point out that there can be at present no binding commitment.' This was precisely what Hogg had called praising with faint damns. Hinchingbrooke put down an amendment calling on the government to set up forth with a Ministry of Social Security, as Beveridge himself had recommended.

Hogg, with forty other Conservatives, had put his name to the amendment and was called on to speak on the second day of the debate. He thus became the Tory Reformers' chief spokesman. Describing the question of post-war recovery as a moral rather than an economic one, he accused the government of being guilty of 'a major political blunder' in not having appreciated that. 'If we are to go to the people of this country and say "You have to look forward to a long period of self-sacrifice and restriction," we can do so only if we offer at the same time a complete measure of social justice to guarantee that we shall all suffer alike.'[12] Beveridge, he said, was not a scheme for the abolition of want in the abstract, but by 'the redistribution of wealth', a phrase he afterwards regretted, because of its socialist ring. Having accused the government of blundering, he went further and shocked the Conservative benches by saying '. . . so long as there remain people who cannot have enough to eat, the possession of private property is a humiliation and not an opportunity'; and 'if you do not give the people social reform, they are going to give you social revolution.'[13]

Hogg's oratory was passionate as well as provocative. It was as strongly felt as any speech he ever made in the House, and it left a deep impression. *The Times* reported: 'The most remarkable speech today came from Mr Quintin Hogg. He was cheered with almost embarrassing fervour from the other side as he called on the government for clear definition and bold action.' The speech must have encouraged Labour backbenchers to vote against the government. One Labour Member asked him to repeat what he had said about the consequences for the Conservative Party if the warnings went unheeded. Hogg obliged, describing himself as a 'despised left-wing Conservative'. His colleagues on the Tory Reform Committee felt equally strongly, but they had no intention of creating embarrassment by dividing the House or voting against the Government. (They thought differently a year later: see p. 93) None the less, when the Greenwood motion was put, 121 votes were cast against the government, 97 of them Labour. The revolt was encouraged not only by the Tory Reformers but also by the ineptitude of Kingsley Wood's contribution. It was prim in style and ominous in intention: 'While I agree that finance should not be our master but rather our servant, that servant must be fairly and properly treated and certainly should not be so dealt with that he breaks or collapses in the course of his work.'[14]

The debate showed the government to be sadly out of touch. Only the Tory Reformers seemed to appreciate the danger of irrelevance facing the Conservative Party. The people were in a hurry and simply not willing to listen to more arguments about belt-tightening and financial stringency. They were too redolent of the thirties. The evangelising editor of *Picture Post*, Edward Hulton, ran a series of pro-Beveridge pieces and a lively correspondence column. The issue of 3 March carried a carefully selected group of letters, from a sailor, a soldier, a wage-earner and three public schoolboys. The boys' letter read: 'We are deeply disgusted with parliament's handling of the Beveridge Report, which shows more strongly than ever that the financial interests and the Baldwin-Chamberlain hangers-on do all they can to delay and destroy any reforms directed to the good of the people. Is this the brave new world we, for instance, will soon be fighting for?'

In the same issue Hogg contributed 'An Open Letter to the Conservative Party'. He called on his fellow members of the party to stop the tactics of a short-sighted and reactionary rump and to go back to Disraeli. 'Tell them they are ruining the party. Tell them to take a long view. Tell them to stick to the principles of Disraeli, and to leave clever party politics alone for the time being.' Hogg dealt gently with the Beveridge debate, saying that Arthur Greenwood's motion was so innocuous that 'some of us younger Tories felt constrained to move an amendment to put a little ginger in it'. He reserved his real strictures for a group of Conservative right-wing backbenchers led by Sir Douglas Hacking, a former chairman of the party. Ernest Bevin, the Minister of Labour, had introduced a Catering Wages Bill to secure minimum wages and conditions in hotels and restaurants. The debate on the Second Reading took place a week before the Beveridge debate. The Tory Reformers had strongly supported the Bill, but Hacking had led a group of more than 100 Conservatives into the 'No' lobby. 'Sir Douglas Hacking', wrote Hogg, 'was blissfully cooking the Conservative goose in a sauce which just suited the Independent Socialist propaganda.' Hogg was referring to an incident in the recent Bristol by-election at which Jennie Lee, Aneurin Bevan's wife, was standing as an Independent Socialist. Hogg went down to support the Government's candidate and was met by cries of: 'What about the Tory MPs who voted against the Catering Bill?' He enjoyed this sort of stumping and was good at it, but he was not alone among the reformers. Peter Thorneycroft also wrote to *Picture Post*. '*We* shall have the Beveridge Report or any adaptation of it that we choose. *They* do not exist who can deny it to us.'

The debates on the Catering Bill and Beveridge had opened up a visible split among Conservatives. The Tory Reformers, whose numbers grew to about 45, were concerned above all to revitalise the party's thinking. On the other side, reactionaries like Hacking threatened to drag Conservatives further towards irrelevance. The reformers were in a hurry to go forth and propagate the gospel, and their fervour could cause irritation in high places, especially when in March 1944 they successfully ambushed the government. During the Committee stage of the Education Bill, Thelma Cazalet Keir, a member of the Tory Reform Committee, put down an amendment for equal pay for women in the teaching profession.[15] R. A. Butler, who had charge of the Bill, made a maladroit speech reprimanding the Tory Reformers for not taking his advice and warning them that a division against the government would be serious. Hogg respected Butler for his liberal outlook and subtle mind. But this was just the sort of thing to make him excited. He took over the case for the amendment with enthusiasm. 'It seems to me a little unjust to suggest that because, as we know, he is a great reformer . . . we should be bound to take his advice on every occasion, or if not on every occasion at least not to disregard it more than once a week.'[16] Butler vainly tried to prevent the rebels from pressing the amendment to a division, saying incautiously of them, 'I understand that discipline among his [Hogg's] followers is of a very high standard.' Butler was rattled and Hogg was not going to let go. The Communist Member, Willie Gallacher, showed what the atmosphere was like: 'I certainly could not compliment the young Tories on their loyalty to their colleagues. Whenever the young Tories get an opportunity, they seize upon some particularly feasible proposal and use it for unscrupulous demagogy . . .'[17] When the House divided, the government was found to have been defeated by Labour backbenchers and Tory rebels by a single vote. Butler saw the Prime Minister that evening and found him in a resolute and jovial mood. Churchill told him that he would seek a reversal of the vote on a confidence motion. He had been waiting for 'the opportunity to rub the rebels' noses in their mess'.[18] He reminded Rab of the strategy at the battle of Dunbar. 'Both sides appealed to Jehovah; and the Most High, finding so little to choose between them in faith and zeal, allowed purely military factors to prevail.' The government had the battalions and got a huge majority.

Butler allowed himself to be upset by the defeat, describing the rebels in his memoirs as 'jubilant and overweening'. It is easy to imagine the young Hogg in full flood meriting these epithets, but for his part he could not understand why Churchill had acted as he had when the issue had nothing to do with the war effort. Both he and Butler failed to put matters in proportion and the Whips let the government down. Churchill put unity first and credibility abroad only slightly behind. The Normandy landings still lay in the future. A series of by-elections were going against the government. The rebels were becoming a nuisance: but with characteristic magnanimity, and perhaps also political opportunism, Churchill took Hogg into the coalition government the following year. The episode, however, revealed a streak of excitability in Hogg which he could not always control.

Hogg also kept his ear to the Tory ground. In February 1944, in the same week as he was elected Chairman of the Tory Reform Committee, he called on Barrington-Ward, the editor of *The Times* and brother of his tutor at Christ Church, to inform him that Beaverbrook was meddling. Barrington-Ward noted Hogg's views in his diary: 'Says the Beaver is trying to "out" Tommy Dugdale [Chairman of the Conservative Party] or get Stephenson of Woolworth's in to supplant him; also that he (B) is moving Bracken [Minister of Information] to come out against the White Paper on health and resign; the Beaver wants to get hold of the party machine.' Barrington-Ward did not believe the story, but it was confirmed a few days later by Henry Willink, the Minister of Health. Hogg was threatening to resign if Beaverbook's plotting bore fruit. Barrington-Ward urged caution, and advised him to talk to Eden and Ernest Bevin. 'He seemed calmer when he left. He is very able but excitable. John (his tutor) told me that they had to nurse him through exams at Ch.Ch.'[19]

But beneath Hogg's excitability, there was an anxiety to uphold legitimate authority. Few really trusted Beaverbrook or his motives, even if he might have energised the moribund Conservative party machine.

The Tory Reformers had no intention of breaking away from their party. They aimed to breathe life into it by taking up Disraelian themes. 'I decided to take a smack at the government,' wrote Hogg, 'and to fly again Disraeli's banner of Young England.'[20] Beveridge was the centrepiece of the reformers' campaign, but it was not the only issue. They supported Bevin's Catering Wages Bill and had shown up the reactionaries in the party. They had justifiable fears about the popular image of Conservatism as the party of wealth and big business with the lingering belief that a measure of want served as a stimulus to effort. That image could lead to electoral disaster, as Hogg wrote in his 'Open Letter to the Conservative Party' in *Picture Post*: 'if . . . the policy . . . of the Conservatives becomes insufficiently progressive, a great electoral defeat is the absolutely inevitable consequence.'

Under the general heading 'Forward – by the Right!' the reformers published a series of pamphlets dealing with employment, land policy, planning, air transport. For research they used the facilities of the Political Research Centre, which was funded by Conservative Central Office. These arrangements ended in April 1944, possibly at the instance of Butler who was anxious about the reformers' ambitions. 'They were very ambitious and it was important that they should not take over the lead, since some of their views did not coincide with the Party's.'[21] The reformers were certainly well organised. They met three times a week, twice in the Commons to discuss their agenda and to decide who should do what, and once over dinner when conversation ranged freely. Although he knew who the leaders of the group were, the Speaker was probably unsure of the identity of all the members and therefore could not always ration their speeches. The *Manchester Guardian* claimed that the committee whipped its members and commented, 'It is rank rebellion to be voting against the government at all, but to crown the offence with a "whip" of their own is the last offence against orthodoxy.'[22] It is safe to assume that Butler was not alone in being anxious and irritated by turns about their activities.

Hogg's connection with the Tory Reformers ended when he joined the government as a junior minister in April 1945; in any case the committee's work was by then almost over. It lingered on after the General Election, but did little, and was never formally disbanded. Its main purpose had been to promote the implementation of the Beveridge proposals as early as possible. With the publication of a series of government White Papers in 1944, that had effectively been achieved.

Although the work of the Tory Reformers was exhilarating,

personal relations were sometimes strained. In July 1943, Hinching-brooke recorded in his diary that Hogg and Molson were thrashing out the main principles of their policy. 'These two stars are finding it difficult to revolve in the same firmament and being brought into conjunction. Their radiancies are now glowing with a disturbing light.'[23] Hinch himself was forced to leave the Chair as a result of a disagreement with Thorneycroft, and, as mentioned above, Hogg became Chairman in January 1944. A year later he wanted to give up the Chair and he wrote to Hinchingbrooke: 'The ground is mapped . . . I am frankly *tiring*. I get no fresh air and exercise. Sooner or later I shall be driven by poverty back to the Bar. I have made very many enemies and would be quite glad of a relapse into obscurity.'[24] But he allowed that the committee had worked well and on the whole harmoniously. Hogg was fond of Hinchingbrooke and regretted that they later drifted apart. In 1962, he remarked in a letter that friendships in public life are hard to make and harder to keep. Describing himself as at times 'electrically charged', he hoped 'that my friends make allowances for these extraordinary manifestations of nature'.[25]

Hogg summarised his own views on the achievements of the Tory Reformers in an unpublished memoir of 1965.[26] He believed that the group 'upheld the banner of progressive Conservatism while not weakening the war effort.' In his view it was, at least in part, responsible for the bipartisan approach to social, as distinct from industrial, problems during the Labour administration of 1945–1951. Their influence on the subsequent recovery of the Conservative Party was, he thought, more decisive. But for the work of the reformers, the party 'might well have gone the way of the Republican Party in America and identified the public organisation of social services with hostility to privately-owned industry and the development of individual character'. That would have been bad for the party and bad for the country. In preventing it, the reformers enabled the Conservatives to recover in six years from the savage defeat of 1945. Lord Thorneycroft agreed that, without the Tory Reform Committee, the party would probably have been longer in the wilderness.[27]

These are large and, in any case, unprovable claims. To suppose that the beaten Conservatives would have drifted rightwards into a sort of Goldwater inconsequence is to leave out of account the natural tendency of the opposition to be drawn towards the centre by a reforming government. Hogg's view also ignores the re-thinking of the Conservative political programme which was going forward in the opposition years under Butler at the Conservative

Research Department, and the reorganisation of the party machine under Lord Woolton, whom the historian of the Party described as the greatest of all Conservative party managers.[28] The Tory Reformers played little part in these developments. For all that, however, the ginger group had an important effect. They forced themselves on the attention of the coalition, the wiser Ministers in which at least knew that they spoke with first-hand knowledge of the tidal direction of the popular will. And the ginger was real ginger.

Were the Tory Reformers right to embrace Beveridge with such ardour? Was the Welfare State which followed such a blessing to the nation? The shortest answer is that it was inevitable anyway. Even if the policy of implementation had not been adopted by both major parties, the Conservatives could not have stopped it after 1945. The contribution of the reformers could not be put higher than that they ensured that it would never be reversed by a Conservative government. But Hogg believed that in any case the reformers were right in the context of the time. The country would not tolerate a return to the conditions of the thirties. The soldiers, sailors and airmen returning from the war, and their wives and families who had seen its destructive power at the closest possible quarters, were determined to live in a new and better world.

There was, however, one serious flaw. Beveridge had conservatively assumed an unemployment rate of $8\frac{1}{2}$ per cent.[29] No one foresaw that after the war it would not normally exceed 3 per cent. The form of the White Papers and the legislation which followed would, in Hogg's view, have been very different if this had been foreseen. Under conditions of full employment, wage levels were high enough to enable many benefits to be carried by the wage-earners rather than by the State. As a consequence, Hogg considered that the tax system had been so heavily burdened with things it ought not to bear that it had been unable to bear the things it should. 'Can anyone pretend that we have really identified and helped the classes who are really vulnerable – the chronic sick, the handicapped, the very old, the retired on fixed incomes? . . . We cannot afford to clean up our environment, rebuild our hospitals, construct universities and schools, or even keep our houses in proper repair.' Writing in 1965, he concluded that none of this was vouchsafed to anyone in 1943. The rhetorical questions remain.

10

Remarriage and Conservative Defeat

THE same Lady Townsend who had presided over the meeting of
the constituency association at which Hogg was adopted in 1938
as Conservative candidate, and who had upbraided Natalie for
interfering in the constituency, was a great personage in Oxford civic
and Conservative life. She had been Mayor of the city and, when
Quintin Hogg returned from the Middle East, was chairman of the
local party. Her husband was a distinguished physicist. In 1935 she
had chosen her fifteen-year-old niece, Mary Evelyn Martin, to be
her Mayoress. (By convention, when the Mayor is a woman, she
chooses a female relative to act as her consort and 'Mayoress' on
formal occasions.) Mary was born in Dublin of a well-known
Norman-Irish family. Her forebears were supposed to have come to
Ireland with Strongbow. *Humanity Dick* (Richard Martin MP,
1754–1834) the earliest of all campaigners against cruelty to animals,
was a member of the family. Mary's great aunt was Violet Martin,
who made up the Somerville and Ross partnership with Edith
Somerville, also a distant relative. Hogg remembered Edith as an
eccentric old lady who believed in spiritualism and Mussolini; she
wrote under the name 'Somerville and Ross' long after Violet's
death, convinced that her deceased partner was still contributing
distantly to her literary endeavours. Mary's mother, Amy Lambert,
was Lady Townsend's sister and a celebrated horsewoman.

When Mary was less than a year old, the Troubles drove her
parents, who were both Church of Ireland, out of the country. Her
father became a tea planter in Ceylon, where Mary lived until she
was seven. Then she was sent to an English boarding school, living
in the holidays in Oxford with her Aunt May, Lady Townsend.
Through her schooldays she saw nothing of her father and very little
of her mother, who paid only one short visit to England each

summer. After finishing school in France, she went to secretarial college and worked in the intelligence services. Her parents returned to England on the outbreak of the Second World War to live in a London flat. Mary was then twenty. She was an only child and had passed the whole of her adolescence away from her parents. Although she lived with the Townsends as a daughter she missed her parents, and this may help to explain her strong feeling of the paramountcy of her own home and family, and her periodic impatience with the demands of her husband's career. In 1957 she wrote a note addressed to: 'Q: Private – *not* for your office. I am not impressed by the efforts to cut down your engagements, see June 24th onwards, and if your office won't do anything about it, I shall invent engagements (which are purely fictitious) in order to fill up your diary . . . The end justifies the means!'

In 1943 Mary was twenty-three, a young woman of classic good looks and manners. She was working near Oxford and living with her aunt. Lady Townsend was well aware of Hogg's lonely personal life and suggested to her niece that she should try to cheer up the Member for Oxford. Mary was willing. The two had met before, at the time of the 1938 by-election when Mary had helped in the Conservative constituency association. On his side Hogg, who had been divorced for nearly a year, craved female companionship, as was more than natural, but he had doubts about a second marriage. 'You must go into it with illusions shattered a little, and perhaps never with the same romantic trust.' (*Diary* 22 Jan. 1943.) These were abstract speculations, however, and Mary blew them away instantly. He quickly proposed, was accepted as promptly, and they were married in Caxton Hall on 18 April 1944. He had by now stopped keeping a journal, but his engagement diary read: '0945 Savoy Church. Get married Caxton ("Church" crossed out)? 1250 train.'[1] They lived first at the house in Victoria Square, and when the lease fell in in 1946, Lord Hailsham bought them the large and comfortable house in Putney, 13 Heathview Gardens, in which Hogg has lived for the rest of his life.

Hogg's first marriage had been an aberration; his second was a safe anchorage for thirty-four years before Mary's tragic riding accident in Sydney brought it to a sudden end. There were five children, of whom the first, Douglas, was almost a honeymoon baby.

In most ways Mary was the direct opposite of Natalie. She was commonsensical, level-headed and shrewd. She was intelligent, but she had no sort of aspiration to be her husband's academic peer, or to be a political hostess. She would have enjoyed a bright social life but disliked the idea of entertaining. So did he, and he was parsimonious as well; his legendary carefulness with money was a family joke. So there was no political hospitality. It was inconceivable that he would think of ingratiating himself with his colleagues by social efforts. This had its effect on his political career, but it would be wrong to blame Mary for it. She did, however, resent the position she was in and may have felt jealousy for the limelight in which he walked. She was strong-willed and could defend her preserve. In later life, she used to say ironically that people thought of her as a 'battle-axe'. Relations at home were sometimes tense. Neither would give way. Mary never liked Carters Corner, the country house in Sussex. She had not created it and it was a burden to have to run two homes. So she readily agreed to its sale in 1963, and never really understood what the place meant to her husband. This rankled, but he doubtless made matters worse. In spite of the tensions Mary was loyal always. Nor did she give herself airs, as was remarked by the popular press. 'Lady Hailsham has more than a clue about how ordinary people live,' said the *Daily Mail* in 1957, 'because she lives like one herself. I wish there were more human beings in the upper air of politics.'[2]

On his side, Quintin often thought he was put upon and did not realise how much Mary had done for him until it was too late. The most important thing she did was to make good the damage which had been inflicted on him by his first marriage. There was a stable family life and the friendly muddle of the Putney house gave him a proper home for the first time. Hogg owed his father and his brother an incalculable debt for persuading him to take the risk of a second marriage rather than live a life of frustrated celibacy.

★

From the time of his return to England, Hogg threw himself enthusiastically into political and public life. It was not only the Tory Reform Committee. His correspondence with his Oxford constituents was on a huge scale. The letter registers which he kept show that in 1943 there were more than 4200 letters, and nearly 4000 in the following year. He was an excellent Member, following up his constituents' grievances and pursuing the ministers who were responsible with force and tenacity.

In 1943, he took up a case referred to him by the Nuffield Professor of Orthopaedic Surgery. William Highet was a young neuro-surgeon employed at a hospital in Oxford and was invited to form a new centre in South Africa for soldiers injured in the Middle East. It was agreed that he would go with the rank of Major; no less than three Brigadiers and a War Office consulting surgeon had promised it. He was in fact commissioned as a Lieutenant. His ship was torpedoed and he was drowned. When his widow claimed her pension she was told that she was entitled only on the basis that he was a Lieutenant. Hogg took the matter up and, according to the *Daily Mirror*, made one of the most scathing attacks the House of Commons had heard for years:

> This is an injustice. Any decent employer would have done exactly what I am asking. The word of the subordinate would have been kept. Nobody but the Crown would treat an employee in this way . . . It reminds me of a poem by G. K. Chesterton: 'Of all the easy speeches which comfort cruel men' . . . I doubt whether we are dealing with a man so much as a bureaucrat, conceived in a pigeon-hole, swaddled in red tape, educated at the Treasury, and reaching manhood as a civilian in the War Office . . . When, at last, he is removed to another place no doubt there will be written on the tombstone a Treasury Minute instead of an epitaph, 'Passed to you for further consideration and comment'.[3]

The case was reopened.

He wrote and broadcast assiduously. As early as 21 January 1943, within a month of his homecoming, he was recruited for the BBC Brains Trust, a highly popular radio programme in which the members of the trust answered listeners' questions. His fellow 'brains' were Henry Strauss MP, the Parliamentary Secretary designate to the Ministry of Town and Country Planning, Mervyn O'Gorman, a former Chairman of the Royal Aeronautical Society, Commander Campbell, a well-known broadcaster, and Professor C. E. M. Joad, who had spoken against Hogg and in favour of the pacifist motion in the King and Country debate at the Oxford Union. Hogg was introduced by the Chairman as 'one of our youngest and most ferocious Members of Parliament, just returned from active service in the Near East'. In January 1944 Hogg and Joad were again in the Brains Trust team. A listener asked what would be the most suitable war memorial when peace came. Joad suggested that the nation should purchase some parkland for the recreation of the young, and added that there should be no military service. Hogg, who had previously attacked the Professor for talking 'rubbish, pure rubbish and nothing but rubbish', said: 'what a jolly thing for Hitler if we had accepted Professor Joad's suggestion after the last war. What a splendid thing if we'd given up all forms of military training. I must say that I have never been more shocked in my life to hear an old man like Joad making just the same mistakes in propositions for after this war as we made after the last war.'[4]

Hogg explained this intemperate attack by the strength of his feelings about pacifism and unilateral disarmament. These false sirens were 'as much the causes of war of which the victims of attack may be guilty as are aggressive intentions on the part of those who plan and execute aggression.' But his intemperance was not to be explained away. A. J. Cummings of the *News Chronicle* described him as a cocksure young man who had gone to 'the entertainment table with the set intention of taking the skin off Joad'. He had succeeded, wrote Cummings, only in disgusting a large number of listeners. 'Other members of the House of Commons tell me that his lack of self-control and of other parliamentary qualities is already jeopardising his political career.'[5] It was to become a familiar refrain. However just the cause or well-founded the argument, there was this tendency to spoil it with immoderateness. But he was not blacklisted from the Brains Trust, as some correspondents expected, and he remained on friendly terms with Joad – due perhaps to the magnanimity of the professor. A few days after the radio outburst, his engagement diary records: 'Dine Joad. Present John Betjeman, Kingsley Martin, Ifor Thomas and Joad's most attractive daughter.' Nor were his friends in the Tory Reform Committee dismayed, for he was elected Chairman on 9 February.

*

In May 1945, with the ending of the war in Europe, the Labour and Liberal parties left the great coalition, and Churchill formed a caretaker administration for the few month until a General Election could be held. Hogg was taken into the coalition on 12 April, barely a month before its demise, as Under-Secretary for Air, when Rupert Brabner was killed in an air crash. By 1990, Hogg believed himself to be the last survivor of Churchill's coalition government. He enjoyed himself visiting Bomber Command airfields and flying as much as he could, both as passenger and trainee pilot. When the caretaker government was formed he was continued in his post, but with Harold Macmillan rather than Sir Archibald Sinclair as his Secretary of State.

Churchill wanted the coalition to continue at least until the defeat of Japan, and wrote to Attlee seeking to persuade him by promising that a National Government would do its utmost to implement the proposals for social security and full employment.[6] He rightly thought that preoccupation with an impending General Election would distract from the business of finishing off Japan and the new menace of Stalin's Russia. But the Labour Party Conference, held the day after Churchill's letter, would have none of it. The Beveridge debate two years earlier had shown Labour backbenchers what could result from being minority shareholders in an enterprise led by the giant figure of Winston; and in any case the tide running for the Labour party was becoming stronger by the day.

Hogg thought in retrospect that the main responsibility for the crushing defeat which brought Attlee to power in July 1945 had to rest with Churchill himself. As he went about the country during the election campaign, he was told that people wanted a Labour government led by Churchill, and they could not understand why that should be impossible. He revered Winston as 'the only genius whom I can claim to have known well'. He understood how the great man's faults as well as his virtues so perfectly matched the moment when he was called upon to lead, and he aptly quoted the French saying: *Il avait les défauts de ses qualités*. There was much that was Churchillian about Hogg himself, not least the particular flavour of his humour. Hogg loved Churchill stories, and always found time to write them down. One had been told him by Oliver Lyttelton. Lyttelton was with the Great Man on a Whitehall roof during an air raid. Lyttelton was vainly trying to make the Prime Minister take cover. Winston was chewing a cigar as he watched and tried to place the bomb bursts. 'Oliver placed his helmet on W's head; did not fit, much too small. Absurd. "Meet my aide, Sir, John Rodgers." W held out his hand, sideways, still watching bomb bursts. Pause. "What did you say yr. name was?" "John Rodgers, Sir." "Ah, a fine name. The envy of one sex, the delight of the other." '

But when Winston ceased to be the great war chieftain, his faults became liabilities once more. Hogg thought him one of the worst electioneers of the century: 'He had absolutely no idea of how other people felt or thought.' As a result, he personally lost more seats in his career than almost anyone else in Hogg's experience. Worst of all was the famous 'Gestapo' broadcast in June, when he declared 'from the bottom of my heart' that socialism in Britain would require some form of Gestapo, 'no doubt very humanely directed in the first instance'. It was a very serious misjudgment of the British electorate, and Attlee's reply, in the laconic style which he made famous, was simply: 'The voice we heard last night was that of Mr Churchill, but the mind was that of Lord Beaverbrook.' It mattered not that the widely distrusted Beaverbrook had nothing to do with it, or that, as

Hogg thought, the Gestapo taunt contained 'a germ of most important truth'.* The damage was done.

Churchill, who in any case had a monumental conceit, believed that he had unique prestige in having led the country to victory from the very brink of defeat. He was not mistaken. He was after all the greatest living Englishman. But it did not follow that the electorate would entrust his party with the task of rebuilding the peace abroad or, more important, reconstruction at home. Hogg was in the best possible position to appreciate this *non sequitur*. He had first hand experience of opinion in the armed forces; he and his Tory Reform colleagues had warned the Conservative leadership of the consequences of a cool reception for the Beveridge plan. In his own memoirs, however, he gives insufficient emphasis to the underlying movement of opinion, although acknowledging 'the triumph of negativism in the higher echelons of the party'. It was more than that. The memories of the thirties were still fresh and the spirit of 'Never Again' was abroad. Hogg was nearer the mark in 1947 in assessing the causes of defeat than he was as Lord Hailsham in 1990. In *The Case for Conservatism* he wrote: 'The result of the election cannot be explained on any other thesis than one of those massive movements of public opinion away from the men, the principles of policy, and the party by which we had been governed for a generation. Such a movement is too deep seated to be wholly rational, and too natural to be entirely unhealthy.' Nevertheless, he tended to underrate the depths of resentment felt about the Baldwin/Chamberlain era, the widespread feeling that the 'Guilty Men' were as much to blame for what they had left undone at home as abroad. His apprehension of all this was deflected by his reverence for his father's life and achievements in government.

The pamphlet titled *Guilty Men* had been published under the pseudonym 'Cato' just after Dunkirk, and accused Britain's Tory rulers in the thirties of exposing the army to destruction by failing adequately to rearm. It was trenchantly written by Michael Foot and the journalist Frank Owen, and its distorted characterisations of the principal Conservative figures gained considerable currency. Gollancz, the publishers, followed it up with two other polemics, *The Trial of Mussolini* and *Your MP*, both also written under Roman

---

* In *The Case for Conservatism* (1947) p. 58, Hogg wrote: 'The danger is that in its present aims and objects, in its present constitution and its way of doing business, the British Labour Party shows signs of developing many of the defects of totalitarianism'. And in a speech on procedural reform in the House of Commons on 24 August 1945, he said in reference to the Labour Government: '. . . the Gestapo or political police of which they so much resent being reminded are part of the armoury of Socialism in certain countries of the world'. (413 HC Debs.: Col. 1043.)

pseudonyms. These books undoubtedly strengthened the tide running against the Conservatives, and sharpened the distinction in the public mind between Churchill and his party. Churchill's own record in the thirties as an anti-appeaser spoke for itself. Hogg decided to publish a riposte to the Gollancz books. *The Left was Never Right*, his first political book, came out on the eve of the General Election. His thesis was that while the Conservative Party's record on re-armament and appeasement could not be looked back on with satisfaction, the preoccupation of the left in the pre-war years with unilateral disarmament and the mirage of 'collective security' would have led straight to irredeemable disaster. Faber's excited blurb described it as 'a devastating rejoinder' and declared that there had been 'too much shadow-sparring by ingenious flyweights under cover of portentous Roman names'. The other flyweights turned out to be Richard Crossman and Peter Howard.

The thesis was fair. Foot and Crossman had twisted history and caricatured Conservative and Labour alike. Hogg was an effective writer of polemic and, forensically, he was justified in saying 'Very well. Let us have *their* record out for inspection and compare the two . . . If there is to be talk of "guilty men", who are to be put in the dock – the men of the right who, whatever their mistakes, enabled the country to escape defeat, or the men of the left who did everything possible to ensure it?' But he could not wash away the stain of appeasement. The guilty men would always be the Men of Munich, however much pot called kettle black. In any case, in the summer of 1945, the country was more concerned with the peace than with responsibility for the lamentable foreign policy of the thirties.

But it is none the less interesting to compare Hogg's summing up of Munich in *The Left was Never Right* with his defence of the agreement in 1938. In 1945 he wrote: '. . . let Munich be viewed in its true perspective . . . [Chamberlain's decision] such as it was, was a legitimate and necessary step. The humiliation of Munich was the result of the persistent refusal of successive governments, of diverse parties, indeed of the whole nation, to realise from 1929 onwards the menace represented by a re-emergent Germany . . .' This was not and could not have been what he told the electors of Oxford in October 1938.

Hogg had none of Churchill's failings as an electioneer and he fought Oxford City in 1945 as much on his record as a good constituency member and a Tory reformer, as on a party platform. He was a well-known public figure. Within less than a year of returning to England, he had broadcast 21 times; he wrote frequently for the *Spectator* and the popular press, and he was one of the top scorers in the columns of Hansard. He had become a very effective speaker in the Commons. *The Evening Standard* ran a Westminster Diary, and on 13 December 1943 Lady Apsley, the diarist and Member for Bristol Central, described his impromptu speech on an amendment to the Address* as 'one of quite the best short speeches I have ever heard – effective, audible, sincere, and delivered with the ease and polish of a great orator'. His opponent at Oxford was Frank Pakenham who had secured the reversion of the Labour nomination, as Hogg had guessed he would at the time of the Munich by-election. The result (Hogg 14,314; Pakenham 11,451; Wing Cdr. Norman, Liberal, 5,860) was a credit to Hogg. His majority was almost the same as in 1938, while across the country the Labour avalanche swept all before it. Labour won 393 seats, the Conservatives 213 and the Liberals 12.

By contrast with the excitement of the Munich by-election, Hogg's first General Election left little impression on his mind: 'one's own contest, so important to oneself and one's own future, is completely lost in the maelstrom of events and the great swings and surges of popular sentiment.' What he did remember were Pakenham's crude and erratic tactics. A less formidable opponent than his wife Elizabeth, who contested the 1950 election at Oxford, he was always liable to be hit by the boomerang effects of some misjudgment. This time he wrote a letter to the *Oxford Mail* for someone else to sign, accusing Hogg of duplicitously allowing his name to go forward as a candidate for the St George's Division of Westminster. Hogg threatened the signatory and the editor with proceedings for libel, since the story was both untrue and damaging, whereupon Pakenham shamefacedly confessed authorship. His candour was engaging and Hogg remained friends with the Pakenhams for life. The quixotic side to Pakenham always appealed to Hogg. In 1985, he wrote to a friend to say that he had been entranced by the revelation in a House of Lords debate that 'poor Frank Longford had spent the night w: a convicted brothel keeper. I am sure I cd: not get away w: it.'

Hogg was now on the opposition benches without hope of preferment for the foreseeable future. His father was a wreck of his former self and tired of life. It could not be long before the son

---

* The speech demolished an amendment to the Loyal Address moved by Sir Richard Acland (Common Wealth) proposing that all substantial resources under private control should be transferred into common ownership. Hogg had beaten Acland in his first attempt on the Presidency of the Oxford Union. He had a friendly acquaintance with him but thought he was a woolly idealist whose party was destined to disappear without trace as soon as the party truce ended. It did.

would become the second Lord Hailsham. He had a new wife and family (Douglas was born in February 1945) and he had to earn his living. The income from a small capital sum provided by his father, together with earnings from writing and broadcasting, were not sufficient. Everything compelled a return to the Bar. It was the first of a series of oscillations between professional and public life which was a recurring theme of his career. The changes of direction, in the timing of which he was to have no say, inflicted damage on both activities. Solicitors expect barristers to whom they send cases to give them undivided attention. Membership of the House of Commons has its own demands. A barrister who is trying to juggle with another career is not thought of as *homme serieux*. Equally, the decision to go back to the Bar, although unavoidable, came at a bad time for Hogg's political ambitions. He had made his mark in the two years since his return, and was being spoken of as a young lion, even a possible future leader. But the enforced return to the Bar meant that he would not be among the leaders of opinion in the party during the years of opposition.

Return to the Bar after a break of six years was not easy. Both sides of the profession had been disrupted by the war, and few of the old personal relationships survived. Hogg recalled that only two firms of solicitors appeared to remember him. He went back to his old chambers in Paper Buildings and set about reconstructing his practice. But work there was concentrated on circuit in the further part of East Anglia. This could not accommodate his parliamentary duties and the insistent demands of the Tory whips; so he moved downstairs to Theo Mathew's old chambers, where he had done his pupillage. He got a warm welcome there from Sydney Aylett, the head clerk, who still reigned unchallenged. Aylett depicted Hogg at that time as 'an explosive extrovert, a brilliant lawyer and an eloquent counsel ... unpredictable perhaps, ... a man of high spirits, given to talking off the top of his head which gave the impression to those who didn't, or hadn't tried to, know him, that he was making quick and unthinking decisions.'[7] Aylett had instinctive perception, and thought this erroneous opinion might have prevented Hogg from attaining the highest political office in the land.

These were impressions from the unusual angle of a barrister's clerk. They were corroborated by Deirdre Shannon, who worked as a secretary in chambers and later became a friend of the family and ultimately Lord Hailsham's third wife. It was her first job and she sat in the tiny room occupied by the clerks. It was an excellent vantage point from which to observe chambers life. While calm prevailed in the book-lined sanctums where Counsel gave advice, the clerks' quarters were the noisy engine room. Here they tried to make sense of the conflicting demands made by solicitors and the Courts for the time of the barristers in their charge, often taking gamblers' risks by double-booking. Here too they negotiated over the telephone with solicitors about what should be paid for advice in cases which the clerks had to pretend to understand. The barristers themselves rushed in and out, throwing over a shoulder the latest news about the progress of cases, or information about where they would be for the rest of the day. Deirdre Shannon thought Hogg forceful, rumbustious, an overwhelming personality 'who made things happen'. His old green car had screeching brakes and his clothes did not stay put properly. He was incorrigibly untidy and could easily become enraged, but the storm would pass quickly. For a girl just out of secretarial college, he was a formidable but exhilarating proposition. In point of personality, he was the exact opposite of Kenneth Diplock, Aylett's other 'flyer'. Diplock was reserved and spoke with polished precision through clenched teeth. His laser intelligence was later to be deployed on the Bench, where he became one of the outstanding analytical minds of his generation. As for Aylett, he was a 'card', who called everyone 'Sir' with an infinite variety of tonal inflections, and believed he was pulling all the strings. He kept the girls in their place as a species of *untermensch*, and was not a little stage-struck about his stars. If a member of chambers was displaced in the queue at the 'Bear Garden' (the ante-chamber in the Law Courts in the Strand where barristers and solicitors wait to see a junior judge in order to resolve some minor, but often significant, point of procedure), Aylett would take perverse pleasure in letting him know that he had allowed himself to be 'bounced'. He controlled the finances of chambers; if one of his men were cross or out of sorts, he would mollify him by producing a cheque with the air of a conjuror. The network through which the barristers' clerks operated was an important source of work. Many solicitors left the conduct of litigation to unqualified managing clerks. Like the clerks, they were men of little formal education and the two groups knew each other well. The destination of many briefs was decided in the taverns around the Temple. Although hair-raising to think about, the system worked quite well.

The Bar exercises a magnetic appeal over its members. The life has colour and permits individualism. Yet it is a closed society with its own conventions and ethic. The barrister is accountable to no one but himself for earning his living. He does not have partners or a bureaucracy to reckon with. He is judged according to stringent standards of diligence and integrity by his colleagues, and from a Bench whose own members are recruited from the same profession. The false gods of place-seeking and time-serving, whose devotees are to be found in public life, are not worshipped at the Bar. Hogg loved the Bench and Bar for what they were, traditional English institutions. Much of what he did and did not do as Lord Chancellor can be explained by a determination to preserve them as they were at almost any cost. When Sir Henry Fisher wanted to resign from the High Court Bench in 1970 to pursue a City career, Hailsham told him that appointment to high judicial office was like ordination to a priesthood (see page 275). The conservation intact of the corps of judges did have an almost sacred importance.

Hogg worked up a good practice. Like his father, he preferred to be an all-rounder. He was retained in a substantial volume of personal injury cases, but he also practised in the criminal and matrimonial courts, and appeared in inquiries and professional disciplinary cases. He had a good quality general common law practice. But he was never in the topmost rank. His volatile and sometimes irascible manner did not commend him to all with whom he came into touch – solicitors, fellow-barristers, judges. Aylett thought his abilities were underrated because of his temperament. But some preferred to deal with a more equable personality. More important, his incursions into politics resulted in his making three entirely fresh starts at the Bar: when he was first called; in 1945 after the Conservative defeat; and in 1964 when the party was defeated again. No one, however able, could expect to rise to the summit by fits and starts. Even when he was in practice, there were the insistent demands of party and constituency to contend with.

11

Politics Practical and Philosophical

AFTER the 1945 election, Churchill took Hogg and Thorneycroft, the two leading Tory reformers, on to the opposition front bench. Although occasionally irritated by Hogg's antics in the ginger group, Churchill recognised his intellect and abilities. He had become an outstandingly forceful speaker and had fulfilled the bright promise of the pre-war years.* In any case, he knew Hogg well and was fond of him. Hogg's uncle Ian, Douglas's brother, had been Churchill's best friend at Sandhurst and afterwards in the Army.

There was soon an opportunity for Hogg to show his paces. Within a month of Labour's victory, Herbert Morrison, the Lord President, put down a motion to appoint a Select Committee to recommend changes 'for the more efficient despatch of business'.[1] This was a radical administration with a lot of business to get through. Morrison admitted that he intended to put the government's suggestions for shortening debate to the Committee. Its composition reflected the balance of the House and it would be likely to accept the government's proposals. The House knew what was up. A. P. Herbert, the Member for Oxford University, visualised Labour Members going back to their constituencies at the weekend and being asked by their supporters: 'What was the first positive thing you did in the Great Palace of Liberty?' They would have to answer, 'Twice a week I voted for the suppression of the individual and the domination of the gang.'[2]

The debate seemed made for Hogg, and Churchill asked him to

---

* In an article for *Harper's Bazaar* in 1933 (reproduced in this book), when Hogg was twenty-six, the Earl of Birkenhead had described him as one of the most brilliant people of his age in England and said, 'there can be no possible doubt in my judgment that he is more certainly earmarked for success than any man I know'. Such assessments were not uncommon.

speak from the Despatch Box. He faced difficulties, however. The government benches were in triumphalist mood and the Conservative ranks were attenuated. The motion asked no more than that an enquiring committee be appointed, and it would be reasonable to defer criticism until the House could see what it recommended. Hogg brushed the objection aside. He had read in Labour pamphlets that the government intended to cut discussion by such devices as grouping clauses and widening the use of the guillotine. The process of a deliberative assembly, he said, was its lifeblood and the House should beware. If revolution were to come in this country, it would not be with drums and marching battalions, 'but by way of a minister of the right or left coming to the House, with crocodile tears in his eyes, with loud praise of the institution he was about to dispatch, and with some apparently trifling procedural change'.[3] The contrivances which the government threatened to use did not even have the respectability due to the antique, but came only out of 'the impact of Irish obstruction on the strong authoritarian mind of Mr Gladstone'. They all tended towards the gradual control of the administration of the business of the House. As to the Labour members, they were a majority with a difference, and Hogg gave them quietus in a phrase which went into the parliamentary vocabulary: 'Lobby-fodder, infinitely patient, all enduring, well-whipped and very gullible'.

It was a good speech which looked forward to Lord Hailsham's idea of the 'Elective Dictatorship', a creeping revolution in which the Commons would little by little surrender its power to a tyrannous executive. Hogg had also generated some excitement: at one point the Speaker intervened: 'I deprecate further interruptions. They only appear to encourage the Hon. Member's exuberance.' The exuberance was well known and appreciated. It never grew less. Early on in the new parliament, he risked calling Bessie Braddock, the hugely formidable Labour Member for Liverpool Exchange, his 'pin-up girl'. She detonated: 'For a long time I have been awaiting an opportunity to tell you that I have often been tempted to grab you by the neck and . . .'[4] A profile published in 1948 commented on Hogg's pugnacity. 'As a parliamentarian Quintin Hogg suffers from what is known as "fatal facility". He scores points too easily, and loses his temper too often (at Oxford he knocked more than one of his contemporaries down). This defect is the reverse side of his deliberate courage, both moral and physical.'[5]

Hogg and Thorneycroft did not last long on the front bench. They soon found that they were too junior to be called on to speak more than occasionally. This would not do for spirits like these, and within a matter of months they moved to the back rows where more opportunity and more freedom were available. Anthony Eden, for one, was disappointed. He wrote to Hogg on 27 December 1945: 'I think that I understand your difficulties. At the same time I cannot but regret your decision . . . all sections of party opinion, and as far as possible all ages should be represented on our front bench. For that reason . . . I was eager to see Peter Thorneycroft join you on that bench . . . It is certainly regrettable that Peter's unhappy judgment should entail your departure too.'[6] Thorneycroft had shown signs of wanting to free himself from the whip, and Hogg may have been influenced by loyalty to his old friend as well as by his own frustration.

Leaving the front bench did not mean that Hogg stopped working for the party altogether. He kept up his always friendly relations with Butler, who was made Chairman of the Conservative Research Department soon after the election defeat; and when in 1949 it was decided to publish a major policy document, the writing of the first draft was, at Lord Woolton's suggestion, entrusted entirely to Hogg. It was hoped that the document, which was eventually called *The Right Road for Britain* would be written in a style which matched that of *The Case for Conservatism*.[7] There were, inevitably, some disagreements on substance, but when the draft was returned to Hogg the prose of the original was unrecognisable.

'My poor Rab,' he wrote, 'Your friends are beyond human aid . . . Your document is now as full of solecisms as a colander of holes, and as impregnated with bromides as a mothball with naphtha. I think it is past saving. 'The "stern realities of the hour" ("dark hours", of course, the present) are "faced" once more and "we set our course" again for new and "wider horizons" (May I suggest here a brilliant reference to the "ship of state" which is inexplicably omitted?). Communism is once more described as "godless" . . . and when we do not know how to begin a sentence we gaily write "Thus it is" . . .'[8] After a long list of examples, he despaired. 'Even the *bourgeois gentilhomme* spoke something more like his native tongue than your friends.'

Butler was amused by the attack, and thought Lord Salisbury, who was responsible for 'godless' Communism, had come off worst. It was an assault to gladden the hearts of Sir Ernest Gowers and cliché hunters everywhere. The document went back to the committee of tinkerers and emerged improved. The next draft, however, was not quite unscathed. 'Many sentences bear unmistakable signs of having been written either by a German or by a Hyde Park orator,' commented the Stylist-in-Chief. But the final version satisfied him. 'You have improved the formal style out of all knowledge,' he complimented Rab. As it finally appeared, it set the standard for a whole series of Party statements.[9]

★

Hogg was difficult to place in the Tory spectrum of indigo to pale pink-blue. His own description of his position before the war, given in *The Door Wherein I Went*, was 'resolutely a man of the centre, somewhere on the left of the Conservative Party, miles to the right of the moderate Labour man . . .' The intellectuals of his generation were mostly left-wing, with a minority on the distant right dabbling with fascism. 'But in one respect I was typical of my generation. The misery of unemployment and depression had made as deep an impression on me as on any of them, left or right.' For all that, he never flirted for a moment with either socialism or fascism, both of which he regarded as authoritarian creeds false to parliamentary government. He put his pre-war view about socialism this way: '. . . the one characteristic of my thinking about home policy was my hatred of unemployment and poverty. I might not accept the socialist remedies. But I accepted many of the premises of my Labour contemporaries.'

By 1942 he was one of the huge majority determined to see that the conditions of the years between the wars should not be carried over into the coming peace. His intention was to achieve this from within the Conservative Party. To soften the hard edges of an unregulated economy by social reforms was within the Tory tradition. In *Sybil* Disraeli had written with splendidly exaggerated scorn of the Liberal Utopia.

> Since the passing of the Reform Act, the altar of Mammon has blazed with triple worship. To acquire, to accumulate, to plunder each other by virtue of philosophic phrases, to propose a Utopia to consist only of wealth and toil, this has been the breathless business of an enfranchised England, until we are startled from our voracious strife by the wail of intolerable serfage.

Hogg quoted this passage in a brilliant chapter on 'The Liberal Heresy' in *The Case for Conservatism*, and asserted: 'It was the Tory Party which took its stand in the nineteenth century against the principles of *laisser faire* liberalism of which it is now accused by its more ignorant opponents of being the sole inventor and patentee.'[10]

Beveridge and the Tory Reform Committee, which Hogg joined as a convert with already-formed opinions, provided the recipe which had to be adopted to avoid a recurrence of the conditions of the thirties. By 1945, however, Beveridge had for the most part been accepted by the Conservative hierarchy. The Tory Reformers were entitled to much of the credit; but the fact was that the two parties went into the election of that year with very little in the way of domestic issues to dispute about. Both were committed to the same schemes of national and industrial insurance; the same National Health Service; the same plan for acquiring land for housing and town planning; and both had publicly declared a common aim of full employment. Family allowances were already on the statute book. Hogg wrote that '. . . over 80 per cent of the field of politics the great mass of decent opinion of all parties was agreed as to the best practicable course to take. Never before perhaps at a great General Election did the intentions of the principal antagonists more closely resemble one another.'[11] What divided the parties was not the objectives, but the means to attain them. Labour was committed to bringing essential industries and services under public control. Conservatives profoundly disagreed, and none was more active than Hogg in exposing the consequences of nationalisation. His arguments were deployed in *The Case for Conservatism*. Nationalisation, he contended, was not a *policy* for an industry, but a mere change in ownership. Its results would be the evils which flow from monopoly, aggravated by the subordination of industrial policy to political expedience. By 1990 there were few of moderate opinion left to disagree.

There was therefore no need to advocate the welfare state. To do so would have been to push at an open door. The Tory Reformers had done their work and had no further programme. They faded away, not individually but collectively. Hogg's only public appearance as a social reformer was as a Tory reformer. For a later indication of his liberal leanings it is probably necessary to go as far as 1968 when, as Shadow Home Secretary, he gave James Callaghan, his opposite number, valuable support against the views of many of the Conservative side in race relations and immigration policy. The isolation of this episode seemed to some to support the view that at bottom he was not on the left wing of the Party. There appeared also to be other straws blowing in the same breeze. He would have no truck with pacifism and consistently took a tough line on foreign affairs. Strongly critical of Labour's behaviour overseas, he condemned communist meddling in Greece and the government's apparent complacency about it; and in *The Case for Conservatism* he savaged British policy in Palestine, describing President Truman as a meddling busybody and his proposal for an Anglo-American

Commission as 'an absurd presumption'. The duty of Britain was to have sought a fresh mandate from the United Nations so that she could continue to govern the country.[12] The same robustness would show up in the Persian oil and Suez crises. But what the public did not know was the agony of conscience he underwent at the time of Suez. Nor that, at the height of the crisis, he had time to write to Butler to press for security of tenure for weekly tenants who were unprotected by the Rent Acts. 'Before the war,' he wrote, 'the working classes were at the mercy of a week's notice – a week's notice to leave their jobs, at least in theory, a week's notice to leave their homes . . . Could you not turn over in your mind a tenant's charter corresponding to the industrial charter . . . ?'[13]

He was also tough about criminal justice. In 1948, he spoke against the proposal to suspend the death penalty for a trial period of five years, saying that although human life was sacred, it was not indefeasibly so.[14] He continued to hold this view. In 1973, in a Cabinet discussion on whether capital punishment should be maintained in Northern Ireland, he said that although it would be difficult to justify a different rule from the rest of the United Kingdom, 'I remain impenitently *for* the death penalty.'[15]

These seemed to be right-wing badges, and Hogg never really threw off the misleading image. He was surprised about it himself. In 1957, in a letter to Constituency Chairmen, he confessed to surprise 'to find myself under attack from the Left as a wild man of the right, a sort of Conservative Aneurin Bevan inside out. Most of my life I have been accused of being mildly pink . . .'[16] Ian Gilmour, who knew him both as a pupil at the Bar and in politics, considered that 'resolutely a man of the centre' applied not only to the pre-war period, but ever afterwards as well.[17]

After 1945 he lacked the opportunity to develop his political ideas from the Front Bench. The necessity of earning his living and the imminence of his father's death drove him from an undivided commitment to politics which could only come from a base in the Commons. His failure to seek or get a position in the 1951 Conservative government surprised and disappointed many. After his powerful speech on the Second Reading of Labour's Trade Disputes Bill in 1946, in which he defended the 1927 Act (which the Bill proposed to repeal) and his father's part in it, George Isaacs, the Minister of Labour, commented that he was 'obviously working his passage back to the Front Bench'.[18] Isaacs had seen Lord Hailsham in the gallery earlier in the day, and generously said that Hogg's tribute to his father had touched the House: 'and I say sincerely that I wish he had been here to hear the defence which his son has put up on behalf of his father'. But a seat on the Front Bench would have to wait another ten years.

Although he had retired to the back benches, he continued to work with Butler in the Conservative Research Department on the reformulation of policy. Butler was shocked when he offered to resign in 1948 after having to miss a meeting. 'I look forward to your visits – though spasmodic – for they enliven our meetings. You must certainly stay.'[19] Nevertheless, it would be wrong to place Hogg's name among the leaders of Conservative opinion who made the years of opposition between 1945 and 1951 so fruitful. This small group, led by Butler, persuaded the Party to stand by the agreement reached in the wartime coalition and so to wipe clean the old pre-war association of Toryism with unemployment and poverty. Although he had given impetus to the movement in his years as a Tory Reformer, Hogg did not continue to lead opinion after 1945. Legal practice claimed too much of his time.

His centrist position owed much to his belief that a two-party system was essential to British parliamentary democracy. The Conservatives, he thought, should be led from left of centre, and the left from its right wing. He liked to quote Macaulay on Conservatism and Radicalism: 'In the sentiments of both, there is something to approve. But of both the best specimens will be found not far from the common frontier. The extreme section of one class consists of bigoted dotards. The extreme section of the other consists of shallow and reckless empirics.' (See Appendix 2, p. 352)

This was not necessarily consensus politics, but it tended to moderate opinion and the isolation of wilder thinking.[20] It also made him a pragmatist. He distrusted political abstractions and -isms; and in *The Case for Conservatism* he elevated this into a positive philosophy. His attitude to capital punishment was a good example. All his life he believed that in principle the state should have the right to take the life of a convicted murderer; but in his latter years he would have voted against the restoration of hanging. The reasons were purely pragmatic. The possibility of a miscarriage of justice had become more serious with the revelations of the Irish bomb trials. Until these cases, he had thought there was little risk of a wrong conviction. He no longer held that view. And he felt it was impracticable to chop and change with the death penalty. In the unlikely event of the House voting to restore it, a future House might again abolish it. Certainty and stability were more important.[21] Each issue should be treated on its merits. That is why his hatred of pre-war poverty and unemployment had not carried over into a wider radical attitude.

(*Left*) Quintin Hogg (1845–1903)

(*Bottom left*) Myssie Brown at her marriage to Archibald Marjoribanks

(*Bottom right*) Douglas Hogg (1872–1950) in the Temple

(*Right*) Neil and
Quintin Hogg, and
Edward and Isabel
Marjoribanks

(*Left*) Neil Hogg

(*Below*) Eton Collegers in 1921. Quintin is ringed

(*Right*) The Earl of Birkenhead's article in *Harper's Bazaar*, November 1933. Those featured are (from top) Frank Pakenham, Lord Dufferin and Ava, Quintin Hogg, Randolph Churchill, the Earl of Birkenhead himself and Evelyn Waugh

MY CONTEMPORARIES

"No One Could Call it a Bad List"

By the Earl of Birkenhead

IT is often suggested in the popular papers that there are no brilliant young men to-day. Is this true? I shall try to show, in selecting a number of clever young men of to-day, and in discussing their qualities and prospects, that it is not.

I begin with the Hon. Quintin Hogg, Lord Hailsham's son. Mr. Hogg is nothing of an advertiser, and it is for this reason that we read less about him in the newspapers than we might. That he is one of the most brilliant people of his age in England there can be no possible doubt; in my judgment he is more certainly ear-marked for success than any man I know. Consider what he has achieved at the age of twenty-four. A scholarship at Eton, a scholarship at Christ Church, Oxford, a double first, the Presidency of the Oxford Union, and a brilliant Fellowship of All Souls. His last achievement was to pass first in all England in the Final Bar examination. We are obviously in the presence of intellect of the highest order. Professor Holdsworth, who examined him for his Fellowship of All Souls, told me that he had been astounded by the depth of Hogg's legal knowledge, particularly in view of the fact that he had been brought up on the classics. Add to this first-class debating powers, an amazing concentration and a mind which absorbs knowledge like a sponge and can quickly grasp the most obscure point, and you will see why I am so certain that Hogg will be one of the great ones of the future.

Mr. Randolph Churchill is a very different type. He has none of Mr. Hogg's learning; in fact he affects to despise deep learning as being unnecessary *(Continued on page 79)*

(Continued on page 79)

Photos: Alfieri, S. & G., Sasha and Karl-Seymor

Reading downwards: The Hon. F. A. Pakenham; Lord Dufferin and Ava; The Hon. Quintin Hogg, and Mr. Randolph Churchill.

The Earl of Birkenhead

Mr. Evelyn Waugh

(*Above*) Edward Marjoribanks

(*Right*) Quintin in the Alps

(*Left*) Natalie

(*Below*) Quintin and Natalie campaigning at the Oxford by-election, 1938

(*Above*) 'The Government candidate at the Oxford By-election.' Quintin Hogg is here shown canvassing a group of laundry girls

(*Below*) The Tory Reform Committee: Quintin Hogg and Lord Hinchingbrooke

Mary

(*Right*)
Quintin Hogg
in 1938: a studio
portrait

(*Left*) As First Lord of the
Admiralty, in action in 1956

Brighton 1957: sea-bathing and other activities. For the photographs below the bell-ringer the newspaper caption reads: 'Above (left), the Minister for Technical Education. Left, the Minister of Cultivation. Above (right), the new Minister of Propaganda and Enlightenment. And above, the recently adopted Minister of Sport and Physical Culture.'

Presenting the new Cabinet

Above (left), the new Minister of Technical Education. Left, the Minister of Cultivation. Above (right), the new Minister of Propaganda and Enlightenment. And above, the recently adopted Minister of Sport and Phsysical Culture.

Equally important was Hogg's sense of loyalty to his party. 'Party is organised opinion' and 'Damn your principles! Stick to your Party' were two of his favourite Disraelian sayings. The organisation of opinion in Disraeli's sense might often involve the subordination of individual views. The first Lord Hailsham, Hogg wrote with justice, 'was a truer blue Conservative than I was or am [1975]. But all the same, I believe he taught me a great deal about sinking my own personal prejudices and convictions in collective discussions and wisdom . . .'

Hogg's vitality and intellect made his pragmatism a dynamic force. Ardour and pragmatism are rare bedfellows, but they co-existed in Quintin Hogg, and the author of his profile in a 1956 issue of the *New Statesman* was justified in entitling it 'The Passionate Pragmatist'.[22] Stimulus was what the Tory Reform Committee was about, and nothing was further from the intentions of its members than disloyalty to the government. Hogg and his colleagues wanted to put some steam into the Conservative upper echelons, and they seized the opportunity offered by the Beveridge Report with both hands. 'Hogg wished to make the movement a kind of Right-wing Fabian Society,' wrote the author of his 1948 Profile, 'a political laboratory and a power-house of ideas.'[23]

★

The Case for Conservatism was published in 1947. Most of it had been written in 1946, but it contained a short epilogue added in the following March with the icy desolation of 'Shinwell's Winter' and its coal crisis starkly in mind. It was brought out as a Penguin Special with a companion volume, *Labour Marches On* by John Parker. The publishers remarked that while Parker had kept closely to the suggested length and could be sold for a shilling, 'Mr Hogg's exposition had run to about double the size we had anticipated', and had to be put in the bookshops at two shillings. This, however, 'does not mean that the publishers wish either to penalise the advocacy of conservatism . . . or to suggest that Labour policy is worth only half as much as Conservative policy!' The rather arch disclaimer did not prevent the book from being too long. Conceived as an extended pamphlet, one of a pair in which rival political cases would be set out for comparison, Hogg's book was much more. It was divided into two parts which did not sit well together. The first was a general statement of the philosophy of conservatism, and the second an attack on socialism and an account of practical politics for the future. The first half of the book was of permanent value, the second ephemeral. When it was revised in 1959 with the help of Peter Goldman and reissued by Penguin under the slightly different title, *The Conservative Case*, the second part was completely re-written and shortened. The result was a better balanced book. The first part was left largely untouched. The author, by then Lord Hailsham and Chairman of the Party, thought it had worn well and felt 'tempted to say that what was then [1947] asserted defiantly as a statement of faith can now be put forward even more confidently as the fruit of experience'.*

The high praise he gave to his own writing was deserved, for the statement of Conservative principles was the best thing he ever wrote. The *Observer* was among the original book's admirers.

His campaign to make the Conservative Party the party of the most intelligent was recently inaugurated by the publication of his Penguin book *The Case for Conservatism*. He applies the principles of Burkeian Conservatism to current politics with an analytical power and forensic skill which few writers on either side can command. Everyone recognises that his book is a 'tour de force'.[24]

It was written when Conservative fortunes were at a low ebb. The country, exhausted by the effort of victory, had decisively turned over its government to the Labour party. As controls multiplied, the defeated Conservatives could see no light in the tunnel and expected to languish in opposition for a long time. Some thought that socialism might make itself irremovable. The extremity of the danger as it was perceived by Hogg comes through in the chapter on 'The Politics of the Next Election'. The real choice, he told his readers, was not so much between private enterprise and nationalisation as between the two-party and a single-party system of government. 'The Labour party almost admittedly aims at the establishment of a single-party system; and it may be said that they are almost within striking distance of their goal.'[25] Organised minorities dominated the Trade Union and Co-operative movements; a great machine designed not to develop foreign or domestic policy but rather to further sectional industrial ends, lay at the mercy of Transport House and its capable political bosses; the vast funds from automatically deducted subscriptions of trade union members subsidised their activities; a large well-disciplined majority dominated the Commons.

* Lord Hailsham did not undervalue his work. When his outstanding historical essay intended to be included in a hardback edition of *The Case for Conservatism* and reproduced here in Appendix 2 was unearthed, he had no recollection whatever of writing it, but said, 'I too am immensely impressed by its quality.' (Letter to the author.)

In sum: 'Never since the days of Cromwell has a single force in this country constituted a more formidable menace to political liberty.'[26]

Did Hogg really think that the Labour government aimed at a one-party totalitarian state? It is easy to dismiss this as alarmist, knowing now how short-lived the Labour regime was to be. It was a black time to have lived through. On one hand, the hopes of 1945 were soon dashed. The wartime spirit of unity seemed to have evaporated in no time. Queueing, restrictions and rationing were worse than at any time in the war. Life was drab. Many things people wanted to buy were labelled 'export only'; Crippsian 'austerity' reached everywhere and the citizenry were encouraged to eat whalemeat, which tasted of cod liver oil, and another repellent species of tinned fish known as 'snoek'. On the other hand, the Government appeared obsessed with extending their plans for nationalisation and the spectre of the dollar gap. Some of its members carried on a shrill class war. Emmanuel Shinwell told the public that it was only the working class that mattered; for the rest he did not care 'a tinker's cuss'. Aneurin Bevan described the Tories as 'lower than vermin'. These infelicities made Attlee's task harder, but they did reflect what John Osborne called ' a new eager divisiveness . . . snatching in the air'.[27] There was bitterness for the legacy of Conservatism and a surge of feeling that 'it was our turn now'. The government, however, seemed to have forgotten that those they abused and visited with privation were also voters. One explanation was that they could afford to do so because of the formidable concentration of power in their own hands. Hogg could be forgiven for not foreseeing how soon the electorate would cast its vote of no confidence in Labour.

The Case for Conservatism begins by setting out the underlying principles of conservatism. The ornate periods of this short essay recall Carlyle, but the thinking derived from Burke and Disraeli. The last forty years, Hogg wrote, were ones of revolutionary change.

> . . . in times like these the signs and symbols which have guided the lives of men for centuries suddenly become unreliable and obscure. Lamps by whose light generations of humble folk have made their way grow dim and fail at last. In the general obscurity all truth seems veiled, and in its eclipse all manner of night birds come out and flap their wings. In the universal deluge of ideas men swim about amid the intellectual wreckage of their culture.[28]

These were times for false prophets, cranks and charlatans, 'of grotesque and perverse fanaticisms, of bigotries which would be contemptible if they were not also dangerous'. It was a vision of a heroic but perilous age, a gothic scene against which to set simple beliefs. In what did Conservatives believe which could stand against such dangers? Conservatives believed neither that politics was the most important thing in life, nor that politics had unlimited power to put things right in this world. Two of the most celebrated phrases in the book occur here: 'The man who puts politics first is not fit to be called a civilised being, let alone a Christian'; and of Conservatives: 'The simplest among them prefer fox hunting – the wisest religion' – in which the absence of a comma before 'religion' caused much misunderstanding of what Hogg meant – and some derision. The party did not believe that it had a monopoly of the truth, indeed philosophy might not even be the right word to use. 'Conservatism is not so much a philosophy as an attitude.' Other parties might wed themselves to theories, nostrums, dogma; the Conservative party did not. 'Its eternal and indispensable role was to criticise and mould the latest heresy of the moment in the name of tradition, as tradition has itself been enriched and moulded by all the transient theories of the past.' For this reason, Conservatives fought the naked *laissez-faire* doctrines of nineteenth century liberals, and then in the following century they fought for economic freedom against the socialists. This was not a reversal of policy. 'In fighting socialism in the twentieth, as they fought liberalism in the nineteenth century, Conservatives will be found to have changed their front to meet a new danger, but not the ground they are defending.'[29]

The blend of pragmatism and respect for tradition was in the mainstream of Tory thought. Burke had written of 'the hocus pocus of abstraction', declaring that 'nothing universal can be rationally affirmed on any moral or political subject'.[30] Disraeli, too, distrusted abstractions. The objectives for his 'reconstructed Tory Party' were to be attained 'rather by the use of ancient forms and the restoration of the past than by political revolutions founded on abstract ideas'.[31] Disraeli's idealised past, however, did not preclude radical policies, for he was nothing if not opportunistic. Harold Macmillan considered Hailsham as a true inheritor of the Disraeli tradition of Tory Radicalism.[32] Lord Hailsham's comment in conversation on this description was: 'I don't think anybody is in the Disraeli tradition. Disraeli was a one-off job. I would put Disraeli's hierarchy: Byron, Disraeli, Oscar Wilde.' He was thinking more about Disraeli's slightly disreputable genius than of his achievements in reconstructing the Tory party. But there was more than a grain of truth in Macmillan's phrase. And in 1943, Hogg was himself conscious of the similarities between the situations faced by the Tory party in Disraeli's time and then. He elaborated them in an article written for the *Spectator* in January 1943 – within weeks of his returning home. Disraeli, he wrote, 'saw that the new was not really the enemy of the old, yet that if the people were not given social reform by the parliament, the parliament would be given social revolution by the people'.* Thus he hit upon the role of Conservatism in revolutionary times – to lead and dominate revolution by superior statesmanship, instead of to oppose it. 'Does it offer any hope for today? Surely it does, almost with mathematical parallelism.'[33]

The Case for Conservatism continued with orthodox Tory views on the religious basis of society, the organic theory of the state, and the Conservative approach to patriotism and the international order. Freedom was defined simply as the diffusion of power, on the straightforward basis that if the concentration of power is corrupting, freedom depends on dispersing it. Liberty thus defined required to be reconciled with the notion of authority, on which Hogg approvingly quoted Lord Hugh Cecil: 'The tradition of authority is naturally a Tory tradition.' The reconciliation of these opposed concepts is one of the less satisfactory aspects of the book. 'In place of the struggle between liberty and authority Conservatism offers as a synthesis the *rule of law*.'[34] But law could not simply be what the sovereign power laid down, because the sovereign might be tyrannical. The synthesis therefore lay in natural law, essentially in the injunction 'Thou shalt love thy neighbour as thyself', of which Hogg said: 'The fundamental thesis on which all societies should pass laws is respect for human personality.'[35] He continued to assert that 'law is natural morality translated into the enforceable'[36] until the last years of his life, but the notion that what parliament can do is limited by 'natural law' (a notoriously slippery concept) does not really bear analysis as a constitutional proposition.

It is equally difficult to accept that Conservatives continue to believe in a religious basis for all civil obligations. Hogg was apprehensive about this chapter of the book, on which he had 'pondered desperately long'. 'There is nothing I despise more', he wrote, 'than a politician who seeks to sell his politics by preaching religion, unless it be a preacher who tries to sell his sermons by talking politics.'[37] It was a telling thrust, as was his assertion of the consequence of irreligion: 'Belsen is the end to which our century of enlightenment has brought us at last.'[38] But he had to concede that his own inability to divorce entirely his political faith from his ultimate view of reality was personal to him. 'I do not pretend that

---

* The origin of the arresting phrase Hogg used in the Beveridge debate (see, p. 91).

this creed is exclusively accepted by Conservatives, or accepted by all Conservatives.'[39]

Stylistically, there are difficulties about *The Case for Conservatism*. It was trying to be two things at once: a Disraelian statement of principle, and a plan for immediate action. This disharmony was reduced in the 1959 revision, but never eliminated. Even in the first and more important part of the book, the point that Conservatism is not an 'ism' at all and takes colour from its political environment, led to a certain sententiousness when blown up into a principle. Trollope's more worldly version of the same idea was that the Tories trimmed to survive. Nothing 'stinks so foully in the nostrils of an English Tory politician as to be absolutely irreconcilable to him,' he wrote in *The Bertrams*. 'When taken in the refreshing waters of office any such pill can be swallowed.'[40] John Osborne, the iconoclast, was a schoolboy when Hogg's book came out, but he and his friends chortled over it. (It is easy to forget that books like this were read in Sixth Forms. The Beveridge Report had a wide circulation in schools.) The target was easy. 'The Conservative does not believe that the power of politics to put things right in this world is unlimited.' It was at once smug and disheartening to say that to a generation emerging from six years of war. Even more complacent was the notion that, somehow, by some means, Conservatives can claim that God is on their side. The Thatcher years may have weakened that idea, but it was abroad in the forties and fifties. These weaknesses may be unavoidable in party political writing. They also show up more sharply in an increasingly cynical and atheist age.

*

In 1956, the *New Statesman* gave Hogg's politics and personality a good rating. 'His politics, therefore, are a mixture of expediency and detachment, the whole suffused by a deep love for and faith in Britain as she has unfolded in the course of centuries. That faith – plus the fact that he is such a warm-hearted, frank and jovial fellow – explain why he is almost universally popular.'[41] This was an impressive testament from the Tuscan ranks. The portrait went on to say that he brought the case against Garry Allighan to the House of Commons, not because Allighan was a socialist, but because he was an MP and had lowered the standards of public life.

Allighan was the Member for Gravesend. In April 1947, Hogg drew the Speaker's attention to an article in *World Press News* under Allighan's name alleging that Members of Parliament had been corruptly taking money in return for confidential information.[42] The case was referred to the Committee of Privileges, who reported in due course the startling conclusion that the only offender was Allighan himself. The Committee found him guilty of a libel on the House and accepting a bribe, aggravated by persistent attempts to mislead the Committee.[43] The House agreed without division to a government motion that he had been guilty of contempt. The case then took a curious turn. A further government motion that Allighan had been 'guilty of dishonourable conduct which deserves to be severely punished' was opposed from the Conservative front bench by J. C. S. Reid, who was later to be appointed a Law Lord and became one of the most distinguished judges of his generation. Reid's argument was that the motion proposed that Allighan be punished for something which was not an offence against the law or against any Order of the House or a contempt. What was or was not 'dishonourable' might be a matter of opinion.[44] This was too pettifogging for Hogg, who supported the government against his own front bench, acting as it were as his Party's censor. It was now the turn of the government to be pusillanimous. Morrison proposed that Allighan be suspended for six months without pay. Hogg moved that instead of suspension he be expelled. 'The whole relationship', he said, 'is an impossible relationship and it ought to be put an end to, both for our sakes and for the reputation which this House holds in the country.'[45] The amendment was carried with the full support of the Conservative front bench.

Hogg confessed afterwards that he had often wondered whether he had not been too harsh. It is certainly questionable whether the moral condemnation of the second motion was either necessary or wise – as Reid argued forcibly. But in opposing suspension for six months as a futile gesture, he was surely right. Expulsion is primarily a remedial, not a punitive, measure. As Winston Churchill observed, 'How can you stigmatize a Member as dishonourable by the most formal and solemn vote and then, after an interval, long or short, immediately resume calling him an honourable Member?'[46]

Hogg's political judgment on the things that matter most was usually sound. His colleagues did not always think so, but Margaret Thatcher did. 'He always got the big questions right,' was her view;[47] and Ian Gilmour put a quotation from Burke at the head of his chapter on Lord Hailsham in his book *Inside Right*: 'Vehement passion does not always indicate an infirm judgement.' It was easy to mistake Hogg's excitability for want of judgment. His brother Neil, who was not interested in politics, put it this way: 'Quintin is emotional but it is near the surface. He has intense superficial sentimentality. His emotions come in gusts but he is pretty well in control and his judgment is very sound.'[48] There was no one else like that in the Tory party, except Churchill himself, and it is not surprising that Hogg could be misunderstood.

★

The General Election of February 1950, in which Hogg defeated his old friend Elizabeth Pakenham at Oxford, destroyed Labour's huge majority and left it with a thin margin of eight seats. The Conservative mood was to use every device to harry the government to early defeat. The atmosphere was rancorous and not conducive to statesmanship or the long view. It was therefore unfortunate that Robert Schuman's proposal for European co-operation in the coal, iron and steel industries came to be debated in the Commons in this atmosphere. It was a 'big question', as Hogg realised. Jean Monnet and Robert Schuman were proposing the first steps in the construction of common political institutions in Europe, starting with supranational control of key industries. Their aim was to remove the causes of conflict within Europe, particularly between France and Germany. On 26 June, Eden moved that the government accept Schuman's invitation to take part in the discussions on his plan, the essentials of which were the pooling of European coal and steel resources and the establishment of a high authority to regulate the industry.[49] Churchill asked Hogg to make the opposition's winding up speech on the first day from his place on the back benches. His stepmother, Mildred, had warned him that his father had had another stroke and might not last long. Hogg knew that this was likely to be his last important speech in the Commons, as it was.

Although Eden moved the Conservative motion, he was cool about Schuman's initiative and distrusted particularly the surrender of British industries to a European authority.[50] He was an olden-day 'Euro-sceptic', and his views were shared by Ernest Bevin, the Foreign Secretary. Some on the government side were worse than sceptical. It was argued variously, and deplorably, that co-operation was only possible with a socialist Europe, that the Plan would result in a Franco-German alliance against Britain, and that it would threaten the standard of living here. Most of these arguments were advanced in an extraordinary and unprincipled speech by Richard Crossman,[51] whom Hogg described as a chameleon-like figure who had 'boxed almost every point in the political compass not only in his short and fascinating career, but also in the space of a 25 minutes' speech'.[52]

Hogg told the House that the matter for discussion was far too momentous to fritter away debating time in taunts and jibes culled from the armoury of party warfare. The Schuman Plan was a step in a limited but decisive sphere, and was 'an experiment which we ought to attempt to make'. It was an historic opportunity.

> We have never achieved liberty except at the expense of a considerable degree of disorder. Nor have we ever built up a system of order without sacrificing some of the essential principles of liberty. Bloodshed has marked the course of our career through time ... But let not Hon. Members seek to minimise the consequences of their decision. Let them not think or flatter themselves that because an opportunity has been missed now, it will necessarily ever recur again in the future.[53]

In the event, the Labour government's motion, effectively a refusal to join in discussions on the Schuman Plan, was carried. It was mealy mouthed in a way destined to become familiar to the proponents of European Union. While welcoming the 'declared readiness' of His Majesty's Government to take a constructive part in discussions, it 'recognised' that it was not possible to take part in international consideration of the Schuman Plan 'on terms which committed them in advance ... to pool the production of coal and steel and to institute a new high authority'. Many on the Conservative side were undismayed. But for Hogg, the way forward had to be through Europe; 'and through Europe we ultimately chose to go, though at a price greater for us and, as I believe, for Europe, higher than either we or they needed to pay.' He saw the Schuman Plan for what it was, a chance to enter the European process at inception, and so to influence its development nearer to the heart's desire than the quarrelsome, bureaucratic association it later became. Twenty years later, when joining Europe was again in issue and he had become Lord Chancellor, Lord Hailsham referred to his speech in the 1950 debate and spoke in similar terms, saying that he could imagine no greater disaster, other than war, than a failure to proceed with our application to join.[54] Ever afterwards, Britain was in the weaker position of supplicant.

In 1950 Hogg was forty-two, of a certain portliness and with 'a premature development of that bowed carriage which might be called statesman's stoop'.[55] Married and now with three children (Douglas, Mary Claire and Frances) he had the embonpoint which accompanies established position. His legal practice was flourishing, but as he knew, time in the House of Commons which he loved was almost up. He would have to develop an affection for his new and involuntary political home in the Lords. Not, however, without fresh controversy.

12

Reluctant Heir

Douglas Hogg died at Carters Corner on 16 August 1950. He had been paralysed down his right side for fourteen years, and all that time had barely been able to speak for more than a few minutes together without losing control. And yet his intellect remained unimpaired. In his tribute in the chamber of the House of Lords, Viscount Maugham remarked that his illness had the result of destroying his superb debating power while not affecting in the least his intellectual capacity.[1] He bore this peculiar frustration and the other indignities of his condition with patient courage. For him and for his son death was a release. It did not come as a shock of bereavement, as had the deaths of Hogg's mother and Edward, and as would Mary's death in 1978. As Neil put it in a letter to his brother: '. . . it is only the parting that is bitter. There is no doubt he was ready to go.'[2] None the less, the loss of the one remaining human being who had known him from the beginning was a landmark in Hogg's life. The filial affection and piety which he always bore his father can hardly be exaggerated and was touching to see.

The similarities between the careers of father and son have often been remarked, but they were very different people. 'Hailsham', Professor Heuston remarked of Douglas, 'was a very straightforward and uncomplicated man. He was in many ways a typical representative of English Conservatism of a kind which his fellow-countryman once admired greatly.'[3] He had little interest in the philosophy either of politics or law. He was not of a reflective cast of mind and his emotions were buried deep under layers of self-control. Hogg said he never knew what his father's own religious beliefs were, and he was puzzled by a remark Douglas made to his stepdaughter shortly before he died, that it did not matter what a man believed so long as he believed something. In fact, Douglas, whose low-church views had gradually broadened, meant that fine points of Christian dogma were not important.[4] His Conservatism was instinctive and unwavering. It was not a thing to entertain doubts about. He cared nothing for show, curbed whatever ambitions he had, and believed that doing his public duty was sufficient reward.

Such a man might seem cold, but he was not. To his four-year-old stepdaughter, coming into a new family and facing formidable and, in Quintin's case, hostile elder brothers, her new father was kind and considerate, taking pains that no one's feelings should be hurt. He had a dry sense of humour, whose unobtrusive asides it was possible to miss, but whose intellect, never flaunted, could not be mistaken.[5]

It was easy to underestimate his talents. The *Manchester Guardian's* obituarist said that he was not a great lawyer: 'one looks in vain among his judgments in the House of Lords for any that are distinguished, far less memorable ... As a politician he was appreciated more by his colleagues than by the public, who never quite got to know him.'[6] Probably he was at his best as an advocate, Lord Denning's Demosthenes, where he could deploy his calmness, quickness of grasp, gift of exposition, and above all his judgment of whether a point was good, bad or indifferent.

The critical obituarist concluded: 'It would not be unfair to say that Hailsham's career was more striking than his achievement.' It might not be unfair to say that of Quintin also. But in almost all aspects of personality the son who revered his father was his opposite. He was complicated, volatile, and ambitious. His father was aware of these sides to his character, some of which had made their first appearance in the nursery. '... I really think you are making a mountain out of a much less important elevation,' he had written in 1934, 'when you think of starting a violent row with central office ... This is eminently an occasion for practising the virtuous and Xtian habit of suffering fools gladly, which is not your strong point and which really is very important for general happiness and success.'[7] Nor were Quintin's virtues the same as his father's. His loyalty was emotional, impulsive, the warmth of his friendship blew in gusts. It is not possible to conceive of the first Lord Hailsham receiving the letter which his son did from a former secretary: 'Some 45 years ago it must be. Remember your suddenly being fed up and taking your secretary on a day trip to Brighton? Happy Christmas to you. Love, Jean.'[8]

The dissimilarities should not, however, be pressed too far. The qualities of loyalty, patriotism and respect for the strength of the institutions of his country were ones which Hogg imbibed directly from his father. The close, admiring attention which he paid to his father's achievements and the steadiness of character which was employed in realising them led to a conscious will to celebrate Douglas's memory by emulation. Father and son forged a single tradition of public service.

*

Hogg's telegram to his father in 1928 to 'reform Lords' had proved harder to achieve than prescribe. The House of Lords was peculiarly resistant to reform. Compulsory elevation now faced him squarely. Hogg had been pondering his prospective fate as a reluctant heir since his father took the peerage, and knew that if the House of Lords was to be reformed, it would be by changing detail to prevent anomaly and injustice rather than by a broad rational scheme. He therefore wrote to the Prime Minister a bare two weeks after his father's death.

He told Attlee that he had no means of judging whether he was a useful Member of the Commons, but he thought he was entitled to assume that those who voted for him wished him to be their representative throughout the life of the current parliament. 'This letter is therefore my formal request to you to let me know whether the government will not be prepared to initiate legislation in such a way as to save Oxford from the inconvenience of a by-election.' The letter was well argued but it ended with a foolish coda.

> If your answer is negative I must tell you frankly that, unless you can justify the present situation as a matter of principle, I shall draw the inference that you and your party prefer to continue a system which is fraught with inconvenience to my former constituents, contrary to the public interest and unjust, in order to maintain a grievance rather than to pursue the public good.[9]

Attlee sent a short friendly note ('I fully understand your feelings and I must say that I have much sympathy with them') to say he would consider the matter. The full reply was disappointing. Attlee thought that the suggestion which had been made was that 'in order to save the City of Oxford from the trouble of a by-election, I should forthwith introduce retrospective legislation to remove the disqualification which you have incurred . . .'[10] This was a misunderstanding for which Attlee could be forgiven but which could easily have been cleared up. The new Lord Hailsham's relations with

Attlee were cordial. When he had congratulated the Labour leader on his victory in 1945, Attlee wrote a charming letter saying how highly he valued the good wishes 'as an instance of the way in which personal regard in the House is not affected by differences of political conviction when they are sincerely held.'[11] But Attlee also knew Hogg's tendency to overstate his case. In September 1949 he had called on Attlee to recall parliament in order to debate devaluation. 'We all know that with a docile majority you can push things through as and when you please, but the ordinary decencies of Parliamentary Government should, I think, allow us to discuss this most important matter before it is quite stale.'[12] Attlee replied in his best terse style: 'I note your view, reinforcing that of Mr Churchill, about the recall of Parliament.'

The Prime Minister told Hailsham that 'the general problem of the composition of the House of Lords' had been discussed with opposition leaders and that it was unfortunate that they did not take up the opportunity which the talks afforded. He suggested that Hogg approach his own party leader. He regretted the 'unwarrantable assumptions' which had been made at the end of Hailsham's letter. 'On reflection you will, I think, realise that this method of approach was hardly likely to conduce to a favourable reception.'

Hailsham realised nothing of the kind and replied without giving himself any chance to reflect. He accused the Prime Minister of misrepresenting his proposal, and resented the suggestion that he was somehow debarred from approaching the head of the Government direct, simply because he happened to belong to another political party. 'The arrogance of Ministers is becoming intolerable.' He characterised Attlee's reasoning as 'one disingenuous and three irrelevant arguments', and felt bound to draw the inference that the Prime Minister had no good reason for rejecting the proposal on its merits. He concluded: 'Since in my view your answer was both discourteous and disingenuous I am sending a copy of the whole correspondence to the Press.'[13]

It was a bad case of a rush of blood to the head and it had malign consequences. A necessary reform was put off for thirteen years. How much needed it was would be proved then, in 1963. In thinking that Hailsham was seeking help with his own special problem at Oxford rather than a general resolution of the difficulties faced by sons of the peerage, Attlee was mistaken. But he was a fair-minded man. For ever afterwards, however, Hailsham thought of Attlee as a 'rather mean-minded, waspish man' whose dishonesty should not be forgiven and contrasted ill with Harold Macmillan's later treatment of Anthony Wedgwood Benn's parallel case.

However, Attlee also had his humour, of a pithy sort, as Hailsham knew, for in 1976 he wrote down a story told him by Arthur Goodhart, a former Master of University College, Oxford. 'AG told me Attlee often stayed in Univ. during AG's mastership. Once during Bevan troubles, Attlee returned from Univ. service evidently pleased. AG asked why. Attlee: "I am not often impressed by such things. But the second lesson contained the text, If thy Nye offend thee, pluck it out." '

In face of Attlee's refusal to help, Hailsham considered that he should make way for Oxford to elect a new member as soon as might be. He therefore applied for a writ to sit and vote in the House of Lords, thereby opening the way for a quick by-election. He could have drawn attention in various ways to the inconvenience caused by his inheritance, but each of them would have involved a period of uncertainty during which his constituents would have been disfranchised. In any case, the law on the subject was clear. In 1895 the Earl of Selborne, on succeeding to the title, had attempted to continue to sit in the Commons. He was challenged and a Select Committee declared the seat vacant.[14]

During November and December 1951 Hailsham and Anthony Wedgwood Benn, an at least equally reluctant heir, co-operated in trying to promote remedial legislation ('the Liberation Bill' Benn called it) as a Private Member's Bill. Hailsham sent Benn a draft he had prepared providing that Peers should not be disqualified either from voting in parliamentary elections or from being elected to the House of Commons so long as they did not also sit in the Lords. The draft also provided for the creation of Life Peerages. But it came to nothing as Benn was unsuccessful in the ballot.[15]

Benn succeeded to the Stansgate title in 1960, having previously made an unsuccessful attempt to renounce the peerage in advance. He did not feel the same scruples as Hailsham, and in 1961 he made sufficient fuss to provoke the change in the law for which Hailsham had unsuccessfully approached Attlee. His tactic was a variant on that tried by the Earl of Selborne. The Committee of Privileges having decided that his seat representing Bristol South East had been vacated by his succession, he stood as a candidate in the resultant by-election and polled the largest number of votes. Although not legally effective, this was an unanswerable demonstration of the electors' will. The unsuccessful candidate petitioned the Election Court which decided that, as a Peer, Benn was disqualified from sitting in the House of Commons.[16] Benn argued the case himself with conspicuous skill and resource, so much so that the presiding judge, Mr Justice Gorman, commented: 'In the course of the delightful manner in which Mr Wedgwood Benn conducted his case he said words to the effect: "I have intended to make the House of Commons my career. It may be that I shall now have to get my living in some other way . . ." Having heard the magnificent way in which this case has been conducted . . . this court has not the slightest doubt that there is another way.' But his argument was hopeless. He was in any case probably more concerned with publicising the justice of his cause than winning in Court.

These antics by unwilling noblemen had left their constituencies unrepresented and done nothing for the reputation of parliament. But Benn, by his determination, had shown that the law ought to be changed, and Hailsham owed him a debt for that. Harold Macmillan, who had already taken one reforming step in 1958 by promoting legislation to create Life Peerages, was persuaded by the Benn case that the anomaly should be tackled. Hailsham, by then Leader of the Upper House, took his opportunity. On 10 April 1962 he moved the appointment of a Select Committee to consider the whole subject,[17] and spoke, this time with grace and dignity.

He began by paying tribute to the traditional strength of parliamentary institutions in Britain, saying that it was surely only the superficial who would mock at their medieval framework. He reminded the House that General de Gaulle had told his audience in Westminster Hall that 'it is a matter of infinite thankfulness to the British people that it has inherited traditional institutions whose inherent authority is beyond dispute.'* But with all the merit due to antiquity, the composition of the House of Lords had never during this century been capable of theoretical justification. It could continue no longer without at least reducing its anomalies. If, for example, Churchill's uncle had died without issue, Churchill would not have been available to lead in 1940, and would never have served in the House of Commons at all. There were other anomalous cases. Only a handful of Scots peers sat to represent the others. Peeresses

---

* Hailsham rightly described De Gaulle's speech (on 7 April 1960) to Members of both Houses as an 'extraordinary tour de force'. Its magisterial measures may be appreciated from a short extract: 'Certainly it is above all your profound national qualities which have enabled you to play this outstanding role at the height of the storm. But, in this achievement of yours, for how much also has counted the value of your institutions! At the worst moments, whoever contested the legitimacy or the authority of the State? . . . Sure of yourselves, almost without seeming so, you put into practice in freedom a well-founded and stable political system. With you, in the political field, tradition, loyalty, and the rules of the game are so strong that your Government is quite naturally endowed with cohesion and endurance . . . Although since 1940 you have undergone the most severe vicissitudes of your history, only four statesmen, my friends Sir Winston Churchill, Lord Attlee, Sir Anthony Eden and Mr Harold Macmillan have conducted your affairs during these twenty extraordinary years.'

were prevented from sitting in either house – 'a sort of floating kidney in the body politic'. He ended movingly:

> It would be difficult, I think, to find four men who differed more completely in temperament or opinion than Lord Hinching-brooke, Lord Altrincham, Lord Stansgate and myself. Yet I doubt not that we have one thing in common, which indeed we share with the great majority of mankind; we all loved our fathers and are proud of the stock from which we came. My Lords, this is no snobbery; it is shared by all classes in every age. It is not foolish pride. It is common piety that we honour our fathers and our mothers ... It has fallen, or will fall to us all in a moment of bereavement – and, believe me, the pain of parting is as great for rich and poor alike, and neither age nor long service, nor a lifetime full of honours really blunt the edge of the axe when it falls – to have to leave or else forswear a life we loved, the ordinary healthy normal business of democratic politics as it is lived today in the Commons or on the hustings, and if we have protested to have to seem in so doing to dishonour our heritage and the families which gave us birth.[18]

Hailsham submitted two memoranda to the joint committee.[19] In the first he argued that the question was not one of injustice to individual heirs, but rather where the balance of public advantage lay. It was to the advantage of the public to elect whom they chose to the Commons, the dominant House; and equally to the public advantage that the most suitable candidate be available. In the second he dealt with the specious argument that the right to disclaim a peerage should be open only to those who had not applied for a writ to sit and vote in the Lords. That argument, if successful, would have barred him.

The Committee reported in December 1962, and recommended that hereditary peers should be entitled to disclaim their peerage for life. The Peerage Act, which implemented the recommendation, came into force on 31 July 1963, just in time for the leadership crisis in the Conservative party when disclaimer of peerages took the centre of a luridly lit stage.

★

The dilemma facing the reluctant heir, which Hailsham described so eloquently when moving the appointment of a Select Committee in 1962, was one by which he had been oppressed for thirty-four years.

His advice to his father in 1928 not to accept the woolsack and the peerage which accompanied it had a double motive. He thought his father should not put himself out of the running for the leadership of the Conservative party; and he did not want to be an hereditary peer himself. The knowledge that he would inevitably become a 'conscripted father' some time, and the threat that it might be sooner rather than later, put his career in a straitjacket which was capable of crippling. The great offices of state were effectively closed to peers. So were the posts of Attorney and Solicitor-General, attractive to political lawyers not only intrinsically but because they were a traditional route to the High Court Bench. With rare exceptions, like Lord Home's appointment as Foreign Secretary in 1960, which was itself anachronistic, no peer could expect to become Prime Minister, Chancellor of the Exchequer, Foreign Secretary, Home Secretary or Law Officer. That was enough to blight the ultimate political ambitions of the young Hogg, but circumstances were even more constricting. Without the threat of involuntary elevation, he might have delayed his entry into public life until his career at the Bar was secured by appointment to silk. Then he could have chosen law or politics and had a steady run at either. As it was, he swung between the two to the advantage of neither. The chance presented by the approach to Attlee might have ended the duality in his professional life: at any rate it would have granted freedom. He spoiled that chance, and it was ironic that Benn, whose tactics he deplored, rescued the chance he had lost. His attribution of Benn's success and his own failure to Harold Macmillan's magnanimity and Attlee's small-mindedness was a distortion. He naturally left out of account his fit of spleen with Attlee. But events also owed something to Benn's persistence and his demonstration in the Bristol by-election that he remained the electors' choice; and to Hailsham's own honourable course of applying for a House of Lords writ as soon as possible to avoid disenfranchising his constituents.

It is idle to speculate what might have been the political career of Quintin Hogg had he been able to disclaim his peerage in 1950 or soon afterwards. What is certain, however, is that one highly explosive element would have been removed from the leadership crisis of 1963.

Although threatening Hogg all those years with political castration, the problem of the House of Lords fascinated him. He wrote a good deal about its place in the constitution, and his opinion about what to do with it fluctuated. Its composition of bishops, senior judges and hierarchical grades of noblemen seemed to have more to do with ceremonial than reality. Even in the early years of the century, it could not be described as an active member of the body politic. 'The House of Peers', wrote W. S. Gilbert, 'throughout the war / Did nothing in particular, and did it very well.' By then, the Parliament Act of 1911 had shorn it of any real power, and it was ever afterwards liable to reform or abolition. The Act's preamble declared that it should become an elective chamber, and that reform 'brooked no delay'. Yet it survived with only small changes. There was something about it which defied reform.

Hogg's opinion was that it had been preserved because the Commons wanted it preserved. The Commons, he thought, were uneasily aware that people would not tolerate a sovereign legislature with unlimited powers, of which it was the only organ. 'It has therefore deliberately kept in being a second chamber of composition so unjustifiable in principle that it could act as a sort of chaperon to the House of Commons without actually challenging its authority.'[20] Our system is a masquerade, a unicameral legislature of two chambers. So the reforms which have been brought in have not been fundamental. They have tinkered about at the margins of the problem. But, Hogg considered, the Lords had some positive virtues beyond being a cover for the Commons. Such value as it had lay in its very irrationality. Although oddly assorted, its members came as individuals and not as delegates.

> The basic difference between the two Houses is not, as is generally thought, the hereditary or official character of most peers, lay, legal or spiritual, but the fact that Members of the House of Lords are summoned individually by the Sovereign, and therefore attend as individuals, and on occasions when they feel that their presence represents a personal contribution or service.

Because of this, the Lords can call on expert opinion. Debates are better informed and more civilised than in the Commons, whose business is characterised by animal noises and low grade advocacy. Even the vaunted Prime Minister's Question Time, he thought in 1976, was a 'twice-weekly exhibition of schoolboy humour'.[21] The Lords can give time to debate, whereas the great limiting factor in the modern House of Commons is the chronic shortage of parliamentary time. Attempts to improve the transaction of business in the Commons by procedural change are, Hogg thought, always to the advantage of government and the prejudice of the opposition and minority views. As he gained experience of practical politics, he came to think of tightening executive control as the biggest single threat to liberty. A parliament without legal limitation on its powers, a House of Commons whose majority was lobby fodder (his phrase), an upper house shorn of power would lead to 'elective dictatorship', another phrase which he made his own, and whose baleful consequences he elaborated in his celebrated Dimbleby Lecture of 1976.

By 1968 at the latest, Hailsham had come to believe that the unwritten British constitution was in danger of breaking down. Attention would have to be paid to the Lords. In a memorandum to the Shadow Cabinet in 1975 he wrote: 'It is my considered opinion that the weakness of the House of Lords as an effective brake on the tyranny of the Commons is more and more apparent.'[22] When the question of Lords reform was debated in the columns of *The Times* the following year, he conceded in a letter to the editor that 'no one, absolutely no one, defends the present composition of the House of Lords, but this does not exonerate it from discharging its existing constitutional functions responsibly . . .'; and he commented angrily that it was not the House of Lords which had nearly brought the country to its knees, devalued the pound, diminished our defences, created a million and a half unemployed, and lost the confidence of the electorate.[23] The real battle was elsewhere than the Lords.

He had told his colleagues in the shadow cabinet in his memorandum that it should be made clear from the conservative benches that 'we would favour a comprehensive reform of the whole constitutional framework of the U.K.', but he did not then say how the House of Lords would fit in to the scheme. He considered that it had had all the tinkering it could take, and if there were to be further change it would have to be by replacing the House. In *The Door Wherein I Went* (1975) he cautiously ventured that 'There may of course come a time when the House of Lords gives place to a Senate elected on some regional or provincial principle.' The tentative view had given way to much firmer conviction within a year, when he gave his Dimbleby Lecture on *Elective Dictatorship* (14 October 1976). Our constitution, he declared then, needed root and branch overhaul. He envisaged 'nothing less than a written constitution for the United Kingdom', with an entrenched Bill of Rights and powers devolved to regional assemblies. The House of Lords should be replaced by a Senate, elected by a system of proportional representation to represent the regions. The Commons would continue to determine the political colour of the executive government and retain control of finance, but the new upper chamber would have a right of veto over legislation. These views were strongly confirmed in 1978 in *The Dilemma of Democracy*, in which he wrote that it had become 'utterly intolerable' that an executive-controlled Commons should have unlimited powers to change the laws of the land. There was 'no genuine alternative' to radical reform of the Lords.[24]

But by the time he came to write his short essay on the constitution (1992) he had dropped any idea of replacing the Lords. He quoted with approval Lord Melbourne's usual response to suggestions for reform, 'Why not let it alone?' and had reached the point where 'I tend to think we have more important things to do than to reform the existing, theoretically indefensible, but practically useful, and arguably indispensable, House of Lords.'[25]

It was uncharacteristic of him to leave a subject dangling like that. The reasons, however, were primarily political. The near despair of the opposition years of 1975/9, which led to the conviction that only constitutional reform could fend off the tyranny of the executive, gave way to a more optimistic outlook during the Thatcher era. Downing Street had its rightful tenant again, pragmatism ruled once more and Lord Melbourne's minimalism was right. In any case, his interest in the House of Lords was always liable to give place to resentment that he should ever have been forced to go there. The last word, perhaps, was said in *The Door Wherein I Went* in 1975: '. . . when I went there, I tried to do my duty as a hereditary legislator. I made clear, however, that if I were ever permitted to escape, I would take the first opportunity to do so . . . So soon as I had an honourable opportunity I disclaimed my hereditary peerage and offered myself for election to the Commons which, in my view, I should never have been compelled to leave.'

13

Carters Corner

DOUGLAS Hogg lies buried at the western edge of Hurstmonceux churchyard, looking out over the flatlands and in sight of Carters Corner Place, his country home. Beside his tomb is that of Edward, the stepson whom he always called his son, and a little distance off, that of Mary, his daughter-in-law, buried in 1978. Quintin, who every Sunday used to cycle with his family the three miles to the ancient church from Carters Corner, reserved a plot next to his wife's remains. There is a strong atmosphere of peace and continuity about the place. The church stands on a rise, in trees, opposite the entrance to the castle. Below are the Pevensey marshes running away to the sea at Norman's Bay, the spot where the Conqueror is supposed to have landed. Soon after the landing, which was unopposed, William rode round the coast on a reconnaissance with a party of his knights, putting fear into the inhabitants. The waters then extended inland from Pevensey and he must have passed close to Hurstmonceux church and the ground where Carters Corner Place was to be built.

Douglas left the house and farm, valued for probate at £15,000 (£300,000 in 1997) to Quintin. It was part of a rearrangement of his affairs in 1947.[1] At the same time, he made gifts to his second wife, Mildred, and to his sons and settled property on his grandchildren. He hoped and thought that he would live long enough for the gifts to escape death duties. In the event a large part of the gifts and of the residue of the estate was swallowed up in tax. He intended that Carters Corner should remain a family home after he had gone; but because of death duties he left it to Quintin, with a request, 'without imposing any trust or legal obligation' that Mildred's possession of the house should not be disturbed for three years. In order to compensate her, he left her a legacy free of death duties of £20,000.

His intentions about Mildred and the farm were made clearer by his leaving her the livestock and other farm assets. The unexpectedly heavy burden of death duties frustrated all these plans. The new Lord Hailsham was immediately faced with difficulties. He wanted to honour his father's wishes and he loved the house and farm. Both, however, needed money to be spent. On top of death duties he had to find £5,000 (£100,000) more or less immediately to meet expenses. Douglas's failure to live five years after 1947 had worked hardly against him. And then there was the request that Mildred should stay on at Carters Corner for three years.

Relations between Mildred and her stepsons had improved since Douglas's second marriage. But they were not kith and kin, and Mildred had a somewhat military style. She had been a Commandant in the women's army corps and used to go to camp at Aldershot every year. It would have been near impossible to establish a harmonious home at Carters Corner with Mildred and Quintin and his family under the same roof. Mildred was well aware of this; but Quintin tried loyally to carry out his father's wishes. She wrote to Quintin in September: 'Much as I appreciate your suggestions that I remain here as mistress of the house, and I do appreciate this very much, I do not think with the best will in the world that it would work.'[2] Her first instinct had been to stay on, but she changed her mind on thinking it through and when she realised that it would involve bearing the running expenses.

Quintin consulted Neil about the whole situation. He could be more open with him than with anyone else. Neil became his closest friend, and when he died in 1995, Quintin wrote: 'I have lost the best of brothers, the most entertaining of companions, by far the most talented human being I have ever known intimately, and the last link with my own childhood. We spent almost all our lives hundreds, even thousands, of miles apart. But there was a tremendous, almost miraculous, empathy between us.'[3] The understanding between the two was there in 1950, a delicacy in dealing with real motives. He asked Neil to come home from Tobago where he was planting cocoa, but this was impossible.

Quintin wrote a long letter in which he set out all his worries, not only about Carters Corner but about what he should now do with his life.[4] He explained how he had put to Mildred the idea that everyone should use the house as a family home, and pool resources. 'She has replied in a most helpful and good-humoured letter flatly turning down this suggestion.' As soon as she realised what the financial position was (paying the outgoings even though rent free) 'she immediately changed entirely round and wrote me straightaway that she must go at once selling out the livestock as she went'. He did not think that he could manage to keep the place on his own resources, although he wanted to. If he tried, with the Putney house to maintain as well, he would be like an animal caught in a trap. What was the way out of the dilemma? 'One thing is quite clear in my mind. My offer to you remains open. I want you back. I want you in the house, and I think we could manage it together.'

In the meantime, he wrote, 'you might care to cast your mind over my personal worries'. Should he stay at the Bar or leave it? There was more to be said for decamping to Carters Corner than appeared. He was interested in scholarship and philosophy. He would have time for reading and study, and would be living a healthy life in the country. He had always wanted to farm and garden. 'I am dead tired having given more in the last twelve years in energy and emotional force than most in a lifetime.' On the other hand, he wanted to succeed at the Bar. He liked London and being at the centre of things, 'even if the part I must now play is a humbler one'. He wondered if leaving would be abandoning his duty: it would at any rate be an emotional anticlimax. He hoped that Neil, with his 'usual clarity of vision' could illuminate these worries.

Now that he no longer kept a diary, it was unusual for him to lay bare so explicitly the anxieties which troubled him most. There was no mention of politics and public life. The straight choice lay between the Bar and the country, life at the centre or in obscurity.

Neil had no doubt how he should choose. He advised selling Carters Corner and staying at the Bar.[5] Their father had failed to leave enough money for the upkeep of the house and farm, which was 'a good rich man's home, while men could be rich, but . . . it will never pay for its upkeep'. 'My guess is that you will be happier and do all things better, even reading, in London. And I believe that you will continue to play a very important part in the public life of the country as long as you can stay there.' Quintin might also 'take a rest from politics for a time'.[6] A few days later Quintin wrote that he would keep Carters Corner as a family home. Neil rejoiced 'in your decision to do the poetically right thing instead of the merely sensible which my croakings have so hoarsely advocated'.

Some of these letters must have crossed and it is unlikely that Quintin had Neil's advice before deciding. The decision, however, was inevitable as well as poetic. He would never have left the Bar as his junior's practice was expanding and an application for silk was imminent. A decent obscurity was not a serious option although it had to be canvassed.

The poetic part was taking on Carters Corner against the financial odds. Neil could not join his brother in a joint venture, and in any case, as a boy, he had not enjoyed the place as had Quintin. He had not been a robust child and remembered Sussex as being dull. He thought the soil 'poor, thin, sour', and that the expense of draining and irrigating it could be crippling. In 1951 he congratulated Quintin on getting mains water and electricity: 'How we managed to spend so much on that house without getting either is a mystery.'[7] Although he knew the difficulties he faced, it looked different to Quintin. As a boy who enjoyed roughing things, he had roamed about with a dog, shooting rabbits, and knew every copse and ditch of the land. Apart from a few fields let on grazing tenancies, the land was not farmed. Much of it was rough woodland and Quintin remembered it in his boyhood as 'extraordinarily wild and pleasant'. Now he wanted to see if he could make a go of the farm and market garden which had been started and carried on in a rather half-hearted way by his stepmother. In *A Sparrow's Flight* he described the land as he found it as 'virtually unfarmable'. But what was decisive was that it was his home and he loved it. Even after he had to leave, he continued to think of it as home, and he told a television interviewer who asked him whether he missed it, that there was never a day that passed when he did not think of Carters Corner.

It is a tall house built in the last year of Elizabeth's reign by an ironmaster called Barton, and was earlier called Barton House. The house Quintin knew and loved had been restored and re-created slowly by his mother, and was her monument. It stands in the parish of Hellingly above the Cowbeech road a couple of miles from Hailsham, hidden from passing traffic. The high gables and brick mullions are characteristic of its period and the local brick with faded blue banding has mellowed to a glorious colour. Like the family graves, it looks out across its lawn to the Pevensey marshes and the sea. It is a handsome place.

So Quintin took on the farm and market garden alone, unsupported by his brother or stepmother. He had never farmed before. It was a hard struggle, as he described it in his memoirs; but it gave him fourteen years of pleasure and satisfaction. 'Since, from the age of ten, I had been brought up in the country, I still think of myself as a country man, and am glad of my recollections of fourteen years of productive farming.' It was true. His engagement diaries of later years are peppered with references to wild life, and until his legs gave out he never lost the sense of pleasurable excitement from walking the countryside as he had walked his farm with his manager weekend by weekend. By the time he left in 1963, he had cleared the woodland and put the land to pasture with a fine herd of 120

Jerseys and a contract to supply bottled milk to a local dairy. He and his family went down virtually every weekend until Mary, who was not emotionally attached to the house as was her husband, felt that she could not bring up five children and run two houses; and Quintin Hoare, cousin, banker and *homme d'affaires*, agreed with her that the prudent course was to sell.

The trouble was that prudence was not the issue. Not only Quintin but his children also thought of Carters Corner as home. Putney was the base from which you went to school: Father was always working: only in Sussex was there a proper family life. It was a noisy, outdoor life. There was a lot of freedom, but infractions of the domestic code were visited with confinement to the 'sulking room', a remote attic where, once incarcerated, you might be forgotten. Father told stories at bedtime from the Old Testament (like his own grandmother) and, acme of sophistication, cycled with his hands behind his back, whistling.[8]

★

Quintin had been at Eton with Anthony Wagner, who in 1951 had become the Richmond Herald at the College of Arms. Although he disapproved of the hereditary principle, particularly as it had applied to himself, he thought the family coat of arms should have the addition of 'supporters' for a monument to his father to be erected at the Polytechnic. He wrote to seek Wagner's advice. The correspondence which ensued might not be believed a hundred years hence were it not recorded.[9] He gave Wagner some background, telling him that Douglas had been an intensely modest man. ('When he first arose to a position of greatness he could hardly believe himself.') 'Hoggs', he added, thinking this might be relevant to the choice of beast as supporter, 'as you may see to this day in any farming paper in the North are yearling sheep, not hogs.' Wagner took the hint and suggested yearling sheep with the Lord Chancellor's purse. Hailsham considered that the Herald should think again because 'sheep are silly animals'; but 'on second thoughts perhaps you could give him horns . . . and possibly the addition of other appurtenances might give him a more masculine vigour . . . what about a yearling ram with horns and very masculine . . . ?' Wagner was enthusiastic. 'I think we have something now.' Also it would give another 'veiled allusion to the Woolsack'. He sent a sketch. Hailsham was startled: 'You certainly have interpreted my instructions regarding the virility of the animals with extreme punctiliousness.' Wagner did not know quite how to take this sally: 'I take it that what we want is definitely a male and unless you let me know otherwise, I will therefore blazon as a ram.' 'Thank you for your letter. Blazon them as yearling rams. Yrs. Q.'

★

In a series of contributions from wives under the general heading 'The Difficult Years' (although none of them conceded that there was any such thing), Lady Hailsham told the *Daily Sketch* (21 May 1953) that she had found her life completely changed in 1950 when her husband succeeded to the title. 'I was faced with the problem of adjusting myself from an active and exciting public life with him . . . to an entirely private one at home with my children.' This was more difficult for him than for her. With the worries over Carters Corner came a change in his political life. It was not only about leaving the House of Commons. His relations with his colleagues and his party were uneasy, and becoming more so. According to his own account, when the 1951 election came he let Randolph Churchill know that he was not eager to join any Conservative government that might be formed by Winston.[10] Whether this message was conveyed with clarity is not known, but Churchill did not strive officiously to keep Hailsham's ministerial career alive. Hailsham would doubtless have preferred the satisfaction of refusing an offer. 'I had hoped that you would not mind the omission to offer you a job,' wrote Hugh Molson, his colleague from Tory Reform Committee days, 'because I thought you had decided to decline any offer.'[11] Molson was one of those who thought Hailsham would be wise not to interrupt his career at the Bar until he could go back into high office with a big position in his profession, 'as Simonds and Walter Monckton have done – not to mention your father'.

Hailsham told Butler at the end of 1952 that he had 'squandered' over half his adult life in public affairs: 'it was an expensive foible' and he would be better off on some quiet judicial bench.[12] A year later he turned down a speaking invitation from Charles Hill. 'It is as well to know when one has missed the bus for once and all, and nothing is more ridiculous and undignified than to go on running after it . . . Our leaders have made it too plain to me that they are neither interested in my views nor careful of the support I was willing to offer.'[13] The thin skin was easily pricked. Sometimes he found offence where there was none, and this could goad him on to impatience, anger or gross exaggeration. These characteristics had been evident since his schooldays.

He was occasionally reminded of this. In 1952 he had a letter from

143

an Eton contemporary urging him to take up the case of Seretse Khama.* 'I actively disliked you at school,' wrote his accuser. 'The occasion when you beat me on a trumped-up charge of being rude to College Watermen was naturally more memorable to me than to you, and in any case there is little likelihood of your seeing me quite from that angle again. *Eheu fugaces posteriores*.'[14] The bearer of these evil memories went on to say that Seretse's case had been bungled by both parties, and that he should be sent back with his wife and children to his own country to take his proper place as chief of his people.

Hailsham replied: 'I quite agree with what you write about Seretse; indeed I said as much when the matter first arose in the Commons nearly two years ago. I am sorry about the watermen; you are quite right. I had forgotten them though not, as you modestly supposed, yourself.'[15]

As he told the victim of the miscarriage of justice, he had spoken up when the Seretse issue was raised in the Commons by Fenner Brockway after much difficulty in the early hours of the morning of 28 March 1950.[16] The Labour government had failed to give any justification for its decision to continue Seretse's exile, and the Conservatives were unwilling to come out plainly for him – as was shown by their continuance of his exile after they came to power in 1951. Hogg (who was still then in the Commons) therefore spoke for himself when he said that the case 'symbolises the determination of this government to override the decision of a native people to accept as their prince and princess the person and his wife whom they would wish to see.'[17] Behind the inhumanity of the decision were wider implications: 'In the long run the future of our country and of its Empire depends very largely on the confidence with which we are regarded by the African race . . .'; and he pointed out that Seretse's cause was being taken up eagerly by communists all over the world. But the appeal fell on deaf ears. Two years later, he was telling Brockway that he still had no support from his party: 'I am feeling very isolated on my perch'.[18] The isolation was to increase.

---

* Seretse Khama, the hereditary chief of the Bamangwato people of Bechuanaland (then a British Protectorate, later Botswana) married a white English woman. A clear majority of his people wanted him to take up his position as their hereditary chief with his white consort. The British Government brought him to London for discussions and then refused to let him return. Churchill fairly described the episode as a 'disreputable transaction'. Seretse was exiled until his country became independent in 1966, when he returned to take his place at the head of its affairs. It was widely suspected that the pusillanimity of British governments (Labour and Conservative alike) was due to apprehensions about the reactions of the new Nationalist administration in South Africa. For a full account see *A Marriage of Inconvenience: the Persecution of Ruth and Seretse Khama*: Michael Dutfield: 1990.

The speech on Seretse was a model: succinct, restrained, thoughtful. He could not always summon up these qualities to order. His gift for invective, however, was unabated and never deserted him. When Lord Ammon asked the Government whether legal action could not be taken against Dr Hewlett Johnson, the 'Red Dean' of Canterbury, for slighting references to British troops, Hailsham said he thought the Dean merely absurd – politically. But the religious problem could not be so easily ridden off. The Dean had caused scandal to the church, and 'we cannot afford to have clowns in gaiters'; it would be a mistake 'if we allowed the mockery which this vain and ridiculous old man must excite to blind our eyes to the dangerous plight' to which the Church of England had fallen.[19]

The speeches on the Schuman Plan for pooling the resources of the European coal and steel industry (see p. 125) and on Seretse Khama had demonstrated a willingness to speak independently of the party line. When commercial television came to be debated in 1953/4 he felt impelled to do so again. This time it brought about a serious breach. There was a powerful lobby in the Conservative party pressing for the BBC's monopoly to be broken at last; and for public service broadcasting to be exposed to competition from television financed by advertising revenue. This lobby persuaded the government to act. In November 1953 a White Paper was published recommending the introduction of an element of competition to 'allow private enterprise to play a fuller part and to reduce the financial commitment of the state'.[20] Hailsham was wholeheartedly and bitterly opposed to this initiative. He joined the National Television Council, a pressure group whose object was to prevent commercial television. Its President was Lord Waverly and Chairman Lady Violet Bonham Carter. Among Hailsham's fellow Vice-Presidents were Lords Beveridge, Halifax and Jowitt; and Julian Huxley, Harold Nicolson, Lady Pakenham and assorted Bishops. A formidable grouping but one in which the Conservative hierarchy was noticeable by its absence.

When the second reading of the Bill was debated in the Lords in July 1954, Hailsham was chosen to wind up for the opponents. They determined to press their hostility to a division. Nothing could have demonstrated more open defiance. Hailsham, however, entered the debate with advantages. He had had more experience of broadcasting than any other Peer; and when the Earl of Selkirk wound up the debate for the Government, he said '. . . it is great fun to listen to Lord Hailsham at any time, especially as he is a television star'. The opponents of the Bill had arguments of real weight. There were dangers inherent in the commercialising of broadcasting: a decline of Reithian values with a concomitant emphasis on prurience, violence and the trivialising of current affairs. Competition, the opponents contended, would be achieved only in a theoretical sense. The viewing public would not have a genuine choice: it would be 'a competition between two things each trying to present the same programme in opposition and trying to capture the same maximum audience'.[21] These arguments still read well in hindsight; and the Government, with what Hailsham called 'inspissated ignorance' appeared to be unaware of the perils. They thought their Bill was a blow for freedom, and their supporters were quoting *Areopagitica*. The situation was made for Hailsham, bursting to explain that the author of the address on the theme of a puissant nation aroused from its slumbers to freedom of speech was 'that ruthless lackey of tyranny John Milton, the Latin Secretary to the Commonwealth'. Unfortunately, however, his speech betrayed the weakness which he sometimes indulged in debate: exaggeration and irresponsibility. He accused the government of having added intellectual perversity to their crimes 'to a degree almost bordering on insanity'; and he stigmatised the (admittedly nonsensical) requirement that commercial programmes should have a tone and style that were 'predominantly British' as 'barbarous, illiterate, cretinous, philistine nonsense, without the benefit of the parliamentary draftsman'.[22] It would have been sufficient to ask, as he did, whether Father Christmas is predominantly British in style and tone. And it did not help his entirely respectable cause to epitomise the Bill as 'a vicious Bill which is wholly contrary to the tradition of British liberty'.

Here was a striking example of Hailsham's ability to 'get the big things right', as Margaret Thatcher was to say of him; but also of his maddening tendency, which broke surface from time to time throughout his career, to allow his enthusiasm for his cause to boil over. When his friends – and enemies – accused him of lacking judgment, they were generally thinking more of how he said things than what he said.

The television debate was a spoiled chance. The opponents were soundly beaten in the division by 130 to 64. 'The general view at the time was that I had badly overstated my case, perhaps from excessive enthusiasm.' The general view was fair. But some of his postbag was not. To a correspondent who maintained that the BBC was part of a conspiracy to line Jewish pockets, he replied: 'Personally I think you are suffering from Jews on the brain. I do not think there is any reason to suppose that the members of this talented race are more numerous in the BBC than any other branch of the entertainment business.' There was an endearing quality which made it hard not to forgive the excesses. He himself thought, however, that he would not be forgiven this time, and that he had 'properly cooked his goose with the powers that be'. He regarded his political handicaps at the time as '(i) my political past in the Commons; (ii) repeated appearances on the television with Edgar Lustgarten, Bob Boothby and Michael Foot; and (iii) a sharp and wholly unsuccessful attempt in the House of Lords to prevent the introduction of commercial television'.[23] It seemed to him that the breach with his party had now widened to the point where it would be wise to leave public affairs and concentrate on the Bar.

★

While Hailsham was wrestling with the money worries of Carters Corner and suffering the disappointments of politics, he was steadily building his practice in Paper Buildings. A quick survey of the Law Reports in the early fifties shows that his traditional personal injuries work was broadening into other fields, and there was evidence of what is sometimes called, a little patronisingly, a 'good quality' practice. His old friends, the solicitors Jacobson Ridley and Herbert Baron, continued faithful, and civil work was beginning to come also from the Crown. His name occurs in the Appeal Cases before the House of Lords and Privy Council and there was a series of appeals from Canada. He was led by Kenneth Diplock in another group of cases from the Treasury Solicitor. Diplock had taken silk and was clearly on his way to the High Court Bench, when Hailsham would become head of chambers. He took a number of pupils in this period, among them Ian Gilmour. The encounter began with a royal dressing down from the pupil master for Gilmour's failure to read any textbooks for the Bar Final Examinations which he had taken shortly before. That cleared the air like a thunderstorm, and they always got on well afterwards. Hailsham spent a lot of time with his pupils in the evenings, talking about his work and about life. A liberal education was his pupil's account. Gilmour loved him from the start.[24]

Hailsham did not become Queen's Counsel until 1953. Lord Simon, who was a personal friend, told him that he could have had silk for the asking when he returned from the war, and his father was disappointed never to have seen him in the front row in Court. But his war service and the Tory Reform Committee intervened. There is also some evidence that his application for silk was delayed because of the nature of his practice. This was largely personal injury work with insurance companies as clients, until the early 1950s. These companies may have indicated that they would not be able to continue to instruct him if he took silk. In any case, that step always involves rebuilding a practice. It was Lord Simonds* who as Lord Chancellor finally gave him silk, and when he retired in 1954, Hailsham wrote a note of thanks: 'I was personally most grateful to you not merely for your positive kindness, but also for your abstention from the easy and popular sport of Hogg baiting which attracts so many of your former colleagues.'[25]

This was a curious letter for the Lord Chancellor to receive. Did Hailsham feel a periodic sense of persecution in his profession as he did in politics? Or was it simply that he could have a bad day in Court in just the same way as he could in parliament? Lord Rawlinson, who was often in both arenas with him, thought him erratic. 'Sometimes he would put in a towering performance, on others disastrous. He was capable of brilliance, or of leaving a situation that was irrecoverable. He was a poor judge of a point; he could be seized by a sudden impulse and go off at a tangent. But he had a broad sweeping intellect which towered over his contemporaries.'[26] Judges can be rough with advocates, nowhere more so than in the highest appellate tribunals. But this is recognised as a fact of life by the Bar; and it is not likely that a man of Hailsham's courage and pugnacity would have allowed himself to be upset by bloody-mindedness from the Bench.

The art of advocacy in Court is different from parliamentary debating skill. Hailsham was probably more at home with the latter. This does not mean that he was not an effective advocate (there are a number of instances in the Law Reports of tributes from Judges to his energy and ingenuity) but he lacked the gentler techniques of 'playing' the Court like a fisherman. An advocate can so contrive his argument that the Judge supplies the conclusion himself. If the Judge is following the argument and makes Counsel's point for him, he is the more likely to be convinced. It is only human nature. But such skills require patience and restraint.

It is possible, none the less, that had Hailsham's practice been left undisturbed after he took silk, he would have been appointed to that 'quiet judicial bench' about which he had written to Butler. That might have been the route to becoming Lord Chancellor. But it was

* The first Lord Hailsham appointed Simonds to the Chancery Bench. He was a forthright Judge of the 'strict constructionist' school, who may be remembered chiefly for his intense hostility to Lord Denning's approach to the law. Intellectual contempt is not too strong a phrase to describe his feeling about what Denning was doing to the development of English law.

not to be. The other magnetic pole in his life began again to exert its attraction, as usual when it was least expected.

14

Suez

ALTHOUGH Hailsham had declared to Butler and others his utter disenchantment with politics in the years following his father's death, there were indications that the game was not quite lost. He told Geoffrey Hirst that 'for a time at least' he would do no more speaking and concentrate on earning his living. 'Whether it is the end or *reculer pour mieux sauter* remains to be seen.'[1] Some of his colleagues refused to countenance failure. 'Failure and Quintin do not go together', Manningham-Buller wrote, and advised him to keep contact with his parliamentary friends, 'for the day may well come when we shall see you on the Woolsack, and a *slight* contact with politics will I am sure help you to get there.'[2] The flare of ambition did not fade more than momentarily. He was attracted by Manningham-Buller's idea, but a political contact which had reduced itself to 'slight' would not have satisfied him for long.

None the less, it was a surprise when Anthony Eden, who had become Prime Minister in April 1955, began to sound him out for a post in government towards the end of the year, using as intermediaries first Harold Macmillan and then Lord Salisbury. Hailsham was not sure. He considered that the Conservatives would lose power within perhaps three years. He was approaching fifty, a new silk and head of chambers, with four children to educate and two houses to maintain. In retrospect, he thought of these years out of office as golden ones, in which, as Molson put it in his friendly letter advising him to stay at the Bar, 'you have given pledges to fortune by repeatedly reproducing your species.'[3] In 1955 Douglas was 10, Mary Claire 8, Frances 6 and James 4. To disturb his practice for a few years would be playing ducks and drakes with his earning power. There would have to be a powerful incentive. The first offer of Paymaster-General just before Christmas 1955 was not that. It carried a stipend of £3,000 a year (£38,000 in 1997) and was an odd-job-man's post in government. After a couple of hours thought in an empty church, he explained to Salisbury that it was an impossible idea, hardly imagining that the stakes would be raised.

Eden then offered the Admiralty. By now it was the spring of 1956. Hailsham was to replace Lord Cilcennin (Jim Thomas) who wanted to go in the summer. This was a different matter. The office of First Lord was ancient and illustrious, even though its importance had been reduced and it did not carry a seat in the Cabinet. He accepted. Mary was happy about it, but he had a miserable time explaining himself to his clerk and the other occupants of Paper Buildings. He pressed Eden to bring in the appointment quickly, for if it were put about that he was leaving the Bar for a government job his practice would be blighted. 'No one was likely to brief as leading counsel a First Lord of the Admiralty in waiting.' Eden understood the 'personal dilemma' and promised to discuss timing with Salisbury. But before he could, the news leaked in the *Observer,* and worse was to come. Just before the time fixed for the handover, there occurred the dismal and humiliating 'frogman' incident. Bulganin and Khrushchev, the Soviet leaders, arrived for a goodwill visit in a cruiser which docked in Portsmouth harbour. During their visit the frogman, Commander Crabb, disappeared, apparently inspecting the bottom of the cruiser's hull. On whose orders, and for what purpose, no one knew. Hailsham thought it one of the most foolish, unedifying and dishonourable episodes in the whole of the post-war period. The immediate consequence, however, was that the handover was again delayed. Eden felt that a change of First Lord while enquiries were pending would be tantamount to an admission that the Minister, or at least the Admiralty, was implicated. '. . . I do not want to be unfair to Jim [Cilcennin]', he wrote on 17 May. 'I do hope it will not upset your plans if we wait a few more weeks.'[4] The date was fixed for the beginning of September. Hailsham chafed. He was left sitting in the air, his practice withering, correcting the proofs of a book he had written on Monopolies and Restrictive Practices.

While he was waiting for September to come, he also began to ponder a plan for the future of the Navy to form part of the impending radical review of the services. He described this in an unpublished retrospect written some ten years later.[5] In Europe a nuclear stalemate had been reached between East and West. The armies which faced each other across the iron curtain were prepared for a war which, because of the nuclear deterrent, would never be fought. The communist strategy was to foment trouble and insurrection wherever it could elsewhere in the world. It must therefore be the strategy of the West to frustrate this ambition. Until now, the colonial powers had relied on military bases retained in their former possessions. A chain of such British bases stretched from Egypt through the Middle East to Hong Kong, and from Cyprus through Africa to the Cape. Hailsham considered these bases to be precarious. 'They could only be retained at the cost of continuous political friction. The economic resources and political regimes they guarded were of doubtful endurance and popular support.' He concluded that the sheer power of the communist forces could only be contained through the Navy: but a Navy with a difference.

He went to see Winston. The Former Naval Person congratulated him, and advised him to get himself a boat because the Navy liked to see its First Lord afloat. Churchill was a hulk of his former self, speech was difficult, and the capacious mind flickered only intermittently. 'His mind was not so much failing as withdrawn into himself, and from the dark caverns where it reposed, it would suddenly return with devastating clarity and perception, only to disappear again as suddenly.' Hailsham asked his advice about the nuclear stalemate. It was given in few words: 'Indestructible retaliation. That is the secret.' Hailsham inferred that Churchill meant a second strike missile launched under water, as Polaris became: something 'which could be trusted to blast any enemy to hell after he had destroyed us'.[6] The new Navy would also need conventional resources with a high degree of mobility: modern carriers to deliver airstrikes and modern transports to provide groundstrikes.

The premises on which this analysis was based were sound, but Hailsham was never to get the chance to argue his case. When, in January 1957, and after Hailsham had been First Lord of the Admiralty for the few months of the Suez crisis, Macmillan heard of his plan for the first time, he is reputed to have said, 'I hear he wants to rebuild the Navy: that will never do'; and he made him Minister of Education instead. Suez, which was to change so much of the political and strategic landscape, would prove how alert Khrushchev's Russia was to stir up trouble for the West wherever opportunity offered; and the lumbering amphibious operation which was finally mounted against Egypt would demonstrate how badly a new and more mobile strike force was needed. The plan was damned by the very crisis which proved its soundness.

The Middle East had been darkening since the early summer, when the last British troops left the Canal Zone and Hailsham was waiting to take up post. In July, John Foster Dulles, the American Secretary of State, withdrew an offer to finance the construction of the Aswan High Dam, a vast project for irrigating the Nile Valley, on which Egypt had depended since beyond historical memory. Within days, Colonel Nasser, the President of Egypt and leader of a group of young army officers who had deposed the corrupt playboy King Farouk, gave his answer. He announced to a huge excited crowd in Alexandria that their government had taken control of the Canal. Eden reacted immediately. 'No arrangements for the future of this great international waterway could be acceptable to Her Majesty's Government', he told the Commons in July, 'which would leave it in the unfettered control of a single power.'[7] He and his French ally, Mollet, belonged to a generation haunted by Munich. For them, Nasser was a latter-day dictator who had to be resisted at all costs, or the malignant consequences of appeasement would repeat themselves. At the same time, Nasser was increasing pressure on Israel. When his proposal that she should relinquish the Negev region in return for peace was inevitably rejected, he set about progressive strangulation.

Contingency plans for armed intervention by Britain and France against Egypt had been under discussion from the time of the nationalisation of the Canal in late July. The Chiefs of Staff, Lord Mountbatten, the First Sea Lord, Sir Gerald Templer and Sir Dermot Boyle had formulated a plan on Eden's instructions with the code name *Musketeer*, for an amphibious assault on Alexandria preceded by an air and sea bombardment. Mountbatten was profoundly unhappy about it. Alexandria is a densely populated city and the bombardment and subsequent fighting in the streets would cause carnage. He thought too that the reaction in Commonwealth and non-aligned countries would be disastrous. While the plan was being prepared, he had tried to put to Eden that the 'absolutely paramount consideration is the marshalling of world opinion on our side', but Cilcennin had told him that, while he agreed with Mountbatten, as a Chief of Staff he should not concern himself with political considerations.[8] Now Cilcennin was to be replaced by Hailsham. According to a note made by Mountbatten in 1966, Cilcennin had 'warned me that Lord Hailsham's articles in the press and his general known view about force would make my position extremely difficult in the Admiralty since he was certain not to agree with my views'.[9] He could have been forgiven for fearing the worst from Hailsham's supposed bellicosity, but the fears turned out to be groundless.

Hailsham took office on 3 September. He spent the first few days finding his bearings and moving his family into a flat over Admiralty Arch. The choice of the flat was apparently Lady Hailsham's. She refused to live in Admiralty House on the ground that it was huge and unmanageable. The flat also had disadvantages. 'It was inconvenient and noisy, and our sleep was much interrupted by the noise of lorries accelerating under the arch, and pigeons making love at unseasonable hours on our windowsill.' Notwithstanding these hazards, he and his family looked forward to the more agreeable consequences of office. He was appointed to the Privy Council and at the same time began to enjoy the Navy's celebrated hospitality. The Navy took to this boisterous, rather porky figure in his plain peaked cap, altogether reminiscent of Winston. Hailsham seemed not to mind making a fool of himself, even risking being winched down on to the deck of a destroyer from a helicopter. He was very evidently enjoying himself. Mountbatten was First Sea Lord (the Hailsham girls learned how to curtsey) and Sir Caspar John, son of the painter Augustus John, the Fifth. But for Suez, life promised to be pleasant.

The new First Lord had not been briefed either by Cilcennin or Mountbatten on the contingency planning, which he knew must have been going on. The first glimpse of what his position would be appeared in a letter he received from Cilcennin in August. 'I am afraid I shall have to withdraw my suggestion', Cilcennin wrote, 'that you should have a preliminary look at certain papers, as I haven't received approval from No. 10. The answer was that as the Suez crisis has postponed the consideration of the Radical Review of the Services until October, you will have plenty of time during September to read yourself in. I am so sorry about this as I know that with all the reading to be done it would have been easier for you to have had a flying start: but there it is.'[10] From the time he took post at the beginning of September until the drama reached its dénouement two months later, Hailsham, in common with the other service Ministers, John Hare and Nigel Birch, was vouchsafed only occasional hints about the evolving situation, military, political and diplomatic. It is difficult to tell from official records exactly what they knew at each stage. But Hailsham wrote two accounts of his own, neither of which is published. The first is part of a memoir written in 1965[11] which remained in draft among his papers. The second was particularly directed to Suez, and came to be written in curious circumstances in 1981.[12]

Towards the end of his life, Mountbatten prepared a series of television programmes of autobiographical material, including his own recollections of the Suez crisis, stipulating that they should not be shown until after his death. The programme on Suez could not be shown because the Cabinet Office withheld consent, but the content gained some notoriety through two articles by Bernard Levin in *The Times*, containing quotations from the transcript of the Suez interview, which had somehow leaked.[13] Hailsham wrote to the newspaper to say that, although he held Mountbatten's memory in the deepest veneration, his account of the Suez affair was entirely inaccurate.[14] On being shown the second of Levin's articles, he chose plainer language to annotate it: 'He does not realise that poor Dickie's account is virtually fiction from beginning to end.'[15] Shortly afterwards, he decided that he should write down his own recollections of the crisis, in phases, with particular reference to his relations with Mountbatten as First Sea Lord. The account was never intended to be published. Its purpose was no more than to correct the inaccuracies of Mountbatten's recollections, if it should ever again be necessary to do so.

Shortly after taking office, Hailsham made a formal request to be told the contingency planning, making it clear that he was not prepared to take 'no' for an answer. Mountbatten told him that the Prime Minister's consent was necessary. Clearance was sought and obtained within 48 hours. In the 1981 document and *A Sparrow's Flight*, Hailsham puts this exchange some weeks after he took office; but it must have been earlier. On the morning of 7 September (four days after Hailsham took office) there was a meeting between Eden and the Chiefs of Staff to discuss *Musketeer*. Mountbatten obtained the Prime Minister's approval to give his political views. He said that in his opinion there would be massive destruction and civilian casualties before the first troops set foot ashore, and that Britain would be taken to the United Nations by Egypt. Templer backed up Mountbatten by saying that the campaign might take two to three months and that it could take as much as 23 days to reach Cairo. Eden was shaken, and the upshot was that the Chiefs were instructed to prepare a new plan (*Musketeer Revise*) which was substantially the one which was implemented in November, with landings at Port Said instead of Alexandria.[16]

According to Mountbatten's biographer, Philip Ziegler, Hailsham told Mountbatten that at a cabinet that afternoon (7 September) Eden had put forward all Mountbatten's arguments of the morning.[17] Whether or not Hailsham attended the cabinet, by then he certainly knew the original *Musketeer* plan and its horrendous potential, for he sent Mountbatten a handwritten note dated 7 September reading: 'I can't thank you enough for what you did today.'[18] He was briefed about the *Musketeer* plan not by Mountbatten himself, but by a young naval captain. When the briefing was finished and Hailsham had learned for the first time that the attack was to be at Alexandria, and not (as he had imagined) Port Said, he asked the young officer what he thought of the plan. The captain said he thought it was madness. 'So do I,' said Hailsham. He had heard accounts from brother officers in the Middle East of the effects of flat trajectory naval bombardments, and he could imagine what it would do to Alexandria, a city that he knew quite well. According to the 1981 document: 'I spoke directly to the PM, and, as a result, and to my intense relief, the attack on Alex was abandoned as the preferred plan and a contingent descent on Port Said substituted.' Hailsham certainly added his voice to the chorus of alarm on 7 September, but he is not entitled to the entire credit for the change of plan.

He was still very far from being fully informed, particularly about the political aspect. What concerned him at this phase was the justification for war. As a *casus belli*, the nationalisation of the Canal was already stale, if it had ever been adequate. 'Such causes', he wrote, 'must be taken up at once or not at all.'[19] According to the 1981 paper, he discussed his anxieties with a number of colleagues and found that they shared his view that a descent on Egypt was not feasible from the point of view of international law and the United Nations Charter. He did not say who these colleagues were, but they must have included Mountbatten, with whom his personal relations were very warm, and would probably have included Monckton, who was Defence Minister uneasily until October, and his fellow service Ministers, Anthony Head (who succeeded Monckton and was replaced by John Hare) and Nigel Birch. It is not clear how plainly these anxieties were voiced to Eden, even by Monckton who was in the cabinet, or, if they were, whether they had any effect on the course he took. Eden had known that Monckton had had doubts about the operation and had wanted to resign since late September; and he finally replaced him on 18 October.[20] In any event, Hailsham was not in the cabinet and not privy to the diplomatic situation as it unfolded.

Israel now moved into the foreground. Since the nationalisation of the Canal, Nasser had openly boasted of an Arab Empire led by Egypt to destroy the state of Israel. The destruction of Israel was not something which Hailsham thought Britain could conceivably contemplate. Israel's right to exist was beyond argument, for Britain particularly so because of the Balfour Declaration. But beyond this, Hailsham was a friend of Jewry. In a speech at a dinner for Chaim Herzog, the Israeli President, in 1984 in Middle Temple Hall, he said, '. . . speaking for myself, and perhaps not only for myself, I think the world owes some reparation to the Jews. They have suffered too long, too continuously, too unjustly and too much.'[21]

He never could understand anti-semitism, so persistent yet so irrational. It could even become fashionable in the hands of writers like Belloc and Chesterton. Religious prejudice was hateful, but prejudice by blood or cultural inheritance, he thought, was just nonsense.[22] Hailsham's magnanimous spirit was greatly appreciated by Jews; after his speech at the Herzog dinner, Sir Harry Woolf wrote: '. . . even by the standards you set, a towering performance . . . appreciated very much by your audience – particularly the representatives present of a small, vulnerable nation and an oversensitive Jewish community.'[23]

On 25 October, Nasser formed a joint General Staff with Jordan and Syria for the purpose of a concerted assault on Israel. Hailsham wrote in retrospect: 'I appreciated (correctly as I believe) that he intended either an attack on Israel or to compel Israel to attack him by closing the Eilat entrance to the Red Sea. I also correctly, in my view, appreciated that, if so, Israel would be entitled to a pre-emptive strike under the self defence article in the Charter and that, having regard to what we had suffered at Nasser's hand we should be extremely foolish not to safeguard the Canal, which would effectively support Israel.'[24] This was very close to the course which events actually took, but the appreciation was Hailsham's own. He was certainly not aware of the Anglo-French-Israeli discussions which led to the secret Protocol of Sèvres of 24 October. 'I am bound to say that if negotiations took place between the three parties at this time, the First Lord of the Admiralty was not on the distribution list of those who were kept informed.'[25]

In the final phase, Hailsham recollected, 'the service Ministers (self, Hare, Birch) were for the first time enlightened as to the true nature of the operation.' In view of his own speculations, Hailsham was not surprised when he was told at this meeting that the intention was to activate the Port Said plan and attack the Egyptian airfields, to coincide with an anticipated Israeli strike across the desert. 'This, however, was almost immediately before the event. Up to that point I had been deliberately kept in the dark by higher authority and I was extremely put out by the deception.'[26]

The belated briefing must have taken place between the date of the collusive agreement between Britain, France and Israel, 24 October, and the Israeli attack across the Sinai peninsula on 29 October. The invasion was followed in rapid succession by the issue of the Anglo-French ultimatum (which had been agreed upon at Sèvres), the departure of the assault convoy from Malta and British bombing of Egyptian targets. While scenes of primal emotion were being played out in the commons, Mountbatten's long unease about the whole affair erupted in what Hailsham described as 'one tense moment of drama'.

On 2 November, Mountbatten wrote to Eden appealing to him to accept 'the resolution of the overwhelming majority of the United Nations to cease military operations and to beg you to turn back the assault convoy before it is too late . . .'[27] The Prime Minister thanked him for his letter, but said that he was not prepared to go back. Mountbatten then turned to the First Lord, who was at that moment on his way down to Carters Corner for a few hours of peace and quiet away from the pandemonium. Somewhere near East Grinstead Hailsham's old Austin was flagged down by a police car and he was told he was urgently needed at the Admiralty. He returned to find the First Sea Lord in an excited state. 'Dickie was having a brainstorm.' A letter awaited him which read in full:

My Dear First Lord,   4th November 1956

On 2nd November 1956 I took the unprecedented course for a serving officer of writing direct to the Prime Minister and reminding him that he had been fully aware of my great unhappiness at the prospect of launching military operations against Egypt.

I admitted that it was not the business of a serving officer to question the political decisions of his government; and told him that I had done everything in my power to carry out his orders, as in duty bound, loyally and to the full in making all the necessary naval preparations for building up a position in which we could have negotiated from strength.

I went on to say that now the decisive step of armed intervention by the British had been taken, now that the bombing had started and now that the assault convoy was on its way from Malta, I was writing to appeal to him to accept the resolution of the overwhelming majority of the United Nations to cease military operations; and to beg him to turn back the assault convoy before it was too late, as I felt that the actual landing of troops could only spread the war with untold misery and world wide repercussions.

He spoke to me on the telephone to thank me for my letter; he said he fully understood my feelings but was not prepared to turn back the assault convoy. He pointed out that our operations had been directed only against military targets and that no civilians had been killed.

The situation is now, however, worse in that General Keightley has telegraphed that any chances of an easy entry into Port Said are removed.

Though I realise as a result of this telegram that everything is being done, within the limits of the current plan, to lessen civilian casualties, I must make it clear that in my view such casualties cannot be avoided and it must in the main fall to the Navy to inflict them.

However repugnant the task the Navy will carry out its orders. Nevertheless as its professional head I must register the strongest possible protest at this use of my service; and would ask you as the responsible Minister to convey that protest to the Prime Minister.

I regret that a serving officer cannot back his protest by resignation at a time like this, so I must ask you to handle this whole matter on behalf of the Navy. Bearing in mind all the implications I must ask you, after consulting the Prime Minister, to give me an order to stay or to go.

> Yours very sincerely
> Mountbatten of Burma[28]

Hailsham 'handled the whole matter' immediately. He sat down and wrote out an admirably economical reply in his own hand, without consulting the Prime Minister or anyone else.

My dear First Sea Lord,   5 November 56

Thank you for your letter of yesterday by hand of officer. I am glad you have taken the step of informing me of your correspondence with the Prime Minister, of which I should not otherwise have been aware.

I think you are well entitled to entrust your doubts, difficulties and protest to me, as the responsible Minister.

It seems to me that the position is quite plain. If anything happens to impair the honour of the Navy I must resign.

In the meantime, you are entitled to be protected by a direct order from me. It is that you remain at your post until further orders.

I will do my best to comply with your request that the Prime Minister is acquainted with your views as soon as possible.

> Your sincerely
> Hailsham[29]

As he had promised, Hailsham at once informed the Prime Minister of this correspondence, and on the following day, 6

November, he wrote again to Mountbatten to let him know that Eden had confirmed the order.[30]

The friendly relations between Hailsham and Mountbatten were undisturbed by this episode. Meanwhile the Suez crisis moved to its ignominious end. Britain and France yielded to the international call for ceasefire on 6 November before the Canal could be militarily secured. The United States, implacably opposed to the use of force, stood by while a run on sterling gathered speed. No one wanted to hold the currency of a country so politically isolated. The Russians, who at the same moment were brutally repressing the Hungarian uprising, threatened rocket attacks against Britain and France. The failure of the United States to support Britain was aggravated by what Hailsham took to be a note of sanctimonious censure. The fighting over, and the Canal blocked by the Egyptian sinking of a large number of vessels, the Americans now joined in the objections to British salvage vessels and crews being employed in clearance. In a speech at Oxford on 30 November[31] Hailsham took the United States to task:

> We do not mind being criticised; we are quite prepared to answer criticism, because we believe that discussion, and that events as they happen, will prove us right. But we will *not* be sermonised. We do not propose to be sent to Coventry, and please we do not wish to hear any moral lectures from those whose moral weakness and incapacity to see the facts was the precipitating factor in the present crisis.

These rousing sentiments were badly needed by his humiliated fellow-countrymen. Then, apparently forgetting his own injunction against sermons, he addressed the Israelis in Old Testament tones:

> I sympathise, never more deeply, with the desire of Jews throughout the world to return to the land of promise after so many years of persecution and exile. But remember the curse of Naboth's vineyard. It would be an ill chance which brought you back to the land of your fathers if you incurred thereby the curse of Jezebel. Be gentle to Ishmael: he is your brother. Let not the ripening of the harvests you gather from the deserts you have reclaimed be at the expense of those who have dwelt in the land for centuries. Resettle the refugees: offer them generous terms of compensation. It would be a small price to pay for the goodwill of your neighbours.

The clearing of the Canal continued to be a live issue weeks after the cease-fire and into December. The Egyptians wanted no part of the Anglo-French salvage fleet which had already started work in the Port Said area. Third world countries including India were outraged by the Anglo-French invasion and supported Egypt. In an effort to restore morale at home. Eden tried to put pressure on Hammarskjöld, the Secretary-General of the United Nations and, through him, the Egyptians, by linking the evacuation of British and French troops to acceptance of the Anglo-French salvage fleet. But General Wheeler, the U.N.'s representative in charge of clearing the Canal and a very capable engineer, did not appear to be in awe of the reputation of the allied fleet, and seemed to Britain too inclined to accommodate Nasser.

In this intractable situation, in which the vital objective was to re-open the Canal to shipping, Hailsham paid a visit to the Mediterranean fleet. There was an unscheduled stop in Port Said, where he was unexpectedly faced by the press and asked about the future of the Anglo-French salvage fleet. General Wheeler was reported to have said that he could assemble a fleet comparable with the Anglo-French one within ten days. Hailsham told the newsmen: 'That is a proposition which could only be greeted with total incredulity by my advisers . . . they tell me it is nonsense.' According to *The Times* he spoke forcefully for ten minutes. Hailsham was understandably anxious to use the Anglo-French salvage vessels and crews to fend off criticism in the press that Nasser was imposing his own terms for clearing the Canal; but the philippic was ill-informed and Wheeler cleared the Canal in under four months at moderate cost.

Suez was an episode which, like Munich, seemed to crystallise the illusions and fears of a whole political generation. It cast a cruel light on Britain's blindness to the new imperatives of super-power politics, and her own diminished standing in the world. Politically, it was a deplorable reverse which could never be righted. Militarily, it was equally a disaster. The delay in acting, from July to November, allowed American and Commonwealth opposition to the use of force to build up, and the ponderous pace of the assault convoy as it wallowed across the Mediterranean virtually ensured that the business would not be completed.

When Hailsham accepted Anthony Eden's invitation to move from the Bar to the Admiralty he had expected to get three years constructive work and then go back to his profession. He could not have foreseen that he would be away for eight years, and he could have had no idea that he would be plunged into a warlike adventure within weeks of taking office. He hated the whole thing as much as did Mountbatten. Politically, he shared responsibility for putting at hazard innocent civilian lives and the outlawing of Britain in the international community. At the same time he was imprisoned in ignorance by his Prime Minister. He had to demand (and make it a resignation issue that he be told) details of the contingency planning when he took office. Only on the very eve of the operation was he finally given the operational details. This was no way to treat a Minister who was politically answerable for the actions of the Navy. He deplored equally the disingenuousness of the Government's diplomacy, and what he called 'our tergiversation when victory was assured'. Doubtful, or worse, about going in, and as doubtful about stopping when we did, his position was one of acute dilemma. Yet he never considered resigning for a moment. That cannot be accounted weakness – a charge of which some members of the Cabinet could not easily be acquitted. It was rather an honourable determination to stay where he was and do his best when his support was urgently needed by his colleagues, the servicemen for whom he was responsible, and his country. The time for resigning, he considered, was either before or after, but not while serving men's lives are put in the balance. He emerged briefly into the limelight after the fighting was ended. Then resignation was equally out of the question. 'I had no doubt of my immediate duty, which was to pick up the pieces as best I could and not allow Britain to remain a scapegoat or to be traduced.' It was an unhappy passage.

15

Education and Party Chairman

QUINTIN Hailsham used to say that there was plenty of evidence for his favourite heresy, that Providence had a sense of humour. If so, it was a cruel joke to drop him unawares and without warning into the storm centre of the two most divisive moral crises to be presented to Britain in this century, Munich and Suez. He was thankful when Suez was over, so that he could get down to the delayed review of the affairs of the Royal Navy. Even that, however, was not in the providential scheme. In January 1957, with the crisis just passed, he was called to Downing Street in the middle of a children's party in Admiralty House, to be told that Eden could not carry on as Prime Minister. The choice of the new leader was supervised by Lord Salisbury, whose celebrated question, 'Is it Hawold or is it Wab?' is likely to stand as the most effective way the Conservative party can devise for securing a smooth succession. Harold Macmillan was quickly chosen. *The Times* announced Eden's resignation on 10 January and Macmillan's succession on the following day. Hailsham hardly knew him but did not think his record over Suez was a creditable one. Macmillan had been strongly for military action against Egypt during the summer and early autumn, but had called for an immediate withdrawal when a run on the pound developed during the operation itself. 'First in, first out' was Harold Wilson's brutal summary. Hailsham considered that, while it would have been legitimate to be either a hawk or a dove throughout, to be a hawk ahead of the event and a dove when success was certain was to get the worst of all possible worlds.

Within a week of the children's party, he was again summoned to No. 10, this time from Carters Corner. He bicycled the six miles to Polegate to take the London train. Macmillan told him that he was to be Minister of Education with a seat in the Cabinet. Hailsham pondered the improbable turn of events as he cycled home in the dark. 'As I laboured up the hill on the return journey, my lamp swayed backwards and forwards on the road in front. I meditated on the fact that after four and a half months in office, I was in the cabinet . . . I would have no chance to rebuild the Navy.'[1]

He and his family had fallen in love with the Navy, and he received the news of his removal with distinctly mixed feelings. It is not obvious why Macmillan did it. David Eccles, the outgoing Education Minister, had acquitted himself well and, as *The Times* pointed out, Education needed more continuity of policy and longer-term thinking than almost any other department.[2] The editor considered that Hailsham was being rewarded for having been an enthusiastic and vigorous First Lord, and for having taken public pride in the salvage fleet he had assembled to clear the Canal – even though it was never used and had to give way to the United Nations fleet. Certainly he had demonstrated a capacity to lift people's spirits at the end of the crisis when no one else did. That would not have been lost on Macmillan. The story that the new Prime Minister was alarmed by Hailsham's drastic plan for rebuilding the Navy may also be true. Macmillan had noted in his diary for 3 February that 'By moving Hailsham from the Admiralty a possible danger was avoided' – without specifying what danger. The most likely explanation, however, was that Hailsham was peculiarly well qualified for the job by virtue of his own academic achievements and his ability to rouse a dispirited educational establishment. In the same entry in his diary, Macmillan added: 'Also I think he will be a first-class Minister of Education. Anyway, he is one of the cleverest men, if not always the wisest, in the country today.'[3]

Hailsham threw himself into his new work with the same enthusiasm he had shown for the Navy. There was not going to be time to put his own education theories to the test, for he was moved on again after eight months. Nor to do anything about the narrow and illogical jurisdiction of the Department. Its function was limited to funding English schools and teaching staff through local education authorities and religious bodies. It had no jurisdiction over universities, which dominated the educational scene but were within the province of the Treasury, nor over industrial training, which was the business of the Ministry of Labour. The immediate problem was the sheer size of the school population. 'The bulge' had arrived in secondary schools, representing serious underestimates in population trends extending over a number of years. Such mistakes have consequences for schools which can be irremediable. The schools needed more buildings, more teachers and smaller classes. The Department was chronically short of cash. Hailsham told the Cabinet that cuts in funding would be opposed by educational opinion across the board, and made much of by the Labour Party. 'Slum schools, overlarge classes, and the shortage of scientists and technologists are the most publicised deficiencies in education; there are many others.'[4] The government was in danger of failing to justify its claim to be introducing the Opportunity State. But he lost his battle with his old friend Peter Thorneycroft, a Chancellor already infected by Treasury orthodoxy and necessarily influenced by the gathering economic storm which broke later in the year.

In May, Hailsham submitted a proposal to Cabinet to extend the teachers' training course from two to three years.[5] The longer course allowed for studies which were not purely vocational and would prevent the launching of teachers into their work at too young an age. It was a proposal to enhance the status and self-respect of the profession and it was strongly supported by educationalists. Cabinet approved. The change was to be brought in from 1960, by when the bulge would be flattening out. This, and the introduction of a standardised and cost-effective design for school buildings were the main achievements of Hailsham's brief period at Education. He had hoped to leave something more enduring as a memorial.

It is tantalising that we cannot know how a man who was himself supremely well educated according to the criteria of his time and whose ruling principle was pragmatism, might have tackled the persistent obstacles facing English education: its tribalism, its divisiveness, its overall poor results and its downgrading of science. All he had as Minister of Education was from January to September of 1957 and from April to October of 1964, when Sir Alec Douglas-Home's short-lived administration fell. There is not much to go on. He advocated what he called 'pluralism', or the right for parents to choose, and he deplored the politicising of education, or the imposition of doctrinaire theories which preferred one type of school to another.[6] Was the one attainable without the other? He told an audience at Birmingham University in 1983 that independent schools were a necessity. 'The great cooks of history would never have created their classic dishes if they had always been condemned to serve prix fixe table d'hôte meals. Probably we should all be eating brown windsor soup.'[7] But how his ideas might have been translated into decision in 1957 and the years following can only be speculated about, because the Prime Minister had other ideas for his Education Minister.

★

On 17 September 1957 it was announced that Hailsham had been appointed Lord President of the Council and was expected to become Chairman of the Party. This was confirmed two days later. Some time during the summer Oliver Poole, then Chairman himself, had advised Macmillan to make Hailsham Chairman in his place, and had disinterestedly offered to serve under him as his deputy. Macmillan put the proposition to Hailsham in the course of a lunch at the Turf Club on 27 August. 'He professed – quite genuinely – inability to do so great a job. But he would think it over,' Macmillan noted in his diary.[8] On 29th Hailsham accepted. It was now two years since he had left the headship of his chambers in the Temple. He had done so thinking it would be only a temporary break. He had not wanted to leave the Navy, even though Education carried a seat in the Cabinet. Now, at a moment when he was just beginning to become absorbed in the problems of schooling, he was to be uprooted again. It was not for this that he had joined the Government. He repeatedly said and wrote that the law was his first love; and perhaps he would have chosen above all else to ascend to the Lord Chancellorship via the High Court Bench. The bewildering changes now thrust upon him must have confirmed that preference.

It was, however, promotion again, at speed. The standing of the government was at a low ebb, and it was not expected to win the next election. Still demoralised in the aftermath of Suez and endeavouring to heal the breach with the United States, Macmillan's administration faced an economic crisis as well. The day after Hailsham's appointment Bank Rate was raised to 7 per cent, the highest since 1921, and cuts were announced in public and private investment in a shock treatment to defend the pound.

Hailsham had for some time been thought of as the most likely source of inspiration in the Party. In a piece entitled 'Lord Hailsham: The Moses of the Moment'[9] the *Yorkshire Post* asked, 'What is it that has brought Lord Hailsham to the fore? It is his capacity to inspire, to confer a glow, to influence with zeal . . . The man exudes courage and conviction . . .' *The Times* also had no doubt that Hailsham was the man of the hour. The editorial spoke of uncertainty and unease among Government supporters. 'Some Conservatives are now looking for a miracle, or a man . . . Everything has been centred on Lord Hailsham. He is apparently the man.' As the newspaper saw it, he was now to join the innermost circle. 'To what may be loosely called the Macmillan–Butler–Thorneycroft triumvirate is now added Lord Hailsham. If the country is going to decide the next general election on leaders, then it is this quartet it will henceforth largely judge.'[10] This was a misconception. Although in September 1957 Butler, Thorneycroft and Hailsham held the key positions under Macmillan for winning the next election, they did not constitute an inner Cabinet. Macmillan did not like cabals. His relations with Thorneycroft, whose personality he described as *cassant*, were about to explode, and he allowed himself to be persuaded by his Chancellor, against his own judgment, that a Bank Rate of 7 per cent was the way to stem a run on the currency.[11] Butler was a loyal lieutenant to whom Macmillan owed much, but their relations were shadowed by the Prime Minister's unshakeable determination that Butler should never become his successor.

The choice of Hailsham as Chairman turned out to be inspired. He made more of the job than anyone since Lord Woolton, and his combination of youthful enthusiasm and prophetic zeal took the party by storm. There were many letters of encouragement and congratulation. Among them were two from his wartime days. 'You go from strength to strength,' wrote Sir John Hackett; and from Sir Edward Spears: '. . . it is good to see your great personal gifts at last recognised, becoming the propelling force projecting you to the top of public life . . . it is a comfort that you are to be the Doctor who will put a shot in the arm of the Conservative Party. The old boy needs it.'[12] The press announcement of Hailsham's appointment made the point that he would 'restore the strong link between the party and the Cabinet which existed in the days of Lord Woolton's tenure'. This gave rise to some specious comment that the Cabinet would pay too much deference to opinion in the constituencies. But in Hailsham's view, unless there were a Cabinet Minister sitting in the room to interpret the Cabinet to the Party and the Party to the Cabinet, it would be difficult to carry out Cabinet policy. His seat in the Cabinet gave him an authority with the local associations which his predecessor, Oliver Poole, lacked.

Poole was an able administrator who had Macmillan's ear. His modesty was an important ingredient in the highly successful partnership with Hailsham. Poole understood how the party worked. Hailsham disliked administration, and for the most part busied himself in field work and in haranguing the Party infantry at area meetings. He introduced a monthly newsletter to constituency chairmen commenting trenchantly on current events and setting out his own impressions of the state of the party. The link between Poole, always in Central Office or his own office, and Hailsham, out most of the time, was Dennis Walters, selected by Hailsham, on being appointed Party Chairman, to be his personal assistant and who in 1963 was to become one of Hailsham's campaign managers.

Poole would tell Walters what he thought should be put into Hailsham's mind, and Walters, who went everywhere with Hailsham and frequently had to put up with the rough edge of his tongue, would attempt this daunting task. Hailsham met Poole only when occasion required, hardly more than once a week and saw the permanent staff in Central Office but rarely. The partnership worked because of the complementary talents of Hailsham and Poole, the capacity of each for hard work and the mutual respect between the two.[13] Hailsham recalled that in the two years during which they were together there was scarcely a cross word spoken.[14]

As was his habit, Hailsham analysed his new job with acuity. The Chairmanship is a non-elective office, in the gift of the Leader. He is in charge of Central Office, but outside he has no constitutional powers: only responsibilities 'which he discharges by sheer bluff'.[15] He has no authority over the members of either House in the party. If things go wrong, he is blamed; if they go well, the credit belongs to the Leader. On the other hand, the Chairman has an important advantage when his party is in power. He is the only minister apart from the Prime Minister whose words on general policy are reported outside his departmental responsibility. He can make the party workers in the country sing a particular tune. The effect of their doing so, he advised his successor, Butler, with the benefit of his own experience, is large indeed, and capable of influencing public opinion in the country.[16]

The Chairman must take plenty of limelight but, at the same time, he should never threaten the Leader as a rival or try to upstage him. It follows that the Chairman should not be in the running to succeed. For a different reason, the Chairman should not also be leader of the House of Commons. The function of the latter, Hailsham thought, was to seek consensus, blur issues and avoid head-on collisions. The leader of the House of Commons should be conciliatory and grave. The Party Chairman, on the other hand, should be partisan and evangelical, even strident, one who sharpens issues and who deflects criticism of the government by attacking the opposition. These two contrasting personalities could not subsist in one person. It was through this reasoning that Hailsham came to play the fat man to Macmillan's trouper in the celebrated double act which pulled off victory in the general election of 1959.

It was evident that the key to success lay in Hailsham's relationship with his Leader. On his side, Macmillan thought Hailsham had the qualities to bring about as dramatic an improvement in party morale as had Lord Woolton after the electoral disaster of 1945.[17] Hailsham was more doubtful about Macmillan. His appreciation of the political scene in 1957 was that, after Suez, the country craved a leader who could touch the imagination, someone in the Churchill mould. While he was Chairman he repeatedly begged the Prime Minister to go for the great phrase, the larger vision. 'I believe you could afford to drop a little bit of the friendly human colour,' he wrote to Macmillan about a forthcoming broadcast, 'to inject this necessary element of gin into the tonic. I think you could also allow yourself a slice of lemon on the top in the form of a slight flavour of uplift and passion – not unbecoming in a national leader, but just falling short of pomposity or unction.'[18] Whether an exhortation so phrased was best calculated to appeal to Macmillan, who had antennae which were sensitive to vulgarity, may be doubted; but in any case he could not emulate Churchill, for all his political skills. He liked to play things down, play them long, play them cool. His long suit was the extempore speech and the adroit reply: he rarely essayed the grand set piece. He was a complex character whose public persona, emerging gradually during his first administration, of an imperturbable Edwardian impresario, was acquired. Hailsham observed that he was the last of the gifted pre-1914 generation to play a part in public life, and he considered that, after the retirement of Lord Salisbury, this fixed a gulf between Macmillan and everyone else. 'It was as if he saw, looking down and commenting on his conduct all that brilliant, but deceased, generation, the Grenfell boys, Patrick Shaw-Stewart, Edward Horner, Raymond Asquith, and instead of encouraging him they seemed to say to him: "Good Lord! Fancy *you* being there". And his words dried up.'[19]

The relations between the two, on which Hailsham's career eventually hinged, were always hampered by mistrust. Hailsham felt he could not always reach his Leader. He knew that he was fundamentally a good man, a fellow Christian, and physically of the bravest. But he disliked his tendency to appease and his Byzantine ways, and he came to realise that his manner was a mask: Macmillan's real feelings and private melancholy were buried beneath fastidiousness. On his side, Macmillan admired Hailsham's uprightness, but was repelled by and feared the consequences of his unpredictable loss of control. Their successful double act was like a stage duo in which, from across the footlights, apparent ease hid personal strains.

The opportunity for the two most famous pieces of business on Hailsham's side of the act came quickly, at the Brighton Party Conference in October 1957. He had been in the job barely a month and decided to impose his personality immediately. He had been chosen to speak at the Conservative Political Centre meeting on the Thursday night of the Conference at the Brighton Aquarium. The

C.P.C. is the educational wing of the Party, founded by Butler in 1945 to stimulate political ideas, a sort of Tory Fabian Society. The audience was small but influential, and Hailsham determined to make the occasion the launch of his campaign to galvanise the party. He gave all that he had to the preparation of his speech, and thought himself that it was one of the best he had ever made, 'intended to appeal to the head, but phrased also so as to move the heart'. Dennis Walters agreed: 'It was a superb speech, both in its content and delivery, and was received with enormous enthusiasm.'[20] Hailsham expounded the conception of Toryism which he had deployed in *The Case for Conservatism*; and in passages of Socialist-baiting he roused the faithful: 'Having turned up the gas under the national kettle, the Labour Party would try to stop it boiling over by sitting on the lid. I predict that this would be a singularly uncomfortable, a blisteringly painful and in the end an utterly futile posture.' The peroration struck the chord which always resonates most at Conservative Party Conferences, the appeal to spiritual values and the threat from the powers of darkness.

> In an age of infidelity, Conservatism is concerned with faith. In an age of dissolving allegiances, it upholds loyalty. In a fog of material considerations, it points to integrity. In an atmosphere of self-seeking, it preaches self-sacrifice.

This was the music which he unavailingly urged on Harold Macmillan, and it was rapturously received. But to believe, as he apparently did, that the speech was the turning point in the fortunes of the party and paved the way for the victory in 1959, was a wild overvalue. The two pieces of pantomime which followed immediately were much more potent.

Hailsham appeared early the following morning on Brighton beach advancing at a smart pace down the pebbles in a striped dressing-gown which concealed an exiguous pair of swimming trunks. With evident relish he plunged into the Channel for a swim of nearly an hour. Whether by accident or design, gentlemen of the press were present in numbers. They waited patiently for his return to dry land, and not a single national newspaper failed to record in pictures the Chairman's total immersion. The ceremony was repeated each morning before breakfast.

The second bit of theatre occurred on the last morning of the Conference. It was, as he afterwards claimed, unpremeditated. Something certainly needed to be done to liven up that low point in the Conference, as it awaits the Leader's messianic coming in the afternoon and drivels itself away in desultory debate on minor matters. Taking up the handbell which by tradition is presented to the Conference Chairman, Hailsham first tinkled it *piano*, offering some conventional compliment to the recipient; then building up a crescendo, he advised her to ring it for victory; finally, in a tone of solemn declamation, he intoned Donne's famous words (or something approximating) to an imaginarily cringing Labour Party: 'Never send to know for whom the bell tolls: it tolls for thee.' By this time, all 4000 delegates were on their feet, stamping and cheering with complete abandon.

These two episodes are the things that everyone knows about Hailsham's political career. The press, the audience and the public drank it down. The fifty-year-old schoolboy with short-back-and-sides haircut and a glint of mischief in his eye became the party's darling and a national image. The image followed him ever afterwards and could not be shaken off. He repeated his bell-ringing the next year at Blackpool in response to popular demand, but Dennis Walters thought it unwise to do so, and told him so. Hailsham first accepted this advice, but was then carried away by the emotion of the moment and succumbed to the temptation of a repeat performance.[21] The Party adored it but Macmillan may have felt upstaged – a cardinal sin in a Chairman, as Hailsham knew.[22] Macmillan's real feelings can only be guessed at. Of the first bell-ringing at Brighton, he wrote in his memoirs: 'Undoubtedly he became the hero of the Conference . . . Indeed so successful was Hailsham's conduct . . . that some of the press and other commentators felt that the new Chairman had put the Prime Minister somewhat in the shade. I had of course no feelings of reproach.' He received a letter of explanation from Hailsham about the 'campanological eccentricities of the Party Manager', which Macmillan recorded as having been written with 'characteristic sensitivity'.[23] But the Macmillan memoirs are an essay in blandness, and it is more likely that Macmillan enjoyed neither the vulgarity nor living in its shadow.

In any event, Hailsham began to get a reputation for self-advertisement. For his part, he thought he was doing a job, no more, and after the election in 1959 he wrote to Macmillan, saying that he hoped 'a deep grave can be dug for the cap and bells'.[24] They were never interred, and, as he said in a television interview many years later, 'that bloody bell hung round my neck as if I were a Swiss cow'. At the same time as Hailsham wrote his letter, Macmillan entered in his diary that Hailsham was 'really not safe'; and that he was 'in a very over-excited condition and keeps giving ridiculous "Press

Conferences"'.[25] The more sober Butler was made Chairman in Hailsham's place.

That, however, was two years away. For the present, Hailsham's chairmanship was off to a powerful start. The party workers went back to their constituencies from Brighton in a mood to win. Hailsham was making the weather. He had given them a lift with vision and leadership. He thought he could do so without getting between the party and its Leader, by vulgarising his own image. It was a dangerous path to tread. It meant that he would be venturing on Macmillan's preserve. The opposition, however, were thoroughly alarmed by the Conservatives' new weapon. The vulgarity which Macmillan disliked had a threatening appeal to their own supporters. Cassandra of the *Daily Mirror* wrote: 'How I welcome Lord Hailsham's accession as the spokesman of the Tory Party. He is bold, indiscreet, courageous, intelligent, belligerent – and wrong.'[26] This was exactly how Hailsham wanted to engage the Labour Party. The *Daily Herald*'s headline was more candid. 'Don't laugh! This man Hailsham is dangerous.'[27]

As so often in public life, the rapture did not last. Early in 1958 a series of by-elections went wrong. There were rumours in the press and mutterings on the back benches that Hailsham had quarrelled with Macmillan, that he was no good and would have to go. But this was as nothing compared with the resignation of the three Treasury ministers.

On 6 January 1958, Peter Thorneycroft and his two lieutenants, Enoch Powell and Nigel Birch, resigned en bloc. The issue was straightforward. The Treasury Ministers were not prepared to approve estimates for Government expenditure for the coming year at a level higher than that for the current year. After an anxious debate in Cabinet over a weekend, the gap had been narrowed to just £50 million. Neither Thorneycroft nor Macmillan would give way. The narrow gap, however, hid wider differences. Thorneycroft thought Macmillan tricky and by instinct an 'uncontrolled spender': the issue for him was not 'how much?' but 'did it matter?'[28] Powell and Birch, with Thorneycroft, considered it an issue of principle, and one in which they were vindicated by subsequent events. In this light, no amount was merely trivial. 'If it is said that the welfare state is sacrosanct,' argued Thorneycroft, and other expenditure similarly so, 'there is someone left at the end of the queue, and that someone is the pound sterling.'[29] Macmillan, who sometimes did not care for Thorneycroft's manner (in 1956 he had written in his diary: 'He shouts at one as if we were a public meeting'),[30] did think it a trivial amount to resign over, and was angered by the brutal way in which the Treasury three were letting down the government at a difficult time.

For Hailsham as Party Chairman the resignations were serious indeed. It looked as if the government might disintegrate and his hopes be blasted. The episode was personally painful as well, for Thorneycroft was an old ally and friend from Tory Reform days. But he could not easily forgive his Treasury colleagues, and thought they were in thrall to their department. He wrote afterwards

> The Treasury, which commands the cream of the civil service, has an almost mesmeric effect on the Ministers who serve there. They have the kind of esprit de corps of a beleaguered garrison, surrounded by the spending departments, and feeling every man's hand to be against them ... Side by side, however, with this curious sense of isolation is the almost messianic conviction that they can save the nation by their courage and rectitude, and that nobody else can do so.[31]

That atmosphere of stoic denial appealed naturally to Powell and Birch, of whom it was said by an anonymous MP immediately after the resignations that they 'would go to the stake for their principles. The only difference between them is that Enoch Powell would ask for the chains to be tightened as he approached the flames.'[32]

Hailsham's task in the crisis was rapid damage limitation. He met Poole at once and made a plan. On the night the resignations were delivered, a telegram went to the Chairman of every constituency association and area, giving the leadership's side of the argument. The Prime Minister was about to leave on a Commonwealth tour, and at Poole's suggestion the entire Cabinet assembled at the airport to see him off. There he made his celebrated remark to the press which did much to make his reputation for being 'unflappable' – an epithet for which Hailsham claimed the credit: 'I thought the best thing was to settle up with these little local difficulties and then to turn to the wider view of the Commonwealth.' The put-down, as his biographer described it, could not have been more effective, but it concealed a nagging worry about the stability of his government.[33] Hailsham shared these worries and thought that, as a description, 'little local difficulties' had more panache than accuracy.

Macmillan had reason to be thankful for what Hailsham and Poole had done, and sent a message of appreciation from Karachi: 'grateful for the way in which you have helped to steady the party throughout the country at rather a critical period'.[34] Hailsham reported back that he had seen Thorneycroft who had struck him as 'in a resentful and sullen mood but he promised he would not attempt any revolt from the party'.[35] Nor did he, and the crisis passed.

The argument on whether the Treasury Ministers were right to resign continues, but Hailsham always maintained that they were wrong to the point of perversity. 'Although social policy must in the end depend on our economic stability,' he told constituency chairmen in his monthly letter, 'permanent changes in our social structure cannot be made simply to depend on the outturn of each set of annual estimates. If we were to do that we should cease to be a party with a social policy at all.'[36] There was perhaps more to it than that. Hailsham was concerned above all with the prospect of a coming electoral victory. The Government was still weak and, as Chairman of the Party, he thought that a 'mere' £50 million was too small a margin to endanger that victory. As a man of firm instinctive loyalty, his job was to promote it. It was inconceivable that he would have joined the dissidents.

★

An unusually difficult and distasteful problem with which Hailsham had to deal during his Chairmanship was the long-running conflict between the Bournemouth East constituency association and its Member, Nigel Nicolson. Nicolson, the son of Harold Nicolson and Vita Sackville-West, was a civilised Tory on the left wing of the Party. He was at odds with his local association over a whole range of issues from hanging and flogging to Suez, on which he attacked Eden's policy from the start. The mésalliance was made worse by Nicolson's patrician manners and open intellectual contempt for the right. By the time Hailsham arrived at Central Office, the thing had been going on for nearly a year, and it continued to trouble him for another eighteen months.

The constitutional position was and is that a constituency association has an unchallengeable right to select its own candidate for an approaching election. Central Office has no standing in the matter, subject only to the condition that a candidate must be on the Party's approved list. This prevents constituencies selecting someone of known bad character, inexperience, or of views clearly at variance with party policy. But the supposition that Central Office can influence the choice of candidate is wrong: attempts to do so are generally counter-productive. If a row develops between a sitting member and his association, Central Office generally supports the member. It had done so in the Bournemouth case, but to no avail. The constituency had exercised its right to select a new prospective candidate who was already on the approved list, though on the far right of the Party. Nicolson organised a series of public meetings in his own cause and secured a long and distinguished succession of Conservative MPs to speak from his platform. Statements were issued and pamphlets published. The row was continuous and bitter. It threatened to assume national proportions. Macmillan favoured Nicolson and was constantly nagging Hailsham to do something for him: but Hailsham, knowing the weakness of his position, kept his head down 'amid universal obloquy' and bided his time.[37]

Finally, and after he had been Chairman for more than a year, he saw his chance. Nicolson's meetings had been disrupted by Empire Loyalists, a lunatic fringe right-wing organisation unfriendly to the Conservative Party. For some obscure reason they published some correspondence between themselves and the prospective candidate for Bournemouth East which seemed to indicate a degree of collusion between him and these untouchables. Hailsham sent for the candidate, who immediately admitted the authenticity of the correspondence and withdrew his candidacy. This was a help, but it still left the dispute between Nicolson and his association unresolved. Hailsham proposed to settle it by means of a plebiscite of all members of the association. It was not easy. The association considered it a surrender to Nicolson; there were difficulties about who could vote, as Nicolson had been actively recruiting supporters during his campaign; and the plebiscite was only agreed to after a meeting chaired by Hailsham which he 'had to sustain with dignity despite the Empire Loyalists chanting their ludicrous slogans out in the street'. Nicolson lost by a narrow margin. Although sympathetic to him, Hailsham considered this to be the best result obtainable in difficult circumstances. For if Nicolson had won and had become the prospective candidate, the situation in the constituency would hardly have borne thinking about.

*

Although the actual run up was short, the whole of Hailsham's chairmanship was in a sense a prolonged campaign to win the 1959 general election. With Macmillan's growing authority in Parliament and in the country through 1958, as he rode the rising tide of affluence, the prospects of victory improved until, in October, Hailsham believed the Conservatives could win by some 30 seats. But both Poole and he advised waiting. There was a minor recession in early 1959, and again they counselled delay. In April, Hailsham advised the Prime Minister that public opinion had not been developing as favourably as he might have hoped. The latest Gallup Poll was pointing to a stalemate and showed that all parties had gained from a reduction in the number of 'don't knows'.[38] It was to be an autumn election. When Macmillan finally went to the country in October, Hailsham was able to promise a majority of 50. In doing so, he relied heavily on the polls. 'I have no patience with those who affect to despise the polls,' he wrote. 'Of course, they are not infallible and, like the Bible, they require to be interpreted by experts.'[39] The experts were in Central Office where a graph was kept showing the results of polls since their inception. 'It was this long series of results plotted against events . . . and checked against the actual results of by-elections and general elections that for the first time provided me with an objective background of argument to meet the pessimists and the cricketers.' (The 'cricketers' were those who said: Put the other side in to bat and they will make such a mess of things we shall soon get them out. Needless to say, Hailsham thought this ignorant nonsense: 'The one sure way to get hurt in politics is not to play to win.')

The actual campaign was exciting enough. Hailsham had intended to stay in London and concentrate on press conferences, but Poole persuaded him to stump the country. He and Macmillan were to concentrate on the mariginals. The Conservatives got off to a bad start. Their tactics were gentlemanly, concentrating on their own programme and avoiding attacks on Labour. This was not Hailsham's own, very effective, brand of electioneering, but he had been converted to it on the principle of advocacy that 'when the court is in your favour (as the polls showed the electorate to be in ours) you say as little as possible'.[40] The television broadcasts which had been recorded on videotape were, in Hailsham's view, 'a series of the most jejune and boring programmes it has ever been my lot to take part in'. All of this had to be changed when, after a week, Poole rang Hailsham from London and told him that they were losing. They decided to take matters into their own hands. The television programmes were scrapped and, much to Hailsham's taste, they began to attack Labour for financial irresponsibility. This yielded an unexpected dividend. Gaitskell claimed incautiously that he could reduce income tax while maintaining his programme. He was not believed and the Conservatives made hay. They won by a majority of a hundred.

During the campaign, Hailsham was struck down by an attack of gastro-enteritis, from which he had suffered on and off since his time in the Middle East. He fought on with characteristic courage; but it left him weak and dispirited after it was all over. For the moment, however, he could enjoy the triumph. Macmillan wrote him a warm letter: 'I am so particularly happy about *your* success. You have shewn, since [on] my persuasion you took that arduous and difficult job, all the qualities that really matter in life – courage, loyalty and imagination. Bless you.'[41] In *A Sparrow's Flight* Hailsham describes this letter as 'reasonably polite'. This was unfair, but his view was coloured by the unexpected demotion which followed the election victory. It was in truth high praise and deserved, for the victory was a famous one.

How should the credit be apportioned between Macmillan and Hailsham or Hailsham/Poole? Hailsham's own assessment of Macmillan was put high. 'As Prime Minister, but in startling contrast to his performance after 1959, Harold Macmillan had hardly put a foot wrong.' It was he who repaired the broken relationship with the United States, re-established Britain's authority in the Commonwealth and who dominated the House of Commons with his incomparable manner at the Despatch Box. No one who saw him could forget the hooded eyes and drawling voice, the disdain he could call up as he dealt with questions. Close observers saw that he would lightly and repeatedly tap the table with his foot as he moved in for the kill. He was the 'Supermac' of Vicky's cartoons. But even this was not enough to come from behind and win an election. For the revival of morale among the foot soldiers of the party and the stirring of the imagination of opinion-makers in the country, much of the credit belonged to Hailsham. When put to the touch, the double act carried all before it. 'I shall never quite be sure', wrote Hailsham, 'what part I played in helping him. But I shall continue to flatter myself that at least I had something to do with it.'[42]

16

Science

THE Conservative victory of 1959 looked convincing. A confident Prime Minister commanded a majority of 100 in the
Commons. In his valedictory letter to constituency chairmen,
Hailsham described it as the most decisive of modern times. 'Our
opponents are in a sorry mess. They must choose between dropping
nationalisation and controls, which means splitting their party, and
keeping them in their programme, which means continued rejection
by the electorate.' The Liberals, too, had failed: '. . . by driving them
into the open as the implacable opponents of our party, we have
made them more of a menace to the Socialists than to us.'[1] The
triumphalism was understandable but it was undermined by events.
Fumbling economics gave the country the impression that the brake
and accelerator were being applied alternately without a clear policy;
de Gaulle's veto of the United Kingdom's application to join the
European Community; failed attempts to settle the British Commonwealth in Africa by federal schemes; and ultimately a series of
degrading scandals all seemed to reflect the lack of grip and
leadership in government. 'The general trend of Macmillan's second
administration was . . . one of slow and irresistible decay,' was
Hailsham's retrospect in *A Sparrow's Flight*.

He himself was sick and exhausted by the effort of the election.
He did not desire or expect to continue as Party Chairman. He had
had enough of politics, particularly the cap and bells, and wanted to
go back to the Bar. Wandering alone round the haunted Gothic
corridors and cathedral nave of the Law Courts in the Strand, he
gave himself over to nostalgia, thinking only of escape from the
buffets and false gods of public life to decent professionalism.
Macmillan wrote to him after the election 'as a very old friend' to
advise him to take a break. 'You gave everything you had to the

election and it must have taken a tremendous lot out of you.'[2] Hailsham agreed. 'You are plumb right. I have never felt more exhausted in my life. But I do not want to leave my wife and, for various reasons, she will find it impossible to go at present. So . . . I must sweat it out . . . the strain has been moral and emotional rather than physical. Oddly enough, I am unusually sensitive to criticism, and the whole essence of the Chairmanship was to attract it to myself deliberately when any was going.'[3] He was both sensitive to criticism and intolerant of it, and he felt, too, that Mary had been unsympathetic. The demands of Party Chairmanship had imposed strains at home. In early 1958, she had scribbled a note listing his known commitments: 'I shall have been alone for ten days. Quite long enough!' Her husband bowed to this and returned home for the weekend. But the demands increased in the run-up to the general election. At the end of 1959, he told Sir Solly Zuckerman, whom he had come to know through being Lord President (an office he had held concurrently with the Chairmanship of the Party), that his main trouble was worry over his private affairs. 'I am paying a pretty heavy price for my neglect of them and do not seem to be getting any nearer getting them right.'[4]

In this dejected frame of mind, he was summoned to Downing Street and, by his own account, received coldly. He could choose between his old job at Education or a new one to be created for Science and Technology, coupled with the office of Lord Privy Seal, a sinecure but one carrying a salary. Either way, this was demotion. Although he would remain in Cabinet, it was a poor reward for the election triumph, and he would cease to be Lord President of the Council. He regained the office of Lord President in the reshuffle of July 1960, but even then Macmillan was nervous about him. 'Alec [Lord Home] and I (with the Lord Chancellor [Lord Kilmuir]) had been discussing whether Lord Hailsham could lead the House of Lords without disaster . . .', the Prime Minister noted in his diary.[5]* These doubts, and Macmillan's discussions with Home about them, persisted into the leadership crisis of 1963.

The early years of Macmillan's second term marked a low point in the relations between the Prime Minister and Hailsham. In spite of his gratitude for electoral victory and his appreciation of Hailsham's talents, Macmillan was apprehensive about his tendency to lose control of himself. He had noted this immediately after the election

---

* Lord Home was leader in the Lords from March 1957, when Lord Salisbury resigned, until July 1960 when he became Foreign Secretary, an appointment which occasioned some surprise. Lord Hailsham succeeded Lord Home in spite of Prime Ministerial doubts.

and it went on worrying him. Hailsham made matters worse by talking at length about his personal problems. On 17 June 1960 Macmillan recorded that 'Lord Hailsham came at 5.00 p.m. and talked about his future for an hour or more. He thinks he might do better by going back to the Bar now.'[6] This was the sort of incident which accounted for the fluctuations in Macmillan's appraisal of him. Hailsham described the movements in the Prime Minister's mind as 'almost Borgia-like behaviour' and 'somersaults', and he attributed the coolness of 1959–60 to a misunderstanding of his role in the divorce of Lady Dorothy Macmillan's sister. Hailsham gave evidence by affidavit in the case. Macmillan apparently thought (wrongly) that Hailsham was siding with the other party to the divorce. The incident may have had some effect, but it seems unlikely that the Prime Minister would have allowed it to weigh so heavily. Macmillan was not particularly decisive. He became less so during his second term, probably as a consequence of the gradual development of the illness which erupted in 1963. He was in any case an introspective and he was torn by the conflicting qualities in Hailsham's personality.

For his part, Hailsham consulted Oliver Poole, on whose oracular judgment he had come to rely: not about the choice of office which had been presented to him, but about whether he should leave politics altogether. Poole, who was himself committed to return to the City, told him that it was unthinkable that they should both leave together, and that it was his duty to stay. This was bleak counsel to someone who felt both that he had been snubbed and that he was distasteful to his leader. He made his feelings plain to Dennis Walters. 'I still wish I had been allowed to do a bunk. Nine days wonder would have followed, and after that, freedom, and peace with honour. There is no future for me in the House of Lords except to embarrass my friends, and I do not wish to do that.'[7] Never the less, he took Poole's advice, and opted for the new Science portfolio.

★

In May 1959, Hailsham had been invited by the Conservative Club of Glasgow University to accept nomination as a candidate for the office of Lord Rector. The election was to take place a few days after the general election. Hailsham obtained the approval of Central Office and accepted with enthusiasm. The Conservative Club was founded in 1837 to elect Peel as Rector and the office had become something of a Conservative Party perquisite. It has no counterpart in English universities. The Rector is a member of the Court, the governing body of the University, and has the right to take the chair. He is also the representative of the students on the Court.

Hailsham's predecessor as Rector was Butler, remembered in this role only for the pictures of his installation, flashed around the world's press, bespattered with flour, tomatoes and fire extinguisher foam. Butler's uncomplaining demeanour on this miserable occasion was a credit to him but it did him no good with the Tory Party. The faithful hoped for stronger things than meek resignation from the man who, as Home Secretary, was responsible for law and order. According to Butler's biographer, Hailsham drew the short straw in allowing himself to be nominated, Macmillan having prudently declined.[8] In fact, the straw was not short. Although he was unwell and in low spirits at the time of the Rectorial election, Hailsham quickly became an enthusiastic and popular Rector. Butler rightly forecast that the students had 'no intention of submitting you to the same tortures as they did me', and he advised Hailsham, apparently without irony: 'What is needed is a continual work of diplomacy in the interests of these charming students.'[9]

The Rectorial election was managed with professionalism by the Conservative Club, and with the aid of a broadsheet called *The Viscount*, Hailsham easily defeated his two adversaries, Billy Butlin and the pacifist divine, Michael Scott. Replying to Butlin's congratulations, the winner wrote: 'I am sorry we could not share the appointment jointly like the Consuls of Ancient Rome'[10] – a prospect to give pause even to a surreal imagination. The main issue facing the new Rector was student independence. He wrote to the Conservative Club saying that a Rector willing to give time and trouble to this question might render the University a signal service. 'To aim at this would certainly be to me a more attractive prospect than a mere pompous dissertation upon one's personal theories about life, faith and morals.'[11] Hailsham's Rectorial Address might not deserve the epithet 'pompous', but it was otherwise just such a dissertation. Entitled 'The Need for Faith in a Scientific Age', its content was rambling, and it ended with a stirring peroration:

> When I survey the emotional, the intellectual, the moral, the political, even the physical litter and chaos of the world today, when truth has almost ceased to be regarded as objective, when kindness is made to depend on political, class or racial affiliations, when only the obvious stands in need of publicity; when I look at popular pin-ups, playboys, millionaires, and actresses with the bodies of gods and goddesses and the morals of ferrets lurching from one demoralising emotional crisis to another and never

guessing the reason; when I view the leaders of great states, the masters of immense concentrations of power and wealth, gesticulating like monkeys and hurling insults unfit for fishwives; when I reflect on the vapidity of so much that is popular in entertainment, the triteness of so much that passes for profundity, the pointlessness and frustration in the popular mood on one side, and the brutality and cynicism on the other; when I consider all this, I can only reflect, without complacency but with a profound sense of thankfulness and peace, not that I am not as other men are, but that being as other men are I have become in addition a citizen of no mean city, where decency and orderliness prevail, where objective truth is honoured, beauty admired, and kindness and human feeling universalised to cover the whole compass of suffering humanity, with a mission to carry on into the modern world the traditions nurtured and fostered in Greece, Rome and Jerusalem, which I hold sacred, believing that these alone, at least in my own experience, can sanctify and therefore civilise the restless and destructive spirit of chaos and mutual hatred which, allowed to develop uncontrolled in modern conditions, could well annihilate the human species upon the planet, or alternatively undo the process of evolution itself and plunge mankind back into the animal status from which it arose.

★

Hailsham's appointment, as he repeatedly insisted, was as Minister *for*, not *of* Science. He and his scientific advisers wholeheartedly agreed that science should be left to the scientists. It was government's job to encourage, facilitate and to fund. But it was emphatically not its role to define the problems to be solved. Government might set the questions for defence, but not in civil science. The basis for Hailsham's view was simply that 'science is primarily about truth, and therefore ought to be intrinsically disinterested, whereas government is amongst other things about power, and is therefore inevitably motivated by the desire of it'.[12] He explained his idea of government's role to a group of scientific journalists shortly after his appointment. 'I regard myself as a public man whose duty it is to see both that the scientists coherently think about the generalised problem of scientific policy and are provided with the political apparatus whereby their thoughts come into reality. I regard myself in that sense as a midwife.'[13]

The ideal midwife would be a senior figure in government without departmental responsibility. He need not be a scientist but he should have the capacity to understand his advisers. Hailsham seemed to have the right qualifications for the model. He had the lawyer's capacity to pick up enough of his client's business to act as his advocate. He had a far ranging mind, was interested in science, and thought of it as a culture and not just practical technology. The chairman of his advisory committee, the distinguished chemist, Sir Alexander Todd, thought him well qualified. 'No scientific knowledge but very able. He fully realised the importance of developing science. Very sympathetic and acute. Not quite so much clout as Salisbury [Hailsham's predecessor as Lord President of the Council] but pretty senior.'[14]

Not everyone agreed that Hailsham's credentials were the right ones. He was a lawyer, philosopher and politician with no academic background in science. By 1963 he had accumulated many other duties. He was Leader of the House of Lords, and the Minister responsible for sport and for the depressed north-east of England. He was an amateur presiding over affairs of state in a field in which the nation's livelihood was at stake. Yet the system by which the relationship between government and civil science was regulated was well tried. What is more, it was considered by the eminent scientists who were most closely concerned in it to be the best that could be devised.[15]

The system was a series of scientific general staffs directing research in separate fields, independent of government and not concerned with bread-and-butter work in those fields. These were the Research Councils: the Department of Scientific and Industrial Research, the Medical Research Council, the Agricultural Research Council and the Nature Conservancy. The thinking behind the creation of these Councils was to separate the activity of research from the executive business of government. Medical research, for instance, was separated from the Ministry of Health, and industrial technology from the Department of Trade and Industry. Each Council was composed of scientists and industrialists, with responsibility for its own research programme and with separate budgets negotiated with the Treasury. All the Councils operated research stations of their own, and made grants for specific research to be undertaken in the universities. All were responsible to the Lord President of the Council, Hailsham's governmental 'midwife'.

The semi-detached relationship between government and civil scientific research was typically English, but it had not just grown up by historical accident. It owed its origins to the administrative genius of Lord Haldane who, in order to counter the advantage which the Germans had secured in the manufacture of military hardware in the

First World War, determined to invigorate British industry through a committee of the Privy Council composed of high-powered scientists. It was this committee which developed into the Department of Scientific and Industrial Research. In this way, the Lord President of the Council came to assume responsibility for the Research Councils.

Hailsham had been Lord President since 1957, during the period when he was also Chairman of the Party. There was therefore little formal change when, in 1959, he became Minister for Science. He continued to have responsibility for the Research Councils. The one change of substance was the addition to his portfolio of the Atomic Energy Authority. Responsibility for nuclear energy gave Hailsham a voice on defence matters, which he used to good effect, even though he was not a member of the Cabinet Defence Committee. It enabled him to give his views on the Skybolt Missile crisis in December 1962. The Americans had indicated that they were cancelling Skybolt, a long-range missile designed to be fired from aircraft. If Britain did not get a substitute, it would have had unilateral nuclear disarmament imposed upon it. Macmillan flew to the Bahamas on 19 December to persuade the Kennedy Administration to give him the Polaris submarine-fired system instead. In a memorandum to Peter Thorneycroft, the Minister of Defence,[16] sent the day before the Prime Minister flew to Nassau, Hailsham defined Britain's 'independent nuclear deterrent' as a substantial and independent contribution to the western deterrent which would ensure that military planning took account of Britain's vital interests. 'I regard it as unacceptable . . . to allow the alliance to develop into one in which all the sophisticated weapons and delivery systems are manufactured in the U.S.A., and Europe became as it were the P.B.I. [Poor Bloody Infantry] of the alliance'. He told Thorneycroft that he had never varied his opinion since the time when he was First Lord of the Admiralty and Winston Churchill had advised him that 'indestructible retaliation' was the key (see p. 152), and that he believed the best value for money was a submarine firing a nuclear missile. He sent a copy of this note to Macmillan who, immediately on his return from Nassau with Polaris secured and his mission accomplished, wrote to Hailsham: 'I have just seen in another box a copy of your Minute of December 18 to Peter Thorneycroft. The fact that this was written at that time is a great encouragement to me for we have really followed your advice.'[17]

Hailsham described the scientific empire which he inherited in 1959 as 'ramshackle and far flung'.[18] It would have been uncharacteristic of him if he had not analysed its faults and propounded a policy for reform. The most obvious defect was that as Science Minister, he was not responsible for higher education, where in the universities and technical colleges most pure and much applied research was done. He fought long and hard to wrest the funding of the universities from the unlikely but prehensile hand of the Treasury. He rightly thought that granting money for the universities sat uncomfortably with the Treasury's main duty as guardian of financial virtue. It was like a secret spending vice, and no good could come of it.

The game of redefining the boundaries of ministerial responsibility seems to exercise a fascination over government. Bits of empire are repeatedly taken away from one minister and given to another, often with little perceptible effect. But Hailsham was convinced that higher education must be taken away from the Treasury and merged with science in a single ministry. In this he had the support of the landmark report of the Robbins Committee on Higher Educa-tion,* and he eventually had his way. In April 1964 he became Minister for Education and Science with responsibility for all phases of education, and with his friend Sir Edward Boyle, whose own passion was education, as Minister of State responsible for univer-sities. Those who thought that Hailsham had used his elbows to supplant Boyle, or that the two got on badly, were wrong. Although people of very different political outlook, they were fast friends, and they made a formidable combination. But their time together was too short before they were consigned to opposition in October 1964.

Hailsham had very little power as Minister for Science. What he could achieve could only be done by persuasion and by such influence as he had over his colleagues. Influence derived from two sources: his own seniority and authority in Cabinet, and the universally respected Advisory Committee which guided him. He was fortunate indeed in his advisers. The Chairman of the Committee was Sir Alexander Todd and his deputy was Sir Solly Zuckerman; two of the most distinguished scientists in the country.

---

* Report of the Committee on Higher Education (Cmnd.2154, October 1963) chaired by Lord Robbins, Professor of Economics at the London School of Economics. The most important public document since Beveridge, it recommended the creation of 6 new universities and the expansion of other existing universities, so that the student population would be increased more than two and a half times by 1980/1. The proposals were immediately accepted by the Government. Predictably, Hailsham did not think that more necessarily meant better. The new institutions of higher learning which followed the adoption of the Robbins recommendations spawned a whole range of pseudo-subjects, of which sociology was the archetype. He told the Birmingham Law Students Society in 1973 that 'such institutions are rapidly becoming soggy-bellied with sociology, which like ginger beer is in danger of distending without stimulating and like methylated spirits intoxicating without civilising'. (HLSM: LC Diaries V: 8 Dec. 1972.)

Although Todd was a chemist and Zuckerman an anatomist, the range of their minds was not constrained by their disciplines. The exceptional qualities of the two were well appreciated by Hailsham who understood that scientists from different fields were frequently unintelligible to one another. Both Todd and Zuckerman had experience of how to get things done in Government. This was particularly true of Zuckerman, who was effectively full time in Whitehall. As well as being Todd's deputy on the civil science committee, he was also Chairman of the parallel Defence Research Policy Committee and Chief Scientific Adviser to the Ministry of Defence. Through this linkage Hailsham, who had no jurisdiction in defence, was able to keep abreast of development there, and ensure that what was happening in civil science was compatible.

The first thing the new Minister for Science did in the autumn of 1959 was to ask his Advisory Committee to review the whole state of scientific effort in the civil field. The Committee's report gave some ground for satisfaction. The balance of effort, which hitherto had been overwhelmingly in favour of defence, was gradually being redressed. In real terms, expenditure on civil science had increased by 40 per cent over three years. Industry was carrying a proportionately larger share of that expenditure. But the Committee pointed to a basic weakness which threatened to undermine these achievements and the whole future of scientific research. This was the shortage of qualified engineers and the concomitant inadequacy of engineering research in the universities and in industry. A single institution in the United States, the Massachusetts Institute of Technology, was producing more engineers than the whole of the United Kingdom.[19]

The truth was that applied science in general, and engineering in particular, was déclassé. As Lord Todd observed in 1984[20] (and as a man who had spent his life in science he was in the best possible position to judge) an anti-industrial bias has marked British society since the middle of the nineteenth century. Since educational patterns rest on social attitudes, schools and universities have continued to show an anachronistic preference for the scholar-administrator over the engineer. In the British public's estimation, science was not something which you needed to understand yourself: the scientists would do that for you. Moreover, science was relatively new to the school curriculum which bore the imprint of the time when it was just added as an extra. It was separated from the arts by the pernicious legend, popularised in C. P. Snow's novels, of the 'two cultures'. Children in schools were compelled at an early age to opt irrevocably for one or the other. 'A' levels and their forerunners made it impossible for sixth formers to get a good grounding in science without abandoning the humanities altogether – a step which many children were understandably not willing to take. 'The time is ripe', Hailsham wrote in 1963, 'for an alliance between the sciences and the arts. We cannot afford a schizophrenic culture.'[21] The failure was most damaging in engineering. Here, Hailsham could not understand the apparent inability (or was it unwillingness?) of the educational establishment to glamorise and make exciting the profession of Brunel.

In all of this the Minister's advisers agreed with him to the hilt. Each year the Advisory Committee reported the continued shortage of engineers. In 1962/3 they pointed to a new and aggravating circumstance, the emigration of highly qualified scientists to the United States, where research facilities and budgets were far more generous.[22] The Committee confirmed the findings of an earlier report by the Royal Society on the subject, and recommended several measures to staunch the outflow. As well as the more obvious steps of upwardly reviewing salaries in the universities and increasing research budgets, they proposed the award, before emigration, of post-doctoral fellowships to persuade the emigrants to return.

Hailsham was alarmed by the new threat, which by now had become known as the 'brain drain'. He allowed himself an incautious remark when the Advisory Committee's report was being debated in the House of Lords on 27 February 1963. Criticising American school standards, he referred to the need of the United States 'to live – and I am compelled to use the word – parasitically on the brains of other nations in order to supply [her] own needs'.[23] By an unhappy conjunction of events this *bêtise*, which caused much offence, was dropped just after the Council of the Senate of Cambridge University had recommended the grant to Hailsham of the honorary degree of Doctor of Law. A letter of protest from 70 dons caused the Vice-Chancellor to withdraw the recommendation for further consideration. The temperature in Cambridge academic circles climbed. In the week before the vote by all senior members of the university, the air was thick with fly sheets and petitions distributed by the opposing factions. A petition against granting the degree was signed by 255 dons, including such disparate figures as E. M. Forster and Kingsley Amis, as well as Francis Crick, the molecular biologist. In favour of Hailsham, but not necessarily his offensive remark, were 109 signatories who included Lords Todd and Adrian and Noël Annan. It was going to be a close thing. *Varsity*, the undergraduate magazine, thought it discourteous to withdraw a recommendation once made and hoped that common sense would prevail 'so that Lord Hailsham gets his degree and the whole affair blows over very quickly'.[24] Hailsham had decided to outface his detractors and, apart from observing mildly when the Vice-Chancellor withdrew the original recommendation, 'I have apparently, if I read the papers right, failed the LL.D. Cambridge, a very distinguished degree to have got',[25] stayed below the parapet and stuck it out. On 11 May, the largest Congregation within memory to meet in the Senate House awarded the Degree by the narrow margin of 304 to 284. The *Daily Mirror* recorded that the honorand grinned while the Latin eulogium was intoned: 'Not without the dust of conflict has the man who is now brought before us won this palm of ours.'[26]

Hailsham's long spell as Lord President and Minister for Science was a satisfying experience. He rated it second only to the Lord Chancellorship, and it was the greatest period of intellectual stimulus since he had been an undergraduate. He was rewarded with a Fellowship of the Royal Society and of most of the Chartered Engineering institutions; and he won the respect and friendship of the scientists who advised him. But an assessment of his achievement is more elusive. The system which he inherited, in which government's role was limited to listening, encouraging and paying, and in which he strongly believed, was in any case nearing its end. The Robbins Report, the adoption of which implied a huge increase in public funding for universities, made it inevitable that government would have closer control over expenditure on research. Even before Robbins, there were doubts about the essentially amateur character of the Haldane model of a semi-detached relationship between government and science. It was true that those scientists closest to it, like Todd and Zuckerman, believed it to be the best achievable; but others like Dr Bowden, the Principal of Manchester College of Science and Technology, were not so sure. Bowden reviewed Hailsham's book *Science and Politics* when it came out in May, 1963.[27] Bowden contrasted the British and Russian systems; and pointed out that the Russian Minister was himself a great engineer, directly controlling a long chain of research stations; and that a third of the Russian Cabinet were engineers or scientists. They were professionals, while Britain still clung to its old cherished amateurism. He doubted whether the great expansion in science which Britain needed could be achieved under our system. 'One can only hope that Lord Hailsham's belief that something can and should be done will be translated into action and that his most interesting philosophical speculations will not of themselves be held to be sufficient to save the nation.'

The book was philosophical. In its emphasis on the corrupting influence of governmental intrusion in the search for scientific truth, it exposed the dilemma at the heart of the relationship between government and science. Only government could bring about the gear change necessary for rapid expansion, but the price would be the loss of academic independence. In Hailsham's time, public (and private) investment in civil research and development increased many times. Public funding was £28.5 million in 1957/8 and £172 million in 1962/3.* He was entitled to credit for that; but what was needed was on a different scale.

Hailsham tried to persuade his colleagues in government that science was everyone's business. He wanted the Ministry of Transport to make use of the Road Research Laboratory; the Housing Ministry to consult the Building Research Station; and to persuade the Minister of Labour that industrial training was not just a function of labour relations. 'I found this extremely difficult to get across to my colleagues during my first two years of office, but in the end it was generally accepted in the government, though not in parliament.'[28] He was up against the prejudice that science is something that we need not try to understand because scientists do it for us. He claimed, however, that the leaven working through government had tangible results: the saving of the VC10 aircraft, the making of nuclear disarmament more likely, the encouragement of the Concorde project, the saving of the advanced gas-cooled reactor. These claims were by their nature incapable of proof; but what is certain is that Hailsham brought to his work boundless energy and enthusiasm. No one could have done more. He himself attributed his success partly to his avoidance of the limelight. 'Publicity was not what I wanted. I wanted action. For this purpose I was willing to work with the scientists, coordinate their ideas, and seek none of the credit for myself.'[29] Charges of gimmickry against the bell-ringer would have been all too easy.

These considerations, however, were eclipsed in the last year of Macmillan's Government, when Hailsham's career took yet another unexpected turn. The Prime Minister appeared to have overcome his reservations about Hailsham's temperament, and assigned to him a series of conspicuous tasks which formed a crescendo to the noisy climax of October 1963.

---

* The later figure included amounts for nuclear science (£48 m.) and grants to universities and learned societies (£26 m.) which were not included in the figures for the earlier year.

17

'A Man of Many Jobs'

THE turning point came at the end of 1962. Macmillan seemed then to put aside his distrust of Hailsham's temperament. Hailsham's own account was that a chance conversation at a cocktail party at about this time exposed the misunderstanding between himself and the Prime Minister about Hailsham's role in the divorce case (see p. 180), and brought their estrangement to an end. This is unlikely to have been the whole truth. Macmillan's mind veered about Hailsham; but whatever the explanation, and as his administration declined steadily in public estimation, he decided to repose confidence in him and entrust to him a series of unusual and newsworthy assignments.

Through 1961 and 1962, Hailsham continued vainly to urge Macmillan to bring vision and inspiration to the administration. In October 1961, he wrote to the Prime Minister about the forthcoming Party Conference, and returned to the old theme. 'I feel very strongly that you should use this annual occasion for something simple and more positively directed than the ordinary Leader's speech *urbi et orbi* which touches on every subject in a statesmanlike manner but does not move to action.' He went on to warn Macmillan of the mood in the party and the country. 'A feeling of fecklessness and disunity seems to be infecting the party at the moment, and this is reflected in the curious, contradictory, irresponsible and I would say dangerous state of public opinion . . .'[1] Although Hailsham asked Macmillan in a postscript to 'forgive this impertinence', and although Macmillan replied 'I value your opinion . . . My thoughts are on the same lines,'[2] the criticism of the leadership was not to be mistaken.

Hailsham's gloomy prognostications, informed by his experience as Party Chairman, were borne out by the events of the first half of

1962. A series of disappointing by-election results, culminating in the disaster at Orpington (a neat and tidy and apparently safe suburban seat, which was won by the Liberal, Eric Lubbock, who converted a Conservative majority of 15,000 into a loss of 8,000), confirmed the unpopularity of the government. The pay policy was the chief culprit, where the government had decreed a 'pause' to combat inflation. The experiments in government by exhortation had not been successful. In December 1961, Dr Charles Hill (who had made himself famous as the 'Radio Doctor') enlisted Hailsham's help in the public presentation of the Pay Pause policy. Hailsham's thoughts were conveyed in a long memorandum[3] which went through several drafts, the first (as usual) in his own hand. He thought that 'the heart of our failure since the war to develop as we would have liked, resides in our failure to control income policy'. Then, in a passage which might have wrung Mrs Thatcher's withers, he proposed the use of moral suasion: 'the moral implication, that those who do snatch some real advantage – whether it is in the form of capital gains, or of easy profit, or of disproportionate wage increases – are simply gaining something unfairly at the expense of their fellow countrymen . . .' In the end, he thought, the problem was: what kind of sanction have we got? Government by advocacy had hardly been a complete success. Something more than precept and more effective than example was needed.

That something would have to wait another seventeen years for the coming of Mrs Thatcher. In the meantime, the Government continued to falter and its leadership to come more and more into doubt. The maladroit executions in the Night of the Long Knives in July 1962, when Macmillan removed a third of his cabinet, did nothing to stem the decline of the government. There was a case for prising Selwyn Lloyd's feeble hand from the Treasury, but the public was unconvinced that the rest of the massacre was inspired by anything but panic. Macmillan began to turn to Hailsham, who was surprised to survive the slaughter, but whose buoyancy and energy stood out in a lacklustre administration. In December 1962, at the time of the Skybolt/Polaris crisis, the Prime Minister sought his help. He told Hailsham that Lord Beaverbrook had been talking as if the discarded Skybolt were an English weapon like the long bow at Agincourt: '. . . it would do an immense amount of good if you felt able to expound in a speech what we have done, bringing out the two concepts of interdependence and independence which you understand so well'.[4] He preferred Hailsham's forceful presentation to any other spokesman for this assignment.

In October, Hailsham submitted a memorandum to the Prime

Minister on the machinery of government.[5] There were things which were as wrong with the mechanics as with the style of government. He drew attention to the backlog in the legislation programme, the physical and moral strain on Ministers which 'converts them progressively into administrative machines, spending their days in committees, their evenings at public banquets, and their nights reading telegrams'; and the piecemeal way in which great decisions were handled in Cabinet. He proposed as solutions, first the establishment of an inter-party Parliamentary committee which could certify uncontroversial Bills for an expedited procedure; second, the promotion of Parliamentary Secretaries to become Deputy Ministers so that Ministers could be freed to think more about the fundamental problems of their Departments; and last, the re-ordering of the Cabinet agenda so that it could examine fewer issues more deeply.

These were sensible suggestions, but they too carried critical implications for the leadership. Macmillan, however, replied fully and courteously in a personal minute, although not writing until January.[6] He thought there was much to be said for the idea of a legislation committee, but it was not the sort of reform which could be carried through in the last eighteen months of the life of a parliament. On the second point, the problem about Deputy Ministers was that 'nearly everybody will refuse to take "No" for an answer unless they have direct access to the Minister ultimately responsible'. The Prime Minister was not put out by what Hailsham had said of his handling of Cabinet business. He conceded that the Cabinet did tend to deal with matters 'ad hoc' as they were put up by Ministers; but he hoped that the new arrangement of only one Cabinet a week would help, and enable more questions to be disposed of in Cabinet Committees. 'One weekly meeting with a small number of items should ensure that each of them gets a good discussion.' Macmillan instanced Hailsham's own recent appointment as Minister responsible for the problems of unemployment in the North East as an example of what he was trying to do. 'As a result of bringing the area as a whole under one Ministry, the Cabinet will be better placed to form a comprehensive view on the problems involved.'

★

The assignment in the North East brought Hailsham out of the back room of civil science into the light. He received a warm welcome from the leading Newcastle newspaper when he took up the job in

January 1963. Under the headline, 'We think you're just the man for the job', the Editor observed that it was a tough assignment, and the penalties of failure would be out of all proportion to the rewards of success. 'But he does not brood on the consequences of failure: he brings enthusiasm at the outset to the task. Lord Hailsham does not have to *affect* enthusiasm and confidence. Those qualities are natural in him and he can inspire them in others.'[7] They were precisely the qualities which had persuaded the Prime Minister to appoint him. 'We have been arguing backwards and forwards about a "Special Commissioner" or some such character to help N. E. Coast where quite a radical approach seems now to be required,' Macmillan wrote in his diary, 'I chose Hailsham, who at once accepted.'[8] On the same day, 11 January 1963, Harold Macmillan stood godfather at the christening in the crypt of Westminster Palace of Hailsham's youngest daughter, Kate.

Not everyone was as welcoming as the Tory *Newcastle Journal*. The response of some of the local Labour Parties was that the job was a piece of electoral public relations. How was it possible that the bellman of Brighton could have practical and realisable ideas on economic or regional planning? Hailsham was well aware that the psychological factor was vital for success, and that if anything would make his mission a failure it would be ridicule from the ruling party in the region. This continued to be a hazard. In April, a local trade unionist gained a lot of publicity by describing Hailsham as 'the Gimmick Man of the Tory Party – the Andy Capp of the aristocracy'.[9] This last was a reference to the occasion when he left his bowler hat in the car on the way to the northbound train on a bitterly cold winter's day, and assumed a flat cap in its place. Reaction was mixed, but there was some derisive comment. It was a silly thing to do. He had to avoid anything which could be interpreted as an endorsement of the stereotype of the North East as cloth-capped, obsolescent and down at heel. Hailsham knew this picture to be a cruel and unjustified caricature invented by television producers and cartoonists, and that it was essential that he break it. 'The region had to be "sold" as a desirable place to live in, a fashionable place to go to, with a population of skilled workers and amenities worth enjoying.'[10] That remained the keynote of his plan.

By 1962 the North East of England was in deep trouble. Of the four most important industries, three – shipbuilding, steel and coal – were contracting simultaneously, and the fourth, chemicals, was affected by the decline in the others. Of male jobs in the region, 34 per cent were in these industries. Unemployment of 4.5 per cent in the region compared with the national average of 2.4 per cent. These were only fractions of what they had been in the thirties: 24 per cent in 1936 compared with a national average of 14 per cent.[11] But it was serious enough. The name of Jarrow and its bitter image of idle plant and men lounging on street corners could still evoke a mood of cynicism and despair.

Hailsham did not want additional powers for his task, and reckoned that they might even be a hindrance if he had them, for he might spend his time acting as a sort of Court of Appeal in hopeless cases from his ministerial colleagues. Nor did he want a large organisation of his own. He intended to work through existing agencies: Ministries, local authorities, trade unions, employers' associations, and the Regional Development Corporation. His own office would be composed of a few officials from the departments concerned. This could then become the nucleus of a permanent agency of government working at first in Whitehall, later in Newcastle. One of the first things to strike him about the organisation of his work was that there was nothing in Britain which corresponded with the region, the *département* or the province of her continental neighbours. Between Westminster at the centre and the County and Borough Councils in the country, there was a void. His remit comprised the Counties of the North Riding of Yorkshire, Durham and Northumberland, with Berwick upon Tweed. Within this area, he had to deal across the board with industry, education, transport, housing, ports, rivers and social amenities. There were nearly 150 local authorities in the area. 'Each activity in which local authorities were interested was connected by a separate umbilical cord to one of a whole range of ministries in Whitehall and sometimes with different officials in the same department.'[12]

Diagrammatically, and in fact, this was a nightmare. The case for devolving powers to a regional authority in Newcastle seemed overwhelming. But he never achieved it. He might possibly have done if Macmillan had stayed on as leader. 'A very good talk with Lord Hailsham . . . and Keith Joseph [Minister for Local Government],' the Prime Minister recorded in September. 'I am very anxious to launch a scheme for Regionalising the Country . . . I hope to get something for Queen's Speech and organised during the next few months.'[13] It was not to be. The most Hailsham could do was to set up a single office in Newcastle where liaison between departments could take place across the corridors of a single building.

Devolution was a theme to which he returned, but on which he never made the slightest headway. In the early 70s, with increasing wealth flowing from the oilfields in the Scottish waters of the North Sea, the demands for self-determination for Scotland became louder and more insistent. Alec Douglas-Home produced a scheme for a directly elected Scottish Assembly in 1970. Hailsham thought it both feeble and misguided. In his view, it was wrong to devolve powers to Scotland without at the same time granting devolution to Wales, Northern Ireland and the English regions. The whole country was over-centralised. In any case, Home's plan did not give the Scots an executive of any kind. Scottish administration would remain responsible to Westminster; whereas 'it is precisely executive functions which are crying out to be devolved'. 'The thing to opt for', he told Home, 'is a regionalism approaching but not quite reaching federation.'[14]

But such radical thinking could never be acceptable to his party, who thought it threatened the break up of the United Kingdom. He nearly resigned from the Shadow Cabinet in 1976 when Scottish and Welsh devolution was proposed by the Labour government. The Conservative plan, still Home's of 1970, was worse than the government's, he thought, and his new leader, Margaret Thatcher, added insult to injury by putting on a three-line Whip to vote against the government's proposals.[15] When he spoke in the Lords in 1976, he described himself as 'a man of known heterodoxy in these matters'[16] and argued that, to be effective, devolution would have to be enshrined in a written constitution.

> The point I am making is that in order to give round wheels to devolution it is necessary to define powers by law and to provide that the courts shall decide questions of *vires*.

No wonder he disclaimed the support of his party for what he said. For it was nothing less than that the powers (*vires*) of both central and regional authorities should be defined in a written constitution to be interpreted by the Courts. The Conservative Party was certainly not ready for limits to be placed on the powers of the Westminster parliament, and for the Judges to be able to say exactly where the boundaries were.

In the meantime, however, in 1963 he agreed a policy for the North East with his little team. There would have to be conscious discrimination by government, particularly the Treasury, in favour of the region at the expense of the more prosperous areas of the South East and West Midlands. But there should be no competition between the North East and the other areas of high unemployment: South West Scotland, Northern Ireland, South Wales and Mersey-side. Economic regeneration was not enough of itself: the whole quality of life would have to be raised. There was to be no propping up of what was likely to fail: the emphasis should be on accelerating what was likeliest to succeed.

These principles were translated into the practical proposals in the Report which Hailsham had been commissioned to make. The Report was not presented until November,[17] by which time Edward Heath had taken over responsibility for regional development in Sir Alec Douglas-Home's new administration. But the authorship was Hailsham's. In its introduction, the Report made the point that the North East was not so much in decline as in transition − from traditional industries to advanced technologies in industrial production. From his experience of science and government, Hailsham was in a good position to guide this process, and to appreciate the importance for it of higher education in the region. Newcastle University was established independently of Durham, and the Report emphasised that both institutions had a strong tradition of interest and research in matters relevant to current North East problems.

In the opinion of at least one Labour MP from the region, Hailsham and Macmillan, with his experience of Stockton, were the only Tories who understood its problems.[18] The primary need was to diversify out of the dying capital industries; but an economic miracle was not possible and shipbuilding, coal and steel could not simply be left to die. They had to be helped through the transitional phase, or the region would not recover at all. Hailsham's Report became a blueprint for regional development; and its key findings that communications within the area and to its markets were quite inadequate, and that facilities for industrial training and retraining were a good deal worse than inadequate, were lessons that deserved to be well learned. However, unemployment in the North East was not solved by the Hailsham mission. In the nature of things he could not achieve tangible results in a few months and with a single paper. On the whole, though, he was well received and liked. His Churchillian manner and his infectious enthusiasm were appreciated. And in a debate on unemployment in 1985 in the House of Lords, Lord Glenamara, formerly, as Edward Short, the Labour member for Newcastle Central, advised the Minister in considering the North East to take advice from the Lord Chancellor 'who, in his former role as Minister for the North-East, made a bigger impact on unemployment there than anybody else before or since'.[19]

★

Harold Macmillan must have been pleased that Hailsham had talked himself into the North East assignment by ventilating his ideas in Cabinet. It was in the same way that, almost simultaneously, he acquired the job of Minister responsible for Sport. Both commissions 'flowed naturally from contributions I had made in Cabinet discussions', and from the experience which he had had with science where no single ministry is the natural friend at court. But the assignment for Sport was a bizarre one. Hailsham was the first of a long line of Ministers for Sport, and except by dint of his enthusiasm and capacity to stimulate others, he was almost perversely unsuited for what is in any case a pretty odd job. He abominated what he called 'sporting chauvinism', the elevation of athletic prowess into a measure of value for a school, a university or a nation. He disliked watching sport and regarded compulsory school games as 'an incubus'. He was himself physically clumsy and unathletic, enjoying only climbing and walking ('almost to idolatry'), and swimming. It was not necessary that he should have been an international sportsman, but he listed an impressive number of disqualifications for the job.

He was undeterred. In Cabinet he had argued and 'waxed eloquent' that organised sport 'presented a complex of problems out of which modern government was not wholly free to opt'. Proceeding by analogy from his experience as Minister for Science, he advocated that government's relationship with Sport should be focused in the person of one non-departmental minister, so that there might develop 'a coherent body of doctrine, perhaps even a philosophy of government encouragement'. This was to carry doctrine and philosophy to absurdity. Of all the special assignments which he undertook in the first half of 1963 at the behest of the Prime Minister, there is here a case to answer on the charge of electoral gimmickry; and it is perhaps best to leave Sport, as he did in *The Door Wherein I Went*: 'This particular activity was a minor matter, and I thought comparatively little of it at the time it occurred at a period when other things were preoccupying my mind.'

★

The thing which was most preoccupying his mind, and that of the entire government, was the Profumo affair, last and worst of a succession of security and sexual scandals which dragged Macmillan's administration into the shallows.

Hailsham's part in the affair was peripheral only but it had its effect on his immediate future. He was not involved in any of the enquiries which the government made, but when, in the first days of June,

Profumo confessed that he had lied to the House of Commons, Hailsham was chosen to go on television to be interviewed by Robert McKenzie, an experienced and respected political commentator. 'I was in the Lords,' he wrote shortly afterwards, 'expendable, senior, and therefore to that extent, respectable. I was determined to say 1. that private morality does matter in public men; 2. that the public was entitled to take a high moral line on truth telling, and that it was this (and not adultery) which had ruined Profumo; and 3. that it was time we got back to serious business.'[20]

On 21 March 1963 George Wigg, Labour MP for Dudley, under cover of privilege, raised in the House the rumour that a Minister was implicated in the spiriting away out of the country of Christine Keeler, a witness in a criminal trial concerning a shooting incident. He asked the government either to deny the rumour or to appoint a select committee 'so that these things can be dissipated, and the honour of the minister concerned freed from the imputations and innuendoes that are being spread at the present time'.[21] It was the name of John Profumo, the Secretary of State for War, which was the subject of the imputations and innuendoes. On the following morning, Profumo made a personal statement in the House.[22] This had been prepared under the most ill considered circumstances in the small hours. Profumo and his wife were got out of bed unceremoniously at 2.45 a.m., having taken sleeping pills. He was then taken to the House to be met by an extraordinary selection of his colleagues: the Law Officers (Sir John Hobson and Sir Peter Rawlinson); the Leader of the House (Iain Macleod); the Chief Whip (Martin Redmayne); and the Minister without Portfolio (William Deedes). Profumo's solicitor was also present. The Law Officers and the solicitor drafted the statement, which was then agreed paragraph by paragraph by all present. Lord Denning, who later wrote a report on the whole affair, was satisfied that the meeting was never intended as an investigation into the truth. The Ministers' concern was to refute the rumours as quickly and emphatically as they could. Mrs Profumo (the actress Valerie Hobson) told Lord Denning that 'if it had not been for the extraordinary concatenation of circumstances . . . Jack would never have made that statement. I was there and I knew about the sleeping pills and the tiredness . . .' Had the statement been prepared with less haste, the government might have saved itself much embarrassment.

In his statement in the Commons, Profumo denied that he had anything to do with the disappearance of a witness – which was true. He added that he was on friendly terms with Christine Keeler, having met her nearly two years previously, but that there was no impropriety whatsoever in his acquaintanceship – which was untrue. He concluded: 'I shall not hesitate to issue writs for libel and slander if scandalous allegations are made or repeated outside the House.' But the rumours and suspicions did not abate, and Profumo was in the end compelled to make a clean breast of it and confess that he had lied to the House about his liaison with Miss Keeler.

When Hailsham's television interview started, he found that McKenzie wanted to know how a man like Profumo, prepared to lie to the House and keeping the company he did, could rise to high office in the Conservative Party. Hailsham took McKenzie to be making a party political issue out of the scandal, and lost his temper. Anyone who saw the interview, or a clip from it, could not easily forget the face of his avenging morality, white with anger. Hailsham told McKenzie: 'A great party is not to be brought down because of a squalid affair between a woman of easy virtue and a proved liar.' McKenzie persisted: had not Ministers been gullible? 'Well, that depends on how conceited you are ... if I were you, young McKenzie, I shouldn't make up your mind before you've heard the facts.' 'You feel', put McKenzie, 'that those who've spoken out – the Bishop, *The Times* and so on, have tried to turn it into a party issue?' Hailsham, leaning forward and pointing an accusing finger: 'I think *you* have.'[23]

Hailsham's postbag after the interview was preponderantly favourable. Many thought the conscience of the party should be heard loud and clear. Tim Bligh, the Prime Minister's Principal Private Secretary, thought the broadcast was a 'remarkable effort' and reported to Macmillan: 'He gave nothing away but spoke with burning conviction and great effect.' Macmillan, who had not himself seen the programme, sent Hailsham a note of encouragement: 'I cannot tell you how much I have valued your personal support . . . No one can challenge your moral premises.'[24] Nevertheless, the net effect was damaging. Some cabinet ministers considered that he had been ungenerous to a fallen colleague, others doubted the coolness of judgment of someone whose indignation could so readily boil over in public. That was remembered at Blackpool, barely four months on. The morality misfired as well, in the estimation of some. George Wigg, well known for his muck-raking activities and perhaps the last person in the kingdom to prefer such a charge, described the broadcast as cant.[25]

To try to bring moral precepts into public life is a tricky business. Macaulay had written, 'We know no spectacle so ridiculous as the British public in one of its periodical fits of morality.'[26] But Hailsham was not deterred by the risk of ridicule, and he wrote down what he thought about the morality of the thing. He accepted that the British public adopted a humbugging attitude to the sexual behaviour of public men and women. 'We may as well face the fact that the public imposes on politicians an arbitrary standard of morality which is not its own.' Since there had never been a time when a whole team of frontbenchers could be acquitted of sinning if paraded before the public, there must be a convention that private morals are excluded from public criticism *to some extent*. There had to be a concomitant convention that, if a scandal breaks, the victim loses his place in public life. ' "Thou shalt not be found out", the eleventh commandment, with all the hypocrisy that this entails, is part of the public life of any country, and this is a great but unavoidable misfortune.'[27] Hypocrisy indeed, but there was a third, and overriding, convention which had nothing to do with sex. 'A personal statement by a Member of the House to the House must be, so far as it can be made so, gospel true.' This was plain enough, for John Profumo had transgressed. However, the application of the third convention was not so clear.

Hailsham considered that all that was required in Profumo's statement was his denial that he was in any way involved in an attempt to pervert the course of justice through the removal of a witness out of the jurisdiction. The further denial of any improper relationship with Christine Keeler was, he thought, gratuitous and unnecessary. If only Profumo had limited himself to Wigg's accusation, he would not have lied and brought down the great scandal on the government's head. He put this view to Sir John Hobson, the Attorney-General, after the Denning Report had been published. 'I thought he should have stuck to the point and not stuck his neck out on a subject on which male veracity is notoriously unreliable and complete innocence at least unusual.'[28] Hobson could not possibly have agreed. If Hailsham's argument was that a statement limited in the way he suggested would have kept Profumo clear of the eleventh commandment, it ignored the realities of the situation. Hobson himself knew the rumours about Profumo: as to his dalliance with Christine Keeler; her contemporaneous liaison with the Russian naval attaché in London; and Profumo's helping her to disappear.[29] So did Wigg and many others. A half-denial would have fuelled further questioning – again under the protection of Parliamentary privilege. The Ministers concerned in the preparation of Profumo's statement wanted to scotch *all* the rumours. We must assume that, naïvely or no, they believed Profumo's denials: if so, they were justified in aiming to dispose in one sweep of all the rumours attaching to his name.

A few days after Hailsham's bout with McKenzie, on 17 June, the Prime Minister faced a hostile and sceptical House of Commons. The American Ambassador, David Bruce, forecast that it would be a close thing. 'Current betting here is that Macmillan will survive the storm, but with wings so battered that it may take some time for him to recover enough strength to fly.'[30] This was accurate. The Prime Minister's account commanded sympathy, but his admission that he did not know what was going on at critical times was 'pitiable and extremely damaging'.[31] In what was effectively a motion of confidence, although technically one for the adjournment of the House, the Government majority shrank to 57, the extreme low water mark in Macmillan's leadership.

On 21 June, he appointed Lord Denning to undertake an inquiry into the security aspects of the scandal in order to check the flood of accusation and rumour. It is difficult now to recall the hysterical atmosphere in the country as that spring gave way to summer. No member of the government, it seemed, was free. There were supposed orgies of every sort; a headless man and another in an iron mask; one who served dinner in a pair of tiger skin bathing trunks and another in a masonic apron and nothing else. One of the reasons for the violence of Hailsham's anger was his belief that the spate of prurient stories which 'pullulated and festered below the surface' was being fabricated in a central lie factory, and that there was a conspiracy on foot to destroy confidence in political institutions and leadership. But, as Lord Denning found, it was not so.[32] The rumours were due either to the garrulous speculations of Stephen Ward* and the girls of his string, or the guesswork of their credulous clientele. A morbidly curious newspaper readership had done the rest.

Lord Denning reported in September. The Government decided to publish without expurgation, and the Report became an instant best seller. Hailsham thought it a document of mixed quality.[33] The Judge had got about as near to the truth as was possible 'but it was degrading to public life to submit public men to private interrogation simply because slanderous and lying rumours had been put into circulation against them'. Hailsham hoped it would never be repeated in any other case.

Denning, however, gave a beleaguered government much needed relief. He found no security leak, and he showed where the rumours had come from. In only one particular did he fail to acquit the

* Stephen Ward: osteopath, artist and pimp, who introduced the Profumos to Christine Keeler at a house party at Cliveden. He was convicted of various sexual crimes and committed suicide.

government. He made it pretty clear that he thought Macmillan should have dismissed Profumo in March. In arriving at this damning conclusion, he argued that a Prime Minister is justified in acting against a colleague on a reasonable suspicion.[34] Lord Denning framed his recommendation by suggesting that Parliament might wish to consider whether Ministers had asked themselves the right question; but he made it clear that he thought they had not. By inference, proof was not needed. Hailsham thought this a monstrous proposition. He wrote to Hobson that Denning's approach was 'bad in law and logic' and 'wrong in morals'.

> Mr Gladstone notoriously consorted with prostitutes, in order, as he said, to reclaim them. If Denning had been *censor morum* in Queen Victoria's day, Gladstone would never have held office. In my view, Gladstone's conduct was highly indiscreet as well as probably ineffective, and if Birch had been there he would no doubt have asked 'What are whores about?' But there is a difference between innocence and guilt which should not be obscured even in public life.[35]

The rhetorical question about the uses of prostitution was a reference to Nigel Birch's savage attack on the Government in the Profumo debate in which he accused Ministers of being naïve in accepting Profumo's denial of wrongdoing: 'There seems to me a certain basic improbability about the proposition that their relationship was platonic. What are whores about? Yet Profumo's word was accepted.'[36]

As the perspective of time grew longer, Hailsham's opinion of the Denning inquiry grew harsher, until in *A Sparrow's Flight* (1990) it had become 'a panic measure introduced in the wake of the Profumo affair . . . a ghastly error . . .' His retrospective view was coloured by a healthy scepticism about inquiries. There were too many of them and, whenever government was in a difficulty, it tended to turn instinctively to a Judge. It was too much to ask a Judge to take on the task of reassuring public opinion. The Denning type of private inquiry was offensive to a lawyer as well. None of the evidence was published, only the conclusions, and such a procedure encouraged informers. Hailsham considered, again in retrospect, that the correct approach was that if a crime were suspected, the police should investigate; if a security leak, then it was a matter for the Security Services; and if there had to be an inquiry, then it should be held in public with safeguards for those appearing before the tribunal. But how should government deal with a Profumo-type case, with its pullulation of rumours? He did not say. He may have forgotten that at the time Lord Denning was appointed, he had himself drafted notes for a government statement, which pointed out that the traditional method of investigating rumours and allegations by Select Committee had been shown to be unsatisfactory in party matters; and that there should be an inquiry by a single Judge.[37] It therefore seems likely that Hailsham was among those who advised the Prime Minister that a private inquiry by a Judge, however unsatisfactory from the legal point of view, was the best way of dealing with the unprecedented situation.

The justification for the Denning inquiry was in truth political, not legal. It carried hazards, for as Macmillan himself wrote, 'in the method adopted, the putting of our whole lives and careers in the hands of a judge, we took a risk which showed confidence in our integrity'.[38] He might have added that the trust which the government reposed in Lord Denning was not misplaced. Denning lanced a boil which probably could not have been dispersed in any other way. There could have been no better means of bringing the affair to a rapid and decisive end.

The public recollection of Hailsham's part in the Profumo scandal was of his excoriating censure of his erstwhile colleague on television. There is, however, one postscript which it is pleasant to record. Hailsham, who said in a later television interview that Profumo's conduct after the affair made him a better man than he was, wrote a letter to John Profumo in 1975, which does not survive, and received a reply which read simply: 'Your letter has greatly touched me. I shall treasure it.'[39]

Meanwhile, Macmillan's confidence in Hailsham continued to grow, and he chose him for one last enterprise.

18

Nuclear Test Ban Treaty

THE threat of nuclear war hung like a sinister cloud over the late fifties and early sixties. No realist could imagine such a war without the destruction of our civilisation. In 1962 President Kennedy predicted that twenty to thirty states would soon possess nuclear weapons. Five already had them: the United States, the Soviet Union, the United Kingdom, France and China. Preventing the proliferation of these weapons of mass destruction was therefore vital, but an essential step which would have to be taken first was a moratorium on further testing. This was one of the great purposes which Harold Macmillan set himself. 'I have the feeling', he wrote to Kennedy in March 1963, 'that the test ban is the most important step that we can take towards unravelling the frightful tangle of fear and suspicion in East-West relations – important in itself and all the more important for what may flow from it.'[1] What he hoped might flow was the détente which seemed to be the precondition for the survival of humanity.

Over the years of his leadership, Macmillan had repaired the damaged relationship with the United States, and was now able to draw on a remarkable personal friendship with President Kennedy to help, as an honest broker, bring about a ban on nuclear testing. It was this which, in Ambassador Bruce's words, enabled the Prime Minister to fly again. Sir David Ormsby-Gore, the British Ambassador in Washington, told President Kennedy that Macmillan was 'in such a state of euphoria after the Test Ban agreement that Alec doubts whether he now has any intention of resigning . . .' Hailsham generously wrote of Macmillan's contribution to the agreement: '. . . if nothing else stood to his credit, Harold Macmillan's influence in bringing about the negotiation of the partial Test Ban Treaty would entitle him to be treated as one of the great benefactors of this generation . . . He it was who saw that the time was ripe, and the parties were willing . . .'

The signs were not so clear. By March 1963, an impasse had been reached at the 17-nation conference on disarmament at Geneva. France and China appeared determined to pursue their own individual nuclear ambitions, and Khrushchev continued to send bellicose messages to Washington and London. But both Kennedy and Khrushchev had been jolted by being brought to the brink of war in the Cuban missile crisis of October and November, 1962, and for all his roughness the Russian was ready for a peace initiative by the early summer of 1963. In June, just before the negotiations started, he showed what he thought of Chinese dogma on violent revolution. Only madmen, he said, could hope to destroy capitalism by nuclear war: 'A million workers would be destroyed for each capitalist . . . There are people who see things differently. Let them. History will teach them.'[2]

During the spring and early summer, at the same time as he was being oppressed by the Profumo affair, Macmillan was patiently working to bring the Americans and Russians to the point of agreeing on talks between their respective emissaries and the British. There were formidable obstructions. The military establishments in the Soviet Union and the United States were pressing their leaders to carry out more tests, for fear of losing an advantage in the nuclear race, each motivated by deep seated fear and mistrust of the other. Kennedy was sympathetic to Macmillan's purposes, but 'the rats' in the Pentagon, as Macmillan called them, and their allies in Congress, hampered his efforts. None the less, by the beginning of June, the prospect for talks looked promising. Prompted by Macmillan, Kennedy selected Averell Harriman, an elder statesman and diplomat whose experience of Russia reached back to the time of Stalin and Roosevelt, to lead the United States team. Macmillan had first wanted Sir David Ormsby-Gore, the Ambassador in Washington and an intimate friend of Jack Kennedy, to lead the British delegation, but he had been persuaded that he should choose someone of Cabinet rank.[3]

So Hailsham received another summons to Downing Street. It was Whitsun and the Profumo scandal was boiling. He was anxious about the government's position in the country and was not altogether surprised to be called. 'I expected to be rebuked or consulted, I am not sure which.'[4] But he was thoroughly taken unawares to be told by Tim Bligh, Macmillan's Private Secretary, that the Prime Minister had chosen him to lead the British delegation. The choice was a speculative one. Hailsham had no experience of diplomacy. It was his first (and last) international negotiation. Experience here was more important than the knowledge which he had of nuclear science, which in any case was slight. He would be negotiating by the side of the vastly experienced Harriman, and with Andrei Gromyko, whose stone-faced reputation was a legend. None the less, Macmillan had confidence in him. 'I have decided to send Lord Hailsham as our representative,' he wrote in his memoirs. 'Fortified with the help of so able an Ambassador as Humphrey Trevelyan, I felt sure he would do well. He had qualities of energy and imagination which might appeal to Khrushchev.'[5] Macmillan's biographer, Alistair Horne, considered this one of his 'least inspired appointments' and 'perhaps indicative of the pressures on him, and his lassitude at the time'.[6] But there is no evidence that the Prime Minister ever doubted his own judgment in choosing Hailsham. Indeed, on 5 September he noted in his diary: 'I sent H to Moscow on purpose, to test his powers of negotiation etc. He did *very* well.'

His hunch that Hailsham might appeal to Khrushchev was a shrewd one. That unpredictable character was amused when Hailsham responded to the accusation that he was an imperialist: 'An imperialist, yes, but without an empire.' Hailsham found Khrushchev a fascinating, ebullient personality whose coarseness of language and anecdote beggared description. 'When he greeted me first, he told me, in front of the press of the world, that for men of my stamp the Russians had internment facilities available. This was reported in the British press as an invitation to stay in Russia. I replied, humbly enough, that he would find my wants comparatively simple. All I wanted was a bed and a meal. "You will be well treated," he replied.'[7] And when Ian Gilmour met Humphrey Trevelyan in October over lunch, Trevelyan told him that Hailsham had been very entertaining in Moscow, and that Khrushchev had said: 'A very able man, Lord Hailsham. I understand he is going to be promoted as a result of what he is doing here.'[8]

Hailsham got on better with Khrushchev than with Harriman. He was more in tune with the rough countryman than the patrician American. Whether or not this showed, and whether it helped or hindered the negotiations, the American team thought very little of Hailsham's performance. Their attitude was coloured partly by the fact that the British were junior partners in the negotiations with the Russians, and partly by their reaction to Hailsham's personality.

The likely attitude of the British came up at a meeting of the U.S. National Security Council in Washington on 9 July. It was thought that Macmillan wanted a tripartite summit conference, even if there was little of substance to discuss. It was also known that the British were particularly anxious to sign a test ban treaty of some sort. Macmillan had said as much in a letter to Kennedy of 1 July. In arguing for a partial ban, if a full ban were to prove unobtainable, he wrote, '. . . we must be practical . . . we should not let slip the very big prize of the modified ban . . . At any rate we must get agreement if we can. For then we may be able to approach much more effectively the problems that we have in France, Germany etc. and Khrushchev also may be able to do something with China. So even the second prize may turn out well worth having and would certainly be fatal to lose.'[9] As for Hailsham, the President concluded that he 'clearly envisages himself as a mediator between us and the Russians. Mr Bundy mentioned Ambassador Bruce's nervousness about the personal attitude of Hailsham.'[10] The reasons for the Ambassador's nervousness were not given in the summary record of the meeting, but they appear from Harriman's briefing papers which included biographical — and personal — details. 'Lord Hailsham is a man of many jobs', the note read:

> Embassy officers believe [him] to combine a high degree of political and intellectual astuteness, together with political ambitions, with just enough instability (or perhaps better, unpredictableness) to permit occasional impetuous actions and public statements which subsequently cause both him and his party much embarrassment and concern . . . Embassy officers find that there is in him more than a suggestion of intellectual arrogance and the consequent tendency to find his own opinions especially congenial and convincing.[11]

The notes added that he had, on occasion, made statements 'which are at least critical of the United States if not actually anti-American', citing his speech on the 'brain drain'.

Harriman also provided himself with informal opinions through his network of contacts with newspapermen. Marquis Childs, the Washington correspondent of the *St Louis Post-Despatch* and a distinguished commentator who later won a Pulitzer Prize, telephoned at the beginning of July, and told Harriman that he had had a talk with Hailsham. What is he like? Harriman asked. 'Childs said he is an odd bird. He has a kind of righteousness which will make him difficult.'[12]

These assessments were disquieting, but shrewd. The Americans found them to be borne out during the negotiations. The delegations met first in London, where the Americans stopped on their way to

Moscow. There was a lunch which Macmillan attended. Carl Kaysen, the executive secretary to the American delegation, recollected that the Prime Minister took Harriman and Hailsham aside and said 'rather brutally' that Hailsham should simply follow the Americans' lead.[13] This was not well received. Then, at the first business session on 12 July, Hailsham led off in his best forensic manner by criticising the draft treaty which had been tabled by the Americans. He was not aware that the British officials had already approved the text, and he had to be headed off.[14]

Kaysen found Hailsham 'querulous and difficult'.[15] Arthur Schlesinger, who remained in Washington, confirmed Kaysen's impressions.

> As for the test ban treaty, I regret to say that he did not make a good impression on the American negotiators. Averell Harriman had had long experience in Moscow and knew how to deal with the Russians. Hailsham, who had little experience, infuriated Harriman by complaining that Harriman was too tough. Averell of course knew precisely what he was doing and carried the negotiations through to a successful conclusion. He was still fuming about Hailsham when he returned to Washington.[16]

Professor Schlesinger nevertheless thought Quintin Hailsham 'a most intelligent, and boisterous, man'; and his contribution to the success of the talks may well have been underrated, particularly by Harriman, whom he succeeded in rubbing the wrong way. As so often, his manner, which was offensive to the Americans, tended to obstruct an objective assessment of his achievement. However that may be, he was not esteemed in Washington after the Moscow talks.

The briefing process in London began in June, and was undertaken by Sir Solly Zuckerman, whom Hailsham already knew well, and Duncan Wilson, an outstandingly able diplomat who was also a member of the British delegation. The most important question was whether a comprehensive ban would prove possible. This would encompass testing in the atmosphere, in outer space, under water and underground. Hailsham's instructions were explicit. The British team were to go for a comprehensive treaty if it were possible. If not, they were to go for a ban on atmospheric tests, whose fallout would contaminate the atmosphere. In the event, underground tests had to be left out, and the partial treaty which was concluded covered tests in the atmosphere, in outer space, and under water – but not underground. Kennedy's advisers were telling him that without adequate facilities for inspection, the Russians might cheat and carry out tests underground without being detected. The Russians considered that inspection was equivalent to licensed espionage: they did not think you could let the cat into the kitchen to hunt the mice without its also drinking the milk.[17] This led to fruitless haggling over the number of inspections to be allowed. The British advisers thought the argument arid, and in May, Zuckerman and Sir William Penney, the distinguished nuclear physicist, minuted the Prime Minister:

> . . . we share the view that the dangers which inspection is intended to obviate are less important than the risk of further proliferation of nuclear weapons if a test ban is not concluded soon. In our view, too, the military significance of clandestine testing which might escape detection can have no effect on the grand balance of military power.[18]

Their opinion was that in order to have value, underground tests would have to be followed by atmospheric tests which were themselves certain to be detected. It followed that underground tests were not crucial and a treaty banning all nuclear tests could be signed without any provisions at all for underground inspection.[19] Unhappily, neither the Americans nor the Russians would agree to such a simple solution and, when the talks began, it was immediately clear that a total ban was out of the question. 'It was obvious to me from almost the very start that the total ban on tests which I had been briefed to propose was a cock that would not fight, for the simple reason that neither the Soviet nor the American team wanted one.'

The most interesting of the preliminary meetings was the 24-hour visit of Kennedy and his entourage to Birch Grove, the Macmillan home in Sussex, at the end of June. It was the last time that Macmillan saw Kennedy, and he could never afterwards think of the visit without emotion. There was, he wrote, a 'fantastic, even romantic, atmosphere that prevailed during those thrilling hours'.[20] Hailsham was just as much affected by Kennedy's personality and aura as Macmillan. The President dominated his enormous staff and his table talk entranced Hailsham. 'Of all the members of that company he was the civilised man, brave, young, handsome and committed, whatever faults or shortcomings he may have been guilty of, to the triumph of the good . . . I have never met a man in public life like him before, and I believe I never will again.'[21]

The talks began on 15 July and lasted ten days. They were opened by Khrushchev, but after the first meeting he handed over the negotiations to Gromyko. Hailsham described the procedure.

We began in the afternoon with a negotiation. The next morning the legal experts would meet and try to reduce what we had agreed to a text. The next afternoon we would start again, revising the lawyers' draft and then breaking new ground as before. After the session the British and American teams would meet in private session to discuss possible courses of action and iron out points of difference between one another. Then we would have to communicate with our respective governments. The most important sessions when things were really tense were three handed with Gromyko, Harriman and I alone together with the interpreters.[22]

There were tense moments, and the success of the talks was by no means a foregone conclusion. One issue was the so-called Multilateral Force, on which the Americans were keen. This would have involved an additional fleet of surface vessels armed with nuclear warheads, and manned by a mixed force from the Western Alliance, including Germans. The Russians would not stomach the idea. Both Hailsham and Macmillan knew that in practice a choice would have to be made between a test ban and the Multilateral Force, and were quite certain that the test ban was more important. That view fortunately prevailed. Then, before negotiations started, Khrushchev announced that he wanted to couple a ban on tests with a non-aggression pact between the Communist bloc and the Western Alliance. Apart from the unpleasant memories associated with the phrase, the idea of any such pact was as unwelcome to the Americans as was the Multilateral Force to the Russians. Carl Kaysen put the American viewpoint: 'It was poison for us, because we knew that the Germans, who were already uneasy, would be outraged by any statement, much less a formal treaty. In 1963, the Germans still interpreted a non-aggression pact between the two alliances as the formal and final recognition of the division of Germany, which they vehemently rejected.'[23] Harriman and Hailsham were able to deflect the proposal by pointing out that it was something which had to be discussed among all the NATO allies. Hailsham argued that the Soviet government would achieve the worst possible results if the allies of Britain and the United States thought a deal was being done in Moscow behind their backs; and Harriman emphasised how important it was not to hold up the signature of the test ban.[24] Eventually, Kennedy and the Russians accepted an anodyne form of wording about a non-aggression pact put forward by Hailsham for inclusion in the communique, but not the treaty.[25]

The last days of the talks were dramatic. '*Bad* telegrams from Moscow this morning,' Macmillan recorded in his diary for 24 July.

'I have told Gore to stay in Washington, postponing his leave. The Americans are being very stubborn . . .' The following day, 'Hailsham foresaw a wrangle and perhaps a breakdown'[26] at the very last afternoon session. The difficulties were caused by 'legalists on Harriman's team', in Macmillan's description. The treaty was to be open to adherence by other countries, a condition vital to inhibit the proliferation of nuclear weapons. But now the Americans asked what was to be the position if a government which was not recognised by any of the three original parties wished to adhere: East Germany, for example? They also proposed a clause which would make clear that nothing in the treaty was to prevent the use of nuclear weapons in war. Macmillan thought these points mere pedantry at the eleventh hour, and the latter one 'so absurd as to be hardly credible'.[27] Hailsham felt the same; and according to Schlesinger's account, he became increasingly restive and unhappy in these last hours. 'Soon he was complaining to London that Harriman's rigidity might lose the whole treaty. His reports disturbed Macmillan, who finally instructed Ormsby-Gore to call on the President and register official British anxiety.'[28]

This episode was not forgotten in Washington. When Hailsham (by then Quintin Hogg again) was invited at speak at the Churchill Library dinner in November, 1964, Averell Harriman made a memorandum for the files. This indicates that Harriman, at least, thought Ormsby-Gore shared his own views about Hailsham's performance in Moscow.

> David Harlech [Ormsby-Gore's hereditary title] . . . recalled that Prime Minister Macmillan had received hectic telegrams from Moscow . . . stating that I was making such demands on the Soviets that the negotiations . . . would fall through. Macmillan had therefore telegraphed the President, which had been transmitted by David, asking the President to call me off. In speaking of this, of course, David knew that Hailsham was grossly exaggerating the situation and had no real understanding of what was going on.[29]

In the end, the differences were blown away by the will to agree. When he finally got through to the President at the end of the afternoon of 25 July, Macmillan learned that everything had been agreed and that the Treaty was about to be initialled.[30] At the same moment as the President and Prime Minister were talking, Carl Kaysen in Moscow was agreeing final textual details with McGeorge Bundy in Washington. Bundy was able to pass Kennedy a note while

Macmillan was still on the line saying all was settled. 'I shall always remember Carl Kaysen's call,' wrote Zuckerman. 'It was made to the White House on an open telephone line from the Spiridonovka Palace. It seemed like a real sign of trust.'[31]

Hailsham and Harriman did not allow the tensions between them to interfere with their mission; but the tensions were serious. Hailsham thought Harriman rigid and pettifogging. This confirmed his general view that Americans tended to be too legalistic, and that this might be due to their written constitution which made it difficult for them to distinguish law from politics – an eccentric objection to written constitutions.[32] On his side, the older Harriman thought Hailsham impetuous, over-anxious to get a treaty at almost any price, and an amateur to boot. Perhaps Harriman knew exactly what he was about, as Professor Schlesinger thought; but it was equally possible that he was too legalistic and had to be rescued more than once by the British. The true effect of tactics in negotiation can never be known. But the weakness in Hailsham's temperament at times of stress was remembered in Washington when he became a candidate for the Tory leadership. Macmillan, however, could 'never be sufficiently grateful both to Hailsham and to Harriman for the energy and imagination with which they conducted this delicate negotiation'.[33]

The treaty, partial though it was, was much more than better than nothing. 'At least we have done something,' Macmillan wrote to Zuckerman. 'Perhaps we have done better than that by accepting the partial ban than by going on with an interminable wrangle about various forms of inspection.'[34] Although everyone concerned in the negotiations deeply regretted that the ban was not comprehensive (Zuckerman thought it 'a world tragedy of the first magnitude'[35]) it was, as Macmillan had foreseen, the first indispensable step in the process of thawing out the cold war. As his biographer claims, it was a last triumph, and he had a hero's reception in the Commons.*

After the initialling ceremony, the chief negotiators were entertained to dinner in the Kremlin, in a small room which had been made for Catherine the Great and in which Churchill, Roosevelt and Stalin had dined together during the war. Hailsham was overcome by the occasion and described how, suddenly, his self-confidence deserted him. 'There was so much I would have liked to say

---

* The file of messages of gratitude to the Prime Minister from heads of state and other dignitaries is a collectors' item. It includes telegrams from the Patriarch of Antioch and All the East, the Supreme Catholicus of All Armenia and the Patriarch of Moscow. The Eastern Church had special reasons to appreciate this first sign of the unfreezing of the ice floes. (PREM 11: 4409.)

both to Harriman and Khrushchev about the future of the world and the future of the human race. But I was tongue tied. I was much the youngest of the three and I was absolutely exhausted by the experience of . . . negotiation with the toughest professionals on earth.'[36]

The test ban negotiation was the last of the special missions which Macmillan assigned to Hailsham. It seemed to confirm his evolving view that, if he should lay down the leadership, those qualities of enthusiasm and imagination which had commended Hailsham for Moscow, made him also the fittest candidate to succeed.

19

The Tory Leadership

THE loss of the Tory leadership was the hinge of Hailsham's career. Before 1963, the highest political prizes were open; afterwards they were closed off and he turned to the law.

The truth about the whole episode is peculiarly elusive. What had happened to allow the unlikely Lord Home to come from nowhere and win in a few short days? Had Macmillan always intended Home to succeed? Or had he used first Hailsham and then Home to stop Butler? Or was opinion in the party so sharply divided between Hailsham and Butler that a compromise was inevitable? Had Hailsham destroyed his chances by his behaviour at the Conference? Was Macmillan, even on his sick bed, still pulling strings like some puppet master or was the Tory party machine at work? Or yet again, did the Tory infantry panic in face of a public contest like an American Party Convention and rally to someone 'safe' who could unite the party? There are almost as many theories as commentators. What is certain, however, is that Hailsham was Macmillan's first choice to succeed him in the summer of 1963 and up to Blackpool; but that within hours of the Party Conference ending, he had lost the Prime Minister's confidence.

Macmillan had been thinking of the succession at least since the beginning of the year. In early January, Butler dined with the Prime Minister at Bucks. As was his habit he made a note of the conversation.[1] Macmillan had just decided to appoint Hailsham as Commissioner for the North East. It was entirely his own idea and he was pleased with it. 'He detailed several possible leaders in our party,' noted Butler, 'the two Peers Home and Hailsham, Maudling, Heath, and was kind enough to mention myself. The Socialists had no such team . . .' (This was a diffident tone for the heir presumptive – if not heir apparent.) Macmillan doubted whether Home would 'take advantage of the new scheme to come down' to the Commons. 'As for Hailsham, the PM said he had deliberately let him in, but thought his uprightness of character would prevent him from deserting the Lords as leader. But whether the new unemployment job will turn him downwards I do not know.'

The 'new scheme' by which the two peers might come down to the Commons was a reference to the Peerage Act which had made it possible from 31 July 1963 for hereditary peers to disclaim their peerages for their own lives, and so become eligible for membership of the House of Commons. There had been a convention, since Baldwin became Leader of the Conservatives in 1923, that a peer could not be Prime Minister.

Butler's note of his conversation continued by reporting that Macmillan had said that the strain of No. 10 was so awful that he had sometimes to resort to Jane Austen. Butler responded that for his part he was then reading Mommsen.

At this stage Macmillan was not thinking of giving up, more of getting the tackle in order for the time when he would go. In March, just before the Profumo scandal broke, the Prime Minister told Butler that he had no intention of retiring but would review the position at Christmas; he thought it 'ridiculous to give way to a younger man now, and then for that young man (if any) to be tarnished by the present difficulties . . .'[2] But by June there was a strong feeling in the party that the leadership should jump to a younger generation, and in the Profumo debate on 17th, Nigel Birch gave bitter vent to his feelings, quoting Browning's *The Lost Leader*.

> . . . let him never come back to us!
> There would be doubt, hesitation and pain,
> Forced praise on our part − the glimmer of twilight.
> Never glad confident morning again!

Early in the same month Macmillan approached Hailsham and told him that he thought him the right man to succeed him. According to Hailsham, the first approach was through Oliver Poole, but it seems clear that there was at least one conversation with Macmillan in June.[3] It seems too that Macmillan frankly told Hailsham that his first thought had been for Lord Home, but that Home was not keen at that stage to disclaim his peerage. Hailsham also had a conversation with Home, which he dates as preceding the Poole/Macmillan approach, in which they agreed that they should not both disclaim their peerages while the succession was in issue, and that they should consult each other.[4]

As has been seen, the Prime Minister's appreciation of Hailsham was mixed. He admired his uprightness, but was irritated by some of his habits, and Butler left a revealing example after a Chequers weekend in April 1963: 'Harold was annoyed with Quintin Hailsham for talking a great deal and very loudly about the book [*Honest to God* by the Bishop of Woolwich] and then acknowledging that he had not read it.'[5]

But Macmillan appreciated Hailsham's staunchness during the Profumo affair. On 7 July he noted in his diary that, after some wavering by some of the younger members, the Cabinet was standing firm against intrigue: 'Lord Hailsham has been splendid throughout.'[6] He knew that the revivalist fervour and genuine passion which Hailsham could harness to his intellect was capable of winning elections, and this was probably the clinching argument in his mind. It continued to weigh with Macmillan. In September he noted in his diary: 'I cannot go on to an election and lead in it. I am beginning to feel that I haven't the strength and that perhaps another leader could do what I did after Eden left. But it cannot be done by a pedestrian politician. It needs a man with vision and moral strength – Hailsham, not Maudling.'[7]

From June until after the Party Conference in October, while the government's stock was being dragged lower by the Profumo affair, Macmillan vacillated between carrying on until the next election and giving way to a successor. On 20 September he told the Queen that he did not plan to call an election that year, but that he would not lead the party when it did take place early in 1964. All this was to be announced at the Party Conference on 12 October.[8] But by 28 September he felt tempted to change his mind: 'I brood about this all the time'.[9] Earlier in the month he had discussed the situation with Butler and Home. He noted in his diary that Butler did not want another unsuccessful bid, and did not expect any real demand for himself. 'He would prefer to be Warwick (which he could be) and not try to be the King (which he can't be). On the whole he is for Hailsham.'[10] Home was distressed to learn that Macmillan had any idea of retiring, but understood the reasons and thought them sound. He too favoured Hailsham, 'but fears there will be complete disunity in the party and that great troubles will follow'.[11] With hindsight, Macmillan's mental drift can be attributed to the onset of his prostate illness which erupted painfully on the very eve of the Conference. It did not make the task of his closest colleagues easier.

At the weekend immediately before the Conference (5/6 October), Macmillan invited his son-in-law and confidant Julian Amery to Chequers. After avoiding the question of the succession through dinner on Friday 4th, and in a long conversation afterwards, Macmillan finally told Amery the next morning that he must resign. Amery doubted if this was wise, but asked whom he would wish to succeed. Macmillan said Quintin Hailsham – because he thought him most likely to win the next election.* Amery argued for Macmillan staying. He thought the odds at an election were in favour of his doing so. Later they were joined by Maurice Macmillan, who supported Amery's line. By the end of the weekend the two were on the way to convincing the Prime Minister that he should stay.[12] Macmillan, however, had suffered agonies of indecision. He did not sleep at all on the Saturday night.[13] He hated the thought that by going he would be letting so many people down, but he was anxious that he might be humiliated if he stayed. He feared that there was no clear successor. He saw Alec Home on Sunday evening, who introduced new doubt. If Macmillan announced on 12 October that he would stand down the following January, the search for a new leader would start at once. On the other hand, if he announced his determination to go on he would have to fight a vocal and substantial minority, and might then suffer defeat in the election. Home did not propound a solution to the dilemma.[14]

Macmillan motored up to London in the morning. He was greeted by Tim Bligh, his Private Secretary, who told him that the Cabinet were 'rallying to him with great enthusiasm'. There were only one or two exceptions.[15] His diary records that he saw Butler ('who would clearly prefer me to go on, for – in his heart – he does not expect the succession *and* fears it'), Dilhorne, the Lord Chancellor ('*all* for going on'), the Chief Whip ('very ready to fight), Sandys ('unhesitating and loyal'), Oliver Poole ('deeply moved and almost in tears', but warned against his going on) and Home ('balanced but on the whole adverse').

The diary contains no mention of a meeting with Hailsham. But Hailsham's account is that 'on the Monday' he was summoned to Downing Street by the Prime Minister. 'I had not the slightest inkling of what was to take place. He told me, formally, that he wished me to succeed him, and gave me to understand that he expected to retire about Christmas.' Macmillan's biographer doubts this account.[16] On the face of it, it seems inconsistent with

---

* Lord Amery put the point more vividly in a conversation with the author. In answer to Amery's question whether Hailsham would make a good Prime Minister, Macmillan replied: 'Dear boy, that is secondary. The thing is, can he win an election?'

Macmillan's decision to go on, taken over the preceding weekend, and for which, according to his diary, he had received very substantial support. Hailsham's autobiography must be treated cautiously. It was written without reference to contemporary documents and his recollection is certainly faulty at some points. It is inherently implausible that on that Monday Macmillan would have made such a forthright statement. But it is not conceivable that Hailsham would have invented the meeting altogether. The fact that there is no mention of the meeting in Macmillan's diary is inconclusive. Diaries are often not comprehensive and are not necessarily authoritative, particularly when, as seems likely in Macmillan's case, they are written to be read by others. In Hailsham's earlier book, *The Door Wherein I Went* (1975), he wrote that he did see Macmillan at the latter's request on that day and was told that the Prime Minister wished him to succeed him if he retired. 'I say "if"', Hailsham added, 'because he had not then determined to do so, and was in any event talking about retiring, if he did, at Christmas.' This account is corroborated in Randolph Churchill's book *The Fight for the Tory Leadership*, written immediately afterwards, and seen and amended by Macmillan before publication in 1964.[17]

In fact, the truth was different from both accounts. Hailsham undoubtedly saw Macmillan on Monday 7 October. They discussed the Prime Minister's dilemma and Hailsham advised him that at the Conference later in the week he could in practice neither announce a January retirement nor that he was going to fight on. A middle way would have to be found. Hailsham confirmed these views in a handwritten letter written the same day which, because of the controversy surrounding the discussion between the two, deserves to be given in full.

7 October 1963

Dear Harold,

I have been reflecting on this morning's conversation.

I have been prevented by numerous and persistent callers from putting pen to paper.

Briefly, my view is this. On Saturday you will not in practice be able to pursue either of the two clear cut extremes. You will therefore be driven to adopt an intermediate position.

This, however, you will only be able to hold

(1) if you obtain the correct formula;

(2) if the policy content of your speech seems new, intriguing and potentially satisfying on the *home* front as well as the foreign and economic;

(3) if you are backed by the Cab.

If I can, I am willing to help with (1) and (2). I would have done so, had I been able to get ten minutes by myself.[18]

According to a note made by Bligh on the following day, 8 October, Butler advised the Prime Minister in a similar sense. 'One did not take a serious decision at a rally,' said Rab prophetically, and he indicated the lines of a possible 'intermediate position': 'You were not going to give up the leadership of the party. (This would occasion great applause). You had a lot of work still to complete . . . when this was satisfactorily completed you would make up your own mind as to your future.'[19]

This was excellent advice from both Hailsham and Butler, and it neatly resolved the dilemma to which Home had pointed during the previous weekend. It is conceivable that during the meeting between Macmillan and Hailsham, the Prime Minister also said that *if and when* he retired, he was minded to put forward Hailsham as his successor. However that may be, events overtook the Prime Minister. During the night he was seized with excruciating pains leaving him unable to urinate without medical help.

Tuesday 8 October

With great courage Macmillan presided at Cabinet in the morning. As his diary relates, he left the room to enable his colleagues to consider his plan to announce at Blackpool later in the week that he would lead at the next election. All except Enoch Powell apparently gave him backing. Most of the Cabinet then left for the Blackpool conference. Meanwhile, Macmillan consulted his doctors who told him that his prostate was inflamed and that he would have to go to hospital immediately. He was admitted to King Edward's Hospital for Officers in the evening. During the day, when he still hoped that the doctors might be able to 'patch him up', he dictated a note to Butler as First Secretary of State: 'We discussed the situation today. As regards the government, I will continue to carry it on unless and until I send you a message and publish it entrusting it to you. *Blackpool* . . . I should hope to get you a message in the course of tomorrow, Wednesday October 9, as to whether or not I shall be able to come . . .'[20]

Wednesday 9 October

This was the first day of the Conference. The news of the Prime Minister's illness had reached Blackpool the previous evening and speculation about his future and the succession had begun to raise the temperature. Ian Gilmour recorded in his diary that Hailsham received 'incomparably the best reception' in the Conference Hall.[21] Later in the day Hailsham gave a speech in the nearby Morecambe constituency, saying 'So now, Harold, get well quick . . . And when you come back we will hand back to you a government and a party in good order . . .'

Meanwhile in London another confusing day passed. According to his biographer, Macmillan wrote from his bed to the Queen, telling her that his resignation was a necessity, and prepared a letter for Home to read out to Conference making it clear that the Prime Minister could not now lead at the next Election.[22] Home visited the hospital but what happened is obscure.[23] According to Home, Macmillan pressed *him* to consider taking on the leadership, but Home said he was reluctant to leave the Lords. Macmillan seemed to accept this and 'after much thought' concluded that Hailsham might be the best choice. Home agreed. Macmillan then asked Home as Conference President for that year to take a message to Blackpool, and to invite 'those whose business it was to do so, to take soundings about the future leadership'.[24] If this is a correct account, Macmillan was thinking of Home as successor as early as the first day of the Conference and before any of the histrionics had started in Blackpool. There is, however, no reference in Macmillan's diary entry for this day to any discussion with Home about his candidacy for the succession. Indeed, the only reference is to Hailsham: 'If *Hailsham* is to be a competitor,' underlined the Prime Minister, 'he must at once give up his peerage and find a constituency.'[25]

After the Conference, Butler made a note about the 'story of Blackpool' in which he gives a different slant to the Macmillan/ Home meeting. He considered, with every justification, that the Prime Minister's message read by Home to Conference on Thursday was the most important event at Blackpool, and had led directly to the heady scenes which were so distasteful to him. His view was that Macmillan should have been given a chance to recover and should not have had to take vital decisions while he was an invalid.

This all came to a head when Alec Home called at the hospital and obtained from him the declaration which is now history, which was read to the Conference on Thursday afternoon. A statement of facts cannot stress too strongly that Alec Home obtained this and himself read it out. The fact that the PM asked for the processes of selection of his successor to be undertaken in the middle of a Party Conference was bound to create consternation and confusion and intrigue, as indeed it did.[26]

In view of what took place as a result of the Prime Minister's declaration to the Party Conference, particularly the impact on Hailsham's candidacy, Butler's note assumes some importance. More generally, the wisdom of Butler's contemporary view has stood the test of time. Macmillan, with or without encouragement from Home, and although weakened by illness, damaged the Party by tossing the succession into the middle of the Conference.

Butler's suspicions about Home are corroborated from an unexpected quarter. After the whole affair was over, Sir John Richardson, Macmillan's personal physician, made his own note of events.[27] He had from the beginning thought that the urologists' view that the Prime Minister would be out of action for two or three months was exaggeratedly cautious. He knew Macmillan's recuperative powers and on the Wednesday (9th) had 'quite bluntly' told him that he did not need more than a few weeks. But by then Macmillan's mind was made up: 'he said that he wished to go and did not wish the expected duration of his illness to be minimised'. Macmillan had by then seen Home and given him the message to Conference. Earlier in the day, and before the Home meeting, Macmillan had been visited by his son Maurice, who later told Richardson that his father 'had no intention of making a public pronouncement to this effect [resignation] at that time'. 'However,' Richardson's note continued, 'after an interview with Lord Home, the letter to Home stating his intention of resigning and not to lead the party at the next election was written. After this was done, Mr Macmillan was clearly anxious for the letter to be communicated to the Tory Party.'

In face of this evidence, it is difficult to accept that Home's part in the developing drama was a purely passive one. Home's own biographer appears to take a similar view.[28] Home had already told Macmillan that he was against his staying on as Prime Minister, and his influence at this point should not be underestimated.

Amery's statement records that he went to see his father-in-law in hospital during the morning: '. . . he confirmed that the doctors said he must have an operation and that he could not go on as leader in the circumstances. I asked him what he wanted me to do. He said go to Blackpool and get Quintin elected. Maurice, whom I soon met up with at Blackpool, had the same instructions'.[29] In that way, Hailsham became the Macmillan family candidate.

Thursday 10 October

In London, Macmillan had his operation. Before doing so, he saw Home again. According to Macmillan's own amendment to the draft of Randolph Churchill's book* he told Home that 'no one was emerging and it would almost certainly be his duty to disclaim his peerage and slip into the front line. Home was still reluctant but said if no one did emerge he would accept a draft.'[30]

This was an odd, but highly important, exchange. As the Conference, and for that matter the Cabinet also, were then still ignorant of Macmillan's intention to resign immediately, it was, to say the least, unlikely that anyone would have 'emerged'. Moreover, only the previous day the Prime Minister had sent his son and son-in-law posting up to Blackpool with instructions to do their best to get Hailsham adopted. Macmillan, it seems, was keeping Home in play and always intended to.

With Macmillan's statement in his pocket, Home went off to Blackpool to deliver it. This he did in the afternoon, a courtly figure peering over half-glasses as he read. In his statement, the Prime Minister told the party that it would be impossible for him to carry the physical burden of leading it at the next General Election. 'In these circumstances I hope that it will soon be possible for the customary processes of consultation to be carried on within the party about its future leadership.' Something close to hysteria overwhelmed the Conference. The statement precipitated a contest under arc lights, more reminiscent of American than English political processes.

Immediately afterwards, Hailsham, who was to speak to the Conservative Political Centre that evening, asked for his supporters' views on what he should do in face of this quite unexpected development. He thought he had three options: disclaim his peerage immediately; announce that he intended to stay in the Lords; do nothing and wait on events. Dennis Walters advised that, if he intended to run for the leadership, in order to have any chance he should announce his disclaimer immediately.[31] Ian Gilmour, who with Walters was closest to Hailsham throughout the contest,

---

* Randolph Churchill submitted at least part of the proofs of his book, *The Fight for the Tory Leadership* to Macmillan for comment before its publication in 1964. Macmillan advised Hailsham that 'you might be wise to get a look at them too.' (Macmillan Archive: Macmillan – QH: 18 Nov. 1963.)

concurred, as did Peter Walker, Anthony Royle and, importantly, Oliver Poole, on whose advice Hailsham was always inclined to rely.

Poole thought that Hailsham should make his announcement at the C.P.C. meeting in order to get his campaign off to a flying start. Walters and Gilmour had reservations about announcing to the Party, and thought a press conference or the issue of a simple statement might be quieter and better. But their more cautious views were overborne by their candidate whose mind was made up. He would make his announcement at the C.P.C. meeting that evening.

Julian Amery and Maurice Macmillan also encouraged him to act, but according to Walters[32] they did not instigate the move for Hailsham to announce his disclaimer immediately: the decision had already been taken. According to Randolph Churchill's account, the advice tendered by Maurice Macmillan and Amery, acting as the Prime Minister's envoys, was that Hailsham should disclaim his peerage immediately and get ready to assume the leadership.[33] Walters thought that that was putting it too high: his recollection was that Julian Amery and Maurice Macmillan confirmed that Hailsham was the family choice and that in their opinion an announcement at the Conference was the right thing.[34] Walters' recollection seems more likely right; but however that may be, indications of that sort from the Macmillan family could hardly be ignored. Only Butler, to whom Hailsham spoke, advised caution. As he wrote later:

> He [Hailsham] had been up to my room that afternoon and asked my advice. I had recommended him to say he was considering his position and no more. He said he thought it very good advice but would not take it. Alec Home gave him similar advice. This all resulted in due course in a slump in support for Hailsham.[35]

In fact, it does not appear that Home gave Hailsham similar advice. He was not then aware that Hailsham was contemplating an immediate announcement.

Hailsham duly made his announcement after his speech to the C.P.C. In content, it was brief and dignified. He paid tribute to his father whose peerage it had been. He explained his initial reluctance to go to the Lords, but how his respect and affection for that institution had grown. He said that until now he could have done nothing which might undermine the Prime Minister's authority. 'But it must be obvious to you that that situation no longer obtains just now. I shall continue to try to serve my country honourably as a friend to my colleagues, but I ought to say tonight that my intention is, after deep thought, to disclaim my peerage.'

It mattered not how dignified the statement read in print. Hailsham was white and tense with excitement. The effect was bound to be pandemonium. Under a banner headline, 'Call me Mister!' the *Daily Express* declared: 'Lord Hailsham threw his coronet over the Tower and announced he is ready to fight as plain Mister Quintin Hogg for the leadership.' In the hall where his statement was made the audience stood and sang 'For he's a jolly good fellow'. The scene deeply upset Butler. 'When I entered the Winter Gardens,' he wrote a few days afterwards, 'he [Hailsham] was emerging surrounded by hysterical and weeping women on the lines of a Hitler campaign.'[36] The image of a Nuremberg rally which passed into popular legend was grotesque and overwrought, but the hierarchy did not like what they saw. Dennis Walters was in the hall and watched the platform party closely. There were clear signs of discomfiture at the top table: 'Geoffrey Lloyd appeared livid; Keith Joseph embarrassed; Toby Aldington . . . , William Rees-Mogg and Peter Goldman all embarrassed; Martin Redmayne, Chief Whip, stony and prefectorial, clearly not best pleased.'[37] The disapproval of Redmayne, soon to play an important role, was ominous, and Hailsham's low flash point was uncomfortably exposed.

The gale did not abate the next day. Randolph Churchill arrived with 'Q' buttons which he pressed on anyone he could, and marched about urging people to 'testify'. Hailsham and his supporters tried to dissociate themselves from these antics, but they can only have made matters worse. The incident, however, which rivalled the previous evening's scene in the Winter Gardens in causing dismay in respectable Tory breasts was Hailsham's appearance in the foyer of the Imperial Hotel with his one-year-old daughter, Kate, mixing baby food in full view of the media. Mary had not been able to find anyone to look after her youngest child, and when her husband asked her to join him in Blackpool she saw no alternative but to bring the baby as well. She was much criticised by her husband's campaign managers for this, and it was at best a silly decision. But Hailsham deeply resented the unfair stories that he had brought his little daughter to the Conference to help his electioneering; unfortunately, however, he gave some colour to the gossip by his behaviour. His detractors made the most of it. Redmayne, who had been thought a Hoggite but considered that 'the cork had popped too soon for Hailsham';[38] Morrison, the Chairman of the 1922 Committee; and Dilhorne (another Hoggite) were the three most influential advisers and pollsters to the Prime Minister. They were all shocked by the scene in the Imperial Hotel and shortly made their dismay plain to Macmillan.

Hailsham certainly went far to destroy his own chances by these excesses. Gilmour could not understand why theatrics should necessarily be a ground for criticism, and thought the ability to excite passion in an audience was one of the tests of leadership. He gave a graphic account of the excitement Hailsham could generate.* On the last day of the Conference he was one of four ministers answering questions from the platform. The Chairman tried to introduce the four collectively to prevent a demonstration. 'In this she failed, as there was a roar of acclamation when she mentioned Q's name, but she cut it off very prematurely by shrieking through the microphone that they must get on and smiling one of her most devotional smiles.'[39] But it was this very capacity to excite, and become excited, with his propensity to let his reactions take on a life of their own, which caused alarm. It was not what the Tory Party wanted then. Butler's view that 'one did not take a serious decision at a rally' was only too true.

Remainder of the Conference

During the Conference conversations took place between Hailsham and Home, as was natural. Because they were, successively, the Prime Minister's choice, the exchanges are of interest. According to Home's memoirs, he walked away from the Conference Hall with Hailsham after reading out Macmillan's message on the Thursday. On that occasion he told Hailsham that he had his support, but apparently he did not then know that Hailsham was about to announce his disclaimer. 'Had I known that he intended to throw his claim to the leadership into the ring within a matter of hours, I would have tried to dissuade him from it then and there, for people never like being bounced, and least of all at a time of emotional stress ... there followed a swift reaction against his candidature.'[40]

There may have been another conversation, mentioned by Hailsham in *A Sparrow's Flight*, or it may have been part of the same exchange, in which Home told his fellow Peer that he was 'under strong pressure to disclaim and throw his hat in the ring'. According to Hailsham, he reminded Home of their previous agreement that both would not disclaim. He then told Home that in any case he did

---

* Lord Gilmour's diary is altogether graphic. He described the lady chairman as being as 'full of ghastly refinement as ever, though mercifully she had discarded the red Biretta with which she had jeopardised the Roman Catholic vote during the first two days'.

not think Home would be a good choice to succeed to the leadership, that he had no experience of home affairs, and that if he did become Prime Minister, he would not last long – unwelcome advice that Hailsham was later to repeat.

On Friday, Maudling's speech on economic affairs was a flop and he virtually dropped out of the reckoning as a candidate for the leadership. Butler's speech on the following day also failed to make the impression it had to if he was to carry the party by storm.

What was emerging from the lobbying and polling which was going on in every corner was that Hailsham had little support among his ministerial colleagues, and that Butler had substantial backing in the Cabinet. Amery records in his note that on receiving his father-in-law's instructions to advance Hailsham's cause, 'I felt bound to do my best and stuck my neck out pretty strongly on Quintin's behalf. This did me no good with my ministerial colleagues but I saw no alternative.' In the constituencies, however, Hailsham was strong. The memory of his rousing period of office as Chairman of the Party remained fresh. On the other hand, opinion among Conservative MPs was divided, sometimes sharply, between Hailsham and Butler. For some, Hailsham was too strong meat, whilst others saw him as a charismatic leader. These differences were looking as if they might be irreconcilable. To many the choice appeared to be between a candidate who had the experience of governing, and the other man who was most likely to be able to retain or win power. It was also known that the Prime Minister had an unshakable objection to Butler succeeding and the Tory right agreed with Macmillan that he did not have the steel for the job. The situation was ripe for a third candidate and Home's support was swelling by the time the Conference ended on Saturday.

The delegates returned home to face 'the customary processes of consultation'. In fact the polling arrangements devised by Macmillan were the opposite of customary. They were unprecedented and never to be repeated.

Monday 14 October

In the evening, the Prime Minister prepared a 'minute of instruction' for approval by the Cabinet. This provided for four separate soundings. The Lord Chancellor, Dilhorne, would sound the Cabinet; the Chief Whip, Redmayne, would canvass MPs; Lord St Aldwyn would approach the active Conservative Peers; and Lord Poole would report on the constituency parties – or do his best to do so, because reports were to be in by the following Thursday (17

October). The Cabinet, presided over by Butler on Tuesday (15th), approved the procedure on the nod.

Earlier in the day, Redmayne and Dilhorne brought the Prime Minister their reports of the Conference. Macmillan noted in the diary that they were both 'Hoggites' in principle, 'but they feel rather upset at the rather undignified behaviour of Hogg and his supporters at Blackpool. It wasn't easy for him, since whenever he appeared he was surrounded by mobs of enthusiastic supporters. But it was thought that he need not have paraded the baby quite so blatantly or talked so much at large. This is said (by both LC and Chief Whip) to be turning 'respectable' people away from Hogg.'[41] Dilhorne was particularly 'respectable', and embarrassed by displays of emotion. He went further and told the Prime Minister that he had tried to calm Hailsham down, 'but he would not listen and was in a state of hysteria, bursting into tears and clutching his baby and generally behaving in a strange way.'[42] Dilhorne, who was to poll the members of the Cabinet, already felt that 'they would be less and less willing to serve under Lord Hailsham. They were anxious about how he would react to a really serious crisis, e.g. Cuba or Kuwait or something of that kind.'

This was damning, and quite enough for Macmillan. 'So Hogg (who really had the game in his hand) had almost thrown it away,' was his conclusion in his diary. The movement away from Hailsham, the Prime Minister's emissaries informed him, had, however, not gone to Butler or Maudling. 'The "draft" Home movement was in reality a "keep out" Butler movement.'[43]

Lord Poole and Maurice Macmillan called at the hospital in the evening. They told the Prime Minister that the basic situation of deadlock was unchanged. The party in the country wanted Hailsham; the Parliamentary party wanted Maudling or Butler; the Cabinet wanted Butler.[44]

By the end of Monday 14th, Macmillan was already convinced that Hailsham had virtually destroyed his chances, and that his son and son-in-law had been right all along in thinking that he himself could have swept the board at Blackpool. 'Now we are in disarray,' he wrote in his diary.[45] Only the results of the four-part poll could have any chance of putting the pieces together.

Tuesday 15 October

Macmillan decided to clear his own mind by preparing a memorandum, which might perhaps be shown to the Queen.[46] The situation in which a Prime Minister resigned from ill health, rather than from defeat or dissension in Cabinet, and where there was no accepted successor, was an unusual one. The closest parallel, Macmillan thought, was Gladstone's resignation in 1894, when there were many contestants, but none outstanding. However, he already had a preliminary view of how this might turn out. The Cabinet would prefer to work with Butler and 'are afraid that Lord Hailsham would be impulsive, even arrogant', largely due to his habit 'when he is not in the chair, of talking a great deal and sometimes without reflection'. On the other hand, his original view that Hailsham would be the better electioneer was unaltered, and he could be the only real champion the party had to fight Harold Wilson.*

Hailsham had another quality which struck a romantic chord with Macmillan. Of all the candidates, he seemed the only one who would try to harness the country's material success to spiritual purposes, and so become the Prime Minister's true heir. They were both patriots of the same sort. At the end of all, the divisions in the party between Hailsham and Butler made it necessary to consider the compromise candidate, Lord Home. He was a popular and effective man; but the Prime Minister noted:

> the important fact in my view is that Lord Home's candidature has not been set forward on his own merits but has been thought of as a last-minute method of keeping out Mr Butler now that Lord Hailsham has (according to the pundits) put himself out of court by his stupid behaviour in the foyer of the Imperial Hotel at Blackpool.[47]

Macmillan concluded his note characteristically be remarking that 'all this' was very familiar to readers of Mommsen and students of the declining period of the Roman Republic.

In the afternoon Macmillan was visited by Home, Macleod, Heath, Maudling and Hailsham and, with Bligh's help, he made records of what they all said. The list included all the 'possibles' with the significant omission of Butler.

Hailsham's account of his visit was that the Prime Minister 'said nothing to me of the slightest importance. Least of all did he refer to our previous week's meeting in Downing Street [7 October], nor the urgent message he had sent me via Julian [Amery] and Maurice

---

* Wilson had been leader of the Opposition only since February and was seen as a young formidable opponent. On Wilson's defeat of George Brown in the Labour Party ballot, Hailsham wrote a somewhat qualified letter of congratulation: 'I thought you would win, and you did. I am sure your followers chose their ablest man. I hope that history will also say you were their best.' (*Wilson*: Philip Ziegler: p. 137.)

on the eve of the operation. I had the distinct impression that he had done another of his famous somersaults.' Macmillan's note was that Hailsham was 'quite relaxed, although I thought rather white'.

> As regards his own declaration [to disclaim the peerage], he said that he was advised to make it by Lord Poole and by Maurice Macmillan . . . Although I tried to lead him on as to the interpretations and speechifying which he had made, he did not seem conscious of having done anything unusual . . . He thought his baby had made a diversion rather than being used as a political gimmick. He was obviously not conscious of having lost any ground by his antics . . . At the end of the conversation we turned to much wider issues – the spiritual revival of Britain and so forth and on that he spoke both intelligently and movingly. He is a strange mixture . . . Earlier on, Lord Hailsham said that the position of Lord Home taking over would be absurd.[48]

The gulf of mutual incomprehension had opened again. Hailsham rightly judged that Macmillan had changed his mind, but could not for the life of him see why. Macmillan's questioning was so oblique, and doubtless embarrassed, that its purport was obscure. He certainly gave Hailsham no inkling that he thought Hailsham had 'almost thrown the game away'.

Home's message to the Prime Minister, delivered during his visit to the hospital, was so startling both in its content and its vehemence that Bligh's note of the conversation deserves to be read in full:

> The Prime Minister saw the Foreign Secretary on Tuesday October 15. The Prime Minister told me that the main points in the conversation had been as follows:
>
> (a) David Gore had rung up in a great state to say that if Lord Hailsham was made Prime Minister this would be a tremendous blow to Anglo-American relations and would in fact end the special relationship. It was believed that the Ambassador had been talking to the President. It was agreed that the Ambassador should be asked to come to London right away. The manifest reason would be something else.
>
> (b) The incidents at Blackpool had alarmed Lord Home. He had thought that they might be the result of the man being a show-off. He now believed that it was because the person concerned was actually mad at the time – he had been given much good sound advice by experienced and old friends and he had ignored it because he had not been able to control himself.

(c) He thought the man was regarded as Right Wing and would therefore lose some votes on the Left. Lord Home would be prepared to undertake the task if he was asked by the Prime Minister to do so in order to prevent the Party collapsing.[49]

If there was any doubt in Macmillan's mind about Hailsham's fitness to succeed, this was intended to remove it. There is no evidence that opinion in the Kennedy Administration about Hailsham, coloured by the Washington view of his performance in the Test Ban negotiations in July, had previously been conveyed to Macmillan. It would have been extraordinary if the Americans had seen fit to let the Prime Minister have their views on any of the rival contestants for the leadership, but Macmillan could not fail to be impressed now. The entire message was indeed the more impressive because it came from someone who, although a candidate himself, was known for the moderation of his utterance and the integrity of his character. Amid all the conflicting considerations assailing the Prime Minister, Lord Home's offer to be drafted in order to salvage the Party's precarious unity must surely have seemed to represent the best chance of avoiding chaos and defeat.

Wednesday 16 October

The day passed without clear news in the Hailsham camp. *The Times*, which had tipped Home as the Cabinet's man on Monday, switched to Butler as the most likely choice. Ian Gilmour's diary showed some optimism about Hailsham's chances, but Dennis Walters thought 'we are definitely facing a crisis over Home'.[50] Walters was right. During the day Macmillan saw Peter Thorneycroft, Edward Boyle, Christopher Soames, Selwyn Lloyd, John Hare, Henry Brooke and Keith Joseph.[51] Only Thorneycroft, his old friend, supported Hailsham, against whom a new point was now being made. This was that, although it was conceded to be unfair to him, he was widely thought of as right wing and someone who might repel moderates. Home was generally perceived as a unifier, and only Boyle had reservations about him, thinking that he 'would not go very well in Finchley, Orpington and subtopia generally'.[52]

Thursday 17 October

The results of the soundings were brought to the Prime Minister during the day. The Lord Chancellor's polling of the Cabinet was a complicated affair, with first and second choices and tortuous permutations. Although the written results are reproduced in Alistair Horne's biography of Macmillan,[53] and are complex enough, no one can now reconstruct what precise questions Dilhorne put to members of the Cabinet. They appear to have been directed as much to which candidates members of the Cabinet would accept (or tolerate) as to which they would choose.[54] On this dubious basis, Dilhorne had reached the conclusion that the preponderant opinion was for Home. It was implausible, to say the least, that the Cabinet preferred Home to Butler, and the Lord Chancellor's findings have been heavily, even savagely, criticised, notably in Iain Macleod's famous *Spectator* article in which he contended that the real choice had been made by a small social clique;[55] but the relevance of Dilhorne's findings to Hailsham's candidacy is minimal, for after Blackpool, and possibly before, he was never in a position to carry his Cabinet colleagues. The Chief Whip's enquiries in the Commons, which were of more relevance to Hailsham and have also been criticised, yielded a clear preference for Home, with Butler second, and Hailsham third. 'Hailsham', Redmayne reported, '. . . has by far the largest number of declared opponents and makes no real showing at any stage'.[56] Redmayne was impressed by the varying quality of the opposition to the three candidates: in the case of Hailsham and Butler, it was outspoken, but in Home's case 'it is never personal and turns solely on the disadvantages arising from his position'. Hailsham's strength was in the constituencies, and Lords Poole and Chelmer, with Mrs Shepherd, reported that, as expected, he was more popular than Butler. The question of Lord Home was not very clear, because at Blackpool it had not been thought that he was a contender. 'However, it appeared to be the general view that it would be a happy solution.'[57]

The consultations concluded with a meeting between the Prime Minister and Dilhorne, Redmayne, Poole and St Aldwyn. Each rapporteur gave his account in the presence of the others and Macmillan chaired the discussion. Knox Cunningham, Macmillan's Parlimentary Private Secretary, took notes. It seems that Poole fought hard for Hailsham[58] but he was overborne. According to an unpublished memoir of Cunningham's, there was a clear consensus for Home[59]

Macmillan, who must have been desperately tired by these exertions so soon after his operation, sat down in the evening to prepare his memorandum to the Queen and his formal letter of resignation. He would advise her to send for Lord Home. In his diary he noted that the weight of opinion in favour of Home was remarkable and unexpected;[60] but it neatly realised his hope that a way could be found out of the irreconcilable differences in the party between the candidacies of Hailsham and Butler.

The news of the results of the soundings leaked out to senior Conservatives by the evening of Thursday. Many were aghast at the prospect of Lord Home leading the party into battle against the young Harold Wilson. The choice seemed to imply that there was no one among the 363 Tory members of the Commons who was fit to lead. Moreover, the hereditary peer, fourteenth in the line, who had been chosen instead, had no experience of home affairs or economics. There seemed to be no corresponding objection to Hailsham, who was regarded as a sort of 'temporary peer'.

The story of the nocturnal meeting at Enoch Powell's house, to try to head off Home's victory, is well known. The participants (Powell, Macleod, Maudling, Erroll and Aldington), described later by Randolph Churchill as 'the Caballeros', tried unavailingly to dissuade Home from going forward. Hailsham was in touch with the Caballeros from his home in Putney, whither Gilmour and Walters had gone to consider ways of stopping Home. His supporters found Hailsham in a genial mood when they arrived. 'Ah, Tadpole and Taper!' he greeted them on the doorstep. Hailsham at once telephoned Home and told him 'calmly and brutally', as Gilmour described it, that it would be a calamity for the party and the Country if Home became Prime Minister. According to Gilmour's diary, when either he or Walters said that Hailsham had 'pitched it very strong' in his conversation with Lord Home, he replied: 'Of course I pitched it strong. Alec and I have known each other for 40 years. We are gentlemen, so we say what we think. If I had been talking to Ted Heath, I should have been more polite.' It was reminiscent of the Gerald Brenan character who claimed that the great advantage of being born a gentleman was that one never need behave like one.

Later in the evening, Hailsham telephoned Butler. He argued forcefully that if he, Rab and Maudling acted together, no one could form a government without their concurrence. Gilmour, who again heard Hailsham's half of the conversation only, described Hailsham as 'repeating aloud what Rab had just said, in the same way as barristers sometimes repeat the answer of a witness when they are particularly contemptuous of it . . . "You must don your armour, my dear Rab, and fight" '.[61] But Butler would not come in.

Friday 18 October

Macmillan heard about the nocturnal rebellion of the unsuccessful candidates the next morning. 'Considering their intensive rivalry with each other, there was something rather 18th-century about this (Fox-North coalition perhaps) and somewhat distasteful,' he wrote in his diary.[62] He was angry and Sir John Richardson, his physician, described him as 'old and grey and furious'; but 'we knew it meant nothing except that he was concentrating with a strength of purpose ordinary people could not understand.'[63]

Home felt like withdrawing, but Macmillan stiffened him up. 'If we give in to this intrigue, there would be chaos. Butler would fail to form a government . . . no one else would succeed. We would have a Wilson government or dissolution; and our party without even a nominal leader.'[64] However, as Butler described it in his memoirs, the truth was that Macmillan had decided to ignore a powerful objection from seven or eight cabinet ministers 'and acted (as he had done in 1962) with utter determination and despatch'.[65]

During the morning, Butler asked Dilhorne to chair a meeting of himself, Hailsham and Maudling – 'since, if there were serious opposition to Home's succession, Macmillan and his friends should know'. The Lord Chancellor tried to obtain approval for this, 'but no reply was vouchsafed to him'.[66] A meeting between the three candidates and Macleod did take place just before lunch but nothing came of it. Events were now moving too fast.

The Queen visited the hospital during the morning to receive her Prime Minister's resignation and advice about his successor. Macmillan told her about the attempted revolt of the disappointed. She thought the conspirators might have behaved foolishly, even childishly, but agreed in any case that Lord Home was the most likely choice to get general support. 'I said that speed was important and hoped she would send for Lord Home immediately – as soon as she got back to the Palace . . . She gave me her hand and left, carrying the memorandum – in an immense envelope – which I could see (as the door opened) she gave to Adeane [Sir Michael Adeane, the Queen's Private Secretary] – which made him look more like the Frog Footman than ever.'[67] The memorandum argued the merits of Butler and Hailsham, but damned both. 'There were those . . . who thought Mr Butler with all his qualities was a dreary figure who would lead the party to inevitable defeat'; and 'I think there is a real sense of alarm lest under the tremendous stress of world politics Lord Hailsham would not be able to remain sufficiently calm to handle the kind of situation which only too frequently arises.'[68]

If the Sovereign was to take the advice only of her retiring Chief Minister, she was left with no choice. Shortly after noon, Home was at the Palace and was asked by the Queen to try to form a Ministry.

Immediately after lunch he moved into No. 10 and began discussions.

Butler, who in the last phase had been Home's only credible rival, reserved his position on two grounds: first, whether it was right for an hereditary peer to succeed, and secondly, whether Home could command enough unity in the Cabinet. Since in the end only Macleod and Powell stood out, these reservations fell away and Butler became Foreign Secretary. Of his own meeting with Home, Hailsham says simply: 'Later that day I agreed to serve Alec in my existing capacity as Minister for Science and Lord President.' He had been under pressure from Amery, and possibly others, since the previous evening to fall in with Home and he must have realised by the afternoon that, given Butler's irresolution, further resistance was futile. Butler had urged him to return to the Lords if the decision went against him 'and do his bit there',[69] but Hailsham did not think this would have been an honourable course, having staked his peerage on his candidature.

One further meeting took place, a 'quadrilateral' one between the four candidates attended also by the Chief Whip, in the evening of Friday,[70] but by then Home was secure. The following day he kissed hands and assumed office.

★

So Hailsham lost his only chance of the highest political office. It was perhaps always a thin chance. He was seen in some quarters in the party as an erratic demagogue with right-wing inclinations. That this perception was unjust was beside the point. He realised that the antics he had sometimes had to undertake as Chairman of the Party were likely to have made him look suspect. 'The advocate may often have to pay a high price for loyalty to his client,' he wrote in rueful retrospect, 'but in political life he is not allowed to forget his role when the case is over.'[71] Nor did he ever have sufficient support in the Cabinet. His temperament was considered suspect by some of his colleagues (a fear which Blackpool confirmed) and he lacked real friends there in sufficient number. The 'friendly chaos' (as Dennis Walters put it) of his Putney home was not a place where colleagues were entertained. Walters says that Mary gave her husband strong support and wanted him to become Prime Minister, but for herself would have hated and dreaded it.[72] Her decision to bring her baby daughter to Blackpool had very unhappy consequences.

Hailsham's strongest points were the support he had in the country and that he started the race wearing the Prime Minister's colours. This gave his campaign a legitimacy, which others – especially Butler – could not claim. But he had difficulties which proved insuperable.

There is an interesting entry in Macmillan's diary for 14 October:

Hogg (with all his absurdities and posturings and emotions) represents what Stanley, and John Loder, and Boothby, and Noel Skelton and I tried to represent from 1924 onwards. Those who clamour for Butler and Home are really *not* so much shocked by Hogg's oddities as by his *honesty*. He belongs *both* to this strange modern age of space and science *and* to the great past – of classical learning and Christian life. This is what they instinctively dislike . . .[73]

That goes far to explain the roots of the opposition to Hailsham.

Macmillan did him the most serious disservice he could by announcing the start of the race in the middle of the Conference. As Butler observed, this was unnecessary and divisive. Macmillan saw it differently. When he concluded (wrongly as it turned out) that he could not continue, he wanted the succession decided with all possible speed. If Butler had been allowed a period as caretaker it might have strengthened his claims. This was the last thing Macmillan wanted. Home's part in the crisis was certainly not passive, and he played his hand with great skill. In any case, the combination of circumstances placed Hailsham in a cruel dilemma. As his supporters told him, the leadership was not going to fall into his lap unless he fought for it. The Prime Minister's emissaries had encouraged him to do so. On the other hand, Butler had warned him against declaring at once and pandemonium was bound to ensue as soon as his hat was in the ring. In his memoirs, Home treats the declaration as a fatal mistake. 'The immediate instinct of his audience was to acclaim but there followed a swift reaction . . . the tactical advantage which he had seemingly tried to gain by instant action fell right away.'[74] It is hard to criticise his decision to declare as soon as possible – even though, in hindsight, it destroyed his chances with frightening rapidity. 'The party machine' represented by Dilhorne, Redmayne, Morrison and Home, were thoroughly alarmed by the hysteria at Blackpool, a conflagration to which Hailsham's own personality added volatile fuel.

Macmillan, who constantly thought that Butler lacked the steel and resolution for the leadership, and who kept Home's reserve candidacy alive throughout, switched to that reserve as soon as he received the damaging reports about Hailsham from his Blackpool envoys. From his hospital bed he pushed Home through with a determination and ruthlessness which is breathtaking. Although Macmillan's motive was to avoid chaos and defeat, it was ruthless none the less. It was understandable that Hailsham, given legitimacy by his Prime Minister, should have thought that Macmillan 'had done another of his famous somersaults' and that, in tendering advice to the Queen from his sick bed, had based himself on 'hearsay evidence prepared for him by others which he apparently had no possible means of verifying . . .' Although Macmillan had to place some reliance on what he was told of events at which he was not present, there was still force in the 'hearsay' point, particularly as the fatal stories of hysteria at Blackpool were carried to him (himself an admirer of stoicism) by Dilhorne, Redmayne and Home, all men who by upbringing and education were antipathetic to (and perhaps frightened by) displays of emotion.

Hailsham rightly thought that the choice of Home was misconceived and a feeble compromise. Macmillan's view that he represented 'the old governing class at its best'[75] was true but at best irrelevant. The old newsreels show how he lacked the common touch. Far from being a 'safe' choice (an ironically dangerous expedient to which the Conservative Party sometimes resorts) Home was, of the four, the candidate least likely to win the election when it came. Hailsham did his best to support Butler as soon as it became clear that the lot was not going to fall to him, and would have served under Butler. But he could not persuade him to grasp his opportunity. 'Ferdinand the bull had preferred to sniff the flowers rather than take what would have been his if he had wished it.' Butler had sufficient support in the Cabinet, as was indicated by the attempted revolt in the night of 17/18 October, and Dilhorne's polling must be treated as unreliable. But Butler's weakness was a debilitating indecision. Macmillan was only too aware of it. 'All this pretence about Rab's "progressive" views is rather shallow,' he noted harshly in his diary after Home had kissed hands. 'His real trouble is his vacillation in any difficult situation. He has no strength of character or purpose and for this reason should *not* be PM.'[76] Macmillan could not understand why Butler had been so inactive during the crisis, and had not even tried to get some method of testing opinion organised.[77] But, unlike Hailsham, Butler hated the excitements. 'There is not much more to record about Blackpool,' he wrote shortly afterwards, 'except the horror of the lights and the perpetual interviewing. I spent most the time in my room to avoid creating the wrong impression.'[78] It was the same when the succession to the leadership had first come up for discussion. In July he had noted: 'To sum up the whole thing, it is no good thinking there is no life left if one is not elected Pope. One can always be a respected Cardinal.'[79] How could he then be papabile? More charitably, Butler was a man of fastidious honour who prized unity. He wrote to Hailsham after the whole affair was over: 'I do not think that any of us behaved dishonourably or without dignity . . . Equally I am sure that both you and I did right at the critical time to support the new regime.'[80]

Blackpool cast a long shadow across Conservative fortunes. They were bundled out of office within a year, and a radical rethinking of their policies was postponed for more than a decade. The consultative processes for selecting a leader which Macmillan devised were never tried again, and the party resorted to a formal ballot of Conservative Members of the Commons, which carried the seeds of different disadvantages.

After it was all over, Hailsham wrote to Gilmour to thank him for his efforts: 'It was worth trying, but I had too many enemies, and the client lost his nerve.' The experience of the contest left a scar on him. He had to bear attacks from within the party that he had somehow behaved discreditably, and he never wrote poetry again.

20

Opposition Interlude

'THE last six weeks have been bloody,' Hailsham wrote to Harold Macmillan in November, 'at the moment I feel like Job among the potsherds.'[1] Failure in open competition was a rare experience for him and the more bitter for that. He was accused of demagogy and unscrupulousness: it was said that the disclaimer of his peerage for the ends of his own ambition showed a careless disregard for his father's achievements. The injustice of this hurt. Some of his friends advised him to forget about disclaiming and stay on as Leader in the Lords. He would not do this either: '. . . when one has put one's stake on the table and lost the coup I do not think it is open to a man of honour to pick up the counters, put them back in his pocket and walk away whistling a merry tune.' There was unhappiness at home as well. The combination of a prudent bank and a firm-minded Mary made him give up his beloved Carters Corner. All in all, he thought he had not felt so miserable since his homecoming in 1942.

Everything which came after Blackpool was an anticlimax. Just as the destruction of his first marriage marked the end of Quintin Hogg's youth, the failure to win the Tory leadership ended the years of expectation. Although only narrowly beaten in the election of 1964, Sir Alec Douglas-Home's short administration petered away to its inevitable end. Hailsham's forecast that the Prime Minister was unqualified for the job and would not last long was depressingly accurate. The loss of Hailsham's own 'coup' proved to be permanent. He was to distinguish himself as opposition spokesman on Home Affairs, and might have become Home Secretary when the Conservatives returned to power in 1970. But there was no realistic chance that he would ever again challenge for the Leadership. Blackpool 1963 determined that thereafter he would occupy what

Bagehot called 'the dignified parts' of the Constitution. Before then, however, there was an interlude of seven years.

In the short term, he had to find a safe seat. Marylebone was his choice. It was not like Oxford had been. Most of the daytime population went home to sleep elsewhere. He had little contact with his electors, but there were family ties with the constituency. 'Three generations of my family have lived there; indeed I had done so before my first marriage. It had been my father's constituency for seven years. At one end of it was the Regent Street Polytechnic . . . At the other end, up the Finchley Road, were the Quintin and Kynaston schools bearing the Christian names of my grandfather and my godfather . . . I was therefore no carpet-bagger.' The apathy of the London constituents, and the fact that some 20 per cent of them changed every twelve months, did not matter. For after the Conservative defeat in October, 1964, he returned yet again to the Bar, this time as Quintin Hogg.

He was welcomed once more by his old clerk, Sydney Aylett, who set about publicising his return in a way which might have raised eyebrows at the Bar Council.[2] Aylett knew that after eight years' absence Hogg's law would be rusty, and that solicitors would be sceptical about his ability to carry off a miraculous third coming. The canny old clerk moved discreetly among the journalists and solicitors' clerks who frequented the watering holes around the Temple. The time had not yet come when it was universally accepted as respectable for partners in the larger City firms to deal with litigation themselves; and quantities of patronage were still dispensed from lower levels. Aylett knew as well as any barrister's clerk how best to channel these streams. After a decent interval, Hogg began to make a name for himself in defamation cases. It began with an action of more interest to the tabloid press than academic legal journals, in which the producers of the film *Antony and Cleopatra*, with Richard Burton and Elizabeth Taylor as stars, sought to restrain the showing of a slapstick parody called *Carry on Cleo*. Hogg's defence was unsuccessful, but his clients did not mind. The case had given the parody enormous, if short-lived, publicity. Aylett described the period of Conservative opposition of 1964 to 1970, when Hogg was again head of chambers, as harvest years, and his practice flourished in a way which was remarkable when his continued presence in the Temple depended only on Harold Wilson's tenure of power. No one doubted that if the Conservatives returned, Hogg would be offered high office. Among his clients was Wilson himself who, on the advice of Lord Goodman, retained him to stop publication of an obscene caricature of the Prime Minister intended to publicise a pop group called The Move. For all his success, he was never a serious candidate for the High Court Bench. Too volatile and too political, he seems never to have been considered.

Return to the Bar was easier than return to the Commons. 'I greatly underestimated the difficulty of returning to the Commons,' he wrote, 'I had expected to be welcomed as an old friend, and so I was, by some individuals. But the House is something altogether different. It never gives an easy reception to those who have an outside reputation.' The same indulgence is not given to a second maiden speech as to the first; and Hogg made a hash of it. In answering a motion as Minister for Education and Science that the Government's failure to raise the school leaving age had impaired secondary education, he mistook the temper of the House and so forgot himself as to address the Commons as 'My Lords'.[3] It was forgivable; but he knew he had made a bad start, and he asked Butler for help. 'You will . . . notice that (predictably) I am running into a bad patch as the new boy from a strange school and would wish to have not only the loyalty but also the advice of my friends, of whom you are one.'[4] It was not so much advice as reassurance that he wanted. As he fairly said, he did not really recover his footing in the Commons until the race relations and immigration debates of 1968.

He ran an excitable campaign in the 1964 Election. At Plymouth, he was asked, what about Profumo? 'Profumo! I would say just one thing. If you can tell me there are no adulterers on the Front Bench of the Labour Party, you can talk about Profumo.' Two libel actions followed, against the *Guardian* and *Private Eye*, both of whom alleged that he had betrayed an indecent interest in muck raking. Both were settled with public apologies to Hogg. Attlee wrote in the *Daily Mirror*: 'Mr Hogg has many amiable qualities . . . But I am afraid he is not always frightfully tactful. I think it is time he grew up.'[5]

After the Election defeat, Sir Alec Douglas-Home assigned 'Special Duties' to Hogg, and when Edward Heath took over the leadership the following year,* he continued the roving commission. One of the topics he took on was industrial relations.

★

* Heath was elected by ballot of the Party in the Commons in August, 1965. He received 150 votes, Maudling 133 and Powell 15. Although the new rules required a larger majority, Maudling immediately withdrew in favour of Heath. Dissatisfaction with the polling arrangements introduced by Macmillan in October 1963 had led a consultative committee to recommend to the Shadow Cabinet in February 1965 that selection should be by ballot of the Commons Party only.

Hogg's interest in the trade unions had first been aroused when his father, as Attorney-General, had been responsible in 1926/7 for carrying the Trade Disputes Bill through the House of Commons. Hogg was then at Oxford, and neither then nor ever after would he accept that the Bill was a vindictive measure to punish the unions for the general strike. Nevertheless, it inflicted a great defeat. For the first time since the nineteenth century, the unions' freedom to act in their members' interests during industrial disputes without fear of the law was cut back. The Second World War and the social revolution it wrought gave them the chance to reverse the defeat; and the new Labour Government of 1945 moved quickly to repeal the Act of 1927. Hogg put up a spirited defence of that Act and his father's part in it. He was not abashed by his formidable opponent, Hartley Shawcross, the Labour Attorney-General, and his speech on the second reading of the Labour Bill is an excellent example of the debater's art.[6]

Although he supported the restrictions imposed after the general strike, Hogg for long opposed more wide-ranging reform. He was against challenging union opinion which he feared would lead to bitterness and industrial unrest. But by the middle sixties, the steady growth of union power was forcing itself on the attention of the country. In 1965, Harold Wilson's Government appointed a Royal Commission under the chairmanship of Lord Donovan to report on unions and employers' associations. By about the same time, Hogg had convinced himself that a review of the legal position of trade unions was inevitable. Their power was exorbitant, and their legal status, neither within the law nor wholly outside it, was anomalous. He undertook the task of explaining the implications to the Shadow Cabinet.[7] There was no statute, he advised his colleagues, regulating the responsibility of union officers or the use of their funds. In such a jungle, 'very disagreeable things occasionally happen in the mangrove swamps and juju huts of unregulated custom, which occasional punitive expeditions by the judiciary . . . do little to regulate.'

Conservative governments had preferred to ignore the problem in the thirteen years between 1951 and 1964. 'We knew that action was necessary,' Lord Hailsham (as he had again become) confessed in the Lords in 1971, 'but rather than impose action upon a reluctant trade union movement, we tried to believe that the trade unions themselves, or the TUC, would put their own house in order.'[8] It was unconvincing. As long before as 1957 when, as Party Chairman, he had asked Conservatives across the country for possible criticisms of party policy, the most frequent response was that the Macmillan Government was not facing up to the unions. Hogg's reluctance, fully shared by Harold Macmillan, to take on the unions, had disappeared by 1965 at latest. He was now advocating 'the definite goal' of a Trade Union Bill to do for the unions what the Companies Act had done for limited liability companies.

A year later, in February 1966, by which time Edward Heath had replaced Douglas-Home as Conservative leader, Hogg wrote another paper for the Shadow Cabinet, *The Trade Unions and the Law – A New Approach*.[9] He and his colleagues felt that they could not afford to wait for the conclusion of Donovan's labours and should produce some robust proposals of their own. They were right. It was another two years before Donovan reported in June 1968. By then, increasing militancy and wildcat strikes had made the Royal Commission's report look outdated. Its conclusions were moderate and reasonable, but not man enough for the job.

Hogg laid out his ideas. In the context of 1966, they were radical. The comprehensive statute which he envisaged would set up a separate Industrial Relations Court, in which the presiding Judge would sit with lay members; the registration of trade unions with a model set of rules would be compulsory; immunity would be withdrawn from unofficial and other defined classes of strike; the Court would have power to forbid strikes of these classes; and there would be sanctions against restrictive practices.

In early 1966, Hogg had been leading Conservative thinking on industrial relations in the approach to the expected General Election. But when it came at the end of March, Wilson increased his majority, and the Conservative legislation was postponed for four more years. Although most of the ambitious programme outlined in Hogg's 1966 paper came to be embodied eventually in the Heath Government's Bill, he played little further part while his party remained out of power. The reasons for this are not clear. As Opposition spokesman for Home Affairs, he might have been expected to speak on the subject he knew so well, but the task fell increasingly to Robert Carr and Geoffrey Howe. Most likely, his burgeoning practice at the Bar kept him away from the Commons; perhaps Edward Heath had already earmarked him as the next Conservative Lord Chancellor.

Although Hogg's ideas for trade union reform, set out in his paper to the Shadow Cabinet, were radical, he did not positively recommend that collective agreements between employers and men should be enforceable like ordinary contracts. Traditionally, they never had been, and many thought it impracticable to try to attach legal sanctions. In 1975, he wrote retrospectively: 'My view has always been that, although the law has a part to play in the prevention of strikes ... no attempt ... to enforce trade union bargains or to prevent strikes by court order is likely to be successful.'

Whether or not he argued this point with his colleagues, provisions making collective bargains enforceable appeared in the Heath Government's Industrial Relations Bill of 1971; and as Lord Chancellor, Hailsham had a hard time defending them in the committee stage in the Lords, during which he spoke no fewer than 232 times in the space of a month. The unwisdom of trying to make collective agreements enforceable was soon demonstrated by events. Within twelve months of the enactment of the Bill, the dockers' strikes showed the consequences of the Courts granting injunctions against strikers and pickets, and Hailsham was as quickly embroiled in these consequences. (see pp. 276ff and 344ff).

★

Clement Attlee, in his schoolmasterly way, had advised Hogg that it was time he grew up, and examples of his clattering about can certainly be found. Some instances occurred in unusual circumstances. There is a story, possibly apocryphal but none the less believable, that he once sneezed when sitting on the Woolsack. 'I sneezed', he turned on the Bench of Bishops, 'and not one of you said, Bless you.' Bishops went on irritating him, particularly those with experimental views. In 1984, David Jenkins, Bishop of Durham (a frequent target) complained about the employment of Ian McGregor, an 'imported' American, by the National Coal Board. Would the Bishop have used similar expressions, Hailsham asked rhetorically in a letter to *The Times* on 25 September, if Mr McGregor had been 'imported' with a dark skin from Asia or Africa? 'But it is possible to hazard a guess as to what the founder of the Christian religion, who did not approve of double standards on the part of ecclesiastical authorities, would have said about the Bishop of Durham.'

Bishops talked of giving a lead, but in reality sounded off at large. 1965 appeared to Hogg to be a vintage year for episcopal *bêtises*. Mervyn Stockwood, the Bishop of Southwark, used inflammatory language, and during the *Lady Chatterley* obscenity trial, John Robinson, the Bishop of Woolwich, claimed that some four-letter passages in the book 'bore some obscure analogy to Holy Communion', or so it seemed to Hogg. Finally, Archbishop Ramsey 'must needs blunder in with provocative references to the use of force.'[10]

What stimulated this last was the Archbishop's public support for the use of force to oppose a threatened unilateral declaration of independence by the white government in Rhodesia. Ramsey's statement followed a resolution of the British Council of Churches that 'Christian faith demanded', as a precondition of independence, that the four million Africans in the country should have a say in its government. Hogg liked and admired Ramsey, not least for his courage, but this was the last straw. 'If the Archbishop had consulted informed lay option on either political side before making his speech,' Hogg wrote in a letter to *The Times* on 1 November 1965, 'he would have infallibly been told to hold his hand while discussions in Salisbury were still proceeding.'

Not contenting himself with *The Times* readership for an audience, Hogg attacked all these mitred offences against well-informed good sense in a populist piece for the *Sunday Express* under the headline, 'Why not *elect* the Bishops?'[11] Cummings contributed a cartoon for the same page, in which a timorous Britannia holds her hands to her ears while Fisher, Ramsey, Woolwich and Southwark tower over her cavorting like dervishes.

Ramsey's biographer fairly describes the article as less than statesmanlike, and equally fairly, calls its author 'pugnacious but not malicious'.[12] The combativeness was never far away. In an article for *Punch* in February 1968, Hogg accused the Court of Appeal of making the Gaming Act unworkable by 'unrealistic, contradictory and, in the leading case, erroneous, decisions'; and advised the Court that 'Silence is always an option'. Raymond Blackburn, a self-appointed tribune of the people, applied to commit Hogg for contempt for this shaft. Lord Denning presided at the hearing. Denning was not like any Judge before or since, and he had his own brand of magnanimity. He remarked mildly that the article was not only critical, but wrong: the decision which Hogg had attacked had not been given by the Court of Appeal at all, but by another Court. In any case, he said 'we will never use this jurisdiction as a means to uphold our dignity. That must rest on surer foundations.' It was the right of every man to make fair comment, even outspoken comment, on matters of public interest. All that the Court asked was that those who criticised its members should remember that they could not reply. 'So it comes to this: Mr Quintin Hogg has criticised the court, but in so doing he is exercising his undoubted right. The article contains an error, no doubt, but errors do not make it a contempt of court. We must uphold his right to the uttermost.' In his book *The Due Process of Law*, Denning was even more generous. Under the heading 'We ourselves are told to be silent', he described the *Punch* article as

At home at Carters Corner

Scenes at the Nuclear Test Ban Treaty negotiations, Moscow 1963.
(*Above*) With Averell Harriman. (*Below*) With Nikita Khrushchev
and Andrei Gromyko

Work and friendship with Harold Macmillan.
(*Above*) In 1957. (*Below*) At the christening of the Hailshams'
youngest daughter, Kate, in 1963.

In Macmillan's view, Home represented 'the old governing class at its best'

At the Blackpool Conference, 1963

With Rab

More scenes at Blackpool, 1963. The two photographs show Hailsham's
two rivals for the leadership, neither looking quite the part

(*Above*) Two Elders of the Law: Lord Hailsham and Lord Denning

(*Below*) Speakers of both Houses: George Thomas and Lord Hailsham.
'The Law is the true embodiment
Of everything that's excellent,
It has no kind of fault or flaw.
And I, my Lords, embody the Law.'

Deirdre

In 1987, on his way to give his
daughter Mary Claire in marriage

'Cowering on the firing step.'
The debate on the Maastricht Treaty in the House of Lords, 1993

On the Woolsack

'exuberant' and its author 'the most gifted man of our time. Statesman, Orator, Philosopher – he has no compare'.[13]

Hogg had publicly enjoined the Bench of Bishops and the Court of Appeal alike to observe silence. Those who admired his gifts must occasionally have wished that he would respect his own injunction.

★

There could hardly be a more dramatic contrast than between the jejune attacks on bishops and judges, and Hogg's handling of the race and immigration crisis of 1968. It lit up the two sides of his personality, so at variance with each other that at times they seemed to belong to two different people.

'I have never chosen race relations as a special subject,' Lord Hailsham said in 1970,[14] 'at least until the subject chose me when I became Shadow Home Secretary.' He had little taste for legislation on 'social engineering', and in any case thought it was misguided to try to deal with race in isolation, rather than with all forms of objectionable discrimination.

In his view, the country's race problems had been almost entirely and unnecessarily brought about by defective immigration and nationality laws, which he described as 'an irrational jumble of legislation explicable only in terms of history and not logic'.[15] Had we had a prudent national immigration law, he thought, it would not have been necessary to legislate at all on racial discrimination.

The troubles of 1968 were the direct consequence of the jumble. In mid-1967 the Conservative Research Department drew attention to the anxieties of the coloured minority.[16] It was colour alone which was making assimilation harder than it had ever been for immigrants into this country. The Labour government had legislated on racial discrimination in 1965 but only in public places. It was now expected that they would propose to widen the Act into the fields of employment, housing, and the provision of credit. The C.R.D.'s view was that any such proposal would have to be backed by the moral authority of the whole country and would not make headway without the support of both major parties. Enoch Powell was known to be pessimistic about the integration of coloured communities, and had already called for a total halt to immigration and for efforts to repatriate some at least of the coloured population. The choice lay between Powell's views and supporting the government's proposals, for unless the coloured minority could be guaranteed the same rights and opportunities as other citizens, it might indeed be better to send them back to the countries from which they had come. The paper concluded: 'It is a policy of doing nothing that will result in the development of coloured ghettos in Britain full of poverty, frustration and wasted human beings.'

Hailsham thought that the C.R.D. paper set out the issues very well.[17] In spite of his natural aversion to the legislation, he advised that 'we should extend a cautious amber light verging on green' to some extension of the Race Relations Act. But he had reservations. The Conservative party should firmly oppose any extensions of the criminal law; a distinction should be drawn between 'the haphazard manifestation of individual prejudice', for example by individual employees or landladies, and systematic discrimination; and an extension of the Act into bank credit would be fraught with difficulties. 'My conclusion is that we should play this more coolly and cautiously, but liberally. We should not shut the door against extension.'

★

By the turn of the year, a new and explosive element had been introduced into the situation. This was the influx of increasing numbers of Kenyan Asians, and the real possibility that the flow might become a flood. As a consequence of the Attlee Government's praiseworthy but misguided idealism, the British Nationality Act of 1948 had conferred an unrestricted right of entry on all citizens of the new states of India and Pakistan, followed by other countries becoming independent members of the Commonwealth. After long years of neglect and pious hoping that social problems caused by the unrestricted immigration of coloured Commonwealth subjects would just go away, rights of entry were eventually cut down by the Conservative government's Commonwealth Immigrants Act of 1962. But whether by accident or design (and that was savagely disputed), a proportion of those born in colonial territories who did not acquire citizenship of those territories when they became independent, retained an absolute right to enter Britain.* In newly independent Kenya, restrictive laws discriminated against the Asian population, and it was estimated that there were some 200,000 East African Asians who could, and might well choose to, come to this country.

* The 1962 Act controlled immigration through a phased employment voucher system, but was found to have holes in it. For example, a Kenyan Asian who had obtained a British passport from the Foreign Office or a High Commissioner of an independent Commonwealth country, rather than from a colonial government, could come in to the United Kingdom, as his passport proclaimed, without let or hindrance.

On 9 February, Enoch Powell sounded an ominous note in a speech at Walsall and on the 21st, Edward Heath publicly stated the Conservative opposition's policy. He made it clear that the rights of the Asians to enter Britain must be respected. If agreement could not be reached with the Kenyan government on the plight of these second class citizens, the government should phase their entry as immigrants. Two days later the government acted and published a new Commonwealth Immigrants Bill which it intended to push through within a week. This proposed to limit unrestricted rights of entry to those who were British by birth, naturalisation, adoption or registration or whose father or grandfather was so qualified. The Home Secretary, James Callaghan, announced that 1500 vouchers would be allocated annually for UK passport holders who did not have an unrestricted right of entry.

The government's proposals presented the Conservatives with a dilemma. The Bill did not respect the rights of the Kenyan Asians, and it was racial in effect if not in letter. But it was simply not practical to suppose that Britain could absorb quickly, or at all, every Commonwealth citizen who had a right to come here. Archbishop Ramsey denounced the proposals as a breach of Britain's pledged word. The press divided by class. The Bill was welcomed by the *Mirror*, *Express*, *Mail*, *Sun* and *Sketch*; and deplored by *The Times*, *Guardian*, *Telegraph*, *Observer* and *Sunday Times*. The Party's Research Department pointed out that the Bill would have been illegal, had Britain by then acceded to the United Nations Covenant on Civil and Political Rights of 1966 or the European Convention on Human Rights.[18]

On 27 February Callaghan moved the second reading of the Bill,[19] opening his speech by saying, 'We are about to discuss one of the greatest issues of our time, an issue which can tear us apart or unite us.' The reply from the opposition benches was awaited anxiously. Hogg began with a tribute.[20] 'No one who has listened to the Home Secretary would or could doubt the sincerity of every word he spoke.' Then, after stating his two basic propositions of tight immigration control and absolute equality of treatment for everyone lawfully in this country, he gave his answer. 'After anxious thought my own feeling is that the Government have been right to legislate.' He confessed that he was not making his argument with any kind of relish, but it came none the less with characteristic force.

To anyone whose conscience in the matter lies on the other side to mine, I would only say, if you intend to vote against this Bill on conscientious grounds, make sure you endure to the bitter end.

Make sure that you are prepared to face the ultimate consequences, because if you legislate too late, getting over your scruples when most of the situation that you wish to avoid has happened already, you will get an element of the worst of both worlds, and that is not an honest thing to do.

The speech drew an immediate handwriten note from Callaghan:

Dear Quintin,
    You were wonderful this afternoon – breadth, depth and compassion. Don't whisper it to anybody – but if you were always like that you would walk away with the leadership.
Ever,
Jim C.[21]

The Bill was given a second reading by 372 votes to 62 and received the Royal Assent on 1 March.

★

But the crisis was by no means over. The opposition still needed a lead from its spokesman on the Race Relations Bill, the second reading of which was to be moved on 23 April. As had been anticipated, the Bill proposed to extend the scope of the law to employment, housing and credit facilities. On the 9th, Hailsham chaired a meeting of the Conservative Parliamentary Home Affairs Committee,[22] and told members that the provisional view of the Shadow Cabinet was that they should abstain on the motion for a second reading, rather than divide the House. He called on speakers for and against the Bill alternately, and the results showed what he doubtless already knew – the party was hopelessly divided, many being actuated more by emotion than reason or sense.

Hogg's object was somehow to preserve party unity, but there were difficulties, whichever way he turned. He advised the Shadow Cabinet that the least of the evils was for Conservatives to abstain on the Second Reading vote. His colleagues, however, thought that this would look like no policy at all, and it was eventually decided to move a reasoned amendent, approving the objectives of the Bill but declining to give it a Second Reading on the ground that it would not promote better race relations. The Shadow Cabinet retired for the short recess in an uneasy mood, and against a background in the country of worsening racial feeling.

Before the debate could take place, the smouldering figure of Enoch Powell erupted. Apart from an occasional innocuous parliamentary question, he had chosen to make all his public statements on race and immigration outside the House, in or near his own West Midlands constituency, where the ethnic minorities were numerous and growing. Hogg knew his views, and disagreed profoundly with his idea of repatriating coloured immigrants. He considered that any such plan would only intensify victimisation. 'If you say publicly to a class or group: "We do not want you here, we want you so little that we will pay for you to go", how can you protect them or their children from insult in the street or the shop or the school?'[23] In any case, he thought the scheme was a foolish and unpractical piece of escapism.

On the Saturday before the debate, 20 April, Powell made his infamous speech in Birmingham. He took pains to ensure that he was not obstructed by Central Office. Instead of following the normal procedure of passing the text of his speech to Smith Square for clearance and circulation, he sent it to the West Midlands Area Office with a request that it be distributed from there. It was received on Friday, and during that afternoon copies were given to the local papers. Television companies had been warned by Powell that 'he might have something interesting to say . . .'[24] Central Office and Hogg, the party's spokesman on home affairs, knew nothing of it. What Powell said was not untrue or even misleading. But in the language and imagery which he chose, he set out quite deliberately to incite nightmares. The vision of a Tiber foaming with blood with which he ended his speech has become part of popular recollection, but the anecdotal material which he used to whip up his audience for his climax is less well remembered. He cited a woman who had become the only white person to live in what had been 'a respectable street' in Wolverhampton. She had become afraid to go out. 'Windows are broken. She finds excreta pushed through her letter box. When she goes to the shops, she is followed by charming, wide-grinning piccaninnies. They cannot speak English, but one word they know. "Racialist", they chant. When the new Race Relations Bill is passed, this woman is convinced she will go to prison. And is she so wrong? I begin to wonder.'

Powell gave his leader no choice. He was dismissed from the Shadow Cabinet the next day. While Powell was speaking, Hogg was out for a day's walking in the fells. When he returned, his host's unusually acute young son asked him if he had heard about the speech, and suggested that he watch the six o'clock television news. It was the first he knew of the business. Hogg never again enjoyed personal relations with Powell which went beyond the frigidly formal. The two men, as Hogg told the Commons, were joined by a common love of classical literature, a common religion, and a common devotion to scholarship. But each thought he saw the other's faults writ large. Powell reckoned Hogg to have one of the outstanding talents of his time, but his tantrums were those of an adolescent. Hogg admired Powell's intellect, but thought him perverse and inconstant.

The perversity was never better illustrated than by the breach between the two over immigration. Powell recalled that during one of the divisions on the Race Relations Bill, he had heard Hogg remark: 'Of course, Enoch's figures are right: we know that.' To Powell, this meant that Hogg had been driven to say things he did not believe.[25] The misunderstanding was almost wilful. Hogg did not disagree with Powell's figures, nor even his basic view on immigration. What he did dispute was Powell's melancholy assessment of the chances of a harmonious multi-racial society in Britain.[26] And what impelled him to tell Heath, unnecessarily as it turned out, that he could not remain in the Shadow Cabinet with Powell, was the hysteria which the Birmingham speech was deliberately calculated to – and did – whip up.

At the Party Conference in October, Hogg advised Powell to remember the ancient Greek injunction to avoid extremes. Harold Macmillan was delighted by Hogg's speech for its philosophy of Toryism. 'As for Powellism,' he wrote to Hogg, 'it is a curious throw-back to Benthamism – understandable in a Liberal but unforgivable in a Conservative.'[27]

At the General Election of February 1974, Powell did the unthinkable and announced that he had voted for Labour and Harold Wilson. The next year, Hailsham wrote: 'Show me the issue on which he has not changed his mind. Show me the cause to which he has been consistently true. Show me the colleague to whom he has not been disloyal . . . And do not forget the curse of Reuben. "Unstable as water, thou shalt not excel".' The break was complete and permanent.

But in October, 1974, they both attended the Requiem Mass for Dermot Morrah, the historian and Herald. On leaving the Cathedral, 'there was Enoch P. I bowed. He held out his hand and said, "We must forgive one another as we would wish to be forgiven." I replied: "Amen" and took his hand.'[28]

★

On 23 April 1968, Callaghan moved the Second Reading of the Race Relations Bill.[29] He told the House that it had rarely faced an issue of greater moment for the country and its children. It was a time for responsibility, for leadership, and 'if I may dare to use the word, for nobility'. Hogg's speech, moving the amendment, took its conciliatory tone from the Home Secretary's own.[30] Michael Foot, a considerable student of parliamentary style, thought it one of the best he had ever heard in the House of Commons; and Arthur Butler, the political correspondent of the *Daily Express* considered it the finest he had listened to in his twelve years in the Press Gallery: 'the House so dead quiet'.

It would be a disaster, Hogg said, if either of the 'great organised bodies of public opinion upon which the country depends for its successive governments' were to exploit the deep feelings which were held on the subject. It was not for that the House was to be divided. The opposition would seek to improve the Bill, and there might be a chance of passing it. 'It depends on the force of our arguments and the attitude with which our objections are met.' But it was no good trying to pass a curate's egg of a Bill. Some Hon. Members did not want eggs for breakfast at all; others were so afraid of offending the Bishop that they would eat almost anything that he put before them. But the great mass, faced with such a dilemma, would say in all humility that they liked eggs, but would prefer fresher ones rather lightly done. He was not making light of his subject, and his hearers knew it.

The House knew also that he would have to deal with Powell's speech. He described the circumstances in which it was made. 'I sometimes found it a little difficult during the week end to realise that I was the official opposition spokesman and that no one else was.'

If one is going to say, and goodness knows many of us have thought, that the streets of our country might one day run with blood – and make no mistake, it is usually the innocent, usually the defenceless, and sometimes just the ordinarily good, who are victims of that kind of violence – then surely one ought to consider whether, in the more immediate future, one's words are more likely to make that happen, or less likely to make that happen.[31]

The opposition amendment was lost by nearly a hundred votes and the Bill received its Second Reading. During the Committee stage,

Hogg tried to broaden the base of the Bill, so that it included not only racial, but all forms of discrimination. His idea for 'fresher eggs lightly done' was a simply stated statute which would protect minorities of all sorts. The amendment which he moved would have broadened the definition of discrimination to include 'race, colour, sex, language, religion, political or other opinion, national or social origin, property, title or other status'. He was ruled out of order. *The Times*, he complained, said that the imagination boggled at the thought of defining and protecting the rights of individuals in this general way.[32] Evidently, the time was not yet ripe for a Bill of Rights.

The Report and Third Reading stages, taken together through a single night, were an unpleasant affair. Callaghan vainly begged the House not to divide on a fundamental issue of human equality, and Hogg could hardly be heard over the baying of rebel Conservative backbenchers as he tried to explain why his party must not vote against the Bill.[33] Many of the rebels ignored the Shadow Cabinet's advice to abstain, and the Bill was given its Third Reading by 182 to 44 votes.

It was fortunate for the country that when this racial and parliamentary crisis broke, James Callaghan and Quintin Hogg were its principal spokesmen. In an emotional minefield and with a riven party behind him, Hogg's soundness of judgment did not desert him. There was a grandeur about the magnanimity of his oratory, and not a trace of the fragility of temperament which his colleagues feared. 'If you were always like that . . .' Callaghan had said.

Hogg expected that he would be Home Secretary in the next Conservative administration, and he had more than one informal talk with Callaghan, with whom he had struck up a warm and confidential friendship, about affairs then current in the Home Office. But, as so often before, the leader of his party had other ideas for his future.

★

Before he was whisked off to the Lords once more to become Lord Chancellor, he published his little collection of verse, *The Devil's Own Song*, and sent copies to his two Oxford women friends, Elizabeth Longford and Helen Asquith. He had affectionate notes from both. 'Dearest Quintinus,' Lady Longford wrote, 'I shall have it as a bedside book . . .' She liked the war poems best, and his own version of *Dies Irae*. Lady Helen Asquith wrote 'I am delighted and honoured – though the inscription is quite inaccurate! I never judge you severely – on the contrary I admire you greatly and still hope to see you PM. Nor would I describe you as exactly "wayward" – emotional yes, occasionally wrong headed – and sometimes mistaken. But who is not?'[34]

21

Lord Chancellor

THE office of Lord Chancellor was the natural culmination of Hailsham's career. It combined law and politics in a single peak; it emulated his father's achievements; it had been talked about for him by his admirers for twenty years or more; it had been at the back of his own mind for at least as long. Yet when it came it was a surprise. There was only one straw in the wind which might have alerted him to the possibility. Shortly before the end of the 1966 Parliament, he was unexpectedly invited to a meal by the Labour Lord Chancellor, Gerald Gardiner. In what he described as 'the austere discomfort' of the flat in the Palace of Westminster, its equally austere tenant was living out a lonely life as a widower. Gardiner told him that he thought the Labour Government would not last long, and that he himself would favour Hailsham's own appointment to the Woolsack. Gardiner, it seems, had been consulted and asked to sound out the candidate. Hailsham (then still Quintin Hogg) was expecting the Home Office, and made only self-deprecatory noises. He had no doubt, however, that if he were offered the Lord Chancellorship, he should accept.

When Edward Heath did invite him in June 1970, he did not hesitate.*

Only his clerk in the Temple, Sydney Aylett, had reservations when the news was out. Mr Hogg, his head of chambers, would be lost to the Bar for ever. On being asked whether he was not none

* The engagement diaries unfortunately do not record Lord Hailsham's first appointment as Lord Chancellor, but there is a laconic entry when Mrs Thatcher appointed him for the second time in 1979:
'1005 10 Downing St. Lord Chancellor
    Ted out, a pity
    1800 Buck Pal – Sworn. No Great Seal – where is it?'
(HLSM: LC Diaries 1/4: 5 May 1979.)

too pleased, Aylett replied, 'Well, Sir, I must congratulate you, and I'm very glad for Mrs Hogg's sake, now she'll be a Lady again.'[1] Mary was indeed pleased. She had not been so happy since they were at the Admiralty in 1956. The unkind cuts of politics would for the most part be behind them. Her husband was a peer again, this time with the title Lord Hailsham of St Marylebone. There was pardonable confusion about the alternating names. An examiner in constitutional law at Reading University passed on to the new Lord Chancellor a student's answer which he had been marking: 'A person who is appointed Lord Chancellor is given the name of Hailsham. Thus Mr Quintin Hogg on his appointment became Hailsham Hogg.'

For Hailsham himself, the Woolsack meant the end of serious political ambition. He could never again aspire to the leadership, or even to one of the other principal bases of political power, Exchequer, Foreign Office or Home Office. Back again in the Lords, he would become more and more remote from the source of authority. As Jowitt put it in a letter to his sister when he became Lord Chancellor in 1945, 'I'm on the shelf now, but it's a comfortable and gilded shelf and there's some work to be done.'[2] Hailsham would have agreed. At sixty-three, he was reconciled to being out of the political mainstream, and the prestige and dignity of the office were more than recompense. He wrote to his friend, Billy Loudon's widow: 'I love climbing and I have to acknowledge that, after years in the forests and undergrowth, & long struggles up the moraine & glacier, I have at last reached the top of some peak or other. I am too busy to enjoy the view, & the fun of climbing down and climbing another the next day but one, is absent.'[3]

However, it was not all pomp and circumstance. Hailsham was to know something of the same lonely austerity which he had noticed in Gardiner's way of life. On 25 June 1971, he entered in his appointments diary:

I live alone in the flat. M. finds journey to Hurlingham with Kate (double journey twice a day) too much for her. My day begins about 0630 when I wake naturally. I turn on BBC4. The farming news most soothing. After the 0700 news, tea. Papers wh. I bring up from downstairs. Read in bed. Breakfast, Scotts porage oats (One teacup to two of water) milk, salt . . . Lunch, flat, self-cooked, usually from fridge. Change into LC uniform about 1410 . . . Woolsack in procession for prayers 1430. Take questions and formal business. Usually leave soon after if not concerned in business (sack taken over by Listowel and Deputies).* Work in office. Bed.[4]

The Lord Chancellor is a singular figure. Once the most powerful of all the Queen's subjects and her most trusted adviser, the office held by Becket, Wolsey and More and going back beyond the Norman conquest has evolved in the hands of a succession of great jurists into the head of the judiciary. Hailsham knew the history of the evolution well. He considered Sir Thomas More to be the first modern Chancellor. Coming from the legal profession, More's judicial work was celebrated both for its incorruptibility and for the rapid despatch of business. In a talk given in 1985, Hailsham drew a striking picture of More's Court of Chancery, with its marble throne and table in the south west corner of Westminster Hall. Before dispensing the system of jurisprudence known as 'equity', representing the royal conscience, More, attended by his retinue, would first enter the Court of King's Bench, in another corner of the Hall, kneel before his old father who was still sitting as Judge, and seek and receive his blessing, which was given by the laying on of hands.[5]

The Lord Chancellor is a constitutional oddity. He participates in each of the three branches of government: as Cabinet Minister, member and Speaker of the House of Lords, and as the most senior Judge. Hailsham saw nothing untoward in bridging all the branches of government by being part of each. Far from that, he held up the office of Lord Chancellor for admiration for its ability to keep the powers separate. 'In the absence of a paper constitution, the separation of powers is the primary function of the Lord Chancellor, a task which he can only fulfil if he sits somewhere near the apex of the constitutional pyramid, armed with a long barge pole to keep off marauding craft from any quarter.'[6] The paradox was not new. Lord Schuster, the most influential of all Permanent Secretaries to the Lord Chancellor, was the first to articulate it clearly. It had been taken up with enthusiasm by Lord Birkenhead, who considered that unless there was someone 'imbued on the one hand with legal ideas and habits of thought, and aware on the other of the problems which engage the attention of the executive government . . . the judiciary and the executive are likely to drift asunder to the point of a violent separation, followed by a still more violent and disastrous collision.'[7] All Lord Chancellors since have accepted this as revealed truth.

---

* This was one of the changes introduced by Hailsham. Relieving himself of the duty of sitting all the time as Speaker enabled him to sit judicially more than his immediate predecessors.

It would need a W. S. Gilbert to explain why, in order to separate the branches of government, one man must represent all three; or how that man who today is called on to make a politically partisan speech can be expected tomorrow to drive politics altogether from his mind. Such abstractions, however, have not troubled Lord Chancellors and they did not disturb Hailsham. His view of the practicalities was simple. The job was to defend the Judges from interference by the executive and its increasingly willing accomplice, the House of Commons. He could best do this from inside government. The Lord Chancellor, he wrote, 'is in the business of defending and preserving the independence and integrity of the judiciary. If he does it well, he is a good Lord Chancellor, whatever his other defects. If he does it ill, whatever his other qualities, he is not.'[8]

There could have been different priorities. The ensuring of a fair trial, or making justice accessible to all were two other possibilities, both within the bailiwick of the Lord Chancellor. But all holders of the office since the war would have agreed with Hailsham that the independence of the Bench was paramount. It did not matter to which political persuasion they belonged, or whether they were radicals or reactionaries. All were of one mind. Hailsham felt as vehemently about it as any of them. The purpose of keeping the Judges free from interference was that only they could protect the individual against the state. And they themselves were vulnerable to it. The 'elective dictatorship' of a House of Commons dominated by the ruling party was capable of anything. Its sovereignty was unlimited and unqualified. It could trammel the powers of the Judges if and as it pleased. Its failure to do so rested on a precarious restraint which at best might be called a constitutional convention. There was force in Hailsham's view that the Lord Chancellor was protector of the Judges, or nothing.

Just because an executive-controlled House of Commons was so powerful, the most dangerous marauding parties would come from that quarter to threaten the independence of the Judiciary. So when Mrs Thatcher's first administration was formed in 1979, and proposed to carry out the promise in the Conservative election manifesto, to appoint Select Committees of the House to scrutinise public spending and the work of government departments, Hailsham asked her to exclude the appointment and performance of Judges from inquiries into the Lord Chancellor's Department. She was so sympathetic that she gave him more than he had asked for, and the Department was altogether exempted from the remit of the new

Select Committees.* It was a remarkable decision. She had no need to leave out the policy, administration and expenditure of the Department, which was by then a heavy spender. Although he was no lover of Select Committees, which he thought an unwelcome importation from the United States, Hailsham would have contentedly accepted some scrutiny, so long as individual Judges were beyond their reach.

In order to defend the Judges, Lord Hailsham thought, it was better for the Lord Chancellor to sit in comparative safety among the innocuous Lords, at one remove from the more intrusive Commons.

> I should regard it as absolutely intolerable if, as would certainly be the case, the person discharging the present duties of the Lord Chancellor were to sit in the House of Commons and be interrogated (as he certainly would be by one device or another and whether or not by the Speaker's permission) not only as to the qualities of particular judges, but as to their possible removal, their observations, whether *obiter*† or otherwise, and as to sentencing and judicial policy in criminal or civil matters in individual cases . . .[9]

There were enough instances of Members of the House trespassing in this way during his time as Lord Chancellor for this to be said with feeling. Professor Heuston has explained[10] that it is not necessary for the Lord Chancellor to be a peer, notwithstanding his title, and that he is only made a Member of the House of Lords by convention to enable him to speak in debate there. This is providential but, as Mr Podsnap remarked, the Englishman's constitution was bestowed on him by Providence.

Hailsham came to the office with outstanding qualifications. He knew politics from the inside and had served as a Cabinet Minister since 1957, with only one break in opposition between 1964 and 1970. As perhaps only Kilmuir and Dilhorne had had to anything like the same degree since the war, he possessed political clout. Equally, he knew the Bar from within and, although he had never been a judge, he knew a good deal about the business of judging. Not only this. The father whom he admired, and whose career had served as his model, had come to politics from being the leading

---

* In May 1991, the Government accepted the recommendation of the Select Committee on Procedure that the Lord Chancellor's Department should become subject to scrutiny, 'excluding consideration of individual cases and appointments . . .' but not excluding *systems of appointment* (emphasis added: Cm. 1532: *The Working of the Select Committee system: the Government's Response*).

† *obiter*: a remark made by a Judge in his judgment which is not essential to the reasoning of his decision.

advocate of the day, eventually to become Lord Chancellor. Quintin Hailsham was the longest serving Lord Chancellor in this century, with two terms, the first under Edward Heath from 1970 to 1974, and the second under Margaret Thatcher from 1979 to 1987. With his strong credentials for the job and his long experience, he was the best equipped holder of the office since the war. His achievements can best be considered under a series of heads rather than chronologically: his relations with the Judges; and with the legal profession; law reform and the accessibility of justice; his judicial work as a presiding Law Lord.

Much of Hailsham's work as Lord Chancellor is publicly known, at least to the profession. There is, however, one new source of much interest. Between 1970 and 1987, he kept appointment diaries. These were large stiff covered books, or files. One double page was devoted to each day. On one side, his officials pasted a typed list of appointments. On the other, Hailsham often wrote a summarised account of his meeting. The diaries contain a good deal more than the 'daily list of engagements, a few amusing anecdotes and a few nature notes' which he describes in *A Sparrow's Flight*. A proportion of the entries, for the most part the longer ones, are written in his own coded shorthand which makes use of the Greek alphabet. The code is not easy to break but it is not impenetrable. These notes include an account of his interview with Sir Henry Fisher, whom he vainly attempted to dissuade from resigning from the High Court Bench only two years after he was appointed; and his discussions with the Lord Chief Justice about what to do with the gladfly Judge James Pickles. Also some items which fell outside the path of duty, often about wild flowers or food and drink. 'Lunch on terrace at Putters first time this year [1974]. I cooked *ris d'agneau à la crème*, flambés before cooking in cream, rice.' On return from Australia in the same year: 'A bottle of priceless Australian *Hermitage* 1965 exploded in my suitcase on arrival at Heathrow and I returned home pouring libations to Antipodean Dionysus.' And a lengthy account of a 'disastrous evening' at the Royal Academy dinner in 1984. Laurie Lee, '(author, am told, of *Cider with Rosie*)', was sitting between Hailsham and the Princess of Wales, and had been assigned to propose the toast to the Academy. He began amusingly enough but it was soon obvious that he was very drunk. He went on adding fuel to the flames after dinner by taking on quantities of whisky, and 'it became apparent to me that I must take him home at once'. Somehow, Hailsham and his driver got him into the car where he slumped across the back seat and muttered thickly 'Elm Park Gardens'. 'When we came to a pub, called I think the "Great Elm", he insisted on getting out & sd. he wd. walk home, but refused to disclose the number of his house . . . He was quite obviously, as Maggie said, "legless" . . . We turned the car round and saw him slumped in a chair outside the pub.' Maggie, Hailsham's resourceful driver, found the publican who immediately recognised him and undertook to take him home. *Sic me servavit Apollo*, the note concludes. For this service, the Lord Chancellor received appreciative letters from Laurie Lee, Hugh Casson and the Prince of Wales.

He made time as well to keep up a lively correspondence with at least one grandchild. He kept her letters from boarding school in his diary. 'Please don't write Latin back,' she wrote, 'because last time Sister Maria translated the bit about herself. Luckily, she laughed and admired your Latin!'

The public perception of Hailsham as Lord Chancellor has inevitably been thrown into relief by his successor Lord Mackay's attempts to reform the legal profession. In this view, the 'Hailsham era' is seen as a do-nothing period of reactionary conservatism, followed by an age of enlightenment in which all the old prejudices and antiquated practices of the profession are at last dragged from their entrenchment and exposed to challenge. Such a view is a good deal less than fair. Hailsham was no Brezhnev, awaiting his Gorbachev. He knew what was going on, and had a coherent and defensible view of his objectives. But he was a conservative at bottom. This was due more than anything else to a romantic view of the Bar and Bench. He conceived this tiny profession as a *corps d'élite* with some of the attributes of philosopher kings in an idealised state. The tightly-knit collegiate character of the Inns was the essential framework for developing independence of mind, and inculcating integrity and dedication in the profession's initiates. Only a small Bar imbued with these standards could provide recruits for the High Court Bench, on whom the liberty of the citizen ultimately depended. For these reasons, Hailsham fiercely defended the Bar's monopoly of rights of audience in the High Court. To tinker with the margins was to embark on demarcation disputes, something at all costs to be avoided.

The outlook was a respectable one. It had served the country well. The Bench and Bar were institutions which had earned the admiration of the world. Hailsham venerated Britain's institutions. His conservatism was rooted in his historical understanding of the value of stability and legitimacy. But it led him to mistake the temper of the times and to miss opportunities. As an 'insider' who was trusted and generally well liked by the profession, he could have encouraged it more positively to secure public confidence by reforming its less defensible practices. The encyclopaedic report of the Royal Commission on Legal Services chaired by Sir Henry Benson[11] gave him just such an opportunity. Its tenor was conservative and it strongly supported the maintenance of the divided profession which Hailsham considered essential. Its recommendations for change were limited and sensible. But Hailsham did not grasp the opportunity. Benson, too, suggested that there should be a thorough review of civil procedure in the Courts.[12] Although the matter lay outside the Royal Commission's terms of reference, the report pointed out, with tactful understatement, that there was a close relationship between procedural rules and the duration and cost of litigation. Hailsham put the review in hand but, like its many predecessors, it achieved little. It was hampered by not being able to include consideration of the vital question of rights of audience. That lay in *terra sancta*. The wilderness that is civil procedure remains to be cleared.

Hailsham's conservative stance, particularly through seven years of the Thatcher administration, built up pressure for change. For Mrs Thatcher herself, there were few, if any, sacred cows. The public took her cue and asked itself why lawyers should be immune. Mackay, her new Lord Chancellor after Hailsham's departure, with his Scots background, came from outside. This gave him detachment, but it also ensured that, when the contest came, it would be fought out with bitterness. It might have been managed differently if Hailsham had been able to apply to the profession and its working practices those standards of rigour and objectivity which were the hallmark of his thinking elsewhere. But this was not possible. His attachment to the traditional Bench and Bar was an emotional one. In personal matters – and in this sense his love of his own profession was a personal matter – emotion was strong enough to warp judgment.

All this is not to say that Hailsham's long tenure as Lord Chancellor was barren. His achievements in law reform and in the ultimately insoluble problem of legal aid, helping those who cannot afford litigation and legal advice, were substantial. And if he is to be judged by his own test of how well he defended the independence of the Judges, he should be accorded the highest marks. That is the natural place at which to begin a more detailed survey.

22

The Lord Chancellor and the Judges

THE testimony to Lord Hailsham's resoluteness in defending the Bench is impressive. Lord Lane, who was Lord Chief Justice during almost the whole of Hailsham's second term, was a Judge who cared deeply about judicial independence and was highly sensitive to any threat of interference. In spite of some adverse publicity at the end of his career, he discharged his arduous duties as Chief with distinction and notable despatch. But, Hailsham thought, he could be unpredictable and difficult in his dealings with the Lord Chancellor and his Department. For his part, however, he harboured no doubts about Hailsham. He thought him the best possible ally to have in a tight corner, and 'absolutely staunch' in his dealings with the Judges. That, he said, is all the Judges require, as the Lord Chancellor is the only one who can defend them.[1] Lord Rawlinson, Attorney-General during Hailsham's first term, was of the same mind. He considered that Hailsham understood completely the importance of preserving the office in its traditional form. Unlike Lord Gardiner, he had political weight and could 'keep politicians off his patch'.[2] No Judge would have disagreed with either assessment.

The opportunity to show how effective he was at keeping his patch clear of politicians came early, with the establishment in 1971 of the National Industrial Relations Court, and the appointment of Sir John Donaldson as its President. Hailsham did not admire the practice of the new Court of dispensing with wigs and gowns, and formal procedures. He thought it deprived the Court of the dignity and authority of the High Court, all of whose powers it was designed to assume. The supposed 'humanising' of the Court also personalised it. The unwise decision to assign only one Judge to preside, rather than sending a series of High Court Judges in rotation, exposed

Donaldson to attack as the personal instrument of the Conservative Government's policy of curbing the power of the Trade Unions. The Court became demonised in popular parlance as 'the Donaldson Court'. There was no doubt about Donaldson's political sympathies, but there was equally no ground for alleging that he allowed his sympathies to obtrude into his judicial work – although some doubted the wisdom of a series of *ex cathedra* pronouncements he made on the importance of the rule of law. True to form, Hailsham leaped to the defence of a Judge who could not defend himself publicly. In June, 1972, a remark by Edward Short that Donaldson had recently been a Conservative party official drew a tart letter from the Lord Chancellor. There was a more serious skirmish in December of the following year, when 182 Labour Members signed a Commons motion demanding Donaldson's dismissal. In a speech to the Junior Carlton Club, Hailsham attacked them for abusing Parliamentary privilege.

> And what of a judge who has been traduced so unjustly, and by a motion every statement of fact in which is false, and could have been ascertained to be false at the time the motion was put down? What then? . . . The symptoms of our malaise may be economic . . . but underlying the symptoms is a disease which has destroyed democracies in the past, and the causes of that disease are not economic. They are moral . . .[3]

The vigour and pugnacity had not been diminished by the dignity of office. Nor had the integrity. In 1973 he had a letter from the philosopher and historian, Sir Isaiah Berlin, praising '. . . your fiery and unquenchable courage and uncompromising assertion of principle at a time when flexibility and accommodation are regarded as invested with profound political and social wisdom and statesmanship.'

Hailsham defended the Judges fiercely, but he was not blind to their faults. Of one Judge who was 'giving trouble', he wrote in his diary 'I must see', and then

> Let us see if Harold can
> Be a little gentleman
> Let us see if he is able
> To sit quiet and still at table.[4]

In 1976, while he was out of office, he received a complaint from a Judge who thought Hailsham had been criticising one of his decisions. Hailsham replied with a personal note which he thought would be accepted. 'Not at all. My essentially private letter . . . taken to meeting of Chancery Judges, bandied about, construed like an originating summons, assessed with pursed lips as if a dishonest affidavit . . . condensed, garbled and made subject of official complaint to LC . . . pompous ass . . . no wonder lawyers get a bad name.'[5]

The Judges could also invite trouble by disturbing the delicate balance of the constitution. Towards the end of his life, Hailsham came to think that the extraordinary growth of judicial review, the procedure by which the Courts scrutinise the behaviour of Government and its agencies, might have gone too far.[6] At least in theory, Parliament is absolutely sovereign, and there is no constitutional court to check the use of its powers. But as Hailsham appreciated more than most, Parliamentary sovereignty was coming more and more to mean the supremacy of the government machine. He warned against it in his celebrated Dimbleby Lecture, *Elective Dictatorship*. Adventurous Judges, thinking to apply some brake on government, were staking out a new empire called judicial review, and arming themselves with power to pass judgment on a whole range of decisions taken by ministers and officials. The enthusiasm of these zealots on the Bench was pushing the boundaries of the empire further and wider. Even if there were no constitutional court, they seemed to be saying, that did not mean that the processes of government could escape judicial scrutiny. What other check on an overmighty executive was there? What other protection for the citizen? Hailsham feared the consequences of such zeal. Frequent anouncements in the press that Ministers had been declared to 'have acted unlawfully' by Judges who, he thought, were not always well informed about constitutional practice[7] were provocative and might bring retribution on their heads. The judiciary is, after all, the weakest branch of government and would prove no match for an aroused government riding under the banner of the supremacy of an elected Parliament.

Relations between the Lord Chancellor's Department and the senior judiciary are generally strained. Many Judges think that the departmental officials are lawyers who have failed in their profession, are consequently jealous of the Judges, and seek to manipulate the Lord Chancellor. The officials resent these attitudes and consider that Judges make little attempt to understand the realities of political life. In particular, they do not realise that the Department is concerned to defend the interests and independence of the Bench against intrusion and influence from other parts of the government machine, especially the Treasury. Inoculated against 'reality', Judges fail to see that all in the administration of justice is not for the best in the best of all possible worlds. The circumstance that these traditional beliefs, on both sides, are exaggerated and sometimes without foundation at all, does nothing to mitigate the tenacity with which they are held.

The Lord Chancellor's Department is not, and never has been, as other Departments are. 'Rum' was Lord Lane's word for it. Until Hailsham's first term, it was a tiny affair: an office rather than a Department. In 1960 there were only thirteen lawyers in the office, but because of the Beeching reforms of the criminal courts, and the growth of legal aid, by the middle eighties it had increased out of all recognition.[8] The senior officials are lawyers and not professional administrators. At least until Hailsham's time, their duties were not primarily administrative. The Permanent Secretary wields great power and influence, particularly in appointments to the Bench. It is just this power and influence of which the Judges are suspicious. Hailsham was in a good position to understand the tensions, and to distinguish the actual from the fantastic; and it is much to his credit that he was both trusted by the Judges and well respected within the Office. He was an intensely loyal man, and it was part of his code to give loyalty not only to his leader, but also to his staff. During his time, he was served by three Permanent Secretaries, Sir Denis Dobson, Sir Wilfrid Bourne and Sir Derek Oulton. Dobson had had personal experience of six other Lord Chancellors: Jowitt, Simonds, Kilmuir, Dilhorne, Gardiner and Elwyn-Jones; and was in no doubt that Hailsham was the best of them all. In Dobson's opinion, he had the widest background and the greatest ability.[9] 'We knew,' Dobson wrote when congratulating him on becoming a Companion of Honour, 'that in your hands the administration of justice would never be devalued.'[10] The Permanent Secretaries of the second term, from 1979 to 1987, Bourne and Oulton agreed with Dobson's view and neither would have wanted to cede place to him in their admiration for his intellect, integrity and general effectiveness. All three were at one in thinking him outstandingly well equipped, but all agreed also that his emotions could get in the way of his talents. Some officials could ride out the tempest better than others; some were irritated or upset by his bullying; some smiled; but no colleague of his working life could say with his hand on his heart that Quintin Hailsham was invariably 'good with people'. One official of the Department gave it as his opinion that, in order to look after Lord Hailsham, one had to be good with children rather than with the elderly. There was a child-like quality about his outbursts; he could be wilful and utterly charming by turns. But for all his foibles, he was a commanding figure who could and did inspire a fierce affection.

The Judges' distrust of the Department occasionally erupted in individual cases of paranoia. Hailsham had no time for these outbreaks, which he called 'Hewartitis', after Lord Hewart's celebrated rush of blood to the head. In December 1934, Lord Chief Justice Hewart stormed down to the House of Lords and made an intemperate attack on the Lord Chancellor's Office, in particular on the Permanent Secretary, Sir Claud Schuster. The conspiracy of bureaucrats which he thought he saw did not exist. Hailsham's attitude was doubtless influenced by the circumstance that his father, who was then Secretary of State for War and a former Lord Chancellor, warmly defended the Department against Hewart's assault, and showed it up for the nonsense it was.[11] When, therefore, Lord Browne-Wilkinson, then the Vice-Chancellor, suggested in a lecture in 1987[12] that the independence of the judiciary was again under threat, this time by reason of the executive's control of finance, Hailsham thought he detected another incipient attack of Hewartitis. The Vice-Chancellor's argument was that: 'Judges are sitting in an environment wholly determined by executive decision in the Lord Chancellor's Department, which in turn is operating under the financial constraints and pressures imposed by the Treasury. The yard-stick for decision taking is financial value for money, not the interests of justice.'

He suggested as a possible remedy that the Judges should be consulted about the preparation and allocation of the budget for the Courts and their administration.

Hailsham delivered his riposte in the next lecture in the series.[13] He described the Vice-Chancellor's suggestion as 'a sort of legal Arcadia', and Hewartitis as a dangerous disease because it was based on a delusion, whose 'immediate activity consists in sawing off the very branch upon which its sufferers sit'. The Lord Chancellor, he declared, is the Judges' friend at Court: 'You may be absolutely certain that he or his officials will fight to the last man and the last round within the councils of government to meet their legitimate demands.'

This was forceful debate, but it showed some complacency. The Judges might not prove to be very good with budgets, as Hailsham confidently thought: but equally the Department's gallantry might not be enough. Lord Browne-Wilkinson's warning was not the result of delusion and it was absurd to compare him with Lord Hewart. In his laudable anxiety to defend the Department, as his father had done in 1934, Hailsham was demonstrating an inflexible attachment to the Schuster-Birkenhead theory that the Lord Chancellor was the only possible bulwark against executive encroachment. It boiled down to the cautionary moral of Jim's sad end: 'And always keep a hold of Nurse, For fear of finding something worse'. Lord Chancellors, not least Quintin Hailsham, had a good record for protecting the Bench; but even so, the Judges were not likely to find the answer convincing. The dispute with the Bar about fees for the legally-aided defence of criminal cases only a year before the Vice-Chancellor's lecture was sobering evidence of the Treasury's power to outgun the Lord Chancellor (see chapter 24). Moreover, conservatism of this sort helped to give Hailsham the name of not looking fairly at proposals for change.

★

Nothing about the Judges has so consistently excited public interest as the way they are chosen. The critics of the system of appointment are many and vociferous. It is said that it is secretive; it depends on a reassuring network of personal friendship and recommendation; the appointments are political since the choice is made by a cabinet minister; in the result the Judges are monochrome, drawn from a narrow section of the population, being predominantly upper middle class, male, white, and of similar educational background; they are accordingly unrepresentative and, worst of all, out of touch. These are the oft-repeated accusations of the press, the television commentator, the sociologists and academics who interest themselves in the topic. It is less often asked whether any of this matters, or whether the quality of justice is any the worse for it.

Formally, High Court Judges and Circuit Judges are appointed by the Queen on the recommendation of the Lord Chancellor. Appointments to the Court of Appeal, the House of Lords (the final appeal court), and the offices of Lord Chief Justice, Master of the Rolls, Vice-Chancellor and President of the Family Division are made on the advice of the Prime Minister, after consulting the Lord Chancellor.

Hailsham's method was to prepare a short list for the Prime Minister. He would have considered resigning if the Prime Minister had rejected all his suggested names and made an appointment from outside his list. Neither Edward Heath nor Margaret Thatcher ever did so. Mrs Thatcher liked to discuss appointments. She thought, he recalled, that 'somewhere above the ceiling' there was always The Best Man, and she did not appreciate the need to balance the Bench.

After one meeting with her, he noted: 'We must be careful in future minutes *not* to pan our candidates, and *not* to put too many names'.[14]

Since 1971, early in Hailsham's first term, appointments to the Circuit Bench have been open to solicitors; and since 1990, Lord Mackay's reforms have made it possible for solicitors to be appointed direct to the High Court Bench. But most appointments to the Circuit Bench, and almost all to the High Court Bench, have thus far been made from Queen's Counsel practising at the Bar. The appointment of Queen's Counsel is also by the Queen on recommendation by the Lord Chancellor. So in all appointments to the upper judiciary, the Lord Chancellor has the most influential, if not the decisive voice. It is equally clear that, although the decision is his, a small group of officials in his Department headed by his Permanent Secretary exercise great influence over appointments. The process is, as it must be, confidential.

So much for the formal position. How does it work in practice? In 1986, the Lord Chancellor's Department published a booklet intended, as Lord Hailsham wrote in the preface, 'to dispel any lingering sense of mystery or obscurity that there may be about how this work is done'.[15] The mystery was not wholly dispelled, but the pamphlet did shed some light on what consultations lead to decision.

It is clear that for appointments to the High Court and above, the views of the Heads of Divisions – the Lord Chief Justice, the Master of the Rolls, the President of the Family Division and the Vice-Chancellor – are crucial. This is confirmed by a study of Hailsham's engagement diaries. He had frequent meetings with the four, and they discussed candidates for promotion exhaustively. Hailsham took immense care, as he did with all appointments, and not seldom had to deal with disagreements between the Heads, or bees buzzing in the bonnets of one or more of them. He was particularly skilful in steering a course through these difficulties, and he was an excellent judge of the right man or woman.[16] He was understanding too. To one Judge, who politely declined an appointment to the European Court in Luxemburg, saying that it would be like exile, he replied: 'That's what I thought you'd say, my boy. Abroad's alright for the hols.'

There were many incidents which illustrate his determination to have the right candidate, come what may. In July 1979, there was a meeting with the Heads of Division. Mrs Butler-Sloss, then a Registrar, was proposed for promotion to the Family Division of the High Court. Hailsham noted: 'Universal acclaim . . . Reasons her excellence and morale of Registrars . . . Bombshell: she turned out to be E. Havers, sister of A-G [Sir Michael Havers, then the Attorney-

General]. Bourne says I shall be accused of nepotism.' [He was, in the *Daily Mirror*.] 'I sd. to hell with that . . . wrong in principle to discriminate against her . . .'[17] In another incident, which it has not been possible to verify but which is so characteristic that it must be authentic, Hailsham was considering the renewal of an appointment as Law Commissioner (a full time appointment to the body responsible for law reform). The candidate was an eminently suitable one who, but for an incurable disease, would have been on the High Court Bench. Hailsham's officials warned him that reappointment might look like helping a lame dog over a stile. The Lord Chancellor is reported to have replied dismissively: 'This is no lame dog. More like a ram caught in a thicket.'

When Hailsham first became Lord Chancellor in 1970, the system for appointing the lower judiciary was somewhat haphazard. If there were a vacancy in the County Court, one of the senior officials in the Department would seek the views of a few County Court Judges in the area, and report them to the Lord Chancellor. The arrangements were elaborated and rationalised to great advantage by Sir Derek Oulton, with the Lord Chancellor's agreement, during Hailsham's first term, and coinciding with the reform of the court system by the Courts Act of 1971. Under these reforms, the process of consultation leading to the appointment of Circuit Judges, Recorders and Assistant Recorders is delegated to the senior officials in the Department. It is a complex affair involving long interviews with the Presiding Judge of each circuit, as well as other Judges and practitioners. The results of the interviews are summarised in notes which are checked by those who have been interviewed, and the whole process is renewed and gone through annually. The result is a filtering, passing through several stages, which takes full account of local knowledge and experience. The appointment of Queen's Counsel, the essential step to the High Court Bench, was correspondingly rationalised during Hailsham's time.

From time to time it has been argued that the work of appointing Judges would be better done by a Committee of Judges, or by a mixed commission of Judges, barristers, solicitors, and laymen, or any combination of these.[18] These changes would, it is claimed, make judicial appointments more open, less political, and result in a more representative Bench. Unsurprisingly, Hailsham did not think these were sound ideas. He considered that if the profession became party to the decision making, it would get at odds with itself, and considerations of self-interest would inevitably obtrude.[19] 'I'm pretty sure', he said in a radio interview in 1972, 'that the system worked out for consultation to take place in layers across a wide front is infinitely more sophisticated and flexible, and far more efficient in selecting the right personnel, with the Lord Chancellor at the top responsible to Parliament, than any system written by an outside body is ever likely to be.'[20] The reformist Lord Mackay agreed. In his opinion a Judicial Appointments Commission would not be better placed to choose. He thought, as well, that it would impair the Lord Chancellor's accountability to Parliament, and expose the Commission, and ultimately the Judiciary, to 'undesirable external pressures'.[21] On this point at least, Lords Hailsham and Mackay were completely at one.

They also agreed that it was facile to say that the attitudes of the Judges were too similar and too conservative. Mackay declined to accept that it was a function of the Bench to be representative of the population as a whole.[22] Hailsham considered that individual opinions and prejudices were irrelevant to the professional business of judging. 'The Bench is not made up of political, religious or social neuters.* Impartiality consists in the capacity to be aware of one's subjective opinions and to place them on one side when one enters the professional field, and the ability to listen patiently to and to weigh evidence and argument and to withhold concluded judgment until the case is over.' Both Lord Chancellors wanted to see greater numbers of women and members of ethnic minorities on the Bench,[23] but it is at least an open question whether this would make any real difference to attitudes or values in the Judiciary.

In the end, criticisms of the system of appointing Judges should be tested by considering the quality of the Judiciary. In common with his predecessors and successors, Hailsham considered that the system deserved to be judged by its product. Are the Judges fair and independent minded, beyond bribery and dedicated to their work? Their critics have rarely tried and, except in the odd isolated case, never succeeded in showing that this was not so.

★

The question of removing Judges is more theoretical than practical. But if it does arise, it is a problem for the Lord Chancellor. Since the Act of Settlement of 1701, the tenure of High Court Judges is secure, and they hold office so long as they are of good behaviour instead of,

---

* The metaphor was congenial to him, and at the Judges' dinner in the Mansion House in 1984, he elaborated it. 'Judges are not political neuters. Unlike the keepers of the seraglio, on appointment they do not have their political or social opinions carefully removed.'

as formerly, at the pleasure of the Monarch. They can now be dismissed only by the Crown on an address presented by both Houses of Parliament. Circuit Judges, however, are removable by the Lord Chancellor on the ground of incapacity or misbehaviour.[24] Unfortunately, Hailsham had to consider the use of this invidious power on more than one occasion.

Judge James Pickles was a Circuit Judge sitting at Halifax. Difficulties with him started in 1980, when, according to the Presiding Judge, Pickles had written a rude letter to the Chief Constable of West Yorkshire, and there had been other 'lapses of taste'.[25] Pickles paid no attention to a warning letter from Hailsham. In March 1985, he wrote an article for the *Daily Telegraph* about government pressure on the Judges to shorten sentences because of overcrowding in prisons.[26] This was contrary to the 'Kilmuir Rules', which precluded Judges from publicising their views without the approval of the Lord Chancellor. The publication drew a letter from the Permanent Secretary warning Pickles that it constituted a prima facie case of misbehaviour, rendering him liable to dismissal. Pickles was undeterred and wrote another piece for the *Telegraph* about delays in bringing cases to trial.[27] In September, Lord Chief Justice Lane saw him, and Pickles gave an undertaking that he would publish no more without first contacting Lord Lane. The undertaking was later withdrawn, and he went on broadcasting his views.

Then, in February 1986, he wrote an extended article for the *Guardian* under the headline 'Kilmuir Rules – OK?'[28] If, he said, the Lord Chancellor were to take action against him, he would be acting as complainant, prosecutor, judge and jury, all in one. Moreover, in upholding rules which prevented Judges telling people what they thought, Hailsham was perpetuating a deplorable attitude: 'Don't let the side down. Keep in line. Don't let the public know more than is necessary.' The article made Pickles a celebrity. The press was naturally enthusiastic about giving space to such unvarnished views from the Bench. In any case, his points could not simply be dismissed as nonsense. He was a thorn in the Lord Chancellor's flesh. The *Sun* called him a 'Plonker'.

Pickles continued troublesome. At the end of 1984, the appointment of a Recorder called Manus Nunan had not been renewed. No reasons were given to Nunan and there was agitation in the media and the House of Commons. It was suggested that the real reason for not renewing the appointment was that Nunan held an Irish passport.[29] Pickles now took up Nunan's cause. He sent a long letter to Hailsham, complaining that he had acted on reports that Nunan had never seen, and that he had never given Nunan an opportunity to be heard in his own defence.*

On 7 May 1986, Hailsham had a meeting with Lord Lane and Lord Justice Watkins about how best to exorcise this spirit. The two Judges considered that Hailsham should use his power of dismissal, for which they thought there was ample ground. Hailsham disagreed. He thought that the BBC and the press would be bound to take up the cudgels on Pickles' behalf, and that Pickles would try to make him disclose confidential information about the Nunan case, under threat of further publicity. Hailsham was sensitive to the charge that he would be acting as judge in his own cause, and preferred to have the matter dealt with by some sort of tribunal of Judges on the pattern adopted in Scotland, Canada and parts of Australia, as he said. The meeting was a difficult one and no agreement on what to do was reached. The Judges thought that the Lord Chancellor was evading his duty, but the officials who were present agreed with their chief, and thought that he would not get away with the summary dismissal which Lane and Watkins were urging.[30]

The division of view neatly but uncomfortably encapsulated the difficulties about removing a Judge for misbehaviour. There were really only two possibilities. Either he could be taken away by the Lord Chancellor into a dark corner and shot, or he could undergo some sort of trial by his peers or superiors.† In each case, the authorities would be relying on confidential reports which could hardly be disclosed to the victim; and in each case there was a risk of judicial review. The victim would complain that he was being denied the protection of natural justice, and overhanging the whole affair was the threat of publicity. The possibility of a Judge reviewing a decision of the Lord Chancellor and finding the dismissal unlawful did not bear thinking about. Judge Pickles remained in office to haunt Hailsham's successors.

An equally difficult but more distressing case is that of a senior Judge whose powers are declining, while he is apparently unaware of it. This occurred in early 1980 when Lord Chief Justice Widgery was suffering from the onset of Parkinson's disease. A number of barristers and of his colleagues on the Bench became concerned about his waning capacity. A group of Judges urged the Lord

---

* Pickles' own account is given in his book, *Judge for Yourself*: 1992.

† The power to remove Circuit Judges in the Courts Act, 1971, is baldly expressed, and contains no safeguards or procedural requirements. It merely states: 'The Lord Chancellor may, if he thinks fit, remove a Circuit Judge from office on the ground of incapacity or misbehaviour.'

Chancellor to act. But Hailsham thought that, as his colleagues, they were failing in their duty of friendship in not speaking frankly to the Chief themselves; and furthermore, 'undermining the independence of the Bench by driving the LC (a member of the Cabinet) to try to make the LCJ resign'.[31] There was a strong feeling that this second point had nothing in it and that, as head of the Judiciary, Hailsham was shirking a painful obligation. In the end, it was Lord Denning who undertook the task of telling Lord Widgery that it was time to go, a task which it is safe to assume he carried out with tact and grace. Hailsham entered in his diary: 'All this goes to show the folly of want of candour between friends';[32] and of the sufferer himself: 'He is a brave man struggling with adversity.'[33]

The argument with James Pickles was about whether Judges should be free to publicise their views, a question covered by the so-called 'Kilmuir Rules'. There were in fact no rules at all, but only a letter dated 12 December 1955 written by the then Lord Chancellor, Viscount Kilmuir, to Sir Ian Jacob, the Director-General of the BBC.[34] Jacob had enquired about the possibility of Judges taking part in a series of lectures projected for the Third Programme about great Judges of the past. After consulting Heads of Divisions, Kilmuir turned the proposal down. He acknowledged that the Lord Chancellor had no disciplinary jurisdiction over the Judges, each of whom would have to decide for himself, if asked to broadcast, 'whether he considered it compatible with his office to accept'. However, his view and that of the senior Judges, was that the Judge concerned ought to consult the Lord Chancellor first. Kilmuir expressed himself sympathetic to the request and sorry to have to decline, but, he said, the overriding consideration was the importance of insulating the Judiciary from the controversies of the day.

> So long as a Judge keeps silent his reputation for wisdom and impartiality remains unassailable: but every utterance he makes in public, except in the course of the actual performance of his judicial duties, must necessarily bring him within the focus of criticism.

The gist of the letter was conveyed to the Judges, and has since been taken to preclude not only broadcasting on the radio and television, but also articles in the press, unless the Lord Chancellor gives his consent. Most Judges at the time were rigid or, as some thought, timorous in their refusal to appear publicly. At the meeting between the Lord Chancellor and Heads of Division on 7 November 1955 which led to Lord Kilmuir's letter, it was reported that one Judge had been asked to conduct Haydn's Children's Symphony on television, but had refused to do so.

Early in Hailsham's first term, the rule came up for review. He annotated a note of 1971 from Sir Denis Dobson: 'It may be the existing rule is right. But the Royal Family have changed their practice with advantage and many of Kilmuir's arguments apply to them.'[35]

His own view was that the rule might be relaxed, but since only a small number of Judges would prove to be satisfactory performers on television or radio, if any change were to be made, he should keep control in his hands.[36] The Heads of Division, however, were resolutely against any relaxation, and the Lord Chief Justice, Lord Widgery, said he would be 'terrified' of any general change.[37]

The rule was reviewed again in 1979, and again the status quo was maintained. Hailsham sent a circular letter to the Judges, saying that he thought they owed each other a duty to follow a common policy; and that as the 'overwhelming majority' of the senior among them had come to the same verdict, the rule should remain unchanged. He repeated Kilmuir's point that he had no power to give directions to fellow Judges.[38] The Judges thought the rule was 'a convenient shield', and Lord Denning's was the only dissentient voice. He considered the question a difficult one because: 'Judges are independent and not in any way subject to any kind of discipline by the Lord Chancellor'.[39] It was a sad irony that Lord Denning's career was to be brought to an undignified end by a breach of the rule (see p. 280).

Hailsham's opinion that Judges might not be able to look after themselves among the predators in the badlands of radio and, particularly, television, was surely right. He was the most experienced broadcaster ever to become Lord Chancellor and he knew the perils. He laid them out graphically for the benefit of one Lord Justice who was thinking of broadcasting:

> The modern television audience has become accustomed to programmes which follow, as a matter of course, a debased form of drama. The essence of drama, for this purpose, is conflict and characterisation. Even when a programme is concerned with fact, not entertainment, those who make it know that the audience will judge its impact according to their perception of conflict and characterisation. When a producer says that he must make his programme interesting, this is what he means ... To make a success of a television appearance requires more than the power of intellect or personality ... It is no light undertaking.[40]

So the rule remained intact throughout Hailsham's time. In 1989, however, Lord Mackay decided that it should be left to the Judges themselves to decide whether they should give interviews to journalists or appear on radio or television.[41] Although he advised them to be very cautious about their exposure to the media, the consequences of relaxing the rule have caused many to suspect that, in spite of the dated tone of the original Kilmuir letter, the old guideline may still be salutary, and Lord Hailsham's apprehensions about the unsuitability of many Judges for broadcasting well founded.

Within a month of Hailsham's receiving the Great Seal in June 1970, an unprecedented situation was brought about by the resignation of Sir Henry Fisher, a High Court Judge with a distinguished academic and professional background, who had been appointed only two years earlier. On 13 July, the engagement diary records a meeting with the Heads of Division about the High Court Bench. 'Fisher (contemplating retirement) I must now see'.[42]

He saw Fisher on the following day alone and not, as would have been usual, with his Permanent Secretary. His purpose was to try to persuade him to change his mind and not leave the Bench for the City, as he intended. Fisher would not do so. The diary records their conversation in a long coded shorthand note.[43] The recusant Judge was in the happy position of being able to choose between two merchant banks. He told Hailsham that he did not think that his resignation would pose serious problems, because the banks would take only those of the very highest calibre. Hailsham wisely ignored the extraordinary self-regard in that observation, and said that that was precisely what he was afraid of. It would be a 'terrible weapon' in City hands if it were known that they could purchase the services of Judges who might be discontented or dissatisfied with their chances of promotion. The Lord Chancellor could not compete in the market with the banks. Fisher was constrained to agree, but pointed out that his own motives were not financial. He was simply bored with being a Judge. He made some remarks about the misuse of judge–power, the nature of which is not recorded, but was probably concerned with the duty of Queen's Bench Judges (of whom Fisher was one) to go out of London on circuit. Fisher summarised his attitude by observing that the judicial office was not like marriage. No, said Hailsham, 'it is more like ordination to a priesthood.' 'With that he did not agree.' Fisher said he would help in any way he could; but as he had already taken the irrevocable step, the Lord Chancellor did not see what help was possible. There was one other point of disagreement. Hailsham thought that, if Fisher were to become disenchanted with the City, a return to the Bar was impossible. Fisher demurred and referred to some seventeenth century precedents. Hailsham responded: 'I said I thought I could persuade the Judges to refuse the right of audience and would do so if I could get public opinion behind me.'*

Hailsham was not exaggerating, still less being facetious, when he described the Bench as a priesthood. He saw it as a close brotherhood, the proper end of a career at the Bar, a duty and an honour to accept, almost unthinkable to leave until elderly retirement. For so long as the profession was divided, and Hailsham believed passionately in the division, the catchment for the High Court Bench was narrow. The Bar was small enough for it to be his constant concern to ensure that it was not denuded by appointments to the Bench; it was his corresponding concern that the Bench should not be starved of recruits by the refusal of successful silks to give up their work for the much less remunerative seat of judgment. Now Sir Henry Fisher's resignation posed a new threat. If his example were followed by others who might be seduced by the salaries and perquisites dangled like sirens by the merchant banks, the carefully composed High Court Bench might itself be denuded, particularly the vital Commercial Court. His fear was not realised, but his anxiety was understandable. After the Fisher incident, he warned all Judges on their appointment that the route to the Bench was a one way street.

★

The relations between Lord Hailsham and Lord Denning, twin Elders of the Law, were of mutual, but not unqualified, respect. Denning thought it unfortunate for the country that Hailsham did not become Prime Minister in 1963, and told him so; but he considered that Hailsham spoilt his unrivalled abilities by being too conscious of them, and too intolerant of any views but his own. Hailsham thought Denning one of the greatest legal intellects of the century but that he was naïve and his genius was flawed by unscrupulousness. His affection, however, was unqualified: 'the man

---

* It seems that Hailsham was right about returning to the Bar. The Code of Conduct of the Bar states: 'The Bar Council does not approve as a matter of principle of former Judges in England and Wales returning to practise at the Bar in any capacity'. (3rd ed. Annex 8, para. 3.) The right of audience in the High Court was a matter for the Judges until the Mackay reforms were enacted in the Courts and Legal Services Act 1990.

who does not love Tom Denning is no good as a man'.[44] The clash between them over the series of dockers' cases in 1972 seemed to confirm the views of each.

By the early 1970s the 'container revolution' in the shipping industry was under way. Seaborne goods were being carried in big steel boxes, which were loaded and unloaded in depots away from the dockside by relatively low-paid workers. This represented a new and potent threat for the traditional dockers, who were in any case in a declining industry. The cases concerned the attempts of the dockers to fend off the threat.

Believing that it had a mandate to curb the overweening power of the Unions, the Heath administration of 1970–74 put industrial relations at the head of its agenda. In February, 1972, the bitterly fought Industrial Relations Act came into force and with it, the National Industrial Relations Court under the presidency of Sir John Donaldson (see p. 262). Many Unions boycotted the Act, and refused to register or recognise the new Court. As Lord Denning said, they did not see it as a regular court of justice at all: 'It was, in their view, a tool used by the Government to enforce a repressive law . . . If it made orders, they would not obey. They would rather go to prison – confident that, if they did so, there would be a general strike which would bring down the Government.'[45] That, in effect, was what happened.

A more detailed account of the dockers' cases is given in Appendix I, but the pattern in all of them was the same. Dock workers picketed the container depots. They did not offer violence, but they made a note of all the lorries crossing the picket line, and blacklisted the firms operating the lorries nationwide. The Union concerned was not registered under the new Act, so the blacking was unlawful. The National Industrial Relations Court, under Sir John Donaldson's presidency, made orders against the Union or the individual pickets, forbidding the picketing and blacking. Disobedience against the orders was a contempt of court, ultimately leading to imprisonment, but by one means or another the Court of Appeal, under Lord Denning's presidency, frustrated the new Court and, with it, the Government's purposes. Denning did not believe that imprisonment should – or could – be used as a legal sanction in industrial disputes, and he succeeded in finding ways of preventing it. In his book *The Due Process of Law* he wrote: 'The lesson to be learned from the dockers' cases is that the weapon of imprisonment should never be used – for contempt of court – in the case of industrial disputes.' And he added disarmingly: 'Some better means must be found. Can anyone suggest one?'

The activities of Denning's Court caused the government and the Lord Chancellor deep concern. Hailsham thought that Denning had exceeded the bounds of propriety by encouraging the bringing of proceedings into his Court, and asked to see him. According to Denning's recollection, he was presiding in the Court of Appeal one morning when his clerk brought him a message that the Lord Chancellor wanted to see him in the House of Lords. Denning sent a message back that he would not adjourn his Court to see Hailsham, but that they could meet instead at Lincoln's Inn just before lunch. This they did in the Council Room in the Inn, when Denning made clear to Hailsham that his Court would decide cases only on the evidence and other materials before the Court.[46] A brief note in the Lord Chancellor's engagement diary indicates only that Hailsham told Denning that it was alleged that he had himself instigated an application to his Court, but that Denning had categorically denied it.[47]

The clash on the Bench between Lord Denning and Sir John Donaldson, and off the Bench between Lord Denning and Lord Hailsham, was serious. The responsibility for it lay with the Government. By attempting to deploy the full range of legal sanctions in the field of industrial relations, it had brought the Judges into the political arena. In a radio interview in the middle of the crisis, Hailsham had difficulty fending off Robin Day's point that the Judges were becoming embroiled in questions relating to industrial and economic policy, in such a way that an order of a single Judge might lead to an industrial crisis which in turn could bring about a run on the pound.[48] Hailsham's personal view that attempts to enforce collective agreements with the Unions as ordinary contracts, or to prevent strikes by court order, were unlikely to succeed (see p. 242) did not go far enough. For, by equipping the National Industrial Relations Court with all the powers of the High Court, the possibility was opened of imprisonment for contempt.

In his valedictory on Lord Denning's retirement in 1982, Lord Hailsham said: '. . . it is given to few men to become a legend in their lifetime. There would be few in this country who would deny that Lord Denning is one of these few.' One of the things for which he was a legend was a disregard, amounting almost to insouciance, of the hierarchical court system. One morning early in his first term as Lord Chancellor, Hailsham had a visit from Lord Devlin, a former Law Lord.[49] Devlin was much put out. While giving judgment in the Court of Appeal,[50] Denning had criticised a speech of Devlin's in an earlier appeal to the House of Lords,[51] and advised Judges to ignore the House of Lords decision. In Devlin's opinion, Denning's publicly expressed views cut against the whole scheme of judicial authority. Hailsham said that as Denning's judgment was going on appeal to the House of Lords, things could be put right then. But Devlin was not satisfied. He pressed Hailsham to 'give a rebuke to Denning MR publicly here and now'. Hailsham thought that there was no future in such a row, in which he could only put himself in the wrong. If the Appellate Committee thought fit to rebuke Denning, another rebuke from the Lord Chancellor would be superfluous. If it did not, 'it would not become the Chancellor to be more royalist than the King'. Devlin was not appeased, but Hailsham, whose touch in these matters was sure, was certain he was right. He decided to preside himself in the forthcoming appeal from Denning's Court. He did so, and included in his own judgment a rebuke to Lord Denning couched in terms of 'studied moderation'.[52] But it was still plain enough: 'it is not open to the Court of Appeal to give gratuitous advice to judges of first instance to ignore decisions of the House of Lords in this way . . . The fact is, and I hope it will never be necessary to say so again, that, in the hierarchical system of courts which exists in this country, it is necessary for each lower tier, including the Court of Appeal, to accept loyally the decisions of the higher tiers.' Denning was contrite. 'Yes – I had been guilty – of lese-majesty. I had impugned the authority of the House. That must never be done by anyone save the House itself. Least of all by the turbulent Master of the Rolls.'[53]

After his conversation with Devlin, Hailsham recounted it to his Permanent Secretary. Dobson told him that he had been speaking to Lord Reid, who had been a party to the appeal which was the object of Denning's criticism. Reid thought that there might be something in the criticisms,[54] and in any case, 'everyone knows Tom has a way of speaking'. Hailsham knew that in Tom Denning he had a man of genius, for whom some allowances had to be made.

But finally Denning committed an indiscretion for which no allowance could be made. His book, *What Next in the Law*, launched in May 1982, contained a passage suggesting that some coloured immigrants were unsuitable to serve on British juries. Two black jurors threatened to sue him for libel, the Society of Black Lawyers called for his resignation, and all copies of the book had to be recalled. It was a wretched and saddening end to the career of a great Judge; but it seemed to bear out Hailsham's opinion that, for all his towering intellect and understanding of humanity, Denning could be naïve. His belief in the greatness of the British race, Hailsham thought, could occasionally betray him into what looked like illiberality.[55]

★

Lord Denning tells the story of the end of his career in his own way in *The Closing Chapter*.[56] There was, however, one last twist not included in his own account, and through which Hailsham was able to ease the passing. On 26 May 1982, Denning called on the Lord Chancellor with his solicitor, Max Williams, and Counsel, Andrew Leggatt QC and David Eady. He had prepared two letters to the Lord Chancellor, one tendering his resignation and the other seeking advice about timing. Hailsham advised an announcement in June and retirement at the end of September. It then emerged that Denning had recorded an interview with Ludovic Kennedy for BBC television, which had been advertised for broadcast the next Sunday. The offending passages in the book were repeated and confirmed in the interview. Leggatt and Williams had advised that there was no defence to the libel case threatened by the jurors. The BBC had refused to withdraw the broadcast, or even to postpone it. The situation looked black. Lord Denning's advisers asked whether the Lord Chancellor could 'suppress broadcast'.

> I sd. v: difficult. Independent BBC. Govt. BBC relations more than usually cool ... Wd I try? Me: Is this an enquiry or a request? Williams: A request. Rang Trethowan [the Director General of the BBC] and told him above facts. He was friendly & cooperative but wished to put out watered down or edited version. I said difficult, what was wrong was the flavour and not excisable passages. He then took it away and phoned back later saying interview wd. not go out.
> A sad end to a *great* career.
> But illustrates value Kilmuir Rules.[57]

Hailsham's true view of the great Judge comes best from a characteristic incident in 1982. He responded to a letter from Michael Meacher, a Labour MP who was critical of one of Denning's judgments, by telling the complainant that Denning's contribution to the development of our jurisprudence in a humane and rational direction was as great as any one man's. Denning was warmly appreciative, and Hailsham noted in his diary: 'Unmerited censure from the irredeemably prejudiced is the penalty paid for being a truly great man of independent and creative views.'[58]

23

The Lord Chancellor and the Legal Profession

THE Lord Chancellor has no more control over the legal profession than he has over the Judges. Apart from one anomaly, his chairmanship over a small committee which used to set the level of solicitors' fees for conveyancing, he has no power to order either branch of the profession to come or go. But he does traditionally exercise influence. He can exhort, cajole, restrain, and his voice is, or should be, listened to. Lord Hailsham was given a golden opportunity to exert his influence by the report of the Royal Commission on Legal Services, chaired by Sir Henry Benson, an outstandingly able and well informed chartered accountant, which was presented in October 1979, at the beginning of his second term. His failure to grasp that opportunity is perhaps the most serious charge which can be made against his Chancellorship.

The division of the profession into barristers and solicitors is, like the odd character of most traditional British institutions, the result of history rather than logic. The Bar is much the older branch. Its origins lie at the end of the thirteenth century when clerics were forbidden by canon law from appearing in secular cases. Its connection with the Inns dates from a few years later, when the crusading order of the Knights Templar was dissolved, and its buildings in 'the Temple' were occupied by lawyers. By the end of the fourteenth century, the four existing societies of barristers had been formed, the Inner and Middle Temple, Lincoln's Inn and Gray's Inn. From an early date the Inns owned the property in which their member lawyers worked, provided libraries, common rooms and meals for them, and made themselves responsible for their wellbeing and education. The collegiate life of the Inns, so akin to the colleges of Oxford and Cambridge, has through its long continuous tradition come to form that emotional bond between members which is the badge of an *alma mater*.

In spite of their affection, though, there was disquiet among barristers about the Inns during the later part of the nineteenth century. The management and discipline of the profession was in the hands of the benchers who ruled from high table in the Inns. They included a significant proportion of Judges and took their decisions behind closed doors without consulting the practising Bar. A number of barristers petitioned the Attorney-General in 1883 to establish a committee to 'collect and express the opinion of members of the Bar upon matters affecting the profession and to take such action as may be deemed expedient'. This was the origin of the Bar Council. In 1966, the Senate of the four Inns was formed so that the Inns could speak with one voice. There were therefore six autonomous bodies, the four Inns, the Senate and the Bar Council, all concerned with the administration of a tiny profession, and one further body, the Council of Legal Education, responsible for its training. It was a recipe for inertia, and worse. In 1970, soon after he had become Lord Chancellor for the first time, Hailsham held several meetings with these bodies to try to stimulate some reason and coherence. But the divided control of the Bar, with its consequences of diffusion of effort, duplication, rivalry and lack of co-operation, was still largely unremedied by the time the Benson Commission reported.

The senior members of the Bar are called King's or Queen's Counsel, or 'silks', from the material from which their gowns are made. They represent about ten per cent of the Bar, and 'taking silk' is normally an essential step in the *cursus honorum* which culminates in appointment to the Bench. The origin of Silk, Hailsham told the new Q.Cs in 1984,

> was to still the importunities of my predecessor, Francis Bacon, who had not, up to that moment, despite frequent and urgent applications, been appointed a law officer. Until well within my father's lifetime, the Crown had the right to pre-empt the services of all Q.Cs. Even after that, it was etiquette to ask for a dispensation before taking instructions against the Crown.[1]

Junior Counsel apply for silk, and the grant is by the Sovereign on the advice of the Lord Chancellor. It has often been remarked that it is strange that promotion in a self-regulated profession is, for practical purposes, in the hands of a Cabinet Minister and his officials.

Stranger still was a series of antique practices relating to silk. It was contrary to etiquette for a QC to go into Court without a junior barrister, who was normally entitled to a fee of two-thirds of that of his leader. In order to protect the position of juniors, silks did not undertake paperwork, and often were not brought into a case until the last stage before trial, a highly inconvenient arrangement which could give rise to disconcerting changes of direction at the eleventh hour. Hailsham's own attitude to these practices may be gauged from a note he made of a meeting with Sir Geoffrey Howe, then Minister for Trade and Consumer Affairs, in 1973: 'Howe: v. outspoken ... regdg. ppsd. ref. to Monopolies Commission of 2 counsel rule & partnerships ... No case for investgn. Any malpractices profn. will deal'.[2]

By the end of the seventeenth century, some formal divisions in the profession had emerged. There were a number of species other than barristers: attorneys, solicitors, notaries, scriveners and proctors. Solicitors were particularly associated with transactions in land. The functions of solicitors, attorneys and proctors were merged in 1873 into the single title of 'solicitor', the Law Society, the governing body of the solicitors' profession, having been granted a royal charter forty years earlier. Although the Law Society has disciplinary powers, solicitors are by tradition officers of the court, and the Judges are still responsible for maintaining standards of conduct in this branch of the profession.

Solicitors have always been more numerous than barristers; at the time of the Benson Report there were some 4000 barristers and 34,000 solicitors. This disparity helped to promote the idea of the Bar as a small élite, socially superior to the other branch. Until a decade or two ago, consultations between solicitors invariably took place in Counsel's chambers, in something of a teacher-pupil atmosphere, and it was thought neither necessary nor desirable for barristers to transact any business by correspondence or over the telephone. Nor do barristers negotiate their own fees, that uncongenial task being left to their clerks, who have no slightest inkling of what individual cases are about. It is fair to say that many of these practices and attitudes have disappeared in the last twenty years or so; but they were potent factors in the relationship between the two branches of the profession until at least the 1960s. When Hailsham first practised at the Bar, it could fairly be said that solicitors were general practitioners and barristers specialists. That was already an over-simplification by the time he first became Lord Chancellor, but his original perception coloured his view throughout his life. Even in

1975, he could still write: 'The one is a man of business; the other, to some extent, an artist and a scholar.'

The clean division between the two branches owed much to the monopoly rights which each possessed. The right of audience in the High Court was a matter for the Judges and they ensured that, apart from those who argued their own cases, only members of the Bar should plead before them. On their side, and with only a few minor exceptions, solicitors had the sole right of access to barristers, and they also had the exclusive right to handle transfer documents for land and buildings, known as 'conveyancing'.

Before the Benson Commission, the question of whether or not the professions of barrister and solicitor should be fused into one was debated with a passion worthy of theological disputation. Hailsham held to the status quo with as much passion as anyone. The full vehemence of his views, and of those who thought likewise, was only felt when the deluge came in 1989. In the debate on the Green Papers which were Lord Mackay's first shot in the war, Hailsham and some senior members of the Judiciary were betrayed into extravagances which they must afterwards have regretted. Hailsham did not go to the melodramatic lengths of some of the senior Judges, but his contribution was at least as memorable. 'The one thing that has worried me about the whole exercise is that one does not know whether the government is sitting on its head or its bottom. Its trouble is it is thinking with its bottom and sitting on its head.'[3] His romantic attachment to his own profession, his 'first love' as he called it, could admit of no other view. The Bar, independent in fact and in mind, the essential prerequisite for an independent Bench, fearless and incorrupt, each member compelled by professional ethic to accept any case which might be tendered, must survive. This was no caricature but his extreme form of conservatism blinded him to the possibility of some useful reform.

Hailsham's conservatism was moderated when it came to the solicitors' side. In the earliest years of his Chancellorship there was increasing dissatisfaction about the way in which solicitors charged for conveyancing. For transactions whose price did not exceed £30,000 there was a sliding scale fee, from which solicitors were forbidden to depart, either upwards or downwards. Solicitors' fees were fixed by a statutory committee consisting of the Lord Chancellor, the Lord Chief Justice, the Master of the Rolls, the President of the Law Society and another solicitor. The Lord Chancellor had a veto power. No other profession had its charges fixed in this way, and Hailsham was anxious to get rid of the anomaly if he could. But before he could do so, he had to get rid of the scale fee, so that charges could find their own level. He recognised, however, that it was an advantage to people buying and selling houses in the lower price range to know at the outset how much their lawyers were going to charge. He therefore proposed that the scale fee should apply only for prices up to £10,000. There was a history of wrangling between the Law Society and the Lord Chancellor about the proper level for conveyancing charges, and, true to form, the Society opposed Hailsham's suggestion. They argued that scale charges up to prices of £30,000 enabled solicitors to recoup at the higher levels what they lost at the lower levels. This was a dangerous tack, for it showed that charges at the higher levels were more than a fair rate for the job; and it enabled Hailsham, with some adroitness and at the cost of an abusive mail from countless solicitors to secure agreement with the profession in 1972 that the scale charge should be abolished altogether. 'It was a most successful exercise in the light of the thinness of the ice', he wrote to Sir Peter Rawlinson, the Attorney-General.[4]

The so-called conveyancing monopoly was a more awkward case. As the Benson Commission remarked, when people are buying or selling a house, they are in most cases engaging in the biggest financial transaction of their lives, in which large sums, borrowed or saved, are at stake.[5] At some stage, these sums are entrusted to the solicitor, whose honesty and competence are essential if his client is not to risk ruin. Conveyancing was the traditional staple of the solicitor's practice and, on the whole, the profession had a good record for probity. The Royal Commission heard a good deal of evidence that the monopoly should be broken and that others, operating under a licensing system, should be permitted to undertake conveyancing for reward. Benson's view, however, was that the restrictions on conveyancing should stand, and should be extended to cover the whole transaction of sale and purchase.

The pressure for competitive conveyancing did not abate, and built up strongly during the Thatcher years. It came from building societies, estate agents and financial institutions, all of whom wanted to offer a combined service including conveyancing. The Government was inclined to yield, but Hailsham was unhappy about the conflicts of interest which would inevitably arise, and which he thought his colleagues did not properly understand. In an internal note to his officials, he wrote: 'As you know, I hate this whole business and sympathise with the President [of the Law Society] . . .'[6] He reluctantly agreed that the monopoly could be broken, but only 'subject to appropriate safeguards', that is, he would make rules for preventing conflicts of interest. Even that did not satisfy the free marketeers in the Cabinet; and Norman Tebbitt wrote: '. . . excessive safeguards could effectively nullify the opportunity provided by this extension . . .'[7] But Hailsham got his way and the legislation included his safeguards.

He thought that to tinker with the restrictions which protected solicitors, as the Thatcher government did, was to embark on 'avoidable demarcation disputes' which were as objectionable as tinkering with rights of audience and appointments to the judicial bench. They upset the *status quo*, for no good reason. Worse than that, they put at risk the way in which buying and selling houses, so important in everyday life, was conducted. On the other hand, he agreed with Benson that the arcane procedures of conveyancing should be improved and simplified, and he thought it scandalous that the system of land registration, which represented the most effective simplification, and had been started in 1925, had not yet been completed. That was unanswerable. Oliver Cromwell had advocated a register of land titles to eliminate the 'ungodly jumble' of land law. More than 300 years later, Hailsham reminded Mrs Thatcher that, as Lord Chancellor, he was head of the Land Registry '(whose failure to complete the task imposed on it in 1925 is a recurring public scandal)'[8]

Hailsham had opposed as foolish and unnecessary the appointment of a Royal Commission in 1976 to look into the legal profession. He feared, as did the Bar and most solicitors, that Benson and his colleagues might recommend the fusion of the two professions and make other radical and unwelcome proposals. In fact, the Report of the Commission, when it came in 1979, was precisely what the profession and the Lord Chancellor wanted – or, at least, should have wanted. Its stance was conservative. It recognised the virtues of and benefit to the public from the existing regime. It made a large number of sensible suggestions for improvement, but none of them endangered the main edifice. It came down firmly in favour of a divided profession, and it recommended the maintenance of the boundaries between the two, including the barristers' monopoly of audience in the High Court. So the Bar was saved from the threat of revolutionary change; but it was told to mend its ways and abolish the more objectionable of its practices. It was difficult to believe that Hailsham could or would demur to any of this.

In May 1979, the Lord Chancellor heard that the Report was 230,000 words long, but not unanimous. He was given an advance copy which he read on his annual holiday visit to his brother Neil in Switzerland. This was accompanied by a helpful letter from Sir

Henry Benson dated 25 July which set out the main recommendations in summary form. Sir Henry offered a personal view about the likely reaction of the profession.

> I would expect on past form that the Law Society, and possibly the Senate [of the Inns] also, will congratulate themselves at beating off the latest assault and will assume themselves safe for the future. Complacency is their greatest enemy. Unless they are driven to make the necessary changes, they will be in trouble again in a short time . . . The recommendations of the Commission in the concluding chapter 44 [headed 'A Programme for the Future'] have been framed in such a way as to enable you, if you think it desirable, to ask the Senate and the Law Society to submit for your consideration their programme for implementing the report; the programme should be updated annually. This will provide one means of keeping them up to the mark.[9]

No warning to the profession could have been more timely, no suggestion to the Lord Chancellor on how to keep his flock 'up to the mark' more useful. Unhappily, neither was heeded. Instead, Hailsham noted in his diary: '. . . finished reading Benson. What are we to do with this immense *tractatus*? Well written, though numerous notes of dissent are *not*.'[10]

There were few mitigating circumstances attending this most unpromising reaction. One was that Benson had recommended the establishment of a Council for Legal Services to keep under review and make proposals about the profession so as to ensure 'the more effective provision of legal services'. It was contemplated that the Lord Chancellor might allocate 'executive functions' to this body.[11] 'Vast new quango (Council on Legal services – 14 areas)' Hailsham noted.

On 30 October, in the House of Lords, Lord Boston remarked, 'What would be most regrettable, and indeed unforgivable, would be if this matter were to be pigeon-holed.' The Lord Chancellor assured him that that was certainly not the Government's intention.[12] But that is what happened. It was not until November 1983 that Hailsham presented the Government Response,[13] and then only under persistent pressure. It was not an impressive document. In the words of one official in the Department, the Report had been played 'long and cool'.

Lord Benson, as he had by now become, was outraged by the treatment accorded to his Commission's report. He felt that the Conservative party had never wanted the Royal Commission and, when they came to power in 1979, were determined to shelve its Report. When he was received by Lord Hailsham to discuss the Report, he had been met with an attitude which was polite but negative. The Lord Chancellor seemed concerned only about the fate of the Inns.[14] In 1981, while still waiting for the Government's response, Benson wrote to *The Times* complaining of the wholly insufficient attention paid by Ministers to reports by independent bodies set up to advise the Government. He described the Government's attitude to his own report as 'supine', and one which compared unfavourably with the responses of two branches of the profession which, he said, had been active in following up the recommendations.[15]

It is indeed unfair to criticise the Lord Chancellor's inertia without considering the response of the profession. Many of Benson's proposals were for the profession to implement. This was particularly so in the case of the Bar for, apart from legal aid, the solicitors had only matters of detail to attend to. Given the intense natural conservatism of its constituency, the Bar Council had made some worthwhile progress by 1983. But much was still undone. The divided control of the Bar was still not solved. The shortage of accommodation, caused by the Inns' insistence that barristers' chambers should be within their own precincts, rendered somewhat hollow the Bar's defence of its monopoly of advocacy on the ground that anyone who wanted to be an advocate could become a barrister. The Bar's response to Benson[16] stated only it had been agreed between the Inns that they should have a common rent policy and would look to expand their own stock of accommodation. The more obvious, but heretical, solution of permitting barristers to practise outside the precincts was not adopted until 1989. And the more absurd features of the clerking arrangements, which included the payment to clerks of a percentage of Counsel's fees, thereby providing a built-in incentive for clerks to push fees upward, elicited a long and unconvincing answer.

These were all questions in which Hailsham, who had spent his life in the profession and was its friend at Court, could have been expected to interest himself and find ways to prod it into action. Lord Benson had even put the means to do so into his hand. Benson's own judgment in hindsight was that the profession was already in danger in 1979, and further delay undid it.[17] It is open to question whether even the adoption of all Benson's proposals would have warded off the reforming zeal of Lord Mackay's Chancellorship, sustained as it was by rising public impatience. But what is certain, and sad, is that an illustrious profession could not see the motes in its own eye, and that the Lord Chancellor was equally blind to its imperfections.

★

Until the end of the Second World War, the representation of poor people before the Courts was considered a charitable obligation of the legal profession. Lawyers either gave their services free or charged fees which involved working at a loss. This applied both to civil and criminal cases. Hailsham knew a good deal about it at first hand from his early days at the Bar. Out of professional obligation and the need to gain experience, he had done much of this work. He had found that on the civil side the cry for help was mainly for divorce. Using the forms of petition set out in the leading textbook on divorce, 'describing the various sexual exploits sometimes both numerous and sophisticated of Adam Alpha, Solomon Sigma, and even Elizabeth Epsilon, many is the petition I devised, free, gratis and for nothing, to satisfy the insatiable demand of the poor for the dissolution of their unhappy marriages.'[18]

This hand-to-mouth arrangement could not go on. It began to break down after the liberalising of divorce law in 1937 led to a big increase in matrimonial work. Further strain was imposed by the frequency of marital breakdown in wartime. In the Commons in 1943, Quintin Hogg drew attention to the situation and asked for an assurance that the post-war reconstruction would include 'the provision of free legal aid for the poor'.[19] As he knew as well as anyone, the Beveridge Report did not touch the problem. Although it assumed for its plan for social security that there would be a national health service, it made no corresponding assumption that the expenses of legal proceedings, civil or criminal, would be provided for. It was not part of Beveridge's attack on want that every man should have his day in Court.

However, while the war was still on, a separate inquiry was set up under Lord Rushcliffe. Its report formed the basis of modern legal aid.[20] It recommended that legal aid in civil cases should be provided in all Courts; it should be available to those of moderate means as well as the poor; those who could not afford anything should receive aid free, and there should be a sliding scale of contributions for those who could afford something but not the whole fee; the scheme would be run by the Law Society which would be answerable to the Lord Chancellor and who would assess the means of the litigant and the merits of the case; and lawyers should have reasonable fees for the work which would be paid predominantly by the state.

These recommendations were adopted entire and embodied in the Legal Aid and Advice Act, 1949. But two other proposals made by the Rushcliffe Committee were not taken up. One was that legal aid should be available in criminal as well as civil proceedings, and that in criminal matters it should be for the Magistrates or Judge hearing the case to grant aid. The Government appeared to think that the existing arrangements for helping poor prisoners were adequate, and it was more than twenty years after Rushcliffe reported before criminal legal aid was at last put on a systemised footing by the Criminal Justice Act of 1967. The other proposal which was not accepted was that legal advice centres should be opened up in deprived areas, staffed by salaried solicitors employed by the Law Society. It was the Law Society, representing the solicitors' profession, which had taken the main initiative in formulating the original scheme for legal aid, in their submissions to the Rushcliffe Committee. They laid emphasis on the need for advice for those who could not afford it, and argued that it was as important as help in going to Court. They failed to gain acceptance of this view in 1949, but they went on trying.

The policy underlying the Rushcliffe Report and the consequent legislation had incalculable consequences. The scheme of aid for civil proceedings covered over half of the adult population. The state took on a financial commitment which was determined by demand and was virtually open ended. The setting up of a universal system of legal aid changed the face of the profession as well. The volume of paid work grew out of all recognition. Between 1960 and 1980 both branches of the profession doubled in size. This was due more than anything else to the combined effect of legal aid and the introduction in 1969 of 'irretrievable breakdown' as the principal ground for divorce, with a consequent upsurge in the number of petitions. Hailsham perceived a change in the character of the profession, too. Its unprecedented growth and its entitlement to real fees for work for the poor, he thought, had been at the expense of a certain idealism and a growing trade unionism among professional bodies, whose members had earlier been accustomed to give many of their services for nothing or next to nothing. Both branches had divided themselves into two: those who depend for their earnings mainly on the state, and those who operate in the free market. None of these changes to the profession was, to his mind, beneficent.

Lord Gardiner thought of legal aid as a form of welfare. Lord Hailsham preferred to think of it as a piece of social justice.[21] Whichever way you look at it, there is an unresolvable dilemma at its heart. Perhaps, as Hailsham increasingly believed, there is no 'right' to a day in Court; but unless a universal service is provided, how is justice to be prevented from becoming the prerogative of the rich? Is it to be administered irrespective of class, colour, creed, and opinion, but respectful of wealth? One day he had a letter from an unknown lady which he thought put the point better than he could: 'Sir, I understand that there is one law for the rich and one for the poor. Can you please tell me the dividing line moneywise?'

Few can afford High Court proceedings out of their own pocket, not so many more can stretch to the cost of a full-scale trial in the County Court. Hailsham considered that this was necessarily so because litigation is intrinsically expensive. The process of sifting fact and applying the relevant legal principles is never easy and cannot be made both cheap and reliable. 'There is no future in the doctrine that, if the result is to be reliable, the thing can be done cheaply at all.' Those who would contest this must continue the elusive search for simplified procedures and different methods of resolving disputes. But even if sensible economies could be made, such as cutting down the time absorbed by lawyers kicking their heels in Court corridors,* nothing could prevent the public cost of legal aid from burgeoning like the green bay tree. The Treasury looms. Legal Aid must compete in a limited fund with other worthy public purposes.† This was forcibly brought home when Hailsham fell out with the Bar in 1986 over fees for legally aided criminal work. It accounts for his successor, Lord Mackay's, increasingly desperate castings about for ways to contain cost.

The Law Society's persistent campaign to include general advice within legal aid eventually persuaded Lord Gardiner to set up an experimental scheme. Before he could do so, however, there was a change of Government (in 1970) and Hailsham became Lord Chancellor. He was enthusiastic about the idea. Sensible advice at the right time might help to curtail litigation and so moderate the charge on the legal aid fund. He was able to bring in a Bill. Its plan was admirably simple. Anyone who could satisfy a solicitor that he had means below a stated level (originally income of £20 a week and

---

* In 1981, the Lord Chancellor's Advisory Committee on Legal Aid noted with dismay that, for the year 1980/1, waiting time in magistrates' courts accounted for about 20 per cent of the amount paid to solicitors from the legal aid fund; or some £8 million representing half a million waiting hours. (31st Report of the Lord Chancellor's Advisory Committee: 28 Oct. 1981.)

† In 1980/1 the cost of the scheme was £108m; in 1990/1: £685m; and in 1994/5 £1.3 billion. In January 1995, *The Financial Times* commented that legal aid consumed more than it would cost to introduce universal nursery provision for all 3 and 4 year olds; and concluded: 'The U.K.'s legal aid scheme is out of control and must be radically recast'. (*Financial Times* editorial: 12 Jan. 1995.)

capital of £125, after making provision for household needs) could obtain £25 worth of free advice. He had to complete a green form, from which the scheme took its name. It was an important step, for it extended the boundaries of the scheme at moderate cost to cover the everyday need for short legal advice.

The Rushcliffe proposal that legal advice centres should be set up in areas of need fell on deaf ears in the immediate post-war period. But Hailsham's Legal Advice Bill in 1972 provided for a salaried task force within the legal aid scheme. Part of its duties would be to help establish advice centres where they were needed. The Law Society, which had been pressing for this reform, had long recognised that, from the viewpoint of most people, the law is a mystery, and lawyers seem remote figures who charge heavily and tend to act in an unsympathetic way. The law centre, it was felt, set up in the heart of neighbourhoods where these prejudices were most widespread, and staffed by people who seemed more accessible than the lawyer of popular conception, was an essential means of developing an understanding of law and its relevance to people's lives.

But this part of the 1972 Act was never activated. Partly this was due to the economic conditions of the seventies, and partly to prejudice against Law Centres. Their critics felt that they could and often did become the focus of political agitation, and that professional standards were not always controlled and maintained. When the Benson Commission reported in 1979, there were 27 Law Centres. They had grown up haphazardly with widely differing structures, funding and functions. Benson proposed that they be brought under the unified control of a central agency whose members would be appointed by the Lord Chancellor, and who would be responsible for funding the centres out of his Vote.[22] No one liked the idea. The Law Society was worried about the growth of law centres outside the main scheme administered by itself. Hailsham's response, which did not come until four years after Benson reported, was to continue temporising. 'These recommendations are under consideration; an announcement will be made in due course.'[23] It never was made. Law centres have remained in limbo, neither integrated in the main scheme nor having a defined position outside, condemned to wander eternally between heaven and earth. Hailsham was not doctrinally opposed to law centres, but he much disliked the way they tended to attract political activists. When his Labour successor, Lord Elwyn-Jones tried to save some money to fund them, by removing legal aid from undefended divorces, he attacked the proposal partly on the ground that it would create a two tier system, lawyers in private practice and law centres, which would discriminate against the poor.[24] It was a pity he was not able to do more to help a beneficial growth of the centres, but there was never money to spare after the insatiable demands of the main legal aid scheme.

Important though law centres were, Hailsham's main preoccupation in the field of legal aid was the impossibility of containing its cost while making it available to all who needed it. The scheme was meant to cover those of moderate means as well as the really poor. This involved pitching the upper limit of eligibility high enough to catch this large class. It could never be done. The effects of inflation and the need for financial stringency meant that the proportion of the population which was eligible for legal aid fell steadily, while the cost, equally steadily, rose. Hailsham grappled manfully with this insoluble problem. In 1973 he put eligibility on an annual footing which would march step by step with social security limits. The effect of doing so was to jerk the levels upward so sharply in 1979 that the Treasury froze the limits in 1980 and 1981.

In 1981, Hailsham adopted Benson's recommendation that he take over responsibility for criminal legal aid from the Home Office. He had advocated this himself since at least 1976, describing the then divided system of responsibility as 'grotesque'.[25] But the move was not well thought out. He did not take with it responsibility for the reform of procedure in the criminal courts, which remained with the Home Secretary. He therefore lost an important means of containing cost, and his financial problems were aggravated.

There was much criticism from the Law Society and from his own Advisory Committee. 'It should have been a consequence of the publication of the [Benson] report in October 1979', the Law Society's Report on Legal Aid for 1980/1 complained, 'that the pent-up demand for change met with some response. In the eighteen months since publication, however, one can discern no progress whatever . . .'. 'Inertia has its own price, paid by people whose rights go unenforced or whose cases go undefended.' The Advisory Committee 'fully endorsed' these strictures. But the severest censure was reserved for the shrinkage in the numbers eligible for aid. The Advisory Committee could conjure up flights of imagery. 'Successive governments have behaved like the Barmecide prince in the Arabian Nights, they remarked in 1975,

> who served a poor man with a succession of illusory dishes, pretending that they contained a sumptuous feast. It may be remembered that this ultimately had sombre results for the prince

when the beggar in the story, entering into the spirit of the joke, pretended to be intoxicated by the imaginary wine offered to him and attacked his host.[26]

The threatening gesture was addressed to Lord Elwyn-Jones, the Labour Lord Chancellor, but it might as well have been addressed to Hailsham, for the complainants made no distinction of government.

Hailsham did his best with the intractable problem of legal aid and was able to make a number of useful reforms. To complement the civil advice scheme which he introduced in his first term, he brought in during his second term legally aided advice and assistance for suspects detained at police stations, an essential adjunct to the suspect's legal right to a lawyer at that critical stage. He tried as well to improve the way in which lawyers were paid for legally aided work, particularly by persuading the Treasury to agree to interim payments during cases. But it was here, on the question of how much should lawyers be paid for state-funded work, that he suffered the most humiliating episode of his long tenure of the Lord Chancellorship.

24

The Dispute with the Bar

IN March, 1986, in the last year of Hailsham's time as Lord Chancellor, he was brought to Court and accused of having acted unlawfully by his own profession, led not by revolutionaries but by moderate men of traditional view. The descending road to this melancholy pass was littered with misapprehension and characterised by a strange want of firmness.

A convenient point at which to start is Margaret Thatcher's request to him in 1982 for material from the Lord Chancellor's Department to include in the Conservative Party manifesto. He replied, on the subject of fees for legally aided work:

> I foresee a long period in which we shall have to negotiate with the professions. We must retain their goodwill. It is vital that we preserve their independence and integrity. We need to continue to recruit the best brains and the most upright people. We cannot disclaim total responsibility because the structure of remuneration for legal aid has grown out of, and is bound up with, the pre-existing structures of privately funded litigation.[1]

That was his consistent view, but the words must have come back to haunt him.

The scale of fees payable to barristers undertaking legally aided criminal defence work was fixed by regulation. After responsibility for criminal legal aid was transferred to the Lord Chancellor in 1981, the regulations were made by him. This applied only to defence work. Responsibility for prosecutions was the Attorney-General's, so that although the amounts paid to barristers out of public funds for prosecution and defence work were closely linked to each other, responsibility for fixing and paying these amounts were in different ministerial hands. In the event, this fatally hampered Hailsham's freedom of movement.

The Legal Aid Act, 1974, said that the regulations for which the Lord Chancellor was responsible must have regard to the principle of allowing fair remuneration for work actually and reasonably done. Nothing was said about whether regard should also be had to the length of the public purse.

Already by 1982 the Bar was dissatisfied with the level of pay. The squeeze on eligibility for legal aid, as the Treasury froze the limits in 1980 and 1981, was reflected by a squeeze on fee levels for legally aided defence work paid to barristers and solicitors. The Legal Aid Report for 1981/2 informed the Lord Chancellor that there had been 'unprecedented expressions of indignation at the Annual General Meeting of the Bar'.[2] Nevertheless, in 1983, 1984 and 1985 the fees were increased by only a small amount, to keep pace with inflation. These increases were reluctantly accepted by the Bar because, with Hailsham's approval, Coopers & Lybrand, accountants and management consultants, had been appointed by the Bar in May 1984 to carry out an analytical survey of the remuneration paid for criminal legal aid, and it was understood that their report would form the basis for a comprehensive review of fee levels. The Benson Commission had recommended that an independent Committee should be set up to advise on fees, but the Lord Chancellor's response was that he preferred to negotiate.[3] The result of Coopers' enquiries was therefore keenly awaited; and the more so since no less than 2000 barristers' practices consisted mainly or entirely of defences in criminal cases paid for out of the legal aid fund.

The consultants' report was ready by September 1985, and the Bar sent copies immediately to the Lord Chancellor and the Law Officers. It recommended that, in order that a barrister, depending mainly on legally aided criminal defence, should keep pace with a senior legal assistant in the civil service, fee levels would have to be raised by 30–40 per cent. The consultants found that an average barrister working in this field and having between ten and fifteen years' experience was earning only £15,900 (£25,100 in 1997 value) after expenses.

The Law Society was not far behind and had commissioned its own investigation. This was ready in November and recommended fee increases for solicitors doing legally aided defence work of 34 per cent in London, and 26 per cent elsewhere. Clearly, the two branches would have to be treated together.

The timetable was tight. The Permanent Secretary, Sir Derek Oulton, told the Bar that the Department would need to prepare the regulations for the following year in early February. Negotiations would therefore have to be completed by the end of January. With that in mind, the Chairman of the Bar, Robert Alexander QC, arranged a special meeting of his committee for 30 January and an Extraordinary General Meeting of the whole Bar on 8 February. No meetings to discuss Coopers' report had, however, been arranged by the beginning of November, and the Bar were becoming anxious. Within the Government, the Lord Chancellor's Department and the Treasury were comparing notes. Both thought that the consultants' analysis was flawed. The Solicitor-General, Sir Patrick Mayhew, wrote to Alexander on 3 December to let him 'have an indication of the general case which you will be invited to meet by the Treasury'. This was that while the 'fundamental premise' of the consultants' report was comparability of earnings, the true criterion was 'of course' affordability.[4] The Treasury did not seem troubled that 'the true criterion' was not to be found in the wording of the Legal Aid Act. A meeting was arranged for 17 December between Coopers & Lybrand for the Bar, and officials of the Lord Chancellor's Department and the office of the Director of Public Prosecutions. It was made clear, however, that it was preliminary only, and not the opening of negotiations.[5] To the Bar's regret, the Treasury declined an invitation. It was the only meeting on Coopers' report which ever took place before the Bar started proceedings.

Meanwhile, the advice to the Lord Chancellor was that, for the present, the profession should be offered only the routine uprating of fees necessary to reflect inflation, approximately 5 per cent. Hailsham thought this too harsh and wanted it to be made clear that it was subject to any further settlement that might be agreed when the accuracy of the consultants' report was ascertained. If this had been put forward diplomatically to the Bar, disaster might still have been averted. But Christmas now intervened and Hailsham was in India between 4 and 10 January attending a Commonwealth conference. On his return, he was met with the Law Society's claim for increased fees, and the news that the Law Officers (the Attorney-General, Sir Michael Havers, and the Solicitor-General) were pressing for a better increase for the Bar than the usual uprating for inflation. A meeting was arranged to hear their views on 15 January. At the same time, increasingly urgent messages were coming in from the Bar and Coopers that the timetable was in jeopardy without further meetings having been arranged. The officials had to stonewall.

Hailsham found that the Law Officers were hot for the Bar. They were closer than he was to opinion in the profession, and they advised him that, unless the moderate leadership under Alexander could deliver a reasonable settlement, the 'wild men' might take over. 'Industrial action' was not impossible and, in any case, the general health of the Bar was at stake. It might seem a flight of fancy to suppose that barristers would do anything voluntarily to deprive themselves of fees, but those in the government who were responsible for prosecuting crime were alarmed. The new Crown Prosecution Service was about to be set up, and it had to be put in a position in which it could pay reasonable fees. It was unthinkable that the Crown should not be able to bring criminal charges to Court. Hailsham allowed himself to be persuaded that an urgent, direct approach to the Prime Minister be made jointly by him and the Law Officers for an immediate interim increase in fee scales of 20 per cent. An indication of the state of his mind in these critical days may be gained from the fact that he had to be restrained by his officials from writing directly to the Prime Minister without first informing the Chancellor of the Exchequer.

The ensuing approach to the Treasury, setting out the case for an interim increase of 20 per cent, met with a bleak response, but the issue went to the appropriate Cabinet Committee on 3 February. Predictably, it went badly. The Treasury, who felt they had been bounced, argued forcefully against the Law Officers and the Lord Chancellor. To the guardians of financial orthodoxy, it looked like panic. Relations with the Treasury were damaged, and Hailsham was left with no more than the routine uprating to offer.

The Extraordinary General Meeting of the Bar was now only five days off. On 7 February Hailsham saw the Chairman and Vice-Chairman of the Bar. 'Bob Alex'r. & Scott QC friendly interview, but strongly expressed criticism of what I was authorised to offer. Solicitors to come.'[6] In *A Sparrow's Flight*, Hailsham gives an account of a meeting *before* Christmas with representatives of the Bar at which, he says, he explained that the issue would have to go to the Prime Minister.[7] Unfortunately his account is imaginary, and the submission to the Cabinet Committee in February, decided on only in January, was quite unknown to the Bar.[8] However that may be, he handed a letter to Alexander at the meeting on 7 February setting out his decision.[9] He was 'yet to be convinced', his letter said, that the consultants' recommendation for an increase of between 30 and 40 per cent in criminal legal aid fees to give fair remuneration, could be justified. He gave some anecdotal evidence, some from his own experience, to suggest that assumptions used by the consultants were wrong, and he said that in reaching his decision he could not ignore the cost of meeting the claim. 'I am therefore proposing to bring forward regulations based on a routine uprating calculated according to the same formula as in previous years. This will allow for a 5% increase overall.' Of his original intention to continue negotiations on the basis of Coopers' report, there was hardly anything left. 'I hope', he said, 'that it may be possible to find a way forward.'

The letter was necessarily written hurriedly and under the stress of events, but it was his own. It was neither written by the Treasury, as he claimed in *A Sparrow's Flight* (except in the sense that it was the Treasury which was now in the driving seat to the exclusion of everyone else) nor by his officials who, as is usual, prepared a draft for him to consider and amend. It was inevitable that it would be read for what it was, a volte face, and equally inevitable that the Bar, in its current mood, would insist that the Lord Chancellor's decision should be tested in Court. The meeting of the Bar took place the next day in an atmosphere of outrage. The feeling was unanimous, and the situation did much to unify those barristers who were struggling with inadequate incomes with the wealthy minority living on fees from the private sector.

An application for judicial review of the Lord Chancellor's decision followed quickly. The Bar's case was a strong one. They argued that no attempt had been made to provide 'fair remuneration for work actually and reasonably done', as the Legal Aid Act required; and that the Lord Chancellor had created a legitimate expectation that there would be proper negotiations, whereas none had taken place. Hailsham appeared to underestimate by a large margin the strength of the case he had to meet, and to take insufficient account of the fact that he could not reveal in open Court the course of events within Government or the power of veto held by the Treasury – although this might be guessed at.

The hearing began on 20 March before Lord Chief Justice Lane, Mr Justice Boreham and Mr Justice Taylor, who was to become Lord Lane's successor. Mr. Sydney Kentridge QC, who presented the Bar's case with restraint and moderation, was heard in sympathetic silence; but it soon became clear when Mr Nicholas Phillips QC, for the Lord Chancellor, began his address on the second day that the Court was hostile to him. He ran into a hail of fire from all three members of the Court. The weakest point was the letter of 7 February. The Lord Chief Justice could not understand why the Lord Chancellor could not simply have said that the Bar should have their 5 per cent uprating, but that time was too short to discuss the consultants' report in detail. It was precisely Hailsham's position before he was blown off course by the Law Officers.

It was clear that if the case were allowed to go on, the Lord Chancellor would lose, and the Court would have to pronounce that he had acted unlawfully. Lord Lane therefore gave a broad hint that the litigants should sit down together outside Court and agree a timetable for further discussions. The hint was taken. A timetable was agreed and the case brought to an end. There was one final painful twist. The Bar asked that the Lord Chancellor be ordered to pay their costs. It was so ordered.

Hailsham's discomfort was increased by a bad press. Under the heading 'Lord Chancellor in the Dock', *The Times* considered that his 'handling of the affair had done his reputation for ministerial competence harm that will not easily be mended.'[10] It had been a bruising affair and it was debatable whether any good came of it. The Bar gained some of their claim in the subsequent negotiations, but in one sense the victory in Court was Pyrrhic. In 1988 new legislation on legal aid made explicit that remuneration would have to have regard to the cost to public funds, and required that all regulations should be subject to the consent of the Treasury.[11] The hidden role of the Treasury in the case was widely resented, and a former Under Secretary to the Treasury, Lord Bancroft, summed it up:

> To call it a system would strain both language and credulity. It places the responsible Minister and his officials in a totally impossible position, by interposing the say-so of the Treasury jack-in-office between them and the professions . . . it allows of no rational process of argument, let alone negotiation. It imposes a government incomes policy, the existence of which is then promptly denied.[12]

On the other hand, the climate for negotiations improved after the litigation, and there was never again a crisis of such severity. The unity within the Bar which was forged under stress served the profession well.

The blow to Hailsham's pride was wounding and took him by surprise. Pressure from the Bar had been building up for years, but he seemed impervious to it. He did not dream that he would be taken to Court. He may even have persuaded himself that the Bar did not have a case. In any event, he expected that the profession would take the Treasury's verdict with sad resignation. He thought the power of patronage and respect for the office of Lord Chancellor were too strong. He was, after all, the guardian of the profession's interests, and thought he was entitled to be regarded as its champion. He had secured interim payments for legally aided work in the teeth of Treasury opposition, and he had reacted to the Benson report in the way most favourable to the profession – by not reacting at all. For the Bar to attack him in Court was an act of personal ingratitude.

In all of this, he laboured under misapprehension, and the realisation was the more painful for the depth of the misunderstanding. His wavering under the force of the Law Officers' arguments, with which he had sympathy anyway, was perhaps a sign of age. His political judgment and resolution would not have weakened so in his first term. He was at first bitter about the humiliation in the Lord Chief Justice's Court, but after an interval he resumed his usual cordial relations with the leaders of the Bar. The annual conference of the Bar took place a few weeks after the hearing, and he attended and spoke at the dinner, acting with a perfect good grace throughout.[13] The tiff was a serious one, but a tiff for all that.

25

The Lord Chancellor and the Law

HAILSHAM saw his immediate predecessor, Gerald Gardiner, as a man with a high sense of purpose and something of an ascetic; but it is as a reformer that he will be remembered. He left Hailsham the two most important legacies in the field of law reform since the war: the Law Commission, the first permanent, full time body of lawyers devoted to keeping the substantive law in good working order; and the Beeching Report, without whose rationalising the criminal courts might have ground to a halt.

Until Gardiner established the Law Commission in 1965, the impetus for reforming the law lay with a small number of public spirited practitioners who could afford to give only an occasional hour or two after their working day. Gardiner had been one of them and he knew the inadequacy of the system. 'The Law Reform Committee did useful work,' he wrote in 1971, 'but the trouble was that it consisted of busy judges, barristers, solicitors and academic lawyers who only met about once a month at 4.30 after a day in court, and at 6.00 someone would say: "I am afraid that I have to go now", and I eventually resigned because I came to the conclusion that you simply cannot reform the law of England in that way.'[1]

The result was that Chancellors could, if they were so disposed, virtually ignore law reform. Men of the cast of mind of former Chancellors Simonds and Dilhorne were content with the old amateur regime, wondering whether Gardiner's idea of a Law Commission was 'worthwhile', and giving it the faintest of faint praise when it was debated in the Lords.[2] Hailsham was then in the Commons as Quintin Hogg, but he took great satisfaction from Lord Wilberforce's maiden speech in the debate, in which he criticised the Conservatives' churlish attitude to Gardiner's initiative.[3]

Hailsham strongly supported Gardiner's proposal and made good

303

use of the Commission's work when he became Lord Chancellor. His record in competing for parliamentary time and bringing forward reform legislation was a good one; and he indignantly repudiated a suggestion in the *Sunday Times* in a 1988 profile of his successor, Lord Mackay, that he himself had presided over a period of lethargy in English law. He claimed that he had been responsible for no fewer than 85 Acts of Parliament during his two terms.[4] Hailsham would come well out of an audit of technical law reform. But in reform with a political content, he would score less heavily; and it is the 'political' reforms, like those affecting the organisation of the profession, which interest the media and the public, and on which reputations are made and unmade.

In spite of Gardiner's exemplary work in the field, Hailsham was under no illusion about the difficulties in the way of reform of the law, even in the technical sense. He enumerated them in a lecture to the Bentham Club in 1981 under the title *Obstacles to Law Reform*.[5] First and foremost was the innate conservatism ('the wrong sort of conservatism') of most of the profession. It is almost impossible to exaggerate the lengths to which these reactionaries were willing to go in order to obstruct change.

In 1980, the Supreme Court Rules Committee, chaired by Hailsham as Lord Chancellor, proposed to remove from the ordinary form of writ the ancient but misleading royal command. A literal reading gave the impression that the Queen herself was personally commanding the defendant to answer the case against him, and so in some way siding with the plaintiff. The proposal to delete these words provoked an avalanche of insensate royalism. Hailsham, who thought it wrong to preserve such antique nonsense, came under heavy attack in the Lords and was accused of offences falling only just short of high treason.[6] The Chief Chancery Master resigned over the issue and was reported in the William Hickey column of the *Daily Express* in terms more redolent of *Private Eye*: 'As the beaks bounce on their benches with rage, the Chief Master of the Supreme Court broke ranks long enough to tell me, "I have said a lot about this already, and if things go a certain way I will be saying a great deal more. Make no mistake. This is the start of a big one."'

The changed nature of the House of Commons, as Hailsham saw it, also militated against law reform. The House had 'long since ceased to believe that its main business is to act as an efficient legislature'.

Almost all its time is taken up with criticisms of executive government, the battle between the parties, the belief, which I believe to be largely false, that it can greatly influence longterm economic trends ... it would be idle to pretend that this is an atmosphere in which it is easy to get resources, time or adequate attention for practical but politically unemotive measures of law reform ...

The fragmentation of policy within government was another obstacle. There was no focus or coherence in attacking obsolete law. No one knew whether the Home Office or the Lord Chancellor was really responsible for reforming the criminal law, one of the worst repositories of outdated lumber. Hailsham thought that the Lord Chancellor should have the initiative for all law reform, whether or not the subject was within his own departmental interests. In 1973, he urged this on his Cabinet colleagues. 'Pressed for a viable Law Refm. programme to be init'd. by me in Lords', he recorded in his diary, '. . . No votes . . . exc. f. assmt . . . of damages (i.e. ante natal injuries) [a reference to the thalidomide babies' cases]. But a sign of good Gov't. to be seen to mend uncontroversial fences'.[7]

Hailsham had for long favoured the codification of the criminal law. In a paper for the Shadow Cabinet in 1966 on the Labour Party's Criminal Justice Bill,[8] he described the proposals as 'a potpourri of suggestions (none, I think, original) which have been current for a long time'. He supported the great majority of the proposals, but they did not go far enough. He proposed instead a radical scheme of reform: 'A penal code and a code embodying the law of evidence in this country are each about fifty, perhaps a hundred, years overdue'.

He was in favour of ending the accused's absolute right of silence; he considered the Judges' rules to be obsolete; prosecution and defence should each be required to disclose its case to the other as early as possible; juries should not try long commercial frauds; the rigid division between civil and criminal jurisdiction was archaic; the English adversarial system was unsuitable for preliminary investigations into crimes before magistrates. All this 'would require a treatise' to justify, but the ideas were both clear and far-sighted. Yet his achievements in law reform, worthwhile though they were, never included any such codification.

In 1985 the Law Commission produced the first part of a criminal code.[9] It came too late for Hailsham and has not yet been implemented. Hailsham pointed the finger of responsibility at the Home Office.[10] It is the Department accountable for law and order, but it does not follow that it should also be responsible for the state of the criminal law. It is, he thought, ill equipped to deal with it. So many of the rules lived on, increasingly difficult to justify. As he told an Australian audience in 1974, 'These facts are difficult to discuss rationally in England, partly because of the intense conservatism of the legal profession and partly because the same professional civil rights lobbies come barging in with shrill and emotional cries that a conspiracy is on foot to subvert our ancient liberties . . .'[11] He continued to lament the lack of progress in the criminal law. 'After all', he wrote in 1987, 'if we have tribunals worthy of confidence, it might be sensible, with the fewest of possible exceptions, to permit these to be the judges of the reliability and weight of evidence, rather than to prevent them from listening to it on the ground that they cannot be trusted to come to a sound conclusion.'[12]

How could such a sane proposition fail to command assent? Hailsham had his answer ready. 'The great pundits of the legal profession would be heard to exclaim in Noodle's famous words: "We will not have the laws of England changed." '

By the 1960s, the ancient and fragmented system of criminal justice was in danger of breaking down under the relentless impact of rising crime. Both the Assizes, by which Judges were sent out to the Shires from London, and Quarter Sessions, in which worthy men appointed to keep the peace met quarterly to dispense justice, had their origins in the early middle ages. Both had become incapable of coping with the volume of criminal business awaiting decision.

In 1966, the Labour Government set up a Royal Commission, and Gardiner, then Lord Chancellor, decided to appoint Dr Richard Beeching to chair it. Beeching, a businessman and physicist, was already well known for the savage, but necessary, surgery he had performed on the railways, and he proved to be an inspired choice to bring order and efficiency to the criminal justice system. His recommendations[13] were immediately accepted by the Labour Government but, before they could be implemented, there was a change of government and Hailsham became Lord Chancellor. It therefore fell to him to promote the Courts Act of 1971, which turned Beeching's proposals into law.*

The Courts Act was the most important reorganisation of the

---

* Although the reforms staved off disaster, they did not eliminate delay. At the beginning of his second term, Hailsham noted: 'Meeting with Circuit Administrators. Backlogs large. e.g. S.E. [South Eastern Circuit] 14,000 awaiting trial. Fewer pleas of guilty, excessive acquittals attributable to delay (jury or memory) (HLSM: LC Diaries √ 5: 6 Jun. 1979). In his 1983 Hamlyn Lectures, he observed that delays in the North East were about half what they were in London and the South East, and that pleas of guilty, of those arraigned in the Crown Court, were 76 per cent in the North East compared with 44 per cent in the South East. He did not venture any conclusion from these statistics.

administration of justice since the civil courts had been re-ordered in 1875, and the most far reaching change in criminal jurisdiction since the twelfth century. The Act created a new superior court of criminal jurisdiction in place of the Assize Courts, Quarter Sessions, and The Central Criminal Court. The new Crown Court was to be staffed by High Court Judges and a new bench to be called Circuit Judges. The country was to be divided up into Circuits, each of which would be managed by a Circuit Administrator who would be responsible for all the courts in his area. The Lord Chancellor was to be ultimately responsible for all the higher courts and County Courts. This transformed at a stroke the Lord Chancellor's staff from a small office to a large, high-spending Department. Hailsham was the first Chancellor to preside over the radical change which was implied. It meant that a new relationship would have to be worked out with the Treasury, and that the Lord Chancellor and his Department would have to accept new budgetary disciplines and procedures. None of this was any more naturally congenial to Hailsham than it would have been to his predecessors.

Some of the Judges feared that the great access of power in the Lord Chancellor's Department and in the Circuit Administrators would erode their control over their own courts. The old nightmares returned. The Lord Chancellor was thought to be bored by administration, and might allow the reins to slip from his hand. But Beeching, and Hailsham, were aware that there had been limits placed upon the powers of the Circuit Administrators. The smooth running of the courts was one thing; but the allocation of available Judges, the orderly maintenance of court lists to avoid delay, and consistency of sentencing between Judges, were all matters for a senior Judge. So Beeching proposed that each Circuit should have a Presiding Judge to see to the proper discharge of judicial duties.[14] The scheme was implemented with this safeguard, and Hailsham's diaries attest to its importance and success. There was frequent contact between the Department and Presiding Judges, particularly about the suitability of individual Judges for classes of case; and Presiding Judges proved to be the single most important source of information on candidates for the Circuit bench. They did much to oil the new machinery and reduce friction between Judges and the Administration.

Although it was not within his remit, which was limited to the criminal justice system, Beeching remarked that the evidence which his Commission had received about delays in civil proceedings revealed a position which was, at best, unsatisfactory, and, at its worst, quite intolerable.[15] Unhappily, this was not new.

It had long been realised that, above all else, it is delay and cost which bar the way to a system of justice which is fair and accessible. There is little point in having a refined system which hardly anyone can afford. Equally, delayed justice is not justice at all. Beeching put the point in this way: 'It is a negation of justice if the legal system permits, when it does not actually cause, delays of such length that witnesses may have forgotten or refurbished their evidence to the point where it is quite unreliable; of such length that there is a probability that the plaintiff will die before the case is heard; or of such length that the residual life over which the benefit of damages received will be enjoyed is materially reduced.'[16]

The most important key to the problem is the simplification of civil procedure. The ground was well tilled. Since the middle of the nineteenth century there had been some 60 reports and inquiries on the subject. Only one resulted in major reforms.* The rest made only marginal improvements or were futile. There is something peculiarly intractable in the subject matter. Why is the way to the Courts a dense undergrowth through which only the expert knows the route, and then only with the aid of a textbook of some 4000 pages issued annually and costing hundreds of pounds? Hailsham did not lack the urge to reform. 'What, exactly, is happening on the civil procedure front?' he demanded of his officials within a couple of months of the publication of the Benson Report.[17] And long before Benson, he had scouted the amalgamation of the High Court and the County Court, noting in red on a memorandum from his officials, 'I am not prepared to let it rest indefinitely.'[18] Unfortunately, it has rested ever since.

Benson had pointed out that there was a close relationship between the rules of procedure and the duration and cost of litigation, and recommended that 'a single standing body' (which might be the Law Commission) should examine the matter.[19] The Government's response, published in November 1983, promised that the Lord Chancellor would undertake a 'complete and systematic review of civil procedure'.[20] There is no reason to doubt that that is what the Lord Chancellor intended, but he knew the difficulties. He minuted his Permanent Secretary, Sir Derek Oulton: 'Please speak. There have been *many* such reviews since the War. Nothing much has emerged from any except small brown mice . . .'[21]

By November 1983, it had been agreed on the Law Commission's initiative that a seminar should be held during the following summer

---

* The Report of the Royal Commission on the Judicature, which led to the consolidation of the Courts of Chancery, Queen's Bench, Common Pleas, Exchequer, Admiralty, Divorce and Probate into a single Supreme Court (1869).

for practitioners, academics and others interested to discuss the whole subject. This would be chaired by the trenchant Lord Templeman, a Law Lord who had been a member of the Benson Commission. Much was expected, but Hailsham was cautious. He told Oulton that the Department 'would have to be courageous in tackling some radical proposals, which would be likely to attract considerable hostility from vested interests'.[22] His view, formed because of the many past failures by the profession to grapple civil procedure firmly, was that the subject could not safely be left to the lawyers. The Department needed no reminding of the importance of the subject and the likely entrenched conservative reaction to be expected from the profession. The example of Beeching as a businessman who could both understand the technical problems and reflect the interests of justice was fresh in mind. But distrust of the profession's will to reform unhappily contributed to the gap between intention and achievement.

The seminar took place on 25 and 26 September 1984, and was attended by a distinguished company of about 40, including officials from the Lord Chancellor's Department. The officials were roughly handled. Many speakers said that the paper which the Department had prepared was inadequate and superficial. On the question of whether the review should be carried out by the Department or by a more broadly based body, the Chairman called for a show of hands and the Department received no support. Sir Michael Kerr, an experienced commercial Judge, said that there was a need to reconsider basic concepts. The traditional adversarial process should not be extended to the earlier pre-trial stages where a more investigative role for the Judge might promote compromise and settlement. Professor Scott of Birmingham said that the State had a duty to supply a civil procedure service; but the resources were limited and claims on the service were unlimited. In order to ration justice, policy decisions would have to be taken. The ideas were put forward by practitioners and academics who really wanted radical change. There was an unusual chance to build on this initiative. But Hailsham remained sceptical. 'This is very depressing reading,' he noted on the draft record of the seminar, 'I feel like Jehovah at the time of the Flood.' He was particularly hard on a detachment of women who urged that the 'ordinary consumer' be heard. 'Who is Sylvia? What is she?' wrote the red pen.[23]

Summarising the discussion in a letter to Hailsham, Templeman said that the consensus was that the review should be undertaken by an 'informed Committee composed of members familiar with the problems of the courts and fortified by one or more experienced and eminent lay members. There was a feeling that the civil servants of the Department . . . lacked the facilities, the time, the experience and the qualifications for assuming charge of such a technical and important subject . . .'[24] The response to this missile went through several drafts. In its final, moderated form, Hailsham warned Templeman of the intractability of the subject, and informed him that control of the review must remain within the Department. Having warmly defended its achievements, he said: 'Until I have determined upon the appropriate methodology and gathered together a body of relevant information so that we can identify some of the real questions and priorities, I think it is idle to question whether the LCD is an adequate instrument or no. At present it is the only one I have got . . . It looks as if we have a long and daunting task before us.'[25]

The view of the officials was that the Department should retain control, but should be assisted by an advisory committee representing the profession and including eminent laymen. Hailsham accepted this advice although he thought the committee unnecessary and possibly dangerous. He agreed with Lord Gowrie, the Chancellor of the Duchy of Lancaster, who disliked the committee idea and considered that quangos should not be multiplied, and he noted his assent on Gowrie's letter, saying that it was only a sop to Templeman.[26] He continued to distrust his fellow lawyers and he told his officials that the greatest obstacle to change was the conservatism of the profession. While there was plenty of material to support this general characterisation, it is a pity that he did not read the account of the seminar as indicating a powerfully unusual will to change.

He then circulated his proposals to ministers and finally sent them to the Prime Minister. Management consultants would first get out some statistical information about actual experiences in civil proceedings. Then the review body would consider in turn five classes of case: personal injuries, small claims, debt, housing, and commercial cases. The process would take 5 years. The review was to be undertaken by the Department, with an advisory committee under the chairmanship of a non-lawyer. Mrs Thatcher thought the timetable ponderous. Was it really to take 5 years? Hailsham annotated the memorandum from the Prime Minister's Office: 'Timescale misunderstood . . . This is a five course meal. The soup & fish will be served I hope in good time. It is only the savoury which will have to wait.'[27] The Lord Chancellor had told the Prime Minister: 'The object will be to attack the long-standing evils of delay, cost and complexity . . . nothing in present arrangements for handling civil business will be immune from the possibility of radical reform.'[28] This was doubtless the sort of manifesto which Mrs Thatcher wanted to hear, but some at least of those who were at the seminar had forebodings. Professor Jolowicz of Cambridge wrote to Sir Derek Oulton to complain that a great opportunity to attack fundamentals had been missed.

The Review took $3\frac{1}{2}$ years and the Report was published in June 1988.[29] Lord Hailsham had by then retired but his successor rightly gave him the credit. The Advisory Committee, which together with officials from the Department formed the Review Body, was chaired by Sir Maurice Hodgson, a former Chairman of Imperial Chemical Industries, and included a Lord of Appeal, a barrister, a solicitor and Professor Scott of Birmingham. Hailsham did not interfere with the work of the Review Body, although he was kept informed of progress. In the words of one of his officials, 'he was not a fussing Minister'.

The main effect of the Review Body's proposals was to push cases downwards from the High Court to the County Court by increasing the jurisdiction of the latter. For instance, it was proposed that all personal injury cases should be started in the County Court. The suggestion for merging the two courts into one was rejected. The proposal might have resulted in an improvement because procedure is simpler in the County Court, but as *The Times* legal correspondent pointed out when the reforms came into effect in 1991, 'unless there are enough circuit and district judges to deal with the work transferred from the High Court, the trial delays of the High Court will only have shifted to the County Court'.[30] The Report also made some sensible but limited procedural suggestions for reducing delay and the tactic of surprise so beloved of litigating lawyers.

With the best will in the world, the Review must be described as disappointing. Its results were far removed from the ringing declaration with which Lord Hailsham had laid his proposals before Mrs Thatcher. It was in fact another small brown mouse. This might not have mattered had not so much been at stake. The cost and delays attending civil proceedings, included even in Hamlet's catalogue of life's burdens, have disfigured our system of administering justice time out of mind. They lie at the root of the problem of the escalating cost of legal aid, the issue of the availability of redress. Professor Scott touched the heart of the matter at the 1984 Seminar when he said that claims on the Courts' service were unlimited, but resources were limited. There are and were only two ways of making these ends meet. One was to reduce the number of cases coming to Court. This could be done by giving redress in other ways, as for example through an insured scheme for personal injuries which did not depend on establishing fault. The other was to simplify the procedure in those cases which still had to come to Court for resolution. The simplification would have to have a real effect on cost and delay. By that test, the Civil Justice Review was an out and out failure.

Hailsham genuinely wanted reform and knew the need for it. Why then were these hopes and intentions frustrated? The answer seems to be partly because Hailsham and his officials were at one in thinking that the subject could not safely be left to the profession. They could be forgiven for thinking that law reform was too serious a subject to be entrusted to lawyers, in view of the lamentable record of lawyers' inquiries into the subject over the previous hundred years, and the implacable conservatism which they frequently met in dealing with the profession. But it did not follow that the Department should be left in charge, and Hailsham gave no weight to the quite unusual urge to reform shown by some of the ablest and most open-minded professionals of the day who took part in the Seminar, led by the Law Commission under the Chairmanship of Sir Ralph Gibson. In his anxiety not to lose control of the inquiry, Hailsham also failed to appreciate the unavoidable shortfall of experience and resource in his own Department to handle an inquiry of such magnitude, complexity and implication.

Hailsham regretted that the Review did not accept his idea for amalgamating the High Court and the County Court in a single civil court, as Beeching had achieved for the criminal courts. 'I was never persuaded', he wrote in 1988, 'that, given the differences in salary, robes, titles, modes of address, the relative importance of the business transacted and the central location of the Royal Courts of Justice, the status of High Court judges could have been adversely affected'.[31] It may be that opposition to the idea came from the Judges, but a far more serious difficulty was that it raised the question of rights of audience, who should be entitled to argue cases in Court. As far as Hailsham was concerned, that question lay in sanctuary and could not be touched. A thoroughgoing review of civil procedure could not avoid the emotive issue of whether the Bar's monopoly of the right to plead should continue. But it was not negotiable, or even discussable, while Hailsham remained Lord Chancellor.

*

Hailsham had never sat in any judicial capacity before he became Lord Chancellor. Unlike most senior members of the Bar, he had not even held a part-time Recordership. But he was eager for the opportunity now open to him. His father had presided over the Law Lords, the Court of final appeal for the whole of the United Kingdom, and over the Judicial Committee of the Privy Council, hearing appeals from many Commonwealth Courts. This he did as often as his health permitted. In those days, it was possible for the Lord Chancellor to preside frequently, because the political sittings of the House of Lords, in which he was Speaker, did not begin until teatime, after the legal sittings were concluded for the day. Hailsham described his father's daily life as Lord Chancellor.

> Appeals to the House of Lords were held in the chamber. The Lord Chancellor, clad in wig, gown and bands, but in long trousers, would come down from the Woolsack (then stuffed with horsehair) and counsel (silks wearing full-bottomed wigs) would address him and his four colleagues from an uncomfortable little box at the Bar of the House. The hearing would stop at 4 p.m. My father would then adjourn the House, don his knee-breeches and silk stockings, drink his cup of tea and resume his seat on the Woolsack at 4.15. Sittings seldom lasted later than 6.30 p.m. . . .
> (*A Sparrow's Flight*)

The second Lord Hailsham would have enjoyed continuing this picturesque tradition, but the War had changed it all. When their own Chamber was destroyed by bombing, the Commons took over the Lords' Chamber. The Law Lords began to sit in two divisions of five upstairs in a committee room, wearing lounge suits; and the political sittings began after lunch. The Lord Chancellor could not be in two places at once, so he seldom sat judicially.

Hailsham considered that it would be a disaster if the Lord Chancellor never sat as a Judge. There would then be nothing to prevent a Prime Minister, swayed by political considerations, from appointing as Lord Chancellor a politician who did not match up to the professional requirements of the office. The appointment of a Chancellor who was more politician than lawyer would be likely to bring in its train political appointments to the Bench, and a greater risk of political interference with the judiciary. Moreover, the Chancellor himself, through ignorance of the leading advocates of the day and by losing touch with developments in the law, would no longer be able to deal adequately with judicial appointments and promotions. It was vital, he thought, that the man entrusted with the appointment of Judges should not only have the confidence of the Cabinet, but also of the Bench.

Hailsham partially resolved his dilemma by appointing a number of Deputy Speakers to relieve him from sitting continually through the lengthening hours of the Lords' political sessions. He considered it a waste of the Chancellor's time to spend so much of his working day listening to debates in which he had no inclination or duty to participate, and over which, unlike his counterpart, the Speaker in the House of Commons, he had no disciplinary control. This freed him to sit in appeals with the Law Lords, although not as often as he would have wished. For of all the work of the Lord Chancellor he enjoyed sitting as a Judge most.

Shortly before he was to sit for the first time, he came across a group of Law Lords having lunch separately in the Lords' dining room, as was their habit. He was already on familiar terms with them and he asked for some practical advice. Should he or should he not read the papers relative to an appeal before the hearing?* One of his brethren said that he *never* read anything beforehand: to do so would predispose his mind. Another said that he liked having his mind predisposed, and *always* read the papers first. The newcomer retired baffled.[32]

Although without judicial experience, Hailsham came to appellate work with good qualifications. In intellect alone, his extraordinary academic distinction promised well. He had thought about the purposes of law, and once told an audience in New Delhi that it was 'the means of robbing liberty of its anarchic tendencies, and removing from authority the elements of caprice'.[33] He detested both extremes. Although intermittently acquired, his practical knowledge of advocacy, with its process of sifting fact and applying principle, stretched back over his working life. He had a wonderful command of English. He had thought too about the business of decision making and, what was particularly relevant to appellate work, the proper limits of judicial lawmaking. In this last, Hailsham was a conservative, and thought that a Judge would usually be wise 'to stick to the particular even when he is being at his most creative, and to observe the fiction that he is only interpreting and systemising existing law when he is fully aware that, by his decision, he cannot avoid breaking new ground'.[34] Hailsham broke no new ground himself. Yet, for all his credentials, Hailsham was not an outstanding Judge. He may not have been able to sit frequently enough to build up a body of jurisprudence bearing his own personal mark, but in any case he lacked the detachment necessary to the judicial

---

* In the oral tradition of the English process, the Judges used to start the hearing without having read anything about the case. In order to shorten hearings and despatch business more efficiently, this tradition has steadily been eroded.

temperament. He talked a good deal during the hearing and few, if any, of his speeches in the law reports are capable of serving as a guiding light.

This was the view of his contemporaries. Lord Wilberforce, who sat with him, thought that although he could not do anything without distinction, Hailsham was not, perhaps, cut out to be a Judge: there was always much of the debating instinct about him. Lord Templeman, whose own style was terse, was critical and described some of his decisions as a 'lucid fog'. Lord Lane made a similar point more gently, saying that Hailsham's opinions were a pleasure to read, but lacked crispness: they would not be of much help to a Recorder sitting in a provincial town trying to make sense of a House of Lords decision and to direct a jury properly.[35]

Here was the rub. With few exceptions, Hailsham's important decisions were in criminal cases. With his well-known impatience about illogical and outdated rules, it was to be hoped that he would bring some clarity to this branch of the law. He knew as well as anyone the importance of avoiding complexity and obfuscation, and he said, in terms that Lord Lane would have applauded: 'The purpose of a direction to the jury is not best achieved by a disquisition on jurisprudence or philosophy or a universally applicable circular tour round the area of law affected by the case'.[36]

Yet he did not always avoid these pitfalls. The law of homicide was a case in point. His own view was that there should be a single offence of homicide. The circumstances in which one person may kill another were so infinitely various that the distinction between murder and manslaughter would be better abolished, leaving the Judge to decide the sentence appropriate to the circumstances of the case.[37] Such a reform would of course be for Parliament rather than the Judges; but when he presided in a difficult borderline case, it was not Hailsham but one of the other Law Lords, Lord Kilbrandon, who pleaded for this eminently desirable reform.[38]

Early in his first term, he presided in an important libel appeal.[39] The case, one of his few civil appeals with wide implications, illustrates well Hailsham's strengths and weaknesses as a Judge. The subject matter was a famous and tragic episode in the naval history of the Second World War. In 1942, a convoy of merchant ships bound for the Soviet Union via the Arctic Circle was under escort by a destroyer force commanded by Commander Broome. As a result of a blunder committed by the Admiralty, the convoy was ordered to scatter, and two thirds of the merchantmen were destroyed. More than 20 years afterwards, a book was written about the episode, quite unjustifiably blaming the disaster on Commander Broome, and stigmatising him as a coward. It was a terrible slur on a brave officer, aggravated by the fact that the libel was put abroad quite deliberately and without concern for its truth or falsity. Neither author nor publisher appeared to care what distress was caused.

Broome sued the author and publisher, and the case was tried by a Judge and jury. It aroused the most powerful emotions. The jury awarded £15,000 compensation and £25,000 as 'exemplary' or 'punitive' damages. The equivalent sums in 1997 would have been rather more than £125,000 and £200,000. Damages of this latter type were a much criticised anomaly, because they confused the function of the civil law, which is to compensate for injury, with that of the criminal law, which is to inflict punishment.

The defendants appealed. They attacked the way in which the Judge had directed the jury on the principles on which exemplary damages should be awarded. In the Court of Appeal, with Lord Denning presiding, the case took a curious turn. Denning's Court upheld the award, but criticised an earlier House of Lords decision,[40] which had codified the circumstances in which exemplary damages could be awarded. Lord Denning described the earlier decision as 'unworkable' and advised Judges to ignore it. It was this which had so annoyed Lord Devlin, the retired Law Lord who was the main author of the earlier decision (see p. 278).

The defendants appealed again, to the House of Lords. Because of Denning's conduct, which called into question the whole hierarchical system of appellate courts; and perhaps also because of the general importance of the case, Hailsham decided to preside himself, over a bench of seven instead of the usual five. His rebuke to Denning, and his reaffirmation of the essential need for Judges to observe the court hierarchy, was impressively done, the more impressive for the restraint of the language he chose. Devlin wrote Hailsham a note of appreciation after judgment had been given. 'There is enough permissiveness in the world today', he remarked rather petulantly, 'without its penetration into the doctrine of precedent.'[41]

Devlin also considered that Hailsham's speech was 'a comprehensive and masterly review of the whole subject', and ranked 'with the best contributions of great Chancellors of the past . . .' This was high praise, coming as it did from a distinguished common lawyer. The speech, which extends over thirty pages of the official report, was indeed well made. There was clarity and intellectual strength about it. But none the less, the result of the appeal leaves a feeling of disquiet. Hailsham's own contribution peters out in an unconvincing upholding of the jury's award. The direction to the jury survived only by the narrowest of margins, four to three; and of the majority,

Hailsham himself confessed to having had 'the greatest difficulty' in accepting the summing up as adequate. His was the casting vote, and if Commander Broome had lost, the legal fees which he would have had to bear might have swallowed up his damages. It is impossible to feel that Hailsham was not influenced by that thought, and by the more general thought that a libel on a brave naval officer must not go unpunished.

More serious for the longer term development of the law was the failure of the Law Lords, under Hailsham's leadership, to grapple definitively with the anomaly of 'exemplary' damages, 'a dark and emotive branch of the Common Law', in the words of another of the Judges. The case left the law in the same unsatisfactory state as it had been before Lord Denning stirred up his hornets' nest. Penal damages, to teach the wrongdoer that tort does not pay, could still be awarded by juries without the safeguards built into the criminal law; and the money exacted would still go, not to the state, but as a windfall to the plaintiff. Neither Hailsham nor any of his colleagues faced these difficulties squarely.

In a diary note which he made between the end of the hearing and the giving of judgment, Hailsham recorded:

> Wilberforce's jgt. in Broome v Cassell. He now thinks appeal shd. be allowed – contrary to his first view. This means it will be 4–3 (assuming the other two are staunch) dismissing the appeal. My present view remains that the S.U. [summing up] will do in the light of the way the D's [defendants] put their case, and the amount though excessive was for the jury.[42]

This illuminating note doubtless shows some partisanship, but it also points to a concern not to upset a jury verdict. In his own speech in the case, and running like a thread through his other decisions, there is an anxiety not to disturb. From the hierarchical system of appeals to the constitutional authority of decisions arrived at through the judicial process, he was careful always to preserve legitimacy. It was all of a piece with his respect for traditional institutions. *Stare decisis*, he said about the system of precedent, 'is still the indispensable foundation of the use by your Lordships of the appellate jurisdiction of the House and its normal practice. Especially must this be so in criminal law, where certainty is indeed a condition of its commanding and retaining respect.'[43]

26

Last Political Years

As Speaker of the House of Lords, the Chancellor is in a very different position from his counterpart in the Commons. He has no power to keep order or to control the sequence or content of speeches. All these are for the House itself. Hailsham thought that in compensation for his impotence the Chancellor had no need to be impartial in debate. He exercised this self-designed privilege more freely than any Chancellor within living memory and, as in the Committee debates on the Industrial Relations Bill in 1971, he could be as pugnacious as if he had been back in the Commons. Nor did he see anything unseemly in taking to the stump at election time and giving his very considerable all to campaigning. 'The emotional, often wayward, but brilliant engineer of the great Conservative revival of the late 1950s', as *The Times* described him during the campaign of October, 1974, could still generate electricity. 'His mastery of oratory and his almost mesmeric ability to hold an audience are undiminished. The scorn still bites, the pauses and witticisms are timed with perfection, and the boorish interrupters savaged into bewilderment . . .'[1]

Hailsham deprecated the habit of keeping private accounts of discussion in Cabinet, particularly with later publication in view. So there is little in the diaries during the Heath and Thatcher years on Cabinet meetings. But we do have a picture of him in his first term as Lord Chancellor in Edward Heath's Cabinet, ebullient, assertive, talking at large, offering instant, gratuitous legal advice to the Government, often usurping the role of the Law Officers.[2]

We also know something of his always perceptive opinion of the leaders he served, and their differing Cabinet styles. Edward Heath, he considered, was a consensus man, scrupulous in taking the views of his colleagues and weighing them, one against the other. A private, involuted personality, he was given to long periods of silence broken by unexpected eruptions. He was not popular either with his own party or his opponents and, Hailsham thought, had never married because of an inability to commit himself completely.

Margaret Thatcher was an aggressive Chairman, who could take pleasure in putting people down and won her arguments by hectoring. But Hailsham's personal relations with her, after the initial shock, were the best he had with any leader from Churchill onwards. He found her a warm hearted woman, considerate of the feelings of those she liked.[3]

The Hoggs were an Ulster Protestant family. They did not forget their origins, and it was natural that Quintin Hailsham should identify himself with the Unionist viewpoint. He told the Conservative Party Conference in 1969 that if his great grandfather, Sir James Weir Hogg, had not gone to make his fortune with the East India Company, he himself would probably have become Master of the Orange Lodge in Lisburn. But his idea of the Union was of Britain and all Ireland. 'I stand for the unity of the British Islands, allowing the maximum degree of devolution compatible with safety from foreign invasion and economic prosperity'. In history's retrospect, this conception became impossible to realise with the failure of Gladstone's first Home Rule Bill of 1886 and the destruction of Parnell which quickly followed. But it was what Unionism meant to the Hogg family. When Douglas made his maiden speech in the Commons in 1922, it was, by a bitter twist, to propose from the Despatch Box the enactment of the Irish Treaty which he detested, but was in conscience bound to support. Here were the origins of the makeshift Union of Great Britain with the six counties, and the beginning of Stormont. The division of Ireland was no more naturally congenial to Quintin Hogg than to a Fenian; and this view never changed. In 1942, while still serving in the Middle East, he included in his diary a brief reflection on Ireland.

> I have always thought that the Irish trouble is due to the fact that we think of a British nation which ought to be governed in the way in which sovereign nations are governed, and the Irish do not merely consider themselves a separate nation . . . but reject all kinship and community of culture between us and them whatever. But I believe in the existence of a British nation and a specifically British culture to which all the component parts of the islands have a specific contribution to offer. And I can never

319

understand these dreadful murders by people professing the Christian religion. (*Diary* 15 Oct. 1942.)

Hailsham saw the situation in Northern Ireland as simple, but intractable. Two peoples lived in six counties. One felt themselves British, the other Irish. These national aspirations were irreconcilable and, in his view, more important than religion, which he thought served to give the conflict its theatricality. Talk of a quick peace was irresponsible. The search was for a way to live together, and to nourish the hope that the border might in time wither away.[4]

There was a series of attempts made during Hailsham's time in government to blur the hard edge of the border, of which the last was the negotiation of the Anglo-Irish Agreement of 1985. He was sceptical – but never opposed to the objectives which London and Dublin had in view, although he did oppose the idea of mixed North and South Courts to try terrorist cases. His views, he said, were settled, but wholly impracticable. The Nationalists and the Unionists were as unlikely to reach a rational agreement as were the Hutus and the Tutsis.

The Irish question always touched his emotions painfully. In 1969, soon after the civil rights movement had given way to violence, he visited Northern Ireland as shadow Home Secretary. Parts of Belfast and Londonderry, the so called 'no-go areas', were barricaded off, inaccessible to police and troops alike. Houses were burnt out and ruined. He went into the Bogside unescorted. Here was a community in outright rebellion. They treated him kindly, gave him chicken sandwiches and tea, and talked to him. The experience moved him powerfully. He returned and made an emotional speech at the Party Conference. His remorse for having condoned, like all Conservatives, the Unionist domination of Stormont over half a century was laid bare. He pleaded for understanding and charity. But his Protestant Unionist hosts were displeased, and their leader Chichester Clark and others walked out.

Pleas like these went unheeded. Arson, murder and bestial cruelty escalated. The Heath Government brought in internment, which Hailsham had to defend as the lesser of evils, but afterwards felt had been mistaken.[5] At the end of his life, he conceded that internment had probably made matters worse. It was of course inconsistent with the rule of law, but imprisonment without trial could be justified in extreme circumstances. However, he thought there was a more important practical objection: when and in what circumstances could or should internees be released? Through February and into March, 1972, there was the worst series of bombing outrages since the beginning of the emergency. The IRA called a halt for 72 hours and demanded the withdrawal of troops and the abolition of Stormont. This was ignored and bombing resumed. Hailsham characterised the situation as a military insurrection led by the implacable enemies of the country, and passively acquiesced in by a large minority. When he later learned that there had been talks with the terrorists, he wrote angrily in his diary: 'Neither I nor Cabt. w: consulted abt. the talks wi. the IRA – in my view a disastrous error'.[6]

Edward Heath met Brian Faulkner, the Prime Minister of Northern Ireland, on 22 and 23 March in an atmosphere of crisis. They agreed that there could be no change to the border without the consent of the people of the six counties, and that internment should be phased out. But Faulkner would not agree that responsibility for law and order should be transferred to Westminster, and was prepared to resign on the issue. For the British Government, it was not tolerable that 17 battalions of troops should be in Northern Ireland and that the Government should not be responsible for security – as Hailsham said forcibly in the Lords.[7] He did not take part in the negotiations with Stormont, but he attended the Cabinet on 23 March, when the decision to assume direct rule was taken. Of the available options, doing nothing, leaving Northern Ireland to civil war, and direct rule, the case for the last, although he hated it, was in his opinion unanswerable. 'Law and Order has broken down and Stormont unable to restore order', he noted in his diary. 'Most tragic day in my public life'.[8] The following day he heard the Prime Minister's statement from the Peers' Gallery. He thought it went reasonably well. Chichester Clark was mildly hostile, Wilson reasonable, Thorpe good. 'B. Devlin silent, scratched, yawned, picked her teeth'.[9] (Bernadette Devlin was the People's Democracy MP for Mid-Ulster. Her termagant personality and high media profile gave her brief fame as a scourge of all three governments in London, Dublin and Belfast.) On the 27th, he was getting his own speech ready for the Lords. 'Speech on N. Ireland in preparation. Walked w. dogs Polesden Lacy. Norbury. Primroses, scented violets. Wood anemones. White and mauve'.[10]

The problem of Ulster continued unyielding through the rest of his public life. There was no right and no wrong, no solution, only the need for a 'modus vivendi', he wrote in *The Door Wherein I Went* in 1975. By then, he had to accept that the twenty-six counties had gone their own way. But he still held to his ideal: 'we are co-partners in Europe. If ever there came a time when they would be prepared to rejoin the family of British Islanders in a sort of loose confederation, I would rejoice . . .'

Edward Heath succeeded where Harold Macmillan failed, in taking Britain into Europe. Hailsham had no moment of doubt that it was the right thing to do so. In the debate on the Schuman Plan in 1950, he had vainly argued that Britain should join the Coal and Steel Communities, and so enter European Union at its threshold. He had feared that the opportunity might not return. When it did, in 1971, he argued with all the considerable force at his disposal that it would be a disaster not to grasp it. 'We must stand up now and be counted. We must make our decision. We are not likely to get better terms if we wait. It is not likely that we shall get any terms if we wait.'[11] He had nothing for the comfort of those who would have stayed outside. The effect, he said, on our own people would be frustration or despair. For our enemies, it would be just another example of our fecklessness; and our friends would be in doubt and bewilderment as to what, after all, we were really playing at.

> My Lords, to be British is a special and not the least honourable way of being European . . . shall we alone stand aloof? Shall Achilles only remain sulking in his tent? I believe we should be false to our past, we should betray our children, if we allowed temporary or merely ephemeral considerations to cloud our judgment in making this historic choice.

And he concluded a powerful piece of oratory with the simple Tudor rhyme: 'He who will not when he may, / When he will he shall have nay'.[12]

There was a good deal about sovereignty in the speech. He was convinced that all ten members were, and would remain, sovereign. The institutions which administered the Common Market, the Court and the Commission, did not, he claimed, impinge on member states' rights to order their own affairs, and the Community had none of the characteristics of a federation. That view has not stood the test of time. In his little book on the Constitution (1992) he acknowledged that membership of the Community 'places limitations on our sovereignty', and that its institutions made up such a curiously balanced structure that it remained to be seen whether it could be made workable at all.[13] Much more accurate was his forecast of how Britain's friends would react to the dithering and bickering that became known as 'Euroscepticism'.

His opinion on Europe did not change. Adam Smith had remarked that Britain must endeavour 'to accommodate her future views and designs to the real mediocrity of her circumstances'. Hailsham considered that that mediocrity would be cruelly exposed by coming out of Europe. Better in with a vote than out without, summarised his stance.[14] In the debate on the Schuman Plan in 1950, he described the 'specific challenge of history' to European civilisation as its inability to solve the problem of peace.[15] That remained the justification for European Union and Britain's membership of it.

The trade unions were the beginning and end of the Heath Administration. It began with the plan for placing them in a comprehensive legal framework, and it ended with defeat at the hands of the miners and the immediate repeal of the Industrial Relations Act. Hailsham offered a justification for the twists and turns in policy between these events in *The Door Wherein I Went*.[16] He did not seek to avoid his share of responsibility. He believed, with his colleagues, that the Unions would accept voluntary wage restraint in return for reduced unemployment. When that failed, he preferred statutory control of incomes to the alternative as he saw it: 'for the public, including the unions, to learn the hard way'. His memories of the 1930s were still too potent for him to accept deflation, mass unemployment, and the possibility of fascism. Finally, after some hesitating, he accepted that the trial of strength with the miners would have to be decided by the electorate. He made clear that the decision to go to the country was taken unanimously in Cabinet. Heath was grateful for his public acknowledgment of that, when *The Door Wherein I Went* was published. 'I am glad you have put yourself firmly on the record', he wrote to Hailsham, 'that we were all involved in the decision to have a general election in February 1974 and that it was the right thing to have done. None of my other colleagues have had the courage to say so.'[17]

In hindsight, it is not so clear that it was the right thing to have done. Early in January, Lord Carrington told Hailsham that he thought 'we must now have a Gen. Election'.[18] Hailsham reflected on the conversation and wrote to Carrington the next day.[19] The letter was 'as much an attempt to clear my own mind as anything else, and certainly implies no dogmatic assertion of correctness'. He was none the less against an election. The only possible favourable outcome would be for the winner to sit out the crisis at whatever cost. In order to conserve coal stocks, and so defeat industrial action by the miners, the Government had ordered a three-day working week. The polls appeared to support the Government, but no one could say that they would continue to do so for the three-week campaign period, during which the full hardship of the three-day week would be increasingly experienced. 'It would take a good deal to convince me that anything short of a cast iron certainty would justify the abandonment of our present even if precarious, majority.' On the other side of the argument, if the Government went to the country, it would be accused, 'with some effect', of abandoning its post in a moment of danger. 'Consider the effect', Hailsham urged his friend, 'on the £ and our balance of payments, of electoral uncertainty, fluctuating opinion polls and continued crisis.'

These were arguments which still ring, but as Hailsham conceded, the correct answer depended on 'the reliability and staunchness of our present troops in the House of Commons'. If they stood firm, well and good. 'But will they? I rather think that the next week or two may sort out the men from the boys.' It was only that week or two before the Whips began to bring stories of wavering in the ranks, and Hailsham's reasoning was overborne – with his own concurrence.

The result of the election was a stalemate: Labour, 301, Conservative, 297; Liberal 14. There were ministerial meetings over the following weekend, and Hailsham analysed the situation in a long note.[20] The alternatives were to resign at once, or to approach the Liberal leader, Jeremy Thorpe. He rejected the first, which he called 'the King's pawn opening'. His view was that an 'immense majority' had voted for Heath's European and statutory incomes policies, and it would be right to try to form a coalition with the Liberals in order to continue them. The Liberals should be offered participation in the Government: '(say one Cab: Min: two Mins. of State: two Undersecretaries)' to make sure they shared responsibility.

But the Liberals wanted electoral reform before they would participate. This was an impossible demand. The Labour Party would put on a three line Whip against it, and the 11 Ulster Unionists were also 'passionately' against it. Hailsham thought that the most that could be offered would be a Speaker's Conference on reform. Thorpe had also suggested a coalition of 'national unity' with Harold Wilson. This was even less realistic. Wilson, predictably, turned it down. Hailsham concluded: 'If the Libs turn us down we shall resign forthwith . . . I think they will turn us down. If they do, I think they will be foolish, as they will have refused a chance of getting experience of Government, and their best chance ever of getting electoral reform.'

The forecast was accurate. There was a Cabinet on 4 March (Monday) when 'it was readily decided that this administration was to come to an end'. Thorpe had persisted in the 'ridiculous' notion of a grand alliance of all three parties.

The Liberals have put Labour in power. In doing so they have done, I believe, damage to themselves. It remains to be seen how far the country and the Conservative Party will suffer too.[21]

The Conservatives were out of office for five years. Harold Wilson formed a minority Government in March 1974 and improved his position in the October election sufficiently to give himself a thin overall majority of 3. Edward Heath, who had then lost three out of four elections, was discredited, but it was far from clear who should succeed him. At a shadow cabinet immediately after the October election, Hailsham recorded that he had spoken up firmly. 'The Party will fall apart unless opposition constant and robust'.[22] Among Heath's opponents for the leadership, Margaret Thatcher was considered an outsider, but when the election came in February, 1975, she won comfortably.* Hailsham had a warm personal note from her. No letter she had received, she said, was kinder, more understanding or more perceptive. She was well aware of the absolute need to succeed in the daunting task ahead. 'People could so easily destroy their own freedom and not realise what they had lost until it was too late.'[23] These were precisely the terms in which Hailsham saw the threat. The crisis was moral, not economic. But although he and his new leader agreed in their diagnosis, he was not ready for her remedies − or her style. She made both felt immediately.

At the beginning of April, Sir Keith Joseph produced a paper for the shadow cabinet entitled 'Notes towards the Definition of Policy'.[24] It was long and comprehensive, and contained much of what was to become known as 'Thatcherism'. The paper attacked consensus politics which, it argued, led only to competing with the Socialists in offering to perform what was beyond the power of government. Prices, subject to competition, and dividends must be allowed to move freely 'so as to perform their functions'. Nothing should be treated as sacred. Joseph asked rhetorically 'if we can really nerve ourselves' to remove supplementary benefit and tax rebates from strikers, or try a voucher experiment for schools? The Conservatives had a superb radical case, he concluded. 'The conjuring trick by which Labour are apparently able to provide a rising real income for their main supporters will soon be shattered by events.'

* In the first ballot, Mrs Thatcher won 130 votes to 119 for Heath. In the second, the results were: Mrs Thatcher 146; William Whitelaw 79; James Prior 19; Sir Geoffrey Howe 19; John Peyton 11.

The paper was debated by the shadow cabinet on 11 April. Hailsham's copy is peppered with exclamation marks, sometimes in pairs. He made a note of the discussion, if that is the right word. Mrs Thatcher quickly smoked out the 'wets'.

Reggie	I do NOT agree with ONE little bit.
Gilmour	Up to 1970 consensus was a *Conservative* consensus, not a Labour one . . .
Margaret	Ian, you *do* believe in capitalism?
Ian	That is almost blasphemy. I don't believe in Socialism.
Raison	Too much misery in Keith's paper. There are matters on which we have *got* to operate a consensus e.g. we must try to persuade Healey to produce a sensible budget.
Maude	That is not on. The right of the Lab. Pty. will always let us down.
Pym	Society is moving more left. There must be continuity – which means a broad measure of agreement – The Keith paper is a recipe for disaster.

There was hardly a dull moment.[25]

The paper and the debate were a shock. The patricians, Hailsham, Carrington and Whitelaw, were thrown off balance by the style and substance of Margaret Thatcher and her guru, Keith Joseph. Their disquiet continued to appear at intervals through the opposition years to 1979. In March 1977, Carrington went to see Hailsham in his room in the Lords. He was disturbed by the way the party was being run, and by its extreme right wing image. Hailsham was of the same mind. 'I said I had warned again and again but had been ignored.' The two agreed, however, that no future change of leader was possible. 'He sd: "Well, what are we going to do after she gets in if she gets in?" I said "all we can do is to see she is surrounded by adequate advisers". P: said "At present there are Keith who is largely to blame, and Angus [Maude] who is not extreme, but bitter . . ." We both agreed Margaret an extremely nice person, but I said that I had never had much confidence in her judgment . . . Keith tho' clever, even brilliant, is dotty & lacks moral fibre for high office.' Carrington reported that 'the big industrialists' resented the way Mrs Thatcher lectured them: '. . . one had said: I wd. not mind being treated as a schoolboy if only she wd. put me in the 6th form. But I do mind being put in the 4th.'[26]

Joseph continued to worry the old guard. They underrated his intellectual contribution to the new Tory radicalism: they even thought that he might bring the Conservatives down. 'Clever-silly.

Attracts Barmies'.[27] The fear was that if the party moved too far right, it would become isolated from moderate opinion. Wilson might even try to detach the resentful, spurned Heath. Hailsham had warned Mrs Thatcher about this possibility in July 1975:

> I am sure you wd: be wise if at all possible (wh: I fear it may not be) to heal the breach with Ted Heath as soon as may be. I do not myself believe that there is an ideological difference between you. On the other hand, in politics, personal difficulties can be as troublesome, and as lasting . . .[28]

Mrs Thatcher was more concerned with the threat of a National Government. The Socialists, she said in her reply, 'would only use the broader base . . . to take us further down the road to irreversible Socialism'. She added: 'On your other point − about healing the breach − I do try, but it takes two.'[29] Hailsham then wrote to Heath to protest that his own willingness to serve in 'the present Shadow' was not in any way 'an act of disloyalty to our friendship', and suggested that they should remain in touch.[30] Heath replied from Cowes reassuringly, but non-committally. 'There is nothing I should like more than for us to have a talk about our present predicament.'[31]

The attempted bridge-building was hopeless. Hailsham was right that the gulf was more personal than ideological, but it was Carrington who caught the exact flavour. 'Peter Carrington is back,' Hailsham noted after the Christmas 1975 recess.

> He had had Ted Heath for the w/end. I sd. I thought he ought to be in the shadow cabt . . . Peter: 'I told him he ought to have gone around . . . being a good loser, kissing Margaret on every possible opportunity and saying what a splendid woman she was'. He looked at me in absolute amazement: 'Why on earth? I don't think she is any good. I am much better and I ought to be there still.' Peter sd. he was in cracking form being rude to everybody.[32]

After Mrs Thatcher took office in 1979, Hailsham came to accept the rightness of her policies. The imperative to turn back from what she had called 'the road to irreversible Socialism' convinced him that a new radical approach was necessary. By casting out consensus politics, and everyone who sailed under that flag, she changed the face of British politics, as he wrote to her in his resignation letter in 1987. He had been unprepared for both the extent and duration of her dominance at home, and the respect and admiration which she won abroad. He paid her a glowing tribute in *A Sparrow's Flight*,[33] and conceded that the 'middle way' of a concordat between rival political philosophies, which he had for so long supported, had been demonstrated by Mrs Thatcher to be a false god, which would lead only to the eventual triumph of Socialism. Hailsham claimed that the fallacy was first exposed in the Heath Government's manifesto of 1970. It may be so, but Mrs Thatcher's Administration was the first to convince its supporters by deed. In any event, Hailsham was willing to say, perhaps for the first and last time in his public life, not only that he had been wrong, but also that he had been converted by force of argument.

Only after her own defenestration, by when Hailsham had left the scene, did he again begin seriously to mistrust Mrs. Thatcher's judgment. Her tendency to rant had become more prominent and, he thought, she had been overtaken by hubris. He 'cowered on the firing step' (his phrase) as she stormed through the Maastricht debate. It saddened him. The Foyles literary lunch in 1994, at which she promoted her own memoirs and her own opinions at a great deal more than heavenly length, was a miserable experience.[34]

During her Administration, there were continuing disagreements, but less frequent. Keith Joseph's idea of withdrawing welfare benefits from strikers came up early in Mrs Thatcher's first term. 'Stormy cab.' Hailsham noted in his diary, 'but killed for the time being crazy idea abt. strikers benefits wh: hits *non* unionists who are also famy. men'.[35] And later, in 1981, he was worried by 'the intellectual arrogance of the reconstituted Cab., its a priori reasoning, its unwillingness to listen to the voice of experience'.[36] He had few reservations about his leader's foreign policy, at least until the last and most extreme phase of her European policy, and he admired her for having done so much to repair Britain's prestige abroad. He experienced no doubts about the Falklands expedition, only some hesitations about where the extraordinary rapport with Ronald Reagan was leading. The Libyan bombings in 1986 rekindled the old fears. 'In the evening (after House) WWW [Whitelaw] came to see me', Hailsham recorded, '. . . and seemed generally disturbed. He said he is increasingly of the opinion that we have a madman in the White House. I share his view.'[37]

Hailsham's growing sympathy with Margaret Thatcher's policies through the eighties was warmed by friendship and mutual regard. She thought him a great public servant who could draw on his knowledge of the classical world and comprehend the moral dimension of politics.[38] He admired her resoluteness. In 1975, the year in which she took over the leadership, he had written: 'It has been a matter of supreme regret to me that my public life has taken place in a period of national humiliation and decline, the like of which I do not know that the British nation has ever experienced in recent history.' Now, from retirement, he saw her as the only post-war leader to have had the capacity to stem that decline. Above all, he admired her Elizabethan courage. When her hotel was bombed during the 1984 party conference in Brighton, he noted: 'The Prime Minister dressed, made herself [up], and did her hair before coming down'; and then went on characteristically:

> In the hospital was a man assumed to be the hall porter of the hotel. All day long he had been receiving compliments for his bravery and marvellous conduct and handshakes from the high & mighty. He was a nameless, passing drunk who had no recollection of how he came to be there.[39]

The previous July, his small terrier, Mini, died. She had been a consolation to him after Mary's death in 1978, always sleeping on his bed. He had a sympathetic note from Mrs Thatcher, saying she knew how unhappy he would be because of the poignant memories. 'In the meantime you know that we *all love* you and will do anything we can to help'.[40] His colleagues did love him. When he took the oath at the table in the House of Lords after the 1983 General Election, there was a spontaneous cheer from all sides. Since becoming Lord Chancellor, he had mellowed. Much of the abrasiveness had gone, but none of the mischief. 'My dear Willie,' he wrote to Whitelaw in 1981, 'what *do* you think you are about resurrecting that hoary (forgive the pun) old fallacy about licensed brothels . . . Incidentally, even Mrs Warren and her girls are against it . . . And do we want to win the General Election or don't we?'[41]

It seems also that Lords Hailsham and Carrington used sometimes to versify during Cabinet or Committee. The following are samples from Hailsham's diary (authorship unknown but guessable).

> If all the good people were clever
> And all clever people were good
> The world would be nicer than ever
> We thought that it possibly could.
> But somehow it's seldom or never
> The two hit it off as they should.
> The good are so hard on the clever
> The clever so rude to the good.
>
> [1982]

And:

I am really quite sorry for Leon,
He's the colleague we all like to p-- on.
For all of us think
That he's near to the brink,
It's a cliff that we'd rather not be on.

[1981]

The tone of Hailsham's writings during this period is much affected by whether the Conservatives were in or out of power. Between 1974 and 1979, when he wrote *The Dilemma of Democracy* and gave his Dimbleby Lecture on *Elective Dictatorship*, the mood is one of grim foreboding. During the Thatcher era which followed, when he gave the Granada Lecture on the future of Cabinet Government, the gloom has lifted and the mood is less sombre.

The Dilemma of Democracy is a book belonging to 1974, the terrible year when, as one reviewer wrote, the British ruling class lost its nerve.[42] The Queen was enthusiastic about it and wrote him a long handwritten letter.[43] She was reading it 'with intense interest and enjoyment', and was sure that it would help 'many slightly muddled, BBC battered people to see things more clearly'. But it is not a good book, and it was hastily contrived. It set out, as the publishers had it, to answer some fundamental questions: 'What has gone wrong with Britain? Why do such a splendid people put up so pathetic a performance? What has got to be done to put things right?' In form, it is a series of short staccato jabs at major topics: democracy, elitism, freedom, law, capitalism, and the like. The reviews were not kind. The blurb, claiming that gusts of commonsense would blast 'the grey smog of boredom that has brooded so long over British politics', was accounted dubious meteorology. 'Lord Hailsham is really more like an electric fan of antiquated but robust design which blasts impartially and in all directions . . . dust, crumbs, various bugs and old cooking smells as well as good fresh air'.[44] He was no longer willing, or perhaps able, to make the effort which an extended work of original analysis called for. And after a life of political dogma and assertion, his style had taken on a certain flatulence.

It is a relief to turn instead to the celebrated Dimbleby Lecture (1976), one of the shortest and most incisive pieces of political analysis which he ever wrote. The argument of *Elective Dicatorship* is straightforward. The powers of Parliament are unlimited, without any legal constraint. The sovereignty of Parliament is effectively the sovereignty of the Commons, but the Commons in turn is under the sway of the Executive. The Government's influence is exerted through a variety of means. Requiring a little over 300 votes for a majority, it has some 130 placemen, in the shape of Ministers of all ranks, and Parliamentary private secretaries, marching obediently through the lobbies in the Commons. The Prime Minister can dissolve Parliament almost at will, his timing usually being determined by adroit short term manipulation of the economy. The Government can curtail debate by use of the guillotine and other procedural devices, against which Hailsham had inveighed in 1945 (see pp. 110ff). By all these means, our system of government had become by degrees more and more oppressive. With the small majority by which Labour ruled between October 1974 and May 1979, the need for discipline was the greater and, Hailsham considered, government the more oppressive.

The conclusion was that the constitution was no longer wind or weather proof. It was exposed to the risk of tyranny, for 'all reason and human experience tend to show that unlimited powers are intolerable'. Hailsham's compendious remedy was a written constitution, a Bill of Rights, devolved powers to the regions, and a reformed House of Lords elected by proportional representation and with the revising powers of a Senate. This was a prescription which had for long been developing in his mind, the elements of which had been provoked by what he had encountered in the course of his public life. The reform of the House of Lords had been germinating ever since his father became Lord Chancellor, and he was threatened with the political impotence of a peerage. The idea of devolving powers to regional institutions came to him first through his experience of the problem of the North East. It was an issue on which he felt strongly, and over which he nearly resigned from the Shadow Cabinet in 1976. But more potent than these was what he saw as the menace of a Socialist government which might abuse its unconfined power and destroy freedom. Our worn out constitution could not withstand such an assault. In constitutional matters, Hailsham was a radical reformer who could never carry his party, or even an influential segment of it, with him. He may still prove to have been a man before his time.

The Granada Lecture of 1987 is an essay of an altogether different stripe. Mrs Thatcher was in Downing Street and freedom was safe, at any rate for the time being. The lecture has a spacious, philosophical air, and it ends with the comforting thought that the British constitution, far from being worn out, is of the utmost flexibility, and that what his audience was witnessing was not the end or decay of Cabinet Government, but only structural change. Cabinet was the subject, but the discourse was more about how political institutions are formed by chance, and develop in a way never intended. Hailsham was at his best in this sort of speculation, and in its historical originality its only rival among his writings is the unpublished essay on the history of the Tory Party, reproduced in Appendix 2.

The English and, more latterly, the British, Hailsham asserted, have the habit of acquiring their institutions by inadvertence. The Cabinet is no exception. The circumstance which secured the continuance of the Hanoverian succession into the twentieth century was not the undoubted Protestantism of the first George, which had attracted him to contemporary society; but the fact that he could speak no English. Forced to converse with Walpole in dog Latin, he had no alternative but to let his Chief Minister take the chair in his place. This chance circumstance did more than anything else to bring about Cabinet Government, characterised by the lecturer as 'perhaps the most striking political gift of the English to the rest of humanity'.

When the first Lord Hailsham joined the Cabinet in 1922, it dealt with practically all government business. By the time his son was admitted to its mysteries in 1957, the Cabinet met only twice a week and could not possibly cope with the vastly increased volume of work. There had by then grown up a system of Cabinet committees, whose existence was unacknowledged publicly, but which already were handling the greater part of government business. By Mrs Thatcher's time, regular Cabinets were reduced to one a week, and the work of the committees was supplemented by a further, and 'perhaps more questionable' practice. Its characteristic was an informal group of Ministers under the chairmanship of the Prime Minister, bypassing the regular committees and taking important decisions itself. The membership of the group was fluctuating, and was dependent on the Prime Minister's confidence. Hailsham commented that the practice weakened the collegiate character of the Cabinet 'to some extent'. He might have put the point more strongly, and doubtless would, had he been lecturing at the time of a Labour Government. But in 1987 the practice, which concentrated yet more power in the Prime Minister's hands, and encouraged the development of an inner group of ministers who had earned their leader's favour, was no worse than 'questionable'.

27

Bereavement, Remarriage, Retirement

Quintin and Mary Hailsham visited Singapore and Australia in May of 1978. On the 10th, they were in Sydney and the intinerary for the afternoon read: 'At leisure: riding in Centennial Park'. Just before leaving England Mary had fallen off her horse in Richmond Park and bruised her back. It was like a premonition. Hailsham recorded the tragedy in Sydney in his diary.[1]

> There were 4 of us, two police officers, she and I. She had been so much looking forward to this ride and getting me on horseback again after 3 years . . . She (and I) had been afraid that I could not take it owing to my back. We walked for about 20 minutes. I then suggested we should trot, and we trotted for about 5 minutes. My right leg was almost useless owing to my ankle. She was so happy and chattering like a child. The officer on my right suggested a canter. Whilst we were still trotting she said gaily to me, I don't believe I have ridden so strong a horse for years. She was referring to the polo ponies in Richmond Park which she had been riding every week. These were the last words she ever spoke to me.

When the little party started to canter, Mary's horse immediately drew ahead. Her husband had some qualms, but she did not seem out of control and she had some experience as a rider. In any case, the police horses were trained and had been chosen for their docility. Mary's horse was soon out of sight round a bend. One of the officers suggested that he follow. It was too late. Her horse had gone off the track on to a tarmac road. When he got up to her, she was lying on her back in the road with legs outstretched, her head in a pool of blood. Although still alive, she never regained consciousness. She was not quite 59.

Hailsham wrote his account on the flight home, travelling with his wife's coffin on the plane. The air hostesses sat beside him, holding his hand as he cried. He paid tribute to their kindness, and to everyone who helped and comforted him, down to a young man 'who was our sort of ADC in Sydney. He was a sort of Jewish boy . . . could not have been kinder. He wished to accompany me to Heathrow, but I refused. I said I wished to be alone. Mary had taken to him at once.'

After he became Lord Chancellor, Mary had become happier than for a long time. She had been appointed a magistrate, which, he thought, 'gave her a really satisfying life after living so long under the shadow of her husband's career'. In 1980, he found a letter he had written to her while she was in Greece in 1977, which he could not bear to destroy. '. . . I miss you so much', he had said, 'and greatly look forward to having you once again at the helm. I am bound to get in a mess without you.'[2] In Sydney, she had been light-hearted and teased him a good deal. Away from the petty stresses of life at home, the days were an Indian summer, among the closest of their marriage. The shock of her death, in front of his eyes, was like a wholly unsuspected physical blow. He was plunged into a grief which shouted aloud. He felt desolate and guilty. Like many widowers, he could not appreciate his wife until it was too late, and only then found 'the virtue that possession would not show us, whiles it was ours'. To his brother-in-law by his first marriage with whom he always remained good friends, he wrote that he never realised how much he loved Mary until she was gone: 'Now I am a pelican (a water bird) in the wilderness, an owl (a woodland bird) in the desert, a sparrow (a gregarious bird) alone on the housetops. I am where the sun does not shine, no bird sings, no flowers bloom, no stars come out at night.'[3] The guilty grief was fearful. He vented it on a few close friends, sitting broken and weeping for hours. He bewildered his children by his apparently insatiable craving for comfort. He complained that his eldest daughter, Mary Claire, was leaving home. His youngest, then only 15, put him right. 'Might I bring up the question of Mary?' she wrote from school. 'You are saying she is deserting you; that is wrong. the fact is that Mary should have left 10 years ago when most girls leave home . . .' She followed up this sane judgment by assuring her father that she would not try to 'train' him and would allow him 'to retreat into a pile of fuming and very smelly compost if the need so arises'. 'The best thing to do is, as you already are, get out, dine with friends, try cases and if you get inspiration write a book.'[4]

Many asked him whether his religion was not a consolation to him. He always answered that it was not; and he disputed the unspoken premise on which the question seemed to be based, that the Christian religion is some kind of analgesic. The passage in C. S. Lewis's *A Grief Observed*, which he quoted in a sermon at All Souls in 1983, put his point.

> Talk to me about the truth of religion, and I'll listen gladly. Talk to me about the duty of religion, and I'll listen submissively. But don't come talking to me about the consolations of religion or I shall suspect that you don't understand.

He found to his surprise that his answer, far from making his questioners shocked or angry, had helped them in their own distress. In fact, he had a rare gift for understanding the bereavement of others. Some of the most touching of the letters he ever received are replies to his messages of consolation. Maurice Macmillan's widow told him that she carried his letter everywhere with her; Lady Spearman that his letter, which had 'so much of yourself in it', was a strength and comfort to her.[5] So many widows of his friends felt they could confide in him completely. One of these was Lady Diana Cooper, a long time friend who, in 1985 was in her 90s, crippled and dying. 'I loved you long ago', she wrote. 'Look in – that I may paint my face an inch thick and pretend in despair.'[6] He visited her soon afterwards. 'She was perfectly composed, not very deaf, a bit confused ... wished for nothing but "complete oblivion", did not wish to see all her friends "queueing up" to greet her on the other side ... Beautiful eyes rather dimmed. Make up good. Wise, intelligent, integrity, as ever.'[7]

Gradually, the storm of grief blew itself out. By 1980, there are occasional diary entries of lunch with Deirdre Shannon, the family friend who had first been his secretary in barristers' chambers. In 1981, he talked over dinner in Judges' lodgings with a twice married lady whose first husband had been killed in the War. She advocated marriage again, even at 73, for the companionship of both. ' "What would I have to offer at 73?" ... I pointed out it could not be long before I needed looking after with all the squalid accompaniments of old age ... I added, "How about the memories?" She then said, "After I married again I always thought [M] was there. There were always the 3 of us." "But did you feel that when you were a widow?" She: "Never. Of course, I have never told my husband nor, as a matter of fact, anyone else. I have never spoken of it before."' He was impressed by the advice, and he ended his note: 'As I approach the third May without darling M, life emptier than ever'.[8] The following year he brought himself to write to Natalie to ask if she had obtained an annulment of their marriage. After all that time, she had not lost her venom. She surmised rightly that he was hoping to marry a Catholic. As their own marriage in 1932 had not been recognised by Rome, how could any question of an annulment arise? Any humble parish priest, she said dismissively, would tell him as much.[9] The rebuff could still hurt, but he wrote to thank her for her letter. 'I hope we may meet again in heaven when all wrongs are forgotten as well as forgiven. I have paid heavily for my own shortcomings.'

He and Deirdre married in 1986. She at once devoted herself to looking after this elderly child, without thought of herself. No one could have done it so selflessly or so well. And in doing it, she surmounted a rare hurdle, by making herself uniformly and unreservedly loved by all five of Mary's children.

In June 1987, after the election, Margaret Thatcher told him that it was time for him to go. He was not expecting it, although afterwards he realised that he should have been ready. But there was no rancour or difficulty. He did not resent his successor being Sir Michael Havers, even though Havers was unwell, unlikely to last long and was made Lord Chancellor so that he could qualify for the pension. Hailsham thought that Havers deserved to be rewarded for his long service as Attorney-General, an office which does not carry a pension.[10]

The letters exchanged between the Prime Minister and her retiring Lord Chancellor were highly characteristic of each.

13 June '87

My dear Margaret,

Thank you so much for our talk this morning.

We both agreed that the time has come to lay aside my wig and put my father's gold robe back in its tin box. I hope I have worn it without dishonouring his memory.

It has been a great privilege to serve under you. At our last Cabinet before the election I told you that you had changed the face of British politics. This is now reinforced by the results of the election.

God bless you, and thank you for your patience and unfailing kindness.

You may always count on me to do anything in my power to help.

Yrs:

Q.

The 'Q' was finished with the famous swirl.

13 June 1987

My dear Quintin,

Thank you for your letter of today.

There can be few people in public life who have provided such service to our country as you have over the last 40 or more years. From your entry into Government in 1945 at the Ministry of Air to Lord High Chancellor of Great Britain, you have graced every office that you have held with supreme distinction and style. Your oratory on state occasions will be remembered always. And your trenchant advice on the issues of our time has been an enormous source of strength to the Government. Without doubt you are one of the great Lord Chancellors. What marvellous service the Hailsham family has given to our country.

I also thank you for the help you have given me personally. Your kindness and your wisdom in Cabinet has been of great value to me during my time as Prime Minister.

We shall all miss you greatly.

Yours ever,

Margaret

Even allowing for the laudatory conventions of such correspondence, every word of the Prime Minister's letter was felt. The old statesman and counsellor was leaving. Despite their disagreements, and unlike all her other Ministers, he could not be replaced. On his side, he dreaded what awaited him: oblivion and the long enfeeblement of age. 'Old age, you know – there's no future in it', he once said.[11] And he liked to tell the story of Lord Russell of Killowen, whose wife taunted him for not being able to hold the office of Lord Chancellor because he was a Roman Catholic. He told her that as Lord Chief Justice he was much better off because he was irremovable, whereas the Lord Chancellor had to go if his party were defeated at a General Election. 'And what', he is said to have asked her grandly, 'is an ex-Lord Chancellor but a seedy old gentleman with a stick and a pension?'[12]

He had his memories. Derek Hill, the painter, recalled how much he had enjoyed painting him towards the end of his time as Lord

337

Chancellor. (The painting is reproduced on the dust jacket of this book.) No wig because it always slipped off. Constant interruptions: the Prime Minister of Malaysia and a group of Indian ladies in saris arrived in turn. 'Come in, come in, I'm being painted!' Did he enjoy all this? Hill asked. No, he said, but Maggie did. 'She didn't want to see them all and I was supposed to be one of the sights of London.'[13] Derek Hill was among those who accompanied Hailsham on a regular summer weekend as the Queen Mother's guests at the Royal Lodge, Windsor. The guests sang ditties to the huge enjoyment of their hostess and themselves, including an irreverent version of 'La Marseillaise', attributed to the hand of Sir Edward Spears. Hailsham could usually be prevailed upon to oblige with a rendering of one or more of these traditional ditties, in which the tune was approximate only. He was a royalist of passionate conviction and admired the Queen Mother as 'a wonderful woman'.

He had his style as well. It was the man. A few weeks after retirement, on his way to give his daughter Mary Claire in marriage, he walks with two sticks, his top hat tilted back and his lace-up boots clearly visible. The dash and the defiance are still there.

Then there was the oratory of which Mrs Thatcher had written that it would always be remembered. The bicentennial celebration in 1981 of the British surrender at Yorktown was such an occasion. Sir Nicholas Henderson, the British Ambassador in Washington, reported to the Foreign Secretary on Hailsham's triumph, and he placed a copy in his diary.[14] The event presented the British with a difficulty, for, as the Ambassador remarked, 'we naturally realised that we could not win something now that we had lost 200 years ago'. But it was still hoped that something might be saved from the wreckage. The British military detachment numbered about 150 and included a regimental goat which, because of import and other restrictions, had to be hired locally 'but performed loyally for his temporary commanders'. The Ambassador had himself approached the Lord Chancellor. 'Ideally suited to the occasion by renown and maternal ancestry he was also able to out-trump two Heads of State [Presidents Reagan and Mitterand] if not in status, then by the personal impact made by having had a gallant forebear serving on the winning side at Yorktown.' (This was Captain Lytle, one of Hailsham's maternal antecedents, whose silver buckles retained by the family in England were said to have been worn by the Captain when he was in the party which received the British surrender.)

It was the personal impact which was decisive. Mitterand's speech, according to the Ambassador, although generous to Britain, was long and pedestrian, and his manner 'stiff and lifeless as if he were prematurely embalmed'. By contrast Hailsham's 'characteristic bravura' accomplished the twin purpose of preventing the French stealing all the thunder and reminding Americans of what their relationship with Britain had been since the dark days of siege. His battlefield speech was a stirring affair, calling up the scene two hundred years before, and contrasting it with the poignancy of revisiting the pastoral scene in time of peace. It ended with a poem of his own composition, the only one since he had stopped writing verse in 1963. 'Indeed', the Ambassador concluded, 'by many he was declared to have stolen the show . . .'

The days of retirement were taken up with writing and broadcasting, as well as faithful attendance every day at the House of Lords. Between 1990 and 1994, he produced two little books on the Constitution and on his philosophical beliefs, (*Lord Hailsham on the Constitution*, 1992 and *Values: Collapse and Cure*, 1994) the latter in facsimile of his own beautiful hand; as well as his principal autobiographical work, *A Sparrow's Flight*. Neither of the shorter books contained much original material. The work on the Constitution returned to the old theme of devolution to the regions, but he was no longer arguing for a written constitution or for a reformed House of Lords, as he had been during the dark days of Labour Government in the 70s. The Constitution, he concluded after thirteen years of continuous Tory Government, was 'essentially sound', although under strain: '. . . therefore reform is properly on the agenda'. The book is more interesting for its shift in the author's position than for the novelty of its analysis.

Values: Collapse and Cure was written in 1992 in a mood of depression. Hailsham at first attributed his low spirits to the political decline of his country since the war and the high hopes with which it ended. Later, he realised that his dejection was due more to the failure of belief which he observed round him in the things which had buoyed him up during his long life. Whatever the cause, the writing of the book served to cheer him up, for by the end he had become more hopeful. The heart of the matter is a restatement of his belief in the validity of value judgments, and his rejection of what he describes as the positivist fallacy that nothing exists which cannot be verified by measurement or observation. Reviewers objected that he was pushing at a wide open door in attacking a theory to which no one had subscribed for at least fifty years. It was, however, a remarkable thing for a Lord Chancellor, writing at the end of the twentieth century, to sustain a philosophical argument; and remarkable too that at the end of his life he should return again for guidance

339

to his grandfather Quintin Hogg's letter to a protegé troubled by religious doubt: 'Whatever else may be shaken, there are some facts established beyond the warrings of the theologians. Forever, virtue is better than vice, truth than falsehood, kindness than brutality.'

Hailsham wrote *A Sparrow's Flight* without verifying a single reference. 'I did not relish the long and tedious research into my own past . . .' he candidly admitted. He told his readers that, like Trollope, he had a certain contempt for autobiography. 'It tends to be either trivial, or self-justificatory or maliciously critical of others'. He explained why, notwithstanding these deterrents, he none the less embarked on a 400-page account of his life from the beginning. In 1975, he had written *The Door Wherein I Went*, intending it to be his last word, and marking the end of his public life. He looked forward to his remaining years, if not as ones of decent obscurity, then of serenity and modest comfort. Three years later, in what he called the greatest spiritual crisis of his existence, he had lost his wife of 34 years. He thought he should describe how he fared in that desperate time and how, after a year or two in opposition, he came to occupy the Woolsack for another eight years. The book, with its self-deprecating title, was not to be 'the ordinary sort of political autobiography'. It would simply tell the story of his life, 'my youth, my family, my friends, my children, my adventures, my pleasures, my thoughts as I remember them now'.

He was as good as his word. There were no revelations or indiscretions from the Cabinet room. He did not give anyone away. The story of his extraordinary life is told in a disarming way. But his decision not to consult any sources, and to rely instead on his formidable but now waning memory led to inaccuracies, some trivial, some not. There are also passages of the self-justification against which Trollope, and he himself, had warned. These were the consequence of a temperament which constrained him almost never to admit that he had been wrong. So, practically alone, he continued until his dying day to defend the Munich Settlement, and to believe and assert that he had been deprived of the Tory leadership by some sort of conspiracy.

The Door Wherein I Went is altogether a more unusual book. There is nothing quite like it among political memoirs. It starts with a declaration that it is a book about religion and philosophy. So it is for the first third of its length. Then it slips into a more conventional type of memoir at the point at which the author is drawn into government in 1956, and he admits, 'I seem to have become far more autobiographical than I had intended . . .'

The religious and philosophical speculations make up the more interesting part. This contains the fullest account of his journey from godlessness back to the faith which sustained him for the rest of his life. He proclaims this faith in a plain, homespun way. Once it was not out of the ordinary for autobiography to contain passages in which the writer bared his soul for the benefit and elevation of his readers. But not in this more sceptical, and perhaps more prim, age. Lord Lambton, reviewing the book for the *Times Literary Supplement*, confessed that he found 'these Christian effusions surprisingly naïve and faintly embarrassing'.[15] Lambton also disliked what he took to be a courtroom style. 'God and Christ and the Holy Ghost are put in the witness box, are fed convenient questions, are aided by convenient witnesses, and leave the Court triumphant. It is a queer sort of trial.' And Peregrine Worsthorne thought there was something 'complacent, even insensitive' about Hailsham's assumption that he could communicate his spiritual experience 'in the bluff and breezy manner chosen here'.[16]

No doubt the reviewers were embarrassed, but they missed some passages of penetrating simplicity: the author's explanation of the Trinity,[17] his account of the limitations of humanism,[18] and his view of Christian love.[19] The Greek word for Christian love, he wrote, was *agapé*, which was both more and less than 'love'. In the Greek sense, love for friends includes 'respect for their personalities as well as liking for them. It is what we feel for our nearest and dearest even when we are most exasperated by them. It is this, God help us, which Christ enjoins us to feel for our enemies. It is this against which there is no law.' There are also passages which are revealing of the author, perhaps more so than he intended. In chapters 10 and 11 he writes about what he calls the 'utility' of Christianity in a way which would hardly command general assent among believers: '. . . it would be an odd sort of religion', he remarks, 'which, though true, was of no practical value . . .'[20]

The faith regained which Lord Hailsham kept as the world around him became more cynical and more pagan was a simple one and, as he saw it, a rational one. 'I came to accept the rationality of the Christian faith . . . what had begun as a theoretical proposition based originally on a scepticism so complete that I was sceptical even of my own doubts became a matter of deepening experimentation and experience, and I could not live without it.'[21] His religion was a garden, he told an old friend, in which he walked alone in the evening with the door locked behind him.

Controversy disturbed the peace of the garden, and there was enough disputation in his life without its invading his beliefs. Argument among differing Christian persuasions always angered him. So when his successor, Lord Chancellor Mackay, was criticised by his own Wee Frees for attending the Roman Catholic requiem for Lord Russell of Killowen, he wrote to *The Times* at once. 'Whether or not the claim of Mr Donald MacLean that the Free Presbyterian Church of Scotland is a branch rather than an offshoot, a twig or a withered leaf of the Christian Church, is a matter of opinion, the answer to which can probably only be given by the Holy Spirit at the end of the present dispensation.' The ecumenical movement might have its faults but it had reintroduced into the Church the supreme duty of obeying the commandment to love one another.[22] He would have approved of Chaucer's Shipman who refused to listen to a preacher chopping doctrinal logic.

> He shal no gospel glosen here ne teche,
> We liven all in the gret God, quod he,
> He wolden sowen some difficultee.

In the end, though, *The Door Wherein I Went* leaves a feeling of some disappointment. Some of it is repetitious or trite, the argument is not coherent as a whole. But it is not for its flaws that it falls short. Its author might have brought to bear his enthusiasm, his philosophical sweep and his vast knowledge of the classical world in an outstanding book of reflections on his life and times. He never did. His best writing, since *The Case for Conservatism*, was always short: nothing as good as the terse, unpublished essay on the origins and history of the Tory party. Perhaps he lacked the inclination to sustain a long work. Perhaps a life in politics with its catch phrases and advertising slogans had induced a certain shallowness. Whatever it was, the failure to write as he surely could (and showed that he could in some passages in *The Door Wherein I Went*) seems to point up something of unfulfilled promise which was more general. Steeped in public affairs since childhood, the best academic achiever of his generation, an orator who could move audiences to their depths, he yet did not attain the highest offices of state. Coming to be Lord Chancellor with the best credentials of anyone since the War, his achievements there are open to debate. He left no monument to a half century as a devoted public servant.

What is the explanation? Partly, it was ill fortune. The chance of birth sent him to the Lords in 1950, just when his political promise might have flowered in the Commons. The chance of politics presented him with Harold Macmillan as leader, when a man less equivocal might have more fairly rewarded him for his part in the brilliant victory of 1959, and then led him with a steadier hand to succeed. Chance again put his candidacy for the leadership under the lights at Blackpool in 1963, the least auspicious circumstances possible. But the fault lay not only in his stars, but in himself. The streak of arrogance, the intolerance of any opinion but his own, the sheer rudeness which showed first in the nursery, was not worn smooth by human contact, at any rate until the mellower days of Lord Chancellorship and retirement. On the one hand was the formidable instrument of his intellect: on the other, emotions so near the surface that they broke through at times of stress and seemed to threaten the quality of his judgment.

Anger and tears, the visible signs of passion and generosity of spirit, are not often congenial to the Conservative party. They were part of the man. The anger had no malice, the passion was inspired by patriotism. He thought of his country in a special way, as having been selected by Providence for an exceptional destiny. He could not bear its slow but apparently inexorable decline, so at odds with its genius. Like Plantagenet Palliser, an inexhaustible love of his country was the ruling principle of his life but, unlike Trollope's Prime Minister, it did not have to be uncovered. Mary Fairfax, reporting for a Sydney newspaper, sat next to him at dinner in 1974, and was bowled over. 'Never in my life have I met a man of such quality . . . I think it is perhaps because he is consumed himself with a sort of holy and perpetual fire. This warmth, this total belief without fanaticism, is his communion . . . At the end of the dinner with this man who has done so much, written so much, and given so much to England, he said to me in his deep sonorous voice: 'I feel like an old man.' I went away feeling exalted, humbled and completely exhilarated.'[23]

Appendix 1

The Dockers' Cases of 1972

IN the first case, *Heatons Transport* v *Transport and General Workers Union* [1972] 3 WLR 73, the road hauliers, whose lorries were blacked by members of the Union, complained to the National Industrial Relations Court in May, 1972. The NIRC made an order against the Union restraining the blacking. But the action was unofficial, i.e. not authorised by the governing body of the Union, which had in fact been unsuccessfully trying to stop it. The blacking continued and the NIRC fined the Union. The Union appealed.

The Court of Appeal, with Lord Denning presiding, allowed the appeal on June 13, and held that the Union was not responsible for the unofficial acts of its shop stewards, which the Union itself had tried to stop. The decision dismayed the Government. *The Times* said that it had driven a coach and six through the new Act. If Unions could not be made responsible for their own shop stewards, complaints would have to be made against the individual men. If, as was most likely, the men refused to comply with orders of the NIRC, they would ultimately be sent to prison for contempt. In the prevailing climate, sending workmen to prison was likely to lead to a widespread strike, accompanied perhaps by violence. *The Times* reported that senior Ministers were shocked by the Court of Appeal ruling and assumed that the issue would be taken to the House of Lords.

The assumption was correct, but in the meantime the second case, *Churchman* v *Joint Shop Stewards Committee* [1972] 1 WLR 1094 had started. The dispute was between two groups of men, the dockworkers and the workers at the container depot, both of whom belonged to the same Union (the Transport and General Workers Union), and the circumstances were similar to those in the *Heatons* case. But this time, in face of the Court of Appeal's decision in

Heatons, the NIRC was unable to fine the Union, and instead it made orders committing three shop stewards to prison. The men were not to be arrested until the following afternoon (Friday 16 June 1972) to give them a final opportunity to desist or explain. At the news that the three were to be sent to prison, 35,000 dockers up and down the country stopped work. More than a hundred ships lay idle in British ports.

It was at this point that the Official Solicitor made his appearance. This officer, of whose existence the public was quite unaware, is a servant of the Court whose duties are to fill gaps in the legal system, and in particular to represent the interests of those involved in legal processes who cannot or will not help themselves; children, the mentally disabled and those, like the three dockers, committed to prison for contempt of court.

On the Friday on which the dockers were to be arrested, just before the Court sittings resumed for the afternoon session, two Counsel who had represented the Union in the *Heatons Case*, Mr Peter Pain QC and Mr Ian Hunter, consulted Lord Denning privately in his room.* They had been following the *Churchman Case* closely but were not representing anyone in it. Since both the liberty of the subject and the national interest were involved, they considered that the case should be brought before the Court of Appeal at once. Lord Denning, who had been joined by his two colleagues, Lords Justices Buckley and Roskill, invited the Official Solicitor to assist.

The Official Solicitor had been sent the Court file by the NIRC and had been considering the case with his own Counsel, Mr Robert Alexander. They had both formed the view that the evidence was insufficient to support the committal orders. Lord Denning suggested that Mr Pain and Mr Hunter should join Mr Alexander in advising the Official Solicitor: if they were all of one mind, his Court would interrupt the case it was hearing that afternoon to deal with the Official Solicitor's application. The application, to free the three men threatened with imprisonment, was made an hour or so later, and was successful. The decision unleashed a torrent of publicity. At first the three were disconcerted. Their martyrdom, and the national strike which they were sure would follow, had been snatched from them. The *Daily Mirror* reported one of them as saying, with unconscious irony, 'It's a bloody liberty!' But on reflection, the dockers claimed the decision as a famous victory.

Although the crisis was averted for the time being, the Lord

* Sir Peter Pain, who later became a High Court Judge, has kindly provided a note of his recollection. With his permission, it is printed at the end of this appendix.

Chancellor was very much concerned. The Denning decision in the *Heatons Case* was dismaying, but the Court of Appeal could not be said to have acted improperly. Its decision was a defensible view of the law. But this was different. Lord Hailsham thought that Lord Denning had instigated the Official Solicitor to act. In any case, there was widespread misconception about the Official Solicitor. He was thought by many to be an agent of the Government who had intervened to prevent the paralysis of the ports. In fact, Ministers knew nothing about the Official Solicitor's move until they read about it in the newspapers the next morning. Lord Denning did his best to stop ill-informed speculation by making a public statement from the bench explaining what had happened,* but misunderstanding continued.

The third case, *Midland Cold Storage* v *Turner* [1972] ICR 230, brought a renewal of the crisis. Proceedings before the NIRC were brought against seven dockers engaged in blacking. The dockers did not appear and were not represented, but the Official Solicitor briefed Counsel to appear as *amicus curiae*. The NIRC took every precaution to prevent a repetition of the *Churchman Case* in which the Court of Appeal had, in effect, told Sir John Donaldson's Court that it had committed the dockers to prison on inadequate evidence. As a result of the Official Solicitor's submissions, two of the seven dockers dropped out, but the remaining five were ordered to be jailed for defiance of the Court's order. Once again the dockers came out on strike.

In his book, *The Closing Chapter* (p. 175) Lord Denning says that on 25 July 1972, four days after the five dockers were committed, his clerk received a message that an application might be made to his Court about the five dockers. But nothing happened. Denning attributes this to 'intense activity behind the scenes'. The next day, the 26th, the House of Lords gave their decision in the *Heatons Case* ([1972] AC 15). In a unanimous judgment they reversed the Court of Appeal and held that the Union *was* responsible for the acts of shop stewards, and they restored the fines against the Union. That afternoon, the Official Solicitor applied to the NIRC for release of the five dockers who had been committed to prison in the *Midland Cold Storage Case*. Sir John Donaldson ordered their release, saying: 'The Lords' judgment makes it clear that the primary method of enforcement contemplated by the Industrial Relations Act is against the funds of organisations rather than against individuals ... This afternoon the situation is entirely changed.' The crisis was defused.

* [1972] 1 WLR 1101: Lord Denning's statement is reproduced at the end of this appendix.

Lord Denning did not conceal his belief that in the *Midland Cold Storage Case* the Official Solicitor was 'told by someone to hold his hand' so that the House of Lords could rush out its judgment in the *Heatons Case* (*The Due Process of Law* p. 39). The effect of that judgment was to enable the NIRC to release the five dockers and avert the industrial crisis, while at the same time shutting out the Court of Appeal.

It is possible that the House of Lords decision was brought forward; but there is no basis whatever for thinking that the Official Solicitor had allowed himself to be influenced by anyone. Mr Norman Turner, who then held that office, acted throughout with commendable independence and complete propriety – under difficult, unprecedented circumstances. He provided himself with the best legal advice at every stage. He has explained that when the committal orders against the five dockers were made in the *Midland Cold Storage Case*, both he and the experienced Counsel whom he briefed, Mr John Vinelott QC and Mr Robert Alexander, were satisfied that there was no ground as there had been in the *Churchman Case*, for an appeal.*

What then happened? It is impossible to be certain, because the evidence is incomplete. On 25 July, four days after the five dockers were committed in the *Midland Cold Storage Case*, and the same day as that on which Lord Denning said his clerk received intimation of a possible appeal, Lord Hailsham's engagement diary records that the Lord Chief Justice, Lord Widgery, telephoned early in the morning. He asked Hailsham whether the Judges did not now have a responsibility to bring the crisis to an end. Hailsham said that that would happen if and when the decision of the Court of Appeal (in *Heaton*) was reversed. He explained that judgment by the House of Lords would be given the next day (26th) 'and it is confidently expected' that the Court of Appeal would be reversed. This might lead to the release of the five imprisoned dockers. The diary entry continues: 'It is important that the House of Lords decision should be given Wednesday [26th] rather than Thursday [27th] when the dockers' delegates are meeting to discuss Jones-Aldington'.†

It may be significant that when the Official Solicitor attempted to apply to the NIRC on 25 July to submit that some term should be put on the incarceration of the five dockers, he was informed that a

---

* I am greatly indebted to Mr Turner for giving his very full recollection of events.

† HLSM: LC Diaries 5. Mr Jack Jones, the General Secretary of the Transport and General Workers Union, and Lord Aldington, the Chairman of the Port of London Authority, had been appointed to make recommendations on severance pay and other terms of service for redundant dockers. Their interim report was made available to both sides of the industry on 24 July and was rejected by the dockers on 27 July.

Court could not be assembled until the following day (the day when the House of Lords decision in *Heaton* was given). It would have been normal in a case of such importance concerning the liberty of the subject to have treated it as one of the first urgency. However, no further degree of certainty is possible.

Note on the Churchman Case by Sir Peter Pain

The National Industrial Relations Court (chairman Sir John Donaldson) made an order committing three dockers to prison for contempt, but directed that it should not take effect before 2 p.m. on a Friday. The contempt consisted in the industrial action which they were taking. His hope and intention was that they should go before the Court of Appeal on Friday and purge their contempt by promising to cease their industrial action.

On the Friday morning the solicitors for the T. & G.W.U. asked me to stand by to make an application to the Court of Appeal on behalf of one of the dockers who was a union member. I asked to see the papers and when I looked at them it appeared that the committal order had been wrongly made. Committal is a highly technical process and there was some error (I forget what) in the procedure. I let the Union know of this. But they said that their member had declined to be represented. So I was without instructions.

It was inevitable that the arrests, if they took place, would lead to a national dock strike. I felt it was disastrous to have a strike over a court order that had been incorrectly made. I therefore went to see Lord Denning privately to explain the difficulty. He saw the point immediately and drew the other Lords Justices, who were sitting with him, into discussion. I volunteered to raise the matter as *amicus curiae* without fee, if they would hear me in open court. Lord Denning said that I should be properly instructed and called upon the services of the Official Solicitor.

One of the functions of the Official Solicitor is to assist those who have been committed to prison for contempt and who are without legal advice. He told me that he was *au fait* with this case and that he had already consulted junior counsel, Robert Alexander (now Lord Alexander). He then formally instructed me to make application to the Court of Appeal with Alexander as my junior. Lord Denning had already indicated that, as this was a matter of urgency, he would adjourn the case he was currently hearing. Meanwhile Miss Caws, who was junior counsel for the applicant, was asked to appear.

In the course of Friday afternoon I made the application and was able to persuade the Court of Appeal that the order of the N.I.R.C. was wrongly made. So the appeal was allowed and the dockers, who had no idea of what had been going on, and who had been expecting to be arrested, remained at liberty.

Lord Denning's Statement from the Bench: 19 June 1972

LORD DENNING M.R. (sitting with Buckley L.J. and Roskill L.J.) Before we start our list today, in view of the speculation which has been going on in some quarters as to how an application came to be made to us on Friday afternoon, June 16, I would just like to say exactly what happened.

On Thursday, June 15, at about midday, our Official Solicitor was invited by the secretary to the National Industrial Relations Court to appear at the hearing in that court which was to be held today (Monday, June 19) and instruct counsel as amicus curiae to assist that court in dealing with the contempt aspect of the case. The Official Solicitor at once retained Mr Robert Alexander as counsel. Both considered the papers overnight ready for a conference. That was held. Each was independently of the opinion that there were grounds for thinking that the orders had not been properly made in the light of the evidence before the court. It was decided to attend on the Monday morning in any case, but both considered that it might well be proper to make an immediate application to the Court of Appeal in the afternoon. Meanwhile that morning Mr Pain and Mr Ian Hunter, who had each been involved in the litigation arising out of the container dispute, had kept themselves informed of developments. They had no instructions from anyone in the matter, but felt that, as the freedom of the individual was at stake as well as the national interest, someone ought to bring the matter before the Court of Appeal at the earliest moment. They therefore decided to ask to see me personally in chambers to inquire what would be a proper course for them to take. They wondered whether they should come to the court as amici curiae. They came to see me a few minutes before two o'clock. My colleagues joined me at once. We felt that it was a case in which the court might invite the assistance of the Official Solicitor and we asked him to come. The Official Solicitor then told us of the steps which he had already taken including the advice which he had received from Mr Alexander. We then invited the Official Solicitor to discuss the matter with Mr Pain and Mr Hunter in order that each might have the benefit of the other's views and that the Official Solicitor should then take such steps as he thought proper. He then received advice from all three counsel, and in the light of that advice he took the decision to apply to the Court of Appeal that afternoon and Mr Pain agreed to accept the leading brief. The rest of the proceedings all took place in open court and are well known.

Appendix 2

This essay was written as an added first chapter for a hardback edition of *The Case for Conservatism* which Faber and Faber intended to publish in 1949. For reasons which cannot now be discovered, it was not proceeded with, and the essay has until now remained unpublished.

The Nature and History of British Conservatism

No free politics have ever existed without a radical and a conservative party. Examples can be given from the days of Greece and Rome to the present. But the classical, and characteristic, development of the never ending and never completed struggle between these two strongly opposed, yet mutually interdependent, policies has been in the rise to fame of the British people. Conservatism exists everywhere. British Conservatism, like British radicalism, is something so intensely national and individual that the history of its outlook and development demand a separate, and impartial, treatment.

British Conservatism is at once the product, and in part the cause, of the peculiar development of the two party system. This British institution, unofficial yet indispensable, often denied yet never long departed from, voluntary yet in control of all the means of power, lies at the heart of our working constitution and our political history. It is seldom praised; it is often misunderstood, but without an understanding of it none of our other institutions is fully intelligible, nor can their operation be possible unless its efficient working were always taken for granted. In the words of Professor Berriedale Keith: 'Party is, as matters stand, the essential mode of working the British Constitution'. Disraeli put the same idea more strongly still: 'You can have no Parliamentary Government if you have no Party Government'.

The survival of the two party system is neither arbitrary nor inevitable. The party line corresponds to deep natural cleavages. But its retention is a matter of conscious policy, a matter requiring the deepest understanding of politics and the most subtle of relationships between political opponents. The division into two parties, one radical, and one conservative, pre-supposed by our working constitution, presents the public with the appearance of a dilemma, the necessity for making a choice, often difficult, sometimes a painful choice between two bodies of men, each sincerely attached to the country's interest. But the necessity for making choices in this world is at once the justification of the system which compels a choice to be made, and the explanation of its continuing success.

At the same time, public opinion is a continuum, not a dichotomy. The necessity for a real and responsible choice is the justification of the division; it remains tolerable only because by custom neither alternative involves the adoption of an extreme. Radicalism is not revolution. Conservatism is not reaction. These are the twin pillars of British Constitutional theory and practice.

To quote Macaulay: 'It would not be difficult to compose a lampoon or a panegyric upon either of these renowned factions. The truth is, and though parties have often seriously erred, England could have spared neither . . . In the sentiments of both, there is something to approve. But of both the best specimens will be found not far from the common frontier. The extreme section of one class consists of bigoted dotards. The extreme section of the other consists of shallow and reckless empirics'.

Extremism and party dogma go well at annual conferences or dinner parties, but moderation and even compromise are the guiding principles of practical statesmen. There are some who claim always that this argues a want of principle, a tendency to be ruled by mere expediency. I reply with confidence that moderation *is* a principle, the principle of Greek philosophy of English political wisdom. Moderation is also one of the guiding characteristics of British Conservatism.

Historians differ as to the date at which it can be said that a Conservative party began to exist in this country.

Their differences, however, can in the main be traced to differences of opinion as to the significance of facts rather than differences as to facts themselves. Some, like Professor Hearnshaw, stress the timelessness of the Conservative attitude to life.

'Conservatism in the sense of a spirit opposed to radicalism, i.e. as a spirit opposed to that of rash innovation – can be traced right back to the Garden of Eden itself. In that visionary abode of bliss Adam was the person who represented the conservative qualities of contentment and stability. Eve was the innovator, eager for novelty, ready for reckless experiment, liable to be led away by any such seductive slogan as 'Eat More Fruit', or 'Free Fig Leaves for All'.

Others, concerned to demonstrate its particular origins in English history, trace its birth, like Professor Feiling, to the religious controversies of the sixteenth century.

If this means that conservative sentiment can be traced to this fount of origin, few will be inclined to differ. On the other hand, we may legitimately demand a greater degree of organisation in tracing the birth of a political party.

But it is fair to see in the Anglican settlement the roots of modern political Conservatism which, like other political differences, can be traced without doubt to the religious revolution at the time of the Reformation and after.

As a result of this revolution England emerged with a Church settlement which was unique. On the continent the dispute between Church and State resolved itself into one of three main solutions. Either the state became purely secular (as in post-revolution France), or the establishment almost entirely Erastian (as in Prussia), or, as in the case of the Catholic Monarchies, the Church remained ultramontane, and therefore potentially hostile to the National State. The Elizabethan settlement was none of these. In its claim to continuity with the pre-reformation Church, in its retention of the Catholic creeds and orders, in its maintenance of legal forms, above all in its claim that the State was not purely secular, nor the Church merely national, it retained much of the spirit of the Middle Ages. Nevertheless it effected substantial change with the minimum interruption of the organic life of the nation. The Elizabethan settlement is the starting point of modern politics, and the unity of the nation which Elizabeth sought to achieve by moderate change the source of inspiration for the great Anglican Conservatives of the seventeenth century.

Nevertheless, we must look to the disputes under the Stuarts before we can assert the existence of any political organisation with any claim to continuity with the modern Conservative party.

There are definite traces of a Party Organisation in Parliament at least as early as the reign of James I. Porritt in his book, 'The Unreformed Parliament', cites one instance in this reign of a written 'Whip' underscored in the modern manner by as many as six lines on behalf of the King's Party.

Here again, however, there is nothing to show continuity between this organisation and what afterwards came to be known as the Tory Party, indeed nothing to show that it was not a mere collection of individuals drawn together by ambition or individual interest to support the policy of the Court.

A political party requires principles as well as organisation. Modern political parties cannot be said to have arisen before the reign of Charles I.

Macaulay and Professor Hearnshaw derive the origin of the Whig and Tory Parties from the Autumn Session of the Parliament of 1641. The first session of the Parliament, which Charles had been compelled to summon in 1640, had united against the King in order to abolish the various innovations which had been introduced into the constitution by the Tudors, and latterly by Charles I and Laud.

Professor Hearnshaw writes: 'Having secured their position by means of a Perpetuation Act and a Triennial Act they proceeded to abolish Edward IV's Council of the North, Henry VIII's Star Chamber, Henry VIII's Council of Wales, Elizabeth's High Commission Court, and sundry other tribunals that lay outside the sphere of the Common Law. Similarly, they declared illegal all those novel or antique devices such as "Ship money" by means of which the King had endeavoured to evade the necessity of summoning Parliament'.

Up to this point, however, 'radicals' and 'conservatives' were agreed. But from September 1641 the famous party division began to appear for the first time in English History.

'The Conservative Reformers – Falkland, Hyde, Colepeper, and their fellows – were satisfied. They felt that Parliament had once again been established in its proper place in the constitution. Hence they cried a halt to opposition. Not so, however, their more progressive puritan and Parliamentary allies – Pym, Hampden, Cromwell, and their friends'.

In his more sonorous prose, Macaulay makes approximately the same point.

Conservatism was from the first, therefore, a constitutional movement. Its earliest leaders adhered to the principles of monarchy as it was then understood. They had no part or lot with the radicalism of the Puritans. None the less, by their action in the first session of the Long Parliament they clearly showed that, faced with a choice between the traditional constitution as they understood it, and an arbitrary rule by a monarch whose title to govern they none the less defended, the leaders of the party favoured constitutional and rejected absolute Government.

The emergence of party strife at the beginning of the Long Parliament was premature, since Parliamentary and Constitutional rule suffered an interruption by reason of the Civil War in which the prototypes of the Conservatives fought with the King, even as the prototypes of all radicals fought with the Parliament. The appeal to arms was uncongenial to the better spirits on both sides. But the decisive movement of public opinion at the Restoration back to legitimate monarchy, no less than Cromwell's repeated groping after a reconstitution of the monarchy with himself as King, proved how well founded and necessary for the times and for the nation were the institutions which the Cavaliers fought and died to save.

In spite of the break created by the Civil War, the continuity of English Conservatism between the first emergence of party in the Parliament of 1641 and the later birth of the Tory party after the Restoration is sufficiently demonstrated that Hyde – one of the younger leaders of the earlier group – re-emerged in 1660 as the first great Minister of the Restoration.

From the reign of Charles II, party history can be treated as almost continuous. Almost from the first, two great parties appeared, corresponding in the broad to the old division between Cavalier and Roundhead. At first these were called the Court and Country parties, then Abhorrers and Petitioners (or more vulgarly Pets and Horrors). But in 1679 the two factions were finally known as Whigs and Tories.

These labels, apparently first used during the struggles about the Exclusion Act, are among the most convenient party names ever devised for the purposes of political controversy. They are short; they are faintly derisory, and, best of all, they are absolutely meaningless, so that what is intended to be a badge of shame may be accepted by those to whom it is applied as an honourable symbol, like Fluellen's leek. Small wonder that they lasted for centuries, and that one, Tory, remains part of the living language to this day.

It may be claimed that up to this stage English Conservatism had pursued a consistent course. It was Anglican, it was Royalist, it was Parliamentarian. Forced to choose between the traditional constitution, and the King, it chose the constitution; but when the choice was the King or Parliament without the King, it chose the King. Finally, forced to choose between the King and the Church of England, it reluctantly chose the Church of England – on the condition that the institution of monarchy was carefully preserved.

The life of the first Tory party may be said to date from 1660 and to last until 1714. Its unique and permanent achievement was the Restoration. Its most lasting contribution to Foreign Affairs was the settlement of Utrecht; its most discreditable episode the means of achieving this settlement – the occasion of its disaster, the Hanoverian succession.

But perhaps the most significant event in its career was the Glorious Revolution of 1688. This, after the Anglican settlement, did more to fix the permanent character of Conservatism in this island than any other factor in our earlier history. Not all the rhetoric of Macaulay alters the fact that the 'Glorious Revolution' was the product of a coalition between the two parties. Burke has proved its essentially conservative character, just as Macaulay emphasised its radical features. The truth is that, faced with a choice between the King, in whose right they believed, and the Church, whose existence the King's policy appeared to threaten, and the unity of the nation, which would have been disrupted by a threat to the Reformation settlement, the majority of Tories abandoned the King. Even when faced with the Hanoverian succession (which all Tories regarded with abhorrence) a large section of them, charmingly known as 'Whimsicals', preferred George I to the Pretender, and an even larger section would not disturb the peace of the realm in order to bring the Pretender back.

Nevertheless, the debacle of 1714 virtually brought the old Tory Party to an end – smashed by the intransigence and Catholicism of the Stuarts, and brought to political ruin by the opportunism and want of principle of Bolingbroke. The long Whig hegemony began and Toryism went underground, with the inevitable result that Parliament, deprived of the healthy competition of two vigorous parties, became corrupt and, ceasing to reflect the genuine clash of ideas in the public mind, fell into disrepute.

The second Tory party was an entity almost entirely separate from the first. Indeed, it is only by a considerable exercise of ingenuity that historians claim to prove its pedigree.

Bolingbroke, pardoned but not reinstated, discredited but still a genius unimpaired, gave to the world a series of political writings which profoundly influenced two younger contemporaries, each of whom, although personally antagonistic to the other, played a decisive part in creating a new Tory party.

The first of these was William Pitt, Earl of Chatham, a Whig, whose belief that the party system was an evil can be traced directly to the inspiration of Bolingbroke's writings. As a result, he favoured a system of Government by the best men of both parties – an attractive chimera which has constantly deceived some of the noblest minds in our history. Chatham's last government was an attempt to form a cabinet above party; the attempt was a spectacular failure, but hastened the collapse of the Whig predominance.

The second personality upon whom the work of Bolingbroke had such a profound influence was George III himself. Bolingbroke's 'The Patriot King' had originally been written for George's elder brother who had died before coming to the throne. George III, the first of the Hanoverians with predominantly English tastes and interests, set himself the task of using the immense patronage and political influence of the Crown to achieve a political connection which would 'dish the Whigs'.

In itself the attempt was as disastrous as it was wrong-headed. Professor Hearnshaw describing the situation writes:

'Not unnaturally the attempt of abnormal incapacity to deal with abnormal complexity resulted in chaos. Rarely has a great nation, in the absence of any sudden catastrophe, sunk so rapidly, or so completely from the summit of prosperity and glory to the abyss of humiliation and disaster as did the British peoples during the two decades of George's personal misrule'.

The ultimate result of the political confusion which followed the successful revolt of the American colonies was the selection by King George III of a young man of twenty-four to be his principal Minister, at first without a majority in the House of Commons. William Pitt the younger became Prime Minister at the end of 1783 as a result of the King's determination to be rid of the Coalition between Fox, Portland and a section of the Tories. Pitt was successful at the election of 1784 and the party which he created was undoubtedly the foundation upon which the Second Tory Party (1792–1832) was built.

The birth of modern Conservatism which sprung from these admittedly inauspicious beginnings is dated by Lord Hugh Cecil from the moment in 1792 when Edmund Burke, hitherto an orthodox Whig, prevailed upon his companions to cross the floor and ally themselves with Pitt. The political alliance thus made formed the hard core of resistance to the sansculottism of the French Revolution and the Caesarist ambitions of Napoleon. It had to face the longest and perhaps the most arduous war in our history. Whatever of pre-eminence for herself and her ideas Britain won in the nineteenth century was founded on the achievements of these fateful years. If in its decadence the second Tory party was misguided, and if its final end was ignominious, the solid foundation which it provided for the conduct of the war, and the secure basis of lasting peace which concluded it, places the nation for ever in its debt. Some of the most illustrious names in British history – Burke,

Canning, Castlereagh, Peel, Wellington, and even young Palmerston, and the youthful Gladstone, were among its members. And if it also numbered its Addingtons and its Liverpools, there can be few political combinations that have not fallen from time to time under the sway of mediocrities.

The final defeat of the Second Tory Party was due to its inability to maintain the early promise of Pitt's proposed reforms, and its consequent failure to solve the demand for a broader basis of political power made by the rising middle class. That this was due to the fear of radical reforms created first by the experience of men who had seen the revolution in France, and then by the need to maintain public order and security during a long and frequently disastrous continental war, may be an explanation, but offers no excuse. After a period of glorious achievement abroad, the Second Tory Party fell, because it failed to learn Burke's lesson that a nation that is without the means of renewing its institutions is also without the means of conserving them. The Second Tory Party went down in ruin before a revived Whig and Liberal Coalition on the issue of reform. Since 1832 there has been no party legitimately entitled to the name, or even the traditions of Tory. Nevertheless the Conservative Party, which succeeded it, can prove its Tory pedigree by the continuity of its leading personalities.

The name, and the fact of modern Conservatism, can be derived from as early as 1834, two years after the defeat of the Tories and the passage of the first Reform Bill.

If this view be right, Peel was the founder of the Conservative Party. Defeated over a single issue, the Tories had to make up their minds whether to lose themselves amid the bogs and quagmires of reaction or to become a rational Parliamentary party, devoted to tradition, but accepting change constitutionally enacted even in their own despite, and playing their own part, in the tradition of Burke, the Revolution of 1688, and the Anglican settlement, in enacting reforms consonant with the National tradition. Peel chose the latter course, and the choice was thrust upon him by the curious events of 1834 which led him to accept office for a short time as Prime Minister to preside over the General Election of that year.

His election Manifesto – the equivalent of 'let us face the future' – took the form of his own election address to his constituents. This document, the Charter of the new Conservative Party, contained the following clear and definite statement which anchors Conservatism to democracy and Parliamentary Government:

'I consider the Reform Bill a final and irrevocable settlement of a great constitutional question – a settlement which no friend to the peace and welfare of this country could attempt to disturb either by direct or by insidious means.'

Peel afterwards claimed that, by his foundation and leadership of this new political connection both in victory, and later in disaster, he prevented the emergence in Britain in a revolutionary form of the continental outbreaks of 1840. There is much to commend it in this claim.

Peel's new Conservative Party achieved one single political triumph – Peel dominated the Government from 1841 to 1846 – and then broke into fragments over the Corn Laws in 1846.

In effect, this collapse was due to a cleavage between the old territorial connection of Toryism and the new manufacturing and commercial class of which Peel and Gladstone were both representatives. Peel claimed that his repeal of the Corn Laws saved England from revolution. I believe this to be true; but in my judgment historians rightly condemn Peel for carrying through the reform himself. Having convinced himself that his election platform was no longer maintainable in the public interest, he should have announced that he had reached this conclusion and resigned, supporting in the lobby a Radical Government for whom repeal of the Corn Laws was consonant with their pledges. Had he done so the political history of the nineteenth century would have been far more evenly balanced.

Indeed, he attempted to take this course, but when Russell, to quote Disraeli's famous phrase, handed him back the poisoned chalice, he elected to carry through the necessary measures himself. The result was that he split his party; and, by a circumstance unfortunate for Peel, the dissidents contained within their ranks not merely the solid platoons of the agricultural members, but a statesman of genius whom his less prudent colleagues had compelled him to exclude from Ministerial office. This was Disraeli, whose brilliant attacks on Peel brought his new Conservative Party to ruin which appeared irretrievable.

By a strange irony, the Conservative Party was destined to have its fortunes restored by the devoted and patient labours, extending over forty years, of the very man who brought Peel down.

In the course of this work, Disraeli was compelled to unlearn much of the philosophy with which he had begun his early career; by the like token it was his own function to educate what had begun as a mere reactionary rump relying on nothing more constructive than the dumb resentment of the countryside against the dominion of urban civilisation, to an understanding of the true function of Conservatism in a democracy.

Although at the head of a party predominantly agricultural and aristocratic, Disraeli realised that the future lay with the 'suffering millions' – the inarticulate proletariat of the towns, to whom, he held, Conservatives must appeal against the smug materialism of the industrial magnate and the man of commerce. This intuition was based on a genuine sympathy, and was always matched throughout his career by a practical programme designed to attract the support of the wage earning class. 'The Palace is not safe', he said with his usual grandiloquence, 'when the cottage is not happy', and it is no coincidence that during his leadership Conservative Governments passed Acts which today form the Charter of freedom for Trade Unions, and the basis of Public Health administration, as well as that Reform Act which first gave the franchise to the weekly wage earner in the towns.

After the debacle of 1846 it took nearly thirty years – until 1874 to be precise – for Disraeli to recreate a party capable of facing its Liberal antagonists almost on equal terms.

The modern Conservative Party is founded upon the solid foundations of this work – surprisingly little improved upon and even now Conservatives refer back to the pre-election speeches of 1870–74 which brought them back into power, for a clear and compendious statement of principle and policy.

Since 1874 the Conservative Party, alternating between office and opposition, has enjoyed a continuous and on the whole prosperous existence as one of the two major parties in the state. It suffered one loss of strength prior to 1906, when a number of its supporters, including Mr Winston Churchill, joined the Liberals on the issue of Free Trade. Three times it gained notable accretions of strength from the internal divisions of its opponents – from the Liberal Unionists during the Home Rule controversy, from the Right Wing Liberals in the years between the wars, and even from a section of the Labour Party in 1931.

It has twice suffered severe electoral defeats – both times after substantial periods of ascendance in 1906 and in 1945. On both occasions, as I maintain, and as many who do not agree will concede, the electoral balance swung so far the other way as to endanger and disturb the fair working of the Constitution.

It has seven times been in opposition – in 1880, for a few months in 1886, in 1892, from 1906–1915, from 1923–1924, and from 1929–1931, and now again from 1945.

It has formed seven administrations, from 1874–1880, from

1886–1892, from 1895–1906, from 1922–1923, from 1924–1929, and (if we omit its political allies) from 1931–1940, and the caretaker Government of 1945.

It has taken part in three coalitions – for a few months in 1885, from 1915–1922, from 1940–1945 – of which the last two involved the most strenuous period of both world wars.

Its catastrophe of 1906 did not, nor need that of 1945 necessarily be expected to, resemble in severity any of the earlier calamities. Experience seems to show that public opinion will always swing back to a great party which remains united and true to a living principle and policy. Periods of opposition for any party are no bad thing in such circumstances. The catastrophe of parties is brought about by inner divisions – such as those on the Hanoverian succession in 1714, or on the fiscal question in 1846. Defeats which do not divide but are followed by constructive leadership, like that of 1832, do not destroy great political connections; and those which, like those of 1906, are accompanied by divisions, are not fatal when other and more fundamental issues supervene.

The role of Conservatism in the politics of a free society is permanent, and in the last resort unchanging. The philosopher Hegel analysed the development of all human thought into three stages – thesis, antithesis, synthesis. He was well aware that in doing so he was making an abstract, and in some ways arbitrary, division of the concrete, and continuous process of logical thinking. Each 'synthesis' becomes in turn the 'thesis' of a new series. Moreover, since the process is continuous, each 'antithesis' can be treated as a thesis, the following synthesis as an antithesis, and the stage after this as a synthesis.

Arbitrary as it may be, the distinction serves well enough to describe the evolutionary nature of the logical process and, expressed in the language of this terminology, the function of British Conservatism is neither compromise nor reaction. It is synthesis, a genuine reconciliation between conflicting principles, based not on expediency, or the higgling of the political market, but on a more profound analysis and a higher level of thought.

In the nineteenth century, the thesis was provided by the traditional society of Britain as that society had developed after the religious changes of the sixteenth, and the political revolution of the seventeenth centuries; a society aristocratic, mercantilist, agricultural, but fundamentally Christian. Liberalism, commercial, industrial, rationalist, capitalistic, was the 'antithesis'. The function of Conservatism in the nineteenth century was to find a synthesis between two Britains. Thanks to the genius of Peel and Disraeli, by the end of the nineteenth century this synthesis was more or less triumphantly achieved.

At this point the new series began to present itself. The thesis of this series was the conclusion of the old – the Liberal secular state more or less successfully grafted on to the traditional British Polity in which laisser faire had become temporarily the predominant economic doctrine.

Of this thesis, Liberal – imperialist, commercial, capitalist Britain, Socialism is the obvious and natural antithesis, presented less by Marxists and Leninists than by the Shaws, the Wellses, and the Webbs. The object of the new Conservatism is the new synthesis, the grafting of the new successfully upon the old.

Yet even as this synthesis is in process of achievement, a fresh series has already begun. The thesis is Fabian Socialism grafted upon the traditionalist – Liberal stock. Of this thesis, Conservatism has to supply the antithesis, the new doctrine which will rid Socialism of its defects, and offer a counterpoise to its excesses and eccentricities. Only so can a new synthesis be looked for in which the essentials of good Government can be secured.

Note on Sources

Papers

The most important source is naturally Lord Hailsham's personal papers deposited in Churchill College Archives Centre, Cambridge, under the code 'HLSM'. These consist of some 1500 files which are uncatalogued but listed by subject in a card index. The references in the Notes are to this index which is provisional only, but when it is replaced by a definitive catalogue, the provisional list will be preserved to help future researchers.

The papers include the highly discursive diary which Lord Hailsham kept while he was in the army, covering the period from October 1941 to December 1942, when he returned home from the Middle East. References in the text are simply to 'diary'. There are also engagement diaries from June 1970, when he was first appointed Lord Chancellor, until June 1987, when his second term as Chancellor ended. The diaries include the period of opposition from 1974 to 1979. They are in two series and are referred to in the Notes as 'LC Diaries I' etc., and 'LC Diaries 1/1' etc. Although intended to serve only as engagement diaries, Lord Hailsham was in the habit of annotating them with brief accounts of the meetings he had, and including personal letters, memoranda, programmes and so on, relating to individual engagements. Many of his own entries are in an obscure personal shorthand making use of the Greek alphabet. Another illuminating section of the personal papers is an unpublished memoir of 1965, which was apparently intended for publication. It is listed as 'HLSM: Y50'. A series of taped interviews which I made with Lord Hailsham are also deposited in Churchill Archives Centre.

The other more important collections which I consulted are the papers of Lord Hailsham's father, Douglas Hogg, the first Lord Hailsham (also in Churchill Archives Centre and catalogued under 'HAIL'); the Prime Ministerial papers, listed under 'PREM', and Cabinet papers, listed under 'CAB', in the Public Records Office; the Harold Macmillan archive (now in the Bodleian); the R. A. Butler papers (Trinity College, Cambridge); the Conservative Party Archive (Bodleian); the Mountbatten papers (Southampton University); the Zuckerman archive (University of East Anglia); the Eton College Collections; the BBC Written Archive; and for the Nuclear Test Ban Treaty negotiations, the Harriman papers in the Library of Congress in Washington D.C., and papers and oral history transcripts relating to the Kennedy Administration in the John Fitzgerald Kennedy Library in Boston, Massachusetts.

For Lord Hailsham's two terms as Lord Chancellor, the records of the Department, referred to in the Notes under 'LCD', were an invaluable source. I was fortunate to be able to see these papers, but the Department stipulated that file numbers and dates should not be given.

Interviews and Correspondence

Lord Hailsham is a man about whom everyone has had some opinion and some item of information. It was very difficult to know when I should call a halt to seeking out his relations, colleagues, opponents, friends and acquaintances. The list which follows of those I talked to or corresponded with is therefore long. I have not included his immediate family.

Lord Alexander; Lord Amery; Lord Armstrong; Lady Helen Asquith; Lord Benson; Sir Wilfrid Bourne; Lord Boyd-Carpenter; Sir Robin Brook; Lord Browne-Wilkinson; Lord Callaghan; Sir Andrew Carnwath; Lord Carrington; Professor Owen Chadwick; Miss Pam Chitty; Mrs Pamela Cooper; Lord Denning; Sir Denis Dobson; Lord Elliot of Morpeth; Lady Egremont; Mr Garret Fitzgerald; Sir Edward Ford; Sir Ralph Gibson; Lord Gilmour; Mr Cyril Glasser; Lord Glenamara; Sir John Hackett; Sir Edward Heath; Lord Henderson of Brompton; Mr Derek Hill; Mr Quintin Hoare; Sir John Nicholson Hogg; Lady Sarah Hogg; Lord Home; Lord Jakobovits; Sir John Junor; Professor Carl Kaysen; Sir Michael Kerr; Lord Lane; Lord Lester; Sir Anthony Lincoln; Lord and Lady Longford; Lady Prudence Loudon; Lord Mackay; Mrs Rosemary Magnus; Lt. Col. F. W. Marten; Mr Anthony Martineau; Sir Harry Melville; Mr Victor Montagu; Mrs Domini Morgan; Mr Niall Morison; Lord Mustill; Sir Patrick Neill; Sir Derek Oulton; Sir Peter

Pain; Rt Hon. J. Enoch Powell; Mr John Profumo; The Countess of Ranfurly; Lord Rawlinson; Lord Roskill; Professor Arthur Schlesinger Jr; Mr Peter Scott; Lord Shawcross; Lord Simon of Glaisdale; Mr David Staff; Mr Richard Stoate; Mr Matthew Sullivan; Lord Templeman; Lady Thatcher; Lord Thorneycroft; Lord Todd; Mr John Townsend; Mr Norman Turner; Sir John Vinelott; Sir Dennis Walters; Sir Tasker Watkins; Mr Richard White; Lord Whitelaw; Mr Compton Whitworth; Lord Wilberforce; Rev. R. D. F. Wild; Sir John Wood; Baroness Young.

Published Works

A small number of the books and published material listed in the Bibliography or referred to in the Notes merit separate mention.

First, Lord Hailsham's own writings. His two books of memoirs, *The Door Wherein I Went* (1975) and *A Sparrow's Flight* (1990) were obvious sources about which I have included some comment in the text, and which I have quoted throughout. But they have to be handled with care. He did not check any of his references and in spite of his formidable memory, there are inaccuracies. On the whole, where he gives two separate accounts of a single episode, the version in the earlier work is to be preferred. However, the value of the memoirs far outweighs their failings if only because of the insight they give into the character of their author. When quotations occur in the text without direct attribution, they are from his autobiographical writings. *The Case for Conservatism* (1947) remains one of the outstanding statements of the philosophy of Conservatism and amply repays re-reading today. As an example of the force which Lord Hailsham could harness to his polemic, *The Left Was Never Right* (1945) is perhaps the best. Indeed, the larger part of his better writings date from the late forties when a furious energy was released by his return to political life after a time of frustration in the Middle East.

In an age when every received view is exposed to the work of revisionist historians, even Munich is not exempt. But R. A. C. Parker's *Chamberlain and Appeasement* (1993) manages to achieve both freshness and balance. It helped me to think about Quintin Hogg's stance in the Oxford City by-election of 1938, a stance which he never changed. Paul Addison's incisive history of domestic politics during the Second World War, *The Road to 1945* (1994) opened up a new subject and explained, among much else, how bitterly opposed were the Conservative rank and file in the Commons to embracing Beveridge entire. Among Addison's sources is an admirable Ph.D thesis in the Library of the University of London by Hartmut Kopsch, 'The Approach of the Conservative Party to Social Policy during World War Two' (1970). This contains a well-researched account of the work of the Tory Reform Committee.

Although Robert Heuston's two volumes on the lives of the Lord Chancellors from 1885 to 1970 tantalisingly stops just short of the subject of this book, they are an indispensable source of information about the curiously unique office of Chancellor, and include valuable material on the first Lord Hailsham.

Notes

Notes to Chapter 1: Family and Beginnings pp. 1–12

1 HAIL: 1/1/4: *Some reminiscences of the family of Hogg of Scotland whose descendants settled in Ulster circa. 16*: Dickie.
2 HAIL: 1/1/4.
3 Shaftesbury Lecture: 17 Oct. 1957.
4 *Proceedings of the International Congress on Technical Education*: 1897: Paper on Polytechnics by Quintin Hogg.
5 *Century Magazine*: June 1890: *London Polytechnics and People's Palaces*: Albert Shaw.
6 HLSM: R 200/2
7 Conversation with Lord Hailsham.
8 Ibid.
9 HLSM: R 200/2.
10 Ibid.
11 *The Nashville Tennessean Magazine*: 15 Dec. 1957: The Story of Myssie Brown: Louise Davis.
12 HLSM: B 20/4.
13 *The Governors of Tennessee*: Margaret Philips: Pelican Publishing Co. 1978.
14 *Enemies of Promise*: Cyril Connolly: Penguin 1961: p. 174.

Notes to Chapter 2: School pp. 13–18

1 *An English Education*: Richard Ollard: Collins 1982: p.192.
2 Ibid.
3 *Eton Voices*: Interviews by Danny Danziger: Viking 1988.
4 Conversations with Mr Anthony Martineau and Sir Robin Brook.

Notes to Chapter 3: Oxford pp. 19–31

1 *Lives of the Lord Chancellors 1885–1940*: R. F. V. Heuston: Oxford 1964: p. 455.
2 *Lord Derby*: Randolph Churchill: p. 460.
3 *The Unknown Prime Minister*: Robert Blake: p. 505.
4 195 HC Debs col. 584: 6 May 1926; 205 HC Debs col. 1314: 2 May 1927.

5   HLSM 43/185.
6   *Neville Chamberlain*: Iain Macleod: Frederick Muller 1961: p. 129.
7   HLSM 43/185: 6 Nov. 1927.
8   Conversation with Lord Hailsham.
9   HAIL 1/1/3: 15 Mar. 1928.
10 HLSM 43/185: 22 Oct. 1927.
11 Conversation with Lady Longford.
12 HLSM 43/185: 1 Mar. 1928.
13 Conversation with Lady Longford.
14 Letter to the author.
15 Campion Hall papers: Lord Hailsham: address for the funeral of Rev. Fr. D'Arcy
    S J: 5 Feb. 1977.
16 *The Catholic Herald*: July 1968: A Tribute to Father Martin D'Arcy on his Eightieth
    Birthday: Lord Hailsham.
17 Ibid.
18 Ibid.
19 HLSM: LC Diaries 1/1A: 22 Feb. 1976.

Notes to Chapter 4: The World Outside *pp. 32–47*

1   HLSM: Press Cuttings (1).
2   Conversation with Mr Matthew Sullivan.
3   Conversation with Mrs Arnold Morgan.
4   HLSM: Press cuttings (1).
5   HAIL 1/2/2: 4 Oct. 1932.
6   HAIL 1/4/27: letter to Neil Hogg; 21 Feb. 1939.
7   Conversation with Neil Hogg.
8   *Under the Wigs*: Sydney Aylett: Eyre Methuen.
9   LCD XC 25358: QH – Lord Hailsham: 8 Jan. 1938. I am indebted to Mr V. V.
    Veeder QC for information about this episode, and for generously providing a
    proof copy of his article on it, intended to be included in *The LCIA Centenary
    1892–1992: The Internationalisation of International Arbitration*: ed Marriott, Hunter
    and Veeder.
10 HAIL 1/3/1: Lord Hailsham – Miss Cheatham; 15 Jan. 1934.
11 HLSM 43/183, 184.
12 Conversation with Lord Hailsham.
13 HAIL 1/4/26: 23 Aug. 1938.
14 *The Oxford Union*: Christopher Hollis: Evans 1965: p. 186.
15 Ibid. p. 190.
16 *The Left was Never Right*: p. 50.
17 HLSM: Y50.
18 HAIL 1/3/11: 11 Nov. 1936.
19 *Lives of the Lord Chancellors 1885–1940*: p. 474.
20 HAIL 1/3/6: Lord Hailsham to Gen. Lytle Brown: 7 May 1935.
21 HAIL 1/4/27: Lord Hailsham – Neil Hogg: 9 Sep. 1938.
22 HAIL 1/4/27: Lord Hailsham – Neil Hogg: 18 Jan. 1939.
23 HAIL 1/3/5: letter to a Mr Stollard: 18 Oct. 1935.
24 HAIL 1/3/11: Lord Hailsham – R. B. Bennett: 13 Jan. 1937.
25 HAIL 1/4/27: Lord Hailsham – Neil Hogg: 26 May 1938.

Notes to Chapter 5: The Oxford By-election *pp 48–57*

1 HAIL 1/4/26: 17 Aug. 1938.
2 HAIL 1/4/26: 15 Sep. 1938.
3 *The World Crisis*: Winston Churchill: V, p. 225.
4 *Old Men Forget*: Duff Cooper: Hart-Davis 1953: p. 229.
5 Quoted in *Chamberlain and Appeasement*: R. A. C. Parker: Macmillan 1993: p. 162.
6 *Why Britain is at War*: Harold Nicolson: p. 84.
7 *Chamberlain and Appeasement*: p. 183.
8 *Daily Herald*: 19 Oct. 1938.
9 *Born to Believe*: Lord Longford: p. 91.
10 *The Pebbled Shore*: Lady Elizabeth Longford: p. 188.
11 HAIL 1/4/26: 19 Oct. 1938.
12 *Conservative Party Archive.*
13 Ibid.
14 *The Times*: 19 Oct. 1938.
15 *The Pebbled Shore*: p. 188.
16 *Oxford Mail*: 26 Oct. 1938.
17 HLSM 27/117: letters from Toby and Sylvia O'Brien, 21 Oct. 1938; and Frank Pakenham, 20 Oct. 1938.
18 *Oxford Times*: 28 Oct. 1938.
19 HLSM 27/117: 28 Oct. 1938.
20 HLSM 26/115: letter from Mrs Stella Gwynne.
21 Conversation with Lady Longford.

Notes to Chapter 6: The Onset of War and the Norway Debate *pp. 58–64*

1 HAIL 1/4/24: 6 Mar. 1939.
2 HAIL 1/4/27: to Neil Hogg: 3 May 1939.
3 HAIL 1/4/27: 21 Jul. 1939.
4 342 HC Debs.: col. 297: 29 Nov. 1938.
5 360 HC Debs.: col. 1093: 7 May 1940
6 HLSM: Y50
7 Ibid.
8 360 HC Debs.: col. 1150.
9 Col. 1321.
10 HLSM: LC Diaries 1/4 (at 5 Dec. 1978): 9 May 1940.
11 HLSM: Y50.

Notes to Chapter 7: Middle East *pp. 65–78*

1 *The Rifle Brigade*: p. 68.
2 Conversation with Lt. Col. F. W. Marten.
3 *The Rifle Brigade*: p. 70.
4 *Eminent Churchillians*: Andrew Roberts: Weidenfeld 1994: p. 248.
5 HLSM: unsorted: 26 Feb. 1942.
6 *War Memoirs: The Call to Honour 1940–1942*: General de Gaulle: Collins 1955: pp. 187, 188.
7 Conversations with the Countess of Ranfurly and Mrs Pamela Cooper.
8 Conversation with Sir John Hackett.
9 HLSM 43/183: 10 Mar. 1942.

10   HLSM: LC Diaries 7: 14 Nov. 1973.

Notes to Chapter 8: Homecoming pp. 79–83

1   Archive of the British Province of the Society of Jesus: 30/1/2.
2   HLSM: 43/183: 12 May 1942.
3   HLSM: 43/184: 27 May 1942.

Notes to Chapter 9: Beveridge and the Tory Reform Committee pp. 84–97

1   *The Road to 1945*: Paul Addison: Pimlico 1994: p. 234.
2   *Dictionary of National Biography*.
3   *Social Insurance and Allied Services*: Sir William Beveridge: Cmd. 6404: Nov. 1942: para 8.
4   Conversation with Lord Thorneycroft.
5   HLSM: Y50.
6   Ibid.
7   *The Road to 1945*: p. 214.
8   Conservative Party Archive: CRD 2/28/6.
9   PREM 4/89/2: 17 Nov. 1942.
10 *The Hinge of Fate*: Winston Churchill: Appx F, p. 862.
11 386 HC Debs.: Col. 1615: 16 Feb. 1943.
12 Col. 1813.
13 Cols. 1815, 1818.
14 Col. 1827.
15 398 HC Debs.: Col. 1356: 28 Mar. 1944.
16 Col. 1375.
17 Col. 1384.
18 *The Art of the Possible*: R. A. Butler: p. 121.
19 R. M. Barrington-Ward: unpublished diary: 11 Feb. 1944: by kind permission of Mark Barrington-Ward.
20 *One Year's Work*: p. 54.
21 Letter to Hartmut Kopsch in connection with his unpublished thesis.
22 *Manchester Guardian*: 29 Mar. 1944.
23 Victor Montagu: unpublished diary: 26 Jul. 1943.
24 Private archive of Victor Montagu: QH – Hinchingbrooke: 5 Jan. 1945.
25 Ibid. QH – Hinchingbrooke: 2 Apr. 1962.
26 HLSM: Y50.
27 Conversation with Lord Thorneycroft.
28 *The Conservative Party from Peel to Thatcher*: Robert Blake p. 259.
29 Cmd. 6404: para 441: assumption C.

Notes to Chapter 10: Remarriage and Conservative Defeat pp. 98–109

1   HLSM: Box 54.
2   *Daily Mail* 6 Jan. 1957.
3   392 HC Debs.: Col. 1617: 21 Oct. 1943.
4   BBC Archive.
5   *News Chronicle*: 11 January 1944.

6 Churchill – Attlee: 18 May 1945: quoted in *The Second World War: Triumph and Tragedy*: W. S. Churchill: p. 515.
7 *Under the Wigs*: Sydney Aylett: p. 121.

Notes to Chapter 11: Politics Practical and Philosophical pp. *110–126*

1   413 HC Debs.: Col. 984: 24 Aug. 1945.
2   Col. 1007.
3   Col. 1039.
4   *Daily Sketch*: 27 Feb. 1946.
5   *The Observer*: 15 Feb. 1948.
6   HLSM 21/97: Eden – QH: 27 Dec. 1945.
7   *The Making of Conservative Party Policy*: John Ramsden: Longman 1980: p. 135.
8   Quoted ibid. p. 137.
9   Ibid. p. 139.
10 *The Case for Conservatism*: p. 51.
11 Ibid. p. 231.
12 Ibid. p. 240.
13 HLSM: R 199/2: QH – Butler: 24 Oct. 1956.
14 449 HC Debs.: Col. 1017: 14 Apr. 1948.
15 HLSM: LC Diaries VI: 11 Apr. 1973.
16 HLSM: R 115/2: letter to Constituency Associations: 2 Dec. 1957.
17 *Inside Right*: Ian Gilmour: Quartet 1978: p. 103.
18 419 HC Debs.: Col. 296: 12 Feb. 1946.
19 HLSM 11/47: Butler – QH: May 1948.
20 Conversation with Lord Hailsham.
21 Ibid.
22 *The New Statesman and Nation*: 13 Oct. 1956.
23 *The Observer*: 15 Feb. 1948.
24 Ibid.
25 *The Case for Conservatism*: p. 304.
26 Ibid. p. 305.
27 *A Better Class of Person*: John Osborne: Faber 1981: p. 84.
28 *The Case for Conservatism*: p. 7.
29 Ibid. p. 53.
30 *An Appeal from the New to the Old Whigs*, 1791.
31 General Preface to the Hughenden edition of the Novels and Tales of the Earl of Beaconsfield: p. xi.
32 *At the End of the Day*: Harold Macmillan: Macmillan 1973: p. 496.
33 *The Spectator*: The New Conservatism: 29 Jan. 1943.
34 *The Case for Conservatism*: p. 69.
35 Ibid. p. 75.
36 *Values: Collapse and Cure*: 1994.
37 *The Case for Conservatism*: p. 16.
38 Ibid. p. 20.
39 Ibid. p. 23.
40 *The Bertrams*: Anthony Trollope: ch. 16.
41 *The New Statesman and Nation*: 13 Oct. 1956.
42 436 HC Debs.: Col. 190: 16 Apr. 1947.
43 443 HC Debs.: Col. 1106: 30 Oct. 1947.
44 Col. 1113.
45 Col. 1165.

46 Col. 1162.
47 Conversation with Lady Thatcher.
48 Conversation with Neil Hogg.
49 476 HC Debs.: Col. 1907.
50 *Anthony Eden*: Robert Rhodes James: Weidenfeld 1986: p. 350.
51 476 HC Debs.: Col. 2036
52 Col. 2046.
53 Col. 2055.
54 323 HL Debs.: Col. 208: 27 Jul. 1971.
55 *The Observer*: 15 Feb. 1948.

Notes to Chapter 12: Reluctant Heir *pp. 127–137*

1   168 HL Debs.: Col. 912: 12 Sep. 1950.
2   HLSM B24B/4: Neil Hogg – QH: 25 Aug. 1950.
3   *Lives of the Lord Chancellors 1885–1940*: R. F. V. Heuston: p. 494.
4   Conversation with Mrs Arnold Morgan.
5   Ibid.
6   *Manchester Guardian*: 17 Aug. 1950.
7   HLSM 14/61: Lord Hailsham – QH: 22 Oct. 1934.
8   HLSM: LC Diaries 1/12: Jean Crawford – QH: 6 Jan. 1983.
9   HLSM: PC 5: QH – Attlee: 2 Sep. 1950.
10 HLSM: B20/2: Attlee – QH: 6 Sep. 1950.
11 HLSM: 21/97: Attlee – QH: 30 Jul. 1945.
12 HLSM: 11/47: 19 Sep. 1949.
13 HLSM: B20/2: QH – Attlee: 7 Sep. 1950.
14 Report of the Select Committee of the House of Commons (Vacating of Seats) 1895 (Appendix 1) (Parliamentary Papers, Commons, Vol. 10).
15 HLSM: 11/48.
16 *In re Parliamentary Election for Bristol South East* [1964] 2 QB 257.
17 239 HL Debs.: Col. 372: 10 Apr. 1962.
18 Col. 380.
19 Report of the Joint Committee on House of Lords Reform [Session 1962–63]: HL 23/HC 38: Appendices 7 and 18.
20 *The Dilemma of Democracy*: p. 149 (1978).
21 *The Listener*: 28 Oct. 1976 (review of *The Governance of Britain* by Harold Wilson).
22 HLSM: LC Diaries 1/1: 6 Nov. 1975.
23 *The Times*: 17 Nov. 1976.
24 *The Dilemma of Democracy*: pp. 151, 152.
25 *On the Constitution*: p. 51.

Notes to Chapter 13: Carters Corner *pp. 138–149*

1   HLSM: R94/2: Will of first Lord Hailsham: 20 Mar. 1947.
2   HLSM: B24B/3: Lady Hailsham – QH: 11 Sep. 1950.
3   Letter to the author: 17 Mar. 1995.
4   HLSM: B24B/3: QH – Neil Hogg: 13 Sep. 1950.
5   HLSM: B24/4: Neil Hogg – QH: 8 Sep. 1950.
6   Ibid.: Neil Hogg – QH: 20 Sep. 1950.
7   Ibid.: Neil Hogg – QH: undated 1951.
8   Conversation with Hon. Mrs Frances Hoare.
9   HLSM: B17A/9.

10 HLSM: Y50.
11 HLSM: 12/51: Molson – QH: 21 Feb. 1953.
12 HLSM: 11/48: QH – Butler: 23 Nov. 1952.
13 HLSM: 12/51: QH – Hill: 28 Jan. 1954.
14 HLSM: Unsorted papers: Ronald Macdonald – QH: 29 Mar. 1952.
15 Ibid.: QH – Macdonald: 1 Apr. 1952.
16 473 HC Debs.: Col. 348.
17 Col. 350.
18 HLSM: R206/2: QH – Brockway: 16 Jul. 1952.
19 177 HL Debs.: Cols. 1150, 1153: 15 Jul. 1952.
20 *Broadcasting: Memorandum on Television Policy*: Cmd. 9005.
21 188 HL Debs.: Col. 391: 11 Jul. 1954.
22 Col. 393.
23 HLSM Y50.
24 Conversation with Lord Gilmour.
25 HLSM: 50/212: QH – Simonds: Oct. 1954.
26 Conversation with Lord Rawlinson.

Notes to Chapter 14: Suez pp. 150–162

1 HLSM: 12/51: QH – Hirst: 29 Apr. 1953.
2 Ibid.: Manningham-Buller – QH: 20 Jan. 1953.
3 Ibid.: Molson – QH: 21 Feb. 1953.
4 HLSM: 3/12: Eden – QH: 17 May 1956.
5 HLSM: Y50.
6 Ibid.
7 557 HC Debs.: Col. 919: 30 Jul. 1956.
8 *Mountbatten*: Philip Ziegler: Collins 1985: pp. 538/9.
9 Mountbatten papers: MB1/N106.
10 HLSM: 3/12: Cilcennin – QH: 16 Aug. 1956.
11 HLSM: Y50.
12 HLSM: LC Diaries 1/6: 10 Jan. 1981.
13 *The Times*: 5 and 11 Nov. 1980.
14 *The Times*: 7 Nov. 1980.
15 HLSM: LC Diaries 1/7.
16 *Suez*: Keith Kyle: Weidenfeld 1991: p. 236; *Mountbatten*: Philip Ziegler: p. 543.
17 *Mountbatten*: p. 543.
18 Mountbatten papers: MB1/N108.
19 HLSM: Y50.
20 *Eden*: Robert Rhodes James: p. 524; *Suez*: Keith Kyle: p. 304.
21 HLSM: LC Diaries 1/14: 28 Mar. 1984.
22 Conversation with Lord Hailsham.
23 HLSM: LC Diaries 1/14: 29 Mar. 1984.
24 HLSM: LC Diaries 1/6. 10 Jan. 1981
25 HLSM: Y50.
26 HLSM: LC Diaries 1/6. 10 Jan. 1981
27 Mountbatten papers: MB1/N106.
28 Ibid.: Mountbatten – QH: 4 Nov. 1956: reproduced by kind permission of the trustees of the Broadlands archive, and HMSO Copyright Unit.
29 Ibid.: QH – Mountbatten: 5 Nov. 1956.
30 Ibid.: QH – Mountbatten: 6 Nov. 1956.
31 HLSM: R196/1.

Notes to Chapter 15: Education and Party Chairman pp. 163–177

1   HLSM: Y50.
2   *The Times*: 14 Jan. 1957.
3   Macmillan Diary: 3 Feb. 1957.
4   CAB 129: C(57)21: 2 Feb. 1957.
5   CAB 129/87: C(57)123.
6   HLSM: LC Diaries 1/17: Edward Boyle Memorial Lecture: 20 Mar. 1985.
7   HLSM: LC Diaries 1/13: 23 Jul. 1983.
8   *Riding the Storm*: Harold Macmillan: Macmillan 1971: p. 416.
9   *Yorkshire Post*: 10 Jun. 1957.
10   *The Times*: 17 Sep. 1957.
11   *Macmillan*: Alistair Horne: Macmillan 1989: Vol. II: pp. 67, 68.
12   HLSM: B3/1: Hackett – QH: 9 Sept. 1957; and Spears – QH: 11 Sep. 1957.
13   Conversation with Sir Dennis Walters.
14   HLSM: Y50.
15   Ibid.
16   HLSM: R116/3: QH – Butler: 19 Jan. 1960.
17   *Riding the Storm*: p. 415.
18   HLSM: R265/4: QH – Macmillan: 29 Nov. 1957.
19   HLSM: Y50.
20   *Not Always with the Pack*: Dennis Walters: Constable 1989: p. 89.
21   Conversation with Sir Dennis Walters.
22   *Not Always with the Pack*: p. 91.
23   *Riding the Storm*: p. 420.
24   HLSM: R116/3: QH – Macmillan: 26 Oct. 1959.
25   *Macmillan*: Alistair Horne: Vol. II: p. 215.
26   *Daily Mirror*: 25 Oct. 1957.
27   *Daily Herald*: 25 Oct. 1957.
28   Conversation with Lord Thorneycroft.
29   Speech at Newport, Monmouthshire: *The Times*: 15 Jan. 1958.
30   *Macmillan*: Alistaire Horne: Vol. II: p. 72.
31   HLSM: Y50.
32   *Manchester Guardian*: 10 Jan. 1958.
33   *Macmillan*: Alistair Horne: Vol. II: pp. 73, 74.
34   HLSM: R266/4: Macmillan – QH: 12 Jan. 1958.
35   Ibid.: QH – Macmillan.
36   HLSM: R115/2: 22 Jan. 1958.
37   HLSM: Y50.
38   Butler papers: RAB G34 22.
39   HLSM: Y50.
40   Ibid.
41   HLSM: 58/259 b: Macmillan-QH 9 Oct. 1959.
42   HLSM: Y50.

Notes to Chapter 16: Science pp. 178–189

1   HLSM: R115/2: Letter to Party Chairmen 14 Oct. 1959.
2   HLSM: R116/3: Macmillan – QH 22 Oct. 1959.
3   Ibid.: QH – Macmillan 26 Oct. 1959.
4   Zuckerman Archive: SZ/ACSP: QH – Zuckerman: 31 Dec. 1959.
5   *Macmillan*: Alistair Horne: Vol II: p. 243.
6   Ibid.

7   Letter QH – Walters 5 Nov 1959, By kind permission of Sir Dennis Walters
8   *RAB*: Anthony Howard: Cape 1987: p. 262 n.
9   HLSM: R253/2: RAB – QH: 5 Nov. 1959.
10 Ibid.: QH – Butlin: 26 Oct. 1959.
11 HLSM: R181/4: 25 Aug. 1959.
12 *Science and Politics*: Lord Hailsham: p. 74.
13 Zuckerman Archive: SZ/ACSP/22/8: Press conference 21 Oct. 1959.
14 Conversation with Lord Todd.
15 Conversations with Lord Todd and Sir Harry Melville.
16 HLSM: R190/7: QH – Thorneycroft: 18 Dec. 1962.
17 Ibid.: Macmillan – QH: 24 Dec. 1962.
18 HLSM: Y50
19 *Science and Politics*: p. 62.
20 449 HL Debs.: Col. 792: 14 Mar. 1984.
21 *Science and Politics*: p. 33.
22 Report of the Advisory Council on Scientific Policy 1962/3: Cmnd. 2163.
23 247 HL Debs.: col. 93.
24 *Varsity*: 11 May 1963.
25 *Daily Telegraph*: 25 Mar. 1963.
26 *Daily Mirror*: 7 Jun. 1963.
27 *The Observer*: 19 May 1963: *Science: Policy for rapid expansion*.
28 HLSM: Y50.
29 Ibid.

Notes to Chapter 17: 'A Man of Many Jobs' *pp. 190–203*

1   HLSM: R276/2: QH – Macmillan: 2 Oct. 1961.
2   Ibid.: Macmillan – QH: 4 Oct. 1961.
3   HLSM: R190/6: QH – Hill: 23 Jan. 1962.
4   HLSM: R190/17: Macmillan – QH: 23 Dec. 1962.
5   HLSM: R191/1: QH – Macmillan: 23 Oct. 1962.
6   Ibid.: Macmillan – QH: 11 Jan. 1963.
7   *Newcastle Journal*: 10 Jan. 1963.
8   Macmillan Diary – 11 Jan. 1963.
9   *Newcastle Journal*: 15 Apr. 1963.
10 HLSM: Y50.
11 *The North East: A Programme for Regional Development and Growth*: Cmnd. 2206 Nov. 1963.
12 *Lord Hailsham on the Constitution*: p. 88.
13 Macmillan Diary: 26 Sept. 1963.
14 HLSM: Y49: QH – Douglas-Home: 4 Apr. 1970.
15 HLSM: LC Diaries 1/2: 20 Dec. 1976.
16 367 HL Debs.: Col. 745: 27 Jan. 1976.
17 *The North East*: Cmnd. 2206.
18 Conversation with Lord Glenamara, formerly Edward Short.
19 464 HL Debs.: Col. 942: 7 Jun. 1985.
20 HLSM: Y50.
21 674 HC Debs.: Col. 725: 21 Mar. 1963.
22 Col. 809: 22 Mar. 1963.
23 Transcript of *Gallery*: BBC-TV: 13 Jun. 1963.
24 Macmillan Archive: Macmillan – QH: 13 Jun. 1963.
25 679 HC Debs.: Col. 100: 17 Jun. 1963.
26 *Moore's Life of Lord Byron*, from Critical and Historical Essays: Lord Macaulay.

27 HLSM: Y50.
28 HLSM: R266/3: QH – Hobson: 25 Sept. 1963.
29 Denning Report: Cmnd. 2152: para 181.
30 Kennedy Library: PoF Box 27: U.S. Embassy London – State Department: 12 Jun. 1963.
31 Ibid.; PoF Box 171: U.S. Embassy London – State Department: 18 June 1963.
32 Denning Report: Chapter XXV.
33 HLSM: Y50.
34 Denning Report: paras 285, 286.
35 HLSM: R266/3: QH – Hobson: 25 Sep. 1963.
36 679 HC Debs: Col 97
37 HLSM: R190/8.
38 *At The End of The Day*: Harold Macmillan: Macmillan 1973: p. 452.
39 HLSM: R266/3: Profumo – QH: 4 Jul. 1975.

Notes to Chapter 18: Nuclear Test Ban Treaty *pp. 204–213*

1   PREM 11: 4593.
2   *One Thousand Days*: Arthur Schlesinger: Fawcett 1971: p. 772.
3   *Macmillan*: Alistair Horne: Vol II: p. 511.
4   HLSM: Y50.
5   *At The End of The Day*: Harold Macmillan: p. 470.
6   *Macmillan*: Vol II: p. 511.
7   HLSM: Y50.
8   Lord Gilmour: unpublished diary: 14 Oct. 1963.
9   PREM 11: 4593.
10 Kennedy Library: NSF Box 317.
11 Library of Congress: Harriman papers: Box 540.
12 Ibid. Box 581: 4 Jul. 1963.
13 Letter from Professor Carl Kaysen to the author.
14 *Monkeys, Men and Missiles*: Zuckerman: Collins 1988: p. 328.
15 Letter from Professor Carl Kaysen to the author.
16 Letter from Professor Arthur Schlesinger, jr. to the author.
17 *One Thousand Days*: p. 773.
18 Zuckerman archive: unclassified: Minute to PM: 15 May 1963.
19 Ibid. N/4.
20 *At The End of The Day*: p. 472.
21 HLSM: Y50.
22 Ibid.
23 Letter from Professor Carl Kaysen to the author.
24 *At The End of The Day*: p. 481.
25 Ibid. p. 482: for the text of the communique, see 681 HC Debs.: Cols. 1952/3: 25 Jul. 1963.
26 Macmillan diary: 24 and 25 Jul. 1963.
27 Ibid.
28 *One Thousand Days*: p. 775.
29 Library of Congress: Harriman Papers: Box 541.
30 *At The End of The Day*: p. 483.
31 *Monkeys, Men and Missiles*: p. 330.
32 Conversation with Lord Hailsham.
33 *At The End of The Day*: p. 480.
34 Zuckerman archive: unclassified: Macmillan – Zuckerman: 27 Jul. 1963.
35 *Monkeys, Men and Missiles*: p. 341.

36 HLSM: Y50.

Notes to Chapter 19: The Tory Leadership pp. 214–237

1   Butler papers (by kind permission of the Master and Fellows of Trinity College, Cambridge): RAB G40: 8 Jan. 1963.
2   Butler papers: RAB G40: 7 Mar. 1963.
3   *A Sparrows's Flight*: p. 348; *Not Always with the Pack*: Dennis Walters: pp. 110, 114.
4   *A Sparrow's Flight*: p. 349; and *Alec Douglas-Home*: D. R. Thorpe: Sinclair-Stevenson 1996: p. 260.
5   Butler papers: RAB G40: 28 April 1963.
6   Macmillan Diary: 7 Jul. 1963.
7   Ibid.: 5 Sep. 1963.
8   Ibid.: 20 Sep. 1963.
9   Ibid.: 28 Sep. 1963.
10 Ibid.: 11 Sep. 1963.
11 Ibid.: 18 Sep. 1963.
12 Memorandum (15 Sep. 1989) prepared by Lord Amery and conversation with him.
13 Macmillan Diary: 6 Oct. 1963.
14 Ibid.
15 Ibid.: 7 Oct. 1963.
16 *Macmillan*: Horne: Vol II: chapter 18, note 33: p. 688.
17 Macmillan Archive.
18 Macmillan Archive: QH – Macmillan: 7 Oct. 1963.
19 Macmillan Archive: Bligh – Macmillan: 8 Oct. 1963.
20 Butler papers: RAB H13 (55).
21 Lord Gilmour: diary.
22 *Macmillan*: Vol II: p. 545.
23 Some further information is given in *Alec Douglas-Home*: op. cit: pp. 280–282.
24 *The Way the Wind Blows*: Lord Home: pp. 181–2.
25 Macmillan Diary: 9 Oct. 1963.
26 Butler papers: RAB G40: note of October 1963.
27 Macmillan Archive: Note of Sir John Richardson.
28 *Alec Douglas-Home*: pp. 293–5
29 Amery memorandum.
30 Macmillan Archive: quoted in *Macmillan*: op. cit. p. 546.
31 *Not Always with the Pack*: p. 123, quoting from Sir Dennis Walters' diary.
32 Conversation with Sir Dennis Walters.
33 *The Fight for the Tory Leadership*: Randolph Churchill: p. 108.
34 Conversation with Sir Dennis Walters.
35 Butler papers: RAB G40: note of October 1963.
36 Ibid.
37 *Not Allways with the Pack*: pp. 124, 125, quoting from Sir Dennis Walters' diary.
38 Quoted in *Macmillan*: Vol II: p. 549.
39 Lord Gilmour: diary.
40 *The Way the Wind Blows*: p. 182.
41 Macmillan Diary: 14 Oct. 1963.
42 Macmillan Archive: note dated 14 Oct. 1963.
43 Macmillan Diary: 14 Oct. 1963.
44 Ibid.
45 Ibid.
46 Macmillan Archive: Memorandum of 15 Oct. 1963.

47 Quoted in *Macmillan*: p. 557.
48 Macmillan Archive: Note of conversation Macmillan – QH: 15 Oct. 1963.
49 Macmillan Archive: Note of conversation Macmillan – Home: 15 Oct. 1963.
50 *Not Always with the Pack*: p. 131.
51 Macmillan Diary: 16 Oct. 1963.
52 Macmillan Archive: Note of conversation Macmillan – Boyle: 16 Oct. 1963.
53 *Macmillan*: pp. 560–563.
54 *Holding all the Strings*: Ian Gilmour: London Review of Books: 27 Jul. 1989.
55 *The Tory Leadership*: Iain Macleod: *The Spectator*: 17 Jan. 1964.
56 Macmillan Archive: Note of Redmayne: 16 Oct. 1963.
57 Macmillan Archive: Note of conversation Macmillan – Lords Poole and Chelmer and Mrs Shepherd: 17 Oct. 1963.
58 *Alec Douglas-Home*: pp. 306–310.
59 *One Man Dog*: Unpublished memoir of Harold Macmillan by Sir Knox Cunningham. The copyright of Sir Knox' estate is gratefully acknowledged. A copy of the memoir is in the Drapers' Company archive.
60 Macmillan Diary: 17 Oct. 1963.
61 Lord Gilmour: diary.
62 Macmillan Diary: 18 Oct. 1963.
63 Note of Sir John Richardson: op. cit.
64 Macmillan Diary: 18 Oct. 1963.
65 *The Art of the Possible*: R. A. Butler: pp. 247–8.
66 Ibid. p. 248.
67 Macmillan Diary: 18 Oct. 1963.
68 Macmillan Archive: Memorandum by the Prime Minister: 18 Oct. 1963.
69 *The Art of the Possible*: p. 247.
70 Ibid. p. 249.
71 HLSM: Y50.
72 *Not Always with the Pack*: p. 113.
73 Macmillan Diary: 14 Oct. 1963.
74 *The Way the Wind Blows*: p. 182.
75 Macmillan Archive: Memorandum of 15 Oct. 1963.
76 Macmillan Diary: 19 Oct. 1963.
77 Ibid.: 20 Oct. 1963.
78 Butler papers: RAB G40: note of October 1963.
79 Ibid.: 31 Jul. 1963.
80 *The Art of the Possible*. p. 250.

Notes to Chapter 20: Opposition Interlude *pp. 238–253*

1 Macmillan Archive: QH – Macmillan: 20 Nov. 1963.
2 *Under the Wigs*: Sydney Aylett: Ch. 8.
3 688 HC Debs: Col. 152: 27 Jan. 1964.
4 Butler papers: RAB E 20/2 (62)5.
5 *Daily Mirror*: 8 Oct. 1964.
6 419 HC Debs.: Col. 285: 12 Feb. 1946.
7 HLSM: R 258/1: LCC (65)9: 11 Feb. 1965.
8 317 HL Debs.: Col. 209: 6 Apr. 1971.
9 HLSM: 74: LCC/E (66) 33: 23 Feb. 1966.
10 *Sunday Express*: 31 Oct. 1965 .
11 Ibid.
12 *Michael Ramsey: A Life*: Owen Chadwick: Oxford 1990: p. 247.

13 *R v. Commissioner of Police* [1968] 2QB 150, 154; *The Due Process of Law*: Lord Denning: Butterworths 1980: pp. 33, 35.
14 *Race Relations and Parliament*: Third Carr-Saunders Memorial Lecture: 5 Mar. 1970: *Race*: Vol. XII No. 1.
15 HLSM: B12A/3: Draft for a speech on second reading of Immigration Appeals Bill.
16 HLSM: B11A/1: CRD Paper ACP(67)37: 28 Jun. 1967.
17 HLSM: B11A/1: 4 Jul. 1967.
18 HLSM: B13/4: CRD Paper: 27 Feb. 1968.
19 759 HC Debs: Col. 1241: 27 Feb. 1968.
20 Col. 1259.
21 HLSM: B12A/3.
22 HLSM: R227/2.
23 Carr-Saunders Lecture: op. cit.
24 Conservative Party Archive: CCO 5005/32/11: Note of R. J. Webster: 22 Apr.1968.
25 Conversation with Enoch Powell.
26 Carr-Saunders Lecture: op. cit.
27 HLSM: R226/3: Macmillan – QH: 15 Oct. 1968.
28 HLSM: LC Diaries 9: 31 Oct. 1974.
29 763 HC Debs.: Col. 53: 23 Apr. 1968.
30 Col. 67.
31 Col. 75.
32 Carr-Saunders Lecture: op. cit.
33 768 HC Debs: Col. 476: 9 Jul. 1968.
34 HLSM: R 226/3: 19 Oct. 1968. By kind permission of Lady Helen Asquith

Notes to Chapter 21: Lord Chancellor *pp. 254–261*

1 *Under the Wigs*: Sydney Aylett: p. 158.
2 Quoted in *Lives of the Lord Chancellors 1940–1970*: R. F. V. Heuston: Oxford 1987: p. 99.
3 12 Jul. 1970: – By kind permission of Lady Prudence Loudon.
4 HLSM: LC Diaries 2: 25 Jun. 1971.
5 HLSM: LC Diaries 1/17: 13 Feb. 1985.
6 Holdsworth Club Presidential Address 1972: *The Problems of a Lord Chancellor*.
7 *Points of View*: Lord Birkenhead: Hodder 1922: p. 92.
8 *The Office of Lord Chancellor and the Separation of Powers*: 8 Civil Justice Quarterly (1989) p. 308.
9 Ibid. p. 311.
10 *Lives of the Lord Chancellors 1940–1970*: p. 3.
11 Cmnd. 7648: October 1979.
12 Ibid. para. 43.3.

Notes to Chapter 22: The Lord Chancellor and the Judges *pp. 262–281*

1 Conversation with Lord Lane.
2 Conversation with Lord Rawlinson.
3 HLSM: LC Diaries 7: 3 Dec. 1973.
4 HLSM: LC Diaries 1/9 3 Nov. 1981.
5 HLSM: LC Diaries 1/2: 19 Nov. 1976.
6 Conversation with Lord Hailsham.

7 Granada Guildhall Lecture: 10 Nov. 1987.
8 *Lives of the Lord Chancellors 1940–1970*: R. F. V. Heuston, p. 32.
9 Conversation with Sir Denis Dobson.
10 HLSM: Dobson – QH: 8 Apr. 1974.
11 95 HL Debs.: Col. 379: 14 Dec. 1934.
12 *The Independence of the Judiciary in the 1980s*: 1989 Public Law p. 44.
13 *The Office of Lord Chancellor and the Separation of Powers*: 8 Civil Justice Quarterly (1989) p. 308.
14 HLSM: LC Diaries 1/13: 28 Oct. 1983.
15 *Judicial Appointments: the Lord Chancellor's Policies and Procedures*: May 1986.
16 Conversation with Sir Derek Oulton.
17 HLSM: LC Diaries 1/5: 23 Jul. 1979.
18 *The Independence of the Judiciary*: Robert Stevens: Oxford 1993: pp. 179–181.
19 Conversation with Lord Hailsham.
20 *The Listener*: 13 Jul. 1972.
21 Speech at Lord Mayor's dinner for the Judges: 7 Jul. 1993.
22 *The Independence of the Judiciary*: p. 178.
23 Speech at the Lord Mayor's dinner: 7 Jul. 1993.
24 Courts Act, 1971, section 17(4).
25 HLSM: LC Diaries 1/9: 3 Dec. 1980.
26 *Daily Telegraph*: 22 Mar. 1985.
27 *Daily Telegraph*: 7 Aug. 1985.
28 *The Guardian*: 14 Feb. 1986.
29 *The Guardian*: 13 Jun. 1986.
30 HLSM: LC Diaries 1/20: 7 May 1986.
31 HLSM: LC Diaries 1/6: 26 Feb. 1980.
32 Ibid.: 4 Mar. 1980.
33 Ibid.: 5 Mar. 1980.
34 The full text of the letter is printed in [1986] Public Law p. 384.
35 LCD.
36 Ibid.
37 Ibid.
38 Ibid.
39 Ibid.
40 Ibid.
41 Ibid.
42 HLSM: LC Diaries 1: 13 Jul. 1970.
43 Ibid.: 14 Jul. 1970.
44 Conversations with Lord Denning and Lord Hailsham.
45 *The Closing Chapter*: Lord Denning: Butterworths 1983: p. 165.
46 Conversation with Lord Denning.
47 HLSM: LC Diaries 5: 25 Jul. 1972.
48 *The Listener*: 13 Jul. 1972.
49 HLSM: LC Diaries 2: 10 Mar 1971
50 *Broome v Cassell* [1971] 2 QB 354
51 *Rookes v Barnard* [1964] AC 1129
52 *Broome v Cassell* [1972] AC 1027, 1054
53 *The Discipline of Law*: Lord Denning: Butterworths 1979 p. 313
54 HLSM: LC Diaries 2: 10 Mar. 1971
55 Conversation with Lord Hailsham
56 *The Closing Chapter* ch.1 'A calamitous fortnight.'
57 HLSM: LC Diaries 1/10: 26 May 1982

58   HLSM: LC Diaries 1/9: 8 Jan. 1982

Notes to Chapter 23: The Lord Chancellor and the Legal Profession pp. 282–295

1   HLSM: LC Diaries 1/15: 1 May 1984.
2   HLSM: LC Diaries 6: 4 April 1973
3   *The Times*: 15 Apr. 1989.
4   LCD.
5   Final Report of The Royal Commission on Legal Services: Cmnd. 7648: para 21.21.
6   LCD.
7   Ibid.
8   HLSM: LC Diaries 1/12: 22 Dec. 1982
9   Lord Benson's papers.
10 HLSM: LC Diaries 1/5: 27 Jul. 1979 [The date appears to be wrong and should be August].
11 Cmnd. 7648: para 6.20.
12 402 HL Debs.: Cols 334, 335.
13 The Government Response to the Report of The Royal Commission on Legal Services: Cmnd. 9077: Nov. 1983.
14 Conversation with Lord Benson.
15 *The Times*: 27 Apr. 1981.
16 Report of The Royal Commission on Legal Services. Comments of the Senate of the Inns of Court and the Bar on the Recommendations with particular reference to those within the prerogative of the Bar to implement.
17 Conversation with Lord Benson.
18 *Legal Aid*: Lord Hailsham: Medical and Scientific Law (1982) Vol. 22 No. 3 p. 169.
19 392 HC Debs.: Col. 257: 22 Sept. 1943.
20 Report of the Committee on Legal Aid and Legal Advice in England and Wales: Cmnd. 6641: May 1945.
21 *Legal Aid*: Lord Hailsham: op. cit.
22 Cmnd. 7648: para 8.25.
23 Cmnd. 9077: chapter 8.
24 371 HL Debs.: Cols. 1220, 1224: 15 Jun. 1976.
25 Ibid.: Col. 1225.
26 25th Annual Report on Legal Aid (HC 629): 9 Sept. 1975.

Notes to Chapter 24: The Dispute with the Bar pp. 296–302

1   HLSM: LC Diaries 1/12: QH – Thatcher: 22 Dec. 1982.
2   32nd Annual Report on Legal Aid (HC 189): 16 Dec. 1982.
3   Cmnd. 7648 and Cmnd. 9077: recommendations 37.18 and 37.19; and response.
4   Bar Council records.
5   Ibid.
6   HLSM: LC Diaries 1/19: 7 Feb. 1986.
7   *A Sparrow' Flight*: p.444.
8   Conversation with Lord Alexander.
9   Bar Council records: 7 Feb. 1986.
10 *The Times*: 27 Mar. 1986.
11 Legal Aid Act, 1988: section 34.

12 475 HL Debs. Col. 991: 4 Jun. 1986.
13 Conversation with Lord Alexander.

Notes to Chapter 25: The Lord Chancellor and the Law
   pp. 303–317

1   *The Role of the Lord Chancellor in the field of Law Reform*: Lord Gardiner: (1971) Law Quarterly Review p. 326.
2   264 HL Debs.: Col. 1140, 1189: 1 Apr. 1964.
3   Ibid. Col. 1171: *Liber Amicorum for Lord Wilberforce*: ed. Bos and Brownlie: Oxford and ILA 1987: p. 6.
4   *Sunday Times*: 18 Dec. 1988.
5   *Obstacles to Law Reform*: Lord Hailsham: (1981) Current Legal Problems: p. 279.
6   404 HL Debs.: Col. 1550: 7 Feb. 1980.
7   HLSM: LC Diaries 6: 7 Mar. 1973.
8   HLSM: B 19/4: LCC (66) 115: 2 Dec. 1966.
9   Law Com. no. 143: 28 Mar. 1985.
10 Conversation with Lord Hailsham.
11 HLSM: Y21/1: Oration in Sydney for the 150th anniversary of the Supreme Court of New South Wales: 16 May 1974.
12 *The Times*: 6 Aug. 1987.
13 *Report of the Royal Commission on Assizes and Quarter Sessions*: Cmnd. 4153: Sept. 1963.
14 Ibid.: paras 256–265.
15 Ibid.: para 412.
16 Ibid.
17 LCD.
18 Ibid.
19 Cmnd. 7648: paras 43.3, 43.4.
20 *Government Response*: Cmnd. 9077: R. 43.1.
21 LCD.
22 Ibid.
23 Ibid.
24 Ibid.
25 Ibid.
26 Ibid.
27 Ibid.
28 Ibid.
29 *Civil Justice Review*: Cm. 394: Jun. 1988.
30 *The Times*: 2 Jul. 1991.
31 *The Times*: 28 Jun. 1988.
32 Conversation with Lord Hailsham.
33 HLSM: LC Diaries 5: 9 Oct. 1972: Nehru Lecture.
34 *Hamlyn Revisited: The British Legal System Today*: Lord Hailsham: Hamlyn Lectures, 1983.
35 Conversations with Lords Wilberforce, Templeman, and Lane.
36 *R v Lawrence* [1982] AC 510, 519.
37 Conversation with Lord Hailsham.
38 *R v Hyam* [1982] AC 55.
39 *Broome v Cassell* (1972] AC 1027.
40 *Rookes v Barnard* [1964] AC 1129.

41 HLSM: LC Diaries 4: Devlin – QH: 27 Feb. 1972.
42 Ibid.: 24 Jan. 1972.
43 *R v Cunningham* [1982] AC 566, 581

Notes to Chapter 26: Last Political Years *pp. 318–332*

1   *The Times*: 7 Oct 1974.
2   Conversations with Lord Whitelaw and Lord Rawlinson.
3   Conversation with Lord Hailsham.
4   Ibid.
5   324 HL Debs.: Col. 186: 23 Sep. 1971; and conversation with Lord Hailsham.
6   HLSM: LC Diaries 5: 21 Jul. 1972.
7   329 HL Debs.: Col. 1157: 29 Mar. 1972.
8   HLSM: LC Diaries 4: 23 Mar. 1972.
9   Ibid.: 24 Mar. 1972.
10 Ibid.: 27 Mar. 1972.
11 323 HL Debs.: Col. 200: 27 Jul. 1971.
12 Col. 208.
13 *Lord Hailsham on the Constitution*: pp. 82, 84.
14 Conversation with Lord Hailsham.
15 476 HC Debs.: Col. 2055: 26 Jun. 1950.
16 *The Door Wherein I Went*: Chapter 43.
17 HLSM: LC Diaries 1/1a: Heath – QH: 4 Nov. 1975.
18 HLSM: LC Diaries 8: 10 Jan. 1974.
19 Ibid.: QH – Carrington: 11 Jan. 1974.
20 Ibid.: 2/3 Mar. 1974.
21 Ibid.: 4 Mar. 1974.
22 HLSM: LC Diaries 9: 22 Oct. 1974.
23 Ibid.: Thatcher – QH: 16 Feb. 1975.
24 HLSM: Y3/5: 4 Apr. 1975.
25 HLSM: LC Diaries 1/1a: 11 Apr. 1975.
26 HLSM: LC Diaries 1/2: 29 Mar. 1977.
27 HLSM: LC Diaries 1/3: 6 Oct. 1977.
28 HLSM: LC Diaries 1/1: QH – Thatcher: 21 Jul. 1975.
29 Ibid.: Thatcher – QH: 27 Jul. 1975.
30 Ibid.: QH – Heath: 29 Jul. 1975.
31 Ibid.: Heath – QH: 3 Aug. 1975.
32 HLSM: LC Diaries 1/1a: 20 Jan. 1976.
33 *A Sparrow's Flight*: p. 407.
34 Conversation with Lord Hailsham.
35 HLSM: LC Diaries 1/6: 18 Dec. 1979.
36 HLSM: LC Diaries 1/9: 24 Nov. 1981.
37 HLSM: LC Diaries 1/19: 14 Apr. 1986.
38 Conversation with Lady Thatcher.
39 HLSM: LC Diaries 1/16: 15 Oct. 1984.
40 HLSM: LC Diaries 1/15: 11 Jul. 1984.
41 HLSM: LC Diaries 1/9: 27 Nov. 1981.
42 *The Spectator*: 22 Apr. 1978: Ferdinand Mount.
43 HLSM: LC Diaries 1/3: HM Queen – QH: 14 Apr. 1978, by kind permission of Her Majesty the Queen
44 *The Spectator*: 22 Apr. 1978: op. cit.

Notes to Chapter 27: Bereavement, Remarriage, Retirement
pp. 333–343

1   HLSM: LC Diaries 1/3: 13 May 1978.
2   HLSM: LC Diaries 1/6: 22 Jul. 1977 (at 17 Jul. 1980).
3   QH – Matthew Sullivan, by kind permission of Mr Sullivan.
4   HLSM: LC Diaries 1/4: 13 Jul. 1978.
5   HLSM: LC Diaries 1/10: Lady Spearman – QH: Apr. 1982; and LC Diaries 1/14: Lady Macmillan – QH: 26 Mar. 1984.
6   HLSM: LC Diaries 1/17: Lady Diana Cooper – QH: 13 Mar. 1985.
7   Ibid.: 12 Apr. 1985.
8   HLSM: LC Diaries 1/8: 10 Apr. 1981.
9   HLSM: LC Diaries 1/11: 24 Mar. 1982.
10 Conversation with Lord Hailsham.
11 Ibid.
12 HLSM: Y23/4: Speech to Magistrates at Hove: 25 Oct. 1974.
13 Conversation with Derek Hill.
14 HLSM: LC Diaries 1/9: British Ambassador, Washington – Foreign Secretary.: 21 Oct. 1981.
15 *Times Literary Supplement*: 10 Oct. 1975.
16 *The Spectator*: 11 Oct. 1975.
17 *The Door Wherein I Went*: p. 47.
18 Ibid.: pp. 65–67.
19 Ibid.: pp. 74–75.
20 Ibid.: p. 49.
21 HLSM: LC Diaries 9: 3 Nov. 1974 (sermon at All Souls).
22 *The Times*: 12 Nov. 1988.
23 *Sydney Morning Herald*: 17 May 1974.

Select Bibliography

Addison, Paul *The Road to 1945: British Politics and the Second World War* Jonathan Cape 1975.

Aylett, Sydney *Under the Wigs* Eyre Methuen 1978.

Bardon, Jonathan *A History of Ulster* The Blackstaff Press 1992.

Benn, Tony *Years of Hope. Diaries, Papers and Letters 1940–62* Hutchinson 1994.

Birkenhead, Lord (F. E. Smith) *Points of View* Hodder 1922.

Blake, Robert (Lord Blake) *The Conservative Party from Peel to Thatcher* Fontana 1985.

Butler, Richard Austen *The Art of the Possible: the Memoirs of Lord Butler* Hamish Hamilton 1971.

Card, Tim *Eton Renewed. A History from 1860 to the Present Day* John Murray 1994.

Chadwick, Owen *Michael Ramsey. A Life* Oxford University Press 1990.

Churchill, Randolph *The Fight for Tory Leadership: a Contemporary Chronicle* Heinemann 1964.

Churchill, Winston S. *The World Crisis 1916–18* Thornton Butterworth 1927. *The Second World War. Vol. 1. The Gathering Storm (1948); Vol. 4 The Hinge of Fate (1951) Vol. 6. Triumph and Tragedy (1954)* Cassell.

Connolly, Cyril *Enemies of Promise* Routledge and Kegan Paul 1938.

Cooper, Duff *Old Men Forget. The Autobiography of Duff Cooper (Viscount Norwich)* Hart-Davis 1953.

Denning, Lord *The Discipline of Law (1979); The Due Process of Law (1980); What Next in the Law (1982); The Closing Chapter (1983)* Butterworth.

Dilks, David (ed.) *Retreat from Power. Studies in Britain's Foreign Policy. Vol. 1 1906–39; Vol. 2 After 1939* Macmillan 1981.

Feiling, Sir Keith *The Life of Neville Chamberlain* Macmillan 1970.

Francois-Poncet, André *The Fateful Years. Memoirs of a French Ambassador in Berlin* Gollancz 1949.

Gaulle, Charles de *War Memoirs: The Call to Honour 1940–42* Collins 1955.

Gilmour, Ian (Lord Gilmour of Craigmillar) *Inside Right. A Study of Conservatism* Hutchinson 1977. *The Body Politic* Hutchinson 1969.

Guinness, Bryan *Personal Patchwork 1939–45* The Cygnet Press 1986.

Hailsham of St Marylebone, Lord (Quintin McGarel Hogg)

    The Law of Arbitration Butterworth 1936.

    One Year's Work Hurst and Blackett 1944.

    The Left was Never Right Faber & Faber 1945.

    The Case for Conservatism Penguin Books 1947 (revised and reissued as *The Conservative Case* 1959).

    The Purpose of Parliament Blandford Press 1948.

    They Stand Apart. A critical survey of the problems of homosexuality Ed. J. T. Rees and H. V. Usill (contribution by Lord Hailsham: 'Homosexuality and Society') Heinemann 1955.

    Science and Politics Faber & Faber 1963.

    The Devil's Own Song and other verses Hodder and Stoughton 1968.

    The Door Wherein I Went Collins 1975.

    The Dilemma of Democracy Collins 1978.

    A Sparrow's Flight Collins 1990.

    On The Constitution Harper Collins 1992.

    Values: Collapse and Cure Harper Collins 1994.

Healey, Denis *The Time of My Life* Michael Joseph 1989.

Henderson, Sir Nevile *The Failure of a Mission. Berlin 1937–39* Hodder & Stoughton 1940.

Hennessy, Peter *Never Again. Britain 1945–51* Jonathan Cape 1992.

Heuston, Robert *Lives of the Lord Chancellors 1885–1940* (1964); *Lives of the Lord Chancellors 1940–1970* (1987) Oxford University Press.

Hollis, Christopher *The Oxford Union* Evans 1965.

Home of the Hirsel, Lord (Sir Alec Douglas-Home) *The Way the Wind Blows* Collins 1976.

Horne, Alistair *Macmillan Vol. 1 1894–1956* (1988); *Vol. 2 1957–1986* (1989, revised 1991) Macmillan.

Hinchingbrooke, Viscount (Victor Montagu) *Full Speed Ahead! Essays in Tory Reform* Simpkin Marshall 1944.

Howard, Anthony *RAB. The Life of R. A. Butler* Jonathan Cape 1987.

Kyle, Keith *Suez* Wiedenfeld & Nicolson 1991.

Lee, J. J. *Ireland 1912–1985* Cambridge University Press 1989.

Longford, Elizabeth *The Pebbled Shore. The Memoirs of Elizabeth Longford* Weidenfeld & Nicolson 1986.

Longford, Lord (Frank Pakenham) *Born to Believe. An Autobiography* Jonathan Cape 1953.

Macleod, Iain *Neville Chamberlain* Frederick Muller 1961.

Macmillan, Harold (Earl of Stockton) *Autobiography Vol. 4 Riding the Storm 1956–59* (1971); *Vol. 5 Pointing the Way 1959–61* (1972); *Vol. 6 At the End of the Day 1961–63* (1973) Macmillan.

Manning, Olivia *The Levant Trilogy* Weidenfeld & Nicolson (*The Danger Tree* 1977; *The Battle Lost and Won* 1978; *The Sum of Things* 1980).

Nicolson, Harold *Why Britain is at War* Penguin Special 1939.

    Diaries and Letters vol. 3 1945–62 Collins 1968.

Nutting, Anthony *No End of a Lesson – The Story of Suez* Constable 1967.

Ollard, Richard *An English Education* Collins 1982

· *Select Bibliography* ·

Parker, R. A. C. *Chamberlain and Appeasement* Macmillan 1993.

Philips, Margaret *The Governors of Tennessee* Pelican Publishing Co. (USA) 1978.

Ramsden, John *The Making of Conservative Party Policy: the Conservative Research Department since 1929* Longman 1980.

Ranfurly, Countess of *To War with Whitaker: the Wartime Diaries of the Countess of Ranfurly 1939–45* Heinemann 1994.

Rawlinson, Peter (Lord Rawlinson of Ewell) *A Price Too High: an Autobiography* Weidenfeld & Nicolson 1989.

Rhodes James, Robert *Anthony Eden* Weidenfeld & Nicolson 1986.

Roberts, Andrew *Eminent Churchillians* Weidenfeld & Nicolson 1994.

Sampson, Anthony *Macmillan: a Study in Ambiguity* Allen Lane The Penguin Press 1967.

Schlesinger, Arthur M. Jr. *A Thousand Days. John F. Kennedy in the White House* Fawcett (USA) 1965.

Shepherd, Robert *Enoch Powell: a Biography* Hutchinson 1996.

Stevens, Robert *The Independence of the Judiciary. The View from the Lord Chancellor's Office* Oxford University Press 1993.

Thatcher, Margaret (Baroness Thatcher) *The Downing Street Years* Harper Collins 1993.

Thorpe, D. R. *Alec Douglas-Home* Sinclair-Stevenson 1996.

Walters, Sir Dennis *Not Always with the Pack* Constable 1989.

Wood, Ethel M. *The Polytechnic and its Founder Quintin Hogg* Nisbet 1932.

Wheeler-Bennett, Sir John *Munich: Prologue to Tragedy* Macmillan 1948.

Willetts, David *Modern Conservatism* Penguin Books 1992.

Ziegler, Philip *Mountbatten. The Official Biography* Collins 1985.

Zuckerman, Solly (Lord Zuckerman) *Monkeys, Men and Missiles. An Autobiography 1946–88* Collins 1988.

Index